Here are your

1998 WORLD BOOK HEALTH & MEDICAL ANNUAL Cross-Reference Tabs

For insertion in your WORLD BOOK set

The Cross-Reference Tab System is designed to help link THE WORLD BOOK HEALTH & MEDICAL ANNUAL's major articles to related WORLD BOOK articles. When you later look up a topic in your WORLD BOOK and find a Tab by the article, you will know that one of your HEALTH & MEDICAL ANNUALS has newer or more detailed information.

How to use these Tabs

First, remove this page from THE HEALTH & MEDICAL ANNUAL.

Begin with the first Tab, **AIRBAG.** Take the *A* volume of your WORLD BOOK set and find the **AIRBAG** article. Moisten the **AIRBAG** tab and affix it to that page by the article.

Glue all the other Tabs in the appropriate volumes.

THE
WORLD BOOK

HEALTH & MEDICAL
ANNUAL

1998

World Book, Inc.
a Scott Fetzer company
Chicago London Sydney Toronto

THE YEAR'S MAJOR HEALTH STORIES

From reports of the first recorded drop in U.S. AIDS deaths to the promise that vitamin E may help treat Alzheimer's disease, it was an eventful year in medicine. On these two pages are stories that editors selected as among the year's most important, memorable, or promising, along with information about where to find them in the book.

The Editors

Airbag safety

Government officials and automakers proposed several new safety regulations in 1996 in an effort to lower the risk of injury and death caused by rapidly deploying automobile airbags. In the Medical and Safety Alerts section, see AIRBAGS: AN EXPLODING CONTROVERSY.

Vitamin E may treat Alzheimer's

Scientific studies reported in 1996 that vitamin E may help treat Alzheimer's disease and may increase the strength of the immune system in elderly people. In the Health Updates section, see NUTRITION.

AIDS deaths drop in U.S.

The number of AIDS deaths dropped by 13 percent in the first six months of 1996, the first such drop since the Centers for Disease Control and Prevention began tracking the disease in 1981. In the Health Updates section, see AIDS.

World Book, Inc.
525 W. Monroe
Chicago, IL 60661

ISBN 0-7166-1198-8
ISSN 0890-4480
Library of Congress Catalog Card Number: 87-648075
Printed in the United States of America

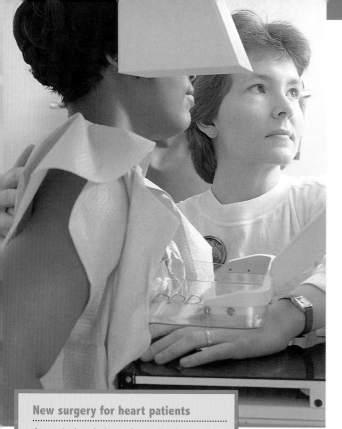

Mammogram controversy

A panel appointed by the National Institutes of Health set off a storm of debate in 1997 after it ruled that women should not begin using mammograms to screen for breast cancer until they reach age 50. In the Health Update section, see CANCER.

Oldest woman to give birth

A 63-year-old woman gave birth in 1996 to a healthy baby girl, making her the oldest post-menopausal woman to have a baby. The birth raised questions about whether there should be an age limit for pregnancy. In the Health Updates section, see MEDICAL ETHICS.

New surgery for heart patients

A surgical technique that gained acceptance in 1997, which involves cutting a wedge of heart muscle out of the left ventricle, may revolutionize care for patients who otherwise would require heart transplant. In the Health Update section, see HEART AND BLOOD VESSELS.

Food poisoning outbreaks

Contaminated produce caused several outbreaks of food poisoning in 1996 and 1997. In March, more than 180 children and adults in Michigan became sick after eating strawberries contaminated with the hepatitis A virus. In the Medical and Safety Alerts section, see HOW SAFE IS OUR FOOD SUPPLY?

Debate on cloning

Scottish scientists reported in February 1997 that they had created a lamb by cloning an adult sheep—the first such cloning of a mammal. News of the experiment stirred public concern—especially over the issue of cloning humans. In the Health Update section, see MEDICAL ETHICS.

CONTENTS

See page 38.

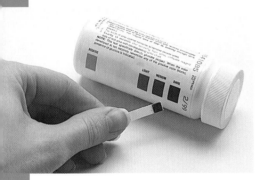

See page 53.

See page 78.

See page 89.

See page 100.

See page 122.

Cross-Reference Tabs: A tear-out page of cross-reference tabs for insertion in *The World Book Encyclopedia* appears before page 1.

See page 144.

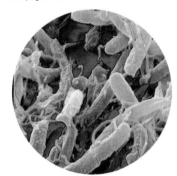

See page 182.

See page 275.

5

STAFF

EDITORIAL ADVISORY BOARD

CONTRIBUTORS

Balk, Robert A., M.D.
Director of Pulmonary Medicine,
Rush-Presbyterian-St. Luke's
Medical Center.
[Health Updates and Resources:
Respiratory System]

Barone, Jeanine, M.S.
Nutritionist, Exercise Physiologist,
Sports Medicine and Nutrition
Editor,
*University of California at Berkeley
Wellness Letter.*
[Consumer Health: *Food: The Best
Source of Nutrients*; Health Updates
and Resources: *Nutrition and Food*]

Benowitz, Steven I., B.S., M.A.
Senior Editor,
The Scientist.
[On the Medical Frontier: *Combat-
ting the Effects of Stroke*]

Birnbaum, Gary, M.D.
Professor of Neurology,
University of Minnesota.
[Health Updates and Resources:
Brain and Nervous System]

Cohen, Donna, Ph.D.
Professor and Chair,
Department of Aging and Mental
Health,
University of South Florida.
[A Healthy Family: *New Options in
Elder Care*]

Crawford, Michael H., M.D.
Robert S. Flinn Professor and
Chief of Cardiology,
University of New Mexico
Health Sciences Center.
[Health Updates and Resources:
Heart and Blood Vessels]

Finberg, Jeanne, A.B., J.D.
Senior Attorney,
Health-Care Policy Analyst,
Head of Health Group,
Consumers Union.
[Spotlight on Managed Care:
*Getting the Most out of Your Health
Plan; Taking Charge of Your Health*]

Friedman, Emily, B.A.
Health Policy and Ethics Analyst,
Health Policy Section Editor,
*Journal of the American Medical
Association.*
[Spotlight on Managed Care: *Un-
derstanding Managed Care; The De-
bate About Managed Care*; Health
Updates and Resources: *Health
Care Issues*]

Gartland, John J., A.B., M.D.
James Edwards Professor
Emeritus of Orthopedic Surgery,
Thomas Jefferson University.
[Health Updates and Resources:
Bone Disorders]

Gerber, Glenn S., M.D.
Assistant Professor,
Department of Surgery,
University of Chicago.
[Health Updates and Resources:
Urology]

Goldstein, Jay L., M.D.
Associate Professor of Medicine,
University of Illinois at Chicago.
[On the Medical Frontier: *Inflam-
matory Bowel Disease*]

Hales, Dianne, B.A., M.S.
Free-Lance Writer.
[A Healthy Family: *Quieting the
Snores*]

Harris, Jules E., M.D.
Samuel G. Taylor III Professor of
Medicine,
Rush University.
[Health Updates and Resources:
Cancer]

Hussar, Daniel A., B.S., M.S., Ph.D.
Remington Professor of Pharmacy,
Philadelphia College of Pharmacy
and Science.
[Health Updates and Resources:
Drugs]

Jones, Cindy, Ph.D.
Free-Lance Writer, Educator.
[Health Updates and Resources:
Skin]

Kass, Philip H., D.V.M., Ph.D.
Associate Professor of
Epidemiology,
University of California at Davis.
[Health Updates and Resources:
Veterinary Medicine]

Klobuchar, Lisa A., B.A.
Free-Lance Writer.
[Health Updates and Resources:
Mental Health]

Levine, Carol, M.A.
Director,
Families and Health Care Project,
United Hospital Fund.
[Health Updates and Resources:
Medical Ethics]

Lewis, David, C., M.D.
Professor of Medicine and
Community Health,
Brown University.
[Health Updates and Resources:
*Alcohol and Drug Abuse;
Smoking*]

Lewis, Ricki, B.S., M.A., Ph.D.
Textbook Author,
McGraw Hill College Publishers.
[Consumer Health: *Dietary Supple-
ments: What Are the Risks?*; Health
Updates and Resources: *Digestive
System*]

Love, Lauren, B.A., M.F.A.
Free-Lance Writer.
[A Healthy You: *Self-Test Kits Bring Medicine Closer to Home*; Health Updates and Resources: *Birth Control; Weight Control*]

Maugh, Thomas H., II, Ph.D.
Science Writer,
Los Angeles Times.
[Health Updates and Resources: *Environmental Health*]

McInerney, Joseph D.,
B.S., M.A., M.S.
Director, Biological Sciences
Curriculum Study.
[Health Updates and Resources: *Genetic Medicine*]

Minotti, Dominick A., M.D.,
Allergist,
Northwest Asthma and Allergy
Center.
[Health Updates and Resources: *Allergies and Asthma*]

Moore, Margaret Eilene,
A.M.L.S., M.P.H.
Head, Education Services,
Health Sciences Library,
University of North Carolina at
Chapel Hill.
[Health Updates and Resources: *Books of Health and Medicine*]

Peters, Victoria M., B.S., M.S.
Free-Lance Writer.
[Medical and Safety Alerts: *Airbags: An Exploding Controversy*; Health Updates and Resources: *Sexually Transmitted Diseases; Stroke*]

Pisetsky, David S., M.D., Ph.D.
Chief of Rheumatology, Allergy and
Clinical Immunology,
Duke University Medical Center.
[Health Updates and Resources: *Arthritis and Connective Tissue Disorders*]

Prinz, Richard A., M.D.
Helen Shedd Keith Professor and
Chairman,
Department of General Surgery,
Rush-Presbyterian-St. Luke's
Medical Center.
[Health Updates and Resources: *Surgery*]

Regan, James K., B.S., M.D.
Fellow in Gastroenterology,
University of Illinois at Chicago.
[On the Medical Frontier: *Inflammatory Bowel Disease*]

Rinehart, Rebecca D.
Associate Director, Publications,
American College of Obstetricians
and Gynecologists.
[Health Updates and Resources: *Pregnancy and Childbirth*]

Roodman, G. David, M.D., Ph.D.
Professor of Medicine,
Associate Chair for Research,
University of Texas Health Science
Center at San Antonio.
[Health Updates and Resources: *Blood*]

Siscovick, David S., M.D., M.P.H.
Professor of Medicine and
Epidemiology,
University of Washington.
[Health Updates and Resources: *Exercise and Fitness*]

Stephenson, Joan, B.S., Ph.D.
Associate Editor,
Journal of the American Medical Association.
[Medical and Safety Alerts: *How Safe Is Our Food Supply?*]

Thompson, Jeffrey R., M.D.
President,
Dallas Kidney Specialists.
[Health Updates and Resources: *Kidney*]

Tideiksaar, Rein, Ph.D.
Director,
Department of
Geriatric Care Coordination,
Sierra Health Services, Inc.
[Health Updates and Resources: *Aging*]

Trubo, Richard, B.A., M.A.
Free-Lance Medical Writer.
[A Healthy You: *How to Travel Well*; Health Updates and Resources: *AIDS; Child Development; Diabetes; Ear and Hearing*]

Van Herle, Andre J., M.D.
Professor of Medicine,
UCLA School of Medicine.
[Health Updates and Resources: *Glands and Hormones*]

Woods, Michael, B.S.
Science Editor, Washington Bureau,
Pittsburgh Post-Gazette.
[Health Updates and Resources: *Dentistry; Eye and Vision, Infectious Diseases; Safety*]

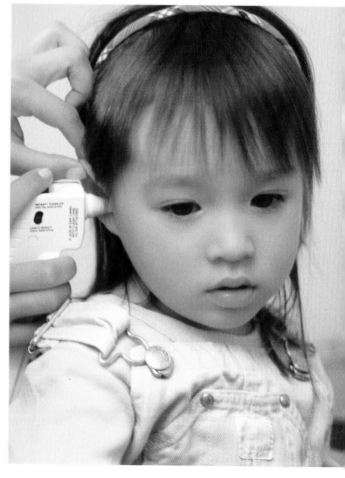

SPOTLIGHT ON MANAGED CARE

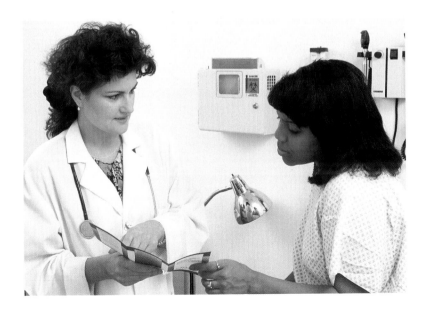

Managed care is changing the way in which millions of Americans pay for and receive medical services.

Understanding MANAGED CARE

By Emily Friedman

A MAJOR CHANGE IS TAKING PLACE in the way in which many Americans pay for health care and receive health services. This change is the shift to managed care, an approach to the delivery of health care that is far different from fee-for-service—the traditional health-care payment system. In the 1990's, millions of people switched from fee-for-service plans to managed care, a system built on the promise of lowering health-care costs to patients, employers, and health-care providers and improving health through better access to preventive care.

Managed care is the term applied to health plans or health insurance programs that give incentives to health-care professionals, such as doctors, to use less expensive treatments and to avoid unnecessary services when possible. Among these incentives are prepayments for health services and discounts negotiated with hospitals or doctors. Prepayment of *premiums,* or patients' insurance fees, can be a powerful incentive for health-care professionals in managed care to keep costs down. By paying costs "up front," purchasers of health coverage set a cap on the amount of money the professionals will ultimately receive.

From a patient's point of view, membership in a managed-care health plan usually means more predictable out-of-pocket expenses over the period of coverage regardless of one's state of health. Payments generally consist of a set monthly payment (the amount varies widely among plans), and a copayment. The *copayment* is a small payment paid by the user of a health service at the time the service is received. Traditional health insurers use a very different system for making payments to hospitals and doctors. In this system, called *fee-for-service,* the patient or patient's insurer pays for services individually, according to a fee structure that links each diagnosis or treatment with a specific cost or fee. For example, if a patient goes to see a doctor because of chest pains, the doctor's office bills the patient or his or her insurance company for the "usual and customary" fee for a doctor's office visit. If the patient undergoes diagnostic tests, the office staff or hospital bills for each of them. This payment method is also known as *indemnity coverage* or, when insurance coverage is involved, *major medical insurance.*

In sharp contrast with managed care, the fee-for-service system gives health professionals little or no incentive to keep costs down. In fact, quite the opposite is true. The more services for which they can bill, the more revenue they will earn. Moreover, health-care providers in the fee-for-service system tend to bill at least some services, such as hospital care, at inflated rates to compensate for patients who cannot pay for the health services they receive.

The origins of managed care

Although fee-for-service was until the 1990's the most common method of payment for health care, it was not the only one. More than 50 years ago, a few doctors and hospitals became involved in

The author:

Emily Friedman is a health policy analyst and health policy section editor of the *Journal of the American Medical Association.*

Rising health costs

Health expenditures in the United States rose sharply and steadily from the early 1940's to the mid-1990's. In 1940 the cost of health-care services made up about 5 percent of the gross domestic product. The figure skyrocketed to nearly 14 percent by 1995.

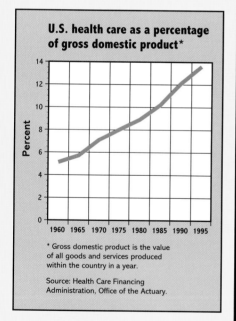

U.S. health care as a percentage of gross domestic product*

Percent

1960 1965 1970 1975 1980 1985 1990 1995

* Gross domestic product is the value of all goods and services produced within the country in a year.

Source: Health Care Financing Administration, Office of the Actuary.

prepaid health plans. These plans developed when an employer, labor union, or other individual or group set up an insurance arrangement in which each member or employer paid a certain amount of money each month to the plan. In return, the plan provided members with all their health care. In these early plans, the doctors were employed by the plan, which typically had its own hospitals, clinics, and other services. By the 1990's, this type of prepaid health plan was called a health maintenance organization (HMO), though this term did not exist before the 1970's.

Most historians consider the first community-based, prepaid health plan to be the Community Cooperative Hospital of Elk City, Oklahoma, which opened in 1931. Each member of the hospital paid $25 a year for all covered health services. In the ensuing years, several other prepaid plans were established in the United States, a few of which are still in existence today. Among them are Kaiser Permanente, the largest managed-care plan in the United States, with 7 million members; the Group Health Cooperative of Puget Sound in Washington state; and the Group Health Association (now known as HealthPartners) in Minnesota.

For the first few decades of their existence, the prepaid plans faced strong opposition from the American Medical Association and many state and county medical societies. Opponents in the medical societies believed that doctors working on salary for a health plan did not serve the best interests of patients or of the medical profession. They contested the legal right of prepaid health plans to exist, resulting in a series of court battles. The prepaid plans eventually won these legal contests, but fee-for-service medicine continued to dominate American health care.

In the 1960's, forces began to emerge that would transform the role of prepaid health plans. Private health insurance costs, for instance, were rising rapidly. Employers—who paid for most private coverage for workers and their dependents, and often for retirees as well—were becoming alarmed at the growing expense. Some began to look around for less expensive ways to provide employee health benefits.

A few employers came to the conclusion that prepaid health plans might provide a solution to the problem of escalating medical costs. An important advocate of this approach was Paul Ellwood, M.D., a Minnesota doctor. Ellwood invented the term HMO to describe prepaid plans. In the early 1970's, he asked President Richard M. Nixon to provide political support for these types of health plans, and Congress then passed the Health Maintenance Act of 1974. This law established standards for prepaid health plans and offered such plans some federal subsidies.

A climate of rapid change

The pace of change in the managed-care health industry accelerated after 1980. One important arena of change concerned the profit status of managed-care companies. Before 1980, virtually all HMO's had been nonprofit, tax-exempt entities. Then in the early 1980's, a new trend emerged: nonprofit HMO's were converting to for-profit status. This trend, which accelerated through the 1980's and into the 1990's, was spurred in part by the federal government's termination of health plan subsidies in 1983.

Furthermore, the traditional model for a managed-care health plan—a range of services provided by a plan that collected the premium, employed the doctors and nurses, and owned the hospitals and other facilities—also began to change. Many of the health plans that emerged in the 1980's did not provide health services themselves, but rather negotiated a contract between the payer (employers, government, or individuals) and health-care professionals. The plan received a portion of the premium; the rest of the money went to the professionals. In other words, whereas managed-care plans had historically been health-care professionals, most new plans were now insurers instead.

This was an important change in three ways. First, many more health-care professionals would get involved in managed care, because health plans could contract with any hospitals and doctors they chose. Second, establishing a health plan would now become much easier, because doing so no longer required hiring doctors, building or acquiring hospitals, or establishing clinics. A plan could simply sign contracts with any number of existing professionals. Third, pro-

Rapid change in America's health care

In the 1990's, millions of Americans shifted from traditional fee-for-service health coverage to the system known as managed care. In 1988, 71 percent of the insured population was enrolled in fee-for-service, though that figure dropped to only 26 percent by 1996.

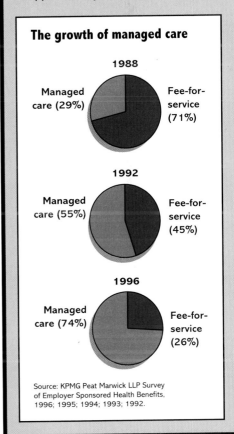

The growth of managed care

1988
Managed care (29%) — Fee-for-service (71%)

1992
Managed care (55%) — Fee-for-service (45%)

1996
Managed care (74%) — Fee-for-service (26%)

Source: KPMG Peat Marwick LLP Survey of Employer Sponsored Health Benefits, 1996; 1995; 1994; 1993; 1992.

fessionals and premiums had become separated, for the organization that collected the premium was not necessarily, or even usually, the organization that provided the care. The ease of establishing such plans resulted in a skyrocketing number of HMO's—from 174 in 1976 to 749 in 1997.

The number of people enrolled in HMO's also skyrocketed in the 1990's, though managed-care growth had been slow in its beginning years. In 1976, only 6 million people belonged to HMO's; in 1980, only 9.1 million did. Then a severe economic downturn in the early 1980's intensified employers' concern about the cost of employee health benefits. Employers turned to managed care as an alternative to expensive traditional coverage. As a result, HMO enrollment jumped during the first half of the decade: by 1985, 21 million people belonged to HMO's.

By late 1996, between 63 and 77 million people were enrolled in HMO's. (Estimates vary widely because researchers define HMO's differently and count HMO enrollment in a variety of ways.)

Total enrollment in all forms of managed care, including HMO's and other managed-care health plans, was estimated to be 153 million in 1996.

Managed care: a brief glossary

Capitation

A prepayment for all the health services that will be rendered to one patient over a period of time, such as a year.

Copayment

A small payment that a patient makes at the time a health service is used.

Fee-for-service

The traditional method of payment for health services, in which patients are charged—or their insurance company is billed—according to a set fee for each diagnosis or treatment. This method is also called the indemnity plan.

HMO (Health maintenance organization)

A tightly organized form of managed care characterized by centralized administration and coordinated patient care.

Managed care

Health plans that use strategies such as prepayment of premiums and control of patients' access to services to hold down costs. Patients in managed care must obtain approval before receiving certain services.

POS (Point of service)

A feature of managed-care health plans that allows patients to consult nonmember doctors or other providers outside the plan, usually for a significant fee.

PPO (Preferred provider organization)

A loosely organized form of managed care, in which patients have inexpensive access to the plan's own network of health-care providers and more costly access to out-of-network providers.

Prepaid health plan

In a strict sense, a precursor of today's HMO. In a general sense, most forms of managed care qualify as prepaid plans.

Managed care in public programs

Although employers led the way in encouraging—or requiring—membership in managed-care plans, the growth of managed care in public programs has been dramatic, too. Managed care has grown in both Medicare and Medicaid populations, with the sharpest increases in enrollment seen in the Medicaid program.

Congress enacted both the Medicare and the Medicaid programs in 1965. Medicare was designed to pay for health care for people over age 65. The intent of Medicaid was to pay for certain health services for some people living in poverty, as well as health coverage such as nursing home costs for people who could not afford them. These programs were soon paying for the care of millions of Americans, and their costs ballooned beyond early projections.

The escalating costs of Medicare and Medicaid eventually made these programs prime candidates for cost-cutting managed care. In 1976, enrollments in managed-care health plans included hardly any Medicare or Medicaid *beneficiaries* (people who receive benefits from these programs). By 1985, however, about 1.1 million Medicare beneficiaries and 600,000 Medicaid beneficiaries belonged to managed-care health plans. By the mid-1990's, approximately 3.6 million Medicare beneficiaries were in managed care. At about the same time, Medicaid enrollment in managed care was sharply higher: about 11.6 million Medicaid beneficiaries—nearly one-third of everyone in the program—were enrolled in HMO's in 1995.

The especially rapid growth of managed care in the Medicaid program can be explained by a simple fact: membership of Medicaid beneficiaries in managed-care plans was mandatory in many states. For Medicare beneficiaries, on the other hand, membership in HMO's or other managed-care plans was still entirely voluntary for beneficiaries in 1997.

Medicaid enrollment focused mostly on low-income families receiving welfare payments. Most recipients requiring specialized or extensive medical care—those in nursing homes, the blind, and the disabled—remained in fee-for-service plans. While managed care is widely viewed as a way to restrain costs, establishing reasonable prepaid premiums or negotiating discounts for these beneficiaries is extremely difficult. Nevertheless, some 20 states have attempted to grapple with this problem, enrolling some elderly or disabled beneficiaries in managed-care plans.

The people who make decisions about health coverage for large populations—employers, government policymakers, and others—continue to view managed care as the best way to cut medical costs, coordinate services, and promote competition in health care. Perceptions such as these guarantee that managed care will remain a prominent feature of the health-care landscape for the foreseeable future. Experts predict that enrollments of both privately and publicly insured patients in managed-care health plans will continue to rise dramatically.

●●●

Types of managed-care health plans

By 1997, the health-care marketplace offered a bewildering variety of managed-care plans. As plans proliferated, many *hybrids* (plans mixing features from various plan types) appeared.

For this reason, health-care analysts find it difficult—if not impossible—to categorize plans neatly or to assign precise enrollment statistics to any one type of plan. Nevertheless, most analysts agree that managed-care health plans share at least the following basic characteristics:

- Patients' access to specialized care, such as costly diagnostic tests or treatment by medical specialists, is controlled. Using such a service may require a doctor's referral, or prior approval from an employee of the plan, or both.
- Payment for services is arranged to give health-care professionals an incentive to avoid unnecessary services. Often, premiums are in the form of a prepayment, such as *capitation* (a prepayment for all the health services to be rendered to one patient over a period of time). Not all managed-care health plans use capitation, however. Some simply negotiate discounts with health-care professionals. Often, these professionals are willing to give significant discounts in return for the volume of patient care offered by a plan.
- Throughout the plan, there is a strong emphasis on containing costs.

HMO's in particular

HMO's exhibit several distinct features beyond the basic characteristics of managed care. In many HMO's, patient care is individually coordinated by health professionals such as doctors or nurses. Typically, the professional who coordinates patient care acts as a gatekeeper in the plan, controlling patients' access to medical services. A doctor who performs this role is designated as the primary-care physician for his or her patients.

Moreover, HMO's have a strongly organized central administration. One important consequence of this structural feature of HMO's is to centralize patients' medical records, making them readily accessible.

Considerable variety exists even among HMO's, however. Virtually all HMO's can be classified according to one or more of four basic organizational models. These models are important, for they significantly affect the way in which health care is delivered to patients:

Staff. In this, the traditional HMO model, doctors and other clinicians are salaried employees of the plan, and they treat plan members exclusively. Here the primary-care physician has a central role as coordinator of each patient's total health care. The staff model is not very common today. In 1996, there were fewer than 50 staff-model HMO's, representing only about 6 percent of HMO enrollment.

Group. Under this approach, the HMO is owned by, or contracts with, one or more group practices—organizations of doctors who own their practice jointly. Each group practice primarily or exclusively treats members of the contracting health plan or plans. Although a long-established feature of the managed-care landscape, the

Organizational models of HMO's

Staff model HMO

The traditional HMO model, in which doctors and other health-care providers are salaried employees of the HMO and treat plan members only.

Group model HMO

A model in which the HMO is owned by, or contracts with, one or more group practices. These practices treat only patients belonging to contracting health plans.

Network model HMO

A model in which an HMO contracts with several group practices, independent doctors, and hospitals. These providers treat both HMO and non-HMO patients.

Individual practice association (IPA)

An HMO that contracts with independent, often unrelated doctors, hospitals, and other services. HMO patients receive treatment on the providers' premises as do non-HMO patients.

Comparing managed care with fee-for-service plans

Feature	Managed care (HMO)	Fee-for-service
Method of payment	Prepaid monthly premium covers all or most health costs.	Pays set fee for each service used.
Doctor choice	Patient selects primary-care doctor from the plan's list.	Patient can use services of any doctor.
Availability of medical services	Controlled by "gatekeeper," typically patient's doctor in the plan.	Wide open—as long as patient has insurance coverage or can pay.
Paperwork	Little or no paperwork.	Insurer requires form, often lengthy, for each service used.
Prevention	Encourages regular doctor visits and provides patient education.	Little or no incentive for prevention.
Appeals process	Each plan has its own process; often difficult and lengthy.	Variable, depending upon insurer; may require persistent effort.

group model today represents only about 13 percent of HMO enrollment.

Network. In this model, an HMO contracts with several group practices, independent doctors, and hospitals, which often offer themselves as a unit or system for contracting purposes. Typically, some or all of these health-care providers have patients who are not HMO members. Network-model HMO's have gained in popularity. In 1997, they represented about 14 percent of HMO enrollment.

Individual practice association (IPA). This model is an insurance arrangement in which the HMO contracts with independent, often unrelated doctors, hospitals, and other services. It is the least tightly structured of the HMO models. The contracting providers in the IPA treat plan members and nonmember patients alike on their own premises. IPA's in 1997 accounted for the lion's share of HMO enrollment, about 67 percent.

Many plans offer a feature known as point of service (POS). POS allows member patients to consult and seek care from doctors or other clinicians outside of the plan, but for a fee that is higher than staying in the network. To protect patient choice, some states have passed laws requiring HMO's and similar health plans to have a POS option.

Other varieties of managed care

Many health-care plans that share characteristics of managed care are organized much more loosely than HMO's. Among such plans, the most popular is the preferred provider organization (PPO).

A PPO is a network of contractual arrangements with doctors, hospitals, and other health-care professionals. It offers member patients inexpensive access to the plan's own network of health-care providers, and more expensive access to out-of-network providers. PPO's provide neither the coordination of care nor the centralized administrative services typical of HMO's. What it does offer is cost control through set monthly premiums and small patient copayments. An estimated 90 million Americans are enrolled in PPO's.

Some health plans do not fit neatly into either the fee-for-service or managed-care category. Managed indemnity, for example, may or may not be a form of managed care—depending upon the observer. It is a traditional fee-for-service insurance plan that includes some type of limit on access and use of services. For example, the plan may require that doctors seek permission from the insurer before hospitalizing a patient.

Many employers with more than 10,000 employees sponsor health plans known as self-insured employer plans. These employers act as their own insurers, collecting premiums and negotiating contracts with health-care providers. Managed-care arrangements are common among self-insured employers, but not required.

The "alphabet soup" of managed-care health plans has confused many patients struggling to adjust to the new system. Experts advise that a patient's best defense against getting lost in the managed-care maze is to become familiar with his or her plan and find out what services and costs it covers before seeking treatment.

The Debate About
MANAGED CARE

Managed care is a
work in progress
with many merits
and shortcomings.

By Emily Friedman

I N 1997, MANAGED CARE WAS RAPIDLY BECOMING the dominant mode of health-care financing and delivery in the United States. As millions of people joined these new systems, a public debate was taking place on the merits and shortcomings of managed care. Supporters credited managed care with lowering the costs and limiting the red tape associated with health care, as well as improving access and coverage for preventive care. Critics charged that the system emphasizes costs over patient welfare.

Managed care's supporters included many state and federal legislators, researchers, economists, health-care analysts, and patients enrolled in managed-care health plans. Advocates emphasized managed care's strong record of holding health costs down. This cost containment, they maintained, benefits employers, individuals, and society as a whole. Moreover, managed-care plans greatly reduce the flood of claim forms issued by traditional fee-for-service insurance plans. Managed care also often encourages patients to adopt preventive behaviors and helps medical professionals practice preventive care. In the long term, these preventive practices lower health-care expenditures as well as save lives.

However, in 1997 a growing number of consumer advocates, doctors, health-care organizations, and members of the press became critical of managed care. Many health-care professionals, as well as patients, claimed that restrictions on treatment options in managed-care plans prevent doctors from providing adequate patient care. Other critics expressed concern about preserving the integrity of the traditional doctor-patient relationship in managed care. Consumer advocates questioned excessive profit-taking in some managed-care companies and raised concerns that many health-care plans restrict or block patients' avenues for appeal.

Areas of controversy

One of the most frequent and serious allegations made about some managed-care plans was that they impose "gag rules" on doctors and other health-care professionals. Gag rule is a colloquial term for a nondefamation clause or a nondisclosure clause. A nondefamation clause prohibits a health plan's contracting professionals from making negative statements about the plan. A nondisclosure clause prevents doctors or other professionals from revealing information such as the full range of treatment options available or financial incentives they may receive under the plan. For example, doctors in a managed-care plan may receive a bonus for limiting the number of referrals they make to specialists. A gag rule prohibits disclosure of such information, even when patients specifically ask for it. Ultimately, the main concern about such rules was that they may result in restrictions on treatment and adversely affect patient care.

Public protest over gag rules grew to such an uproar that one *Time* magazine cover in 1996 depicted a doctor with a gag in his

The author:

Emily Friedman is a health policy analyst and health policy section editor of the *Journal of the American Medical Association.*

mouth. In response to widespread criticism, the American Association of Health Plans (AAHP), the largest managed-care association in the nation, took steps to limit gag rules. It announced in late 1996 that doctors contracting with AAHP member plans would be allowed to reveal information such as provider incentives and all treatment options for a particular condition, including costly "experimental" procedures often denied to patients in managed-care plans.

Health-care professionals and consumers also criticized managed-care policies that limit the amounts and types of treatments offered. In some cases, treatments, drugs, and other services are withheld in favor of alternative, usually less expensive treatments. Moreover, some specialist physicians alleged that primary-care doctors receive inappropriate financial incentives to discourage their referring patients to specialists. The primary-care doctors in strongly centralized health plans such as health maintenance organizations (HMO's) exercise tremendous decision-making power, acting as "gatekeepers" who control access to most medical services. According to some specialists, this power can be abused.

Financial concerns

Another charge leveled by critics of managed care is that some plans are engaged in profiteering. By profiteering, critics mean that the plans withhold too large a part of the *premium* (insurance payment) for profit, administrative costs, and executive compensation. As a result the money available for actual patient care shrinks dramatically. In November 1996, the Association of American Medical Colleges reported that the percentage of premiums spent by health plans on patient care ranged widely, from 59 percent to 94 percent.

The debate over profiteering was especially intense in California. Each year, the California Medical Association (CMA) analyzes data provided to the state by health plans and then publishes a report on the plans' profit margins. In February 1997, the CMA reported that while the nonprofit Kaiser Permanente HMO spent 96.5 percent of its revenue on patient care, several health plans—mostly but not exclusively for-profit plans—spent as little as 72 percent of revenue on patient care. The CMA cautioned that comparisons among plans with very different structures and features could be misleading. Nevertheless, the report received much press coverage and generated criticism of the plans with higher profit margins.

The impetus for cost-cutting in managed care has also resulted in shorter and shorter hospital stays for major surgery and other serious conditions. Under some plans, *mastectomy* patients—women who have a breast removed because of cancer—have been discharged from the hospital on the same day as the surgery. Also, women have been discharged the same day they have given birth, sometimes even when the birth was by *Caesarean section*, a surgical form of delivery. Not all patients were pleased by these policies.

The "pro's" of managed care

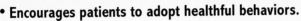

- Often costs less than fee-for-service insurance.

- Shields patients from large unexpected health costs.

- Encourages patients to adopt healthful behaviors.

- Encourages preventive medical care.

- Discourages unnecessary care.

- Coordinates all aspects of patient care.

- Eliminates complicated claim forms.

- Centralizes medical records within a health plan.

Patients and consumer advocates also voiced complaints about the difficulties of appealing health-plan decisions. For example, a doctor or plan administrator may turn down a patient's request for a diagnostic test or consultation with a specialist. Most managed-care plans have a process for appealing unfavorable decisions. However, the appeal process is often difficult and time-consuming.

One common complaint was that plan administrators take too long to respond to an appeal. In April 1997, the Health Care Financing Administration, the agency that oversees Medicare and Medicaid, announced a new appeal rule: plans that deny treatment to Medicare patients in need of urgent care must respond to appeals within 72 hours. The old rule had allowed up to 60 days.

Consumers also expressed concerns about the binding arbitration clauses in many managed-care health plans. *Arbitration* is the hearing and settlement of a dispute by a designated third party, presumed to be impartial. *Binding arbitration* means that the parties in the dispute must accept the arbitrator's decision. In some plans, the arbitration requirement even applies to allegations of medical malpractice, not just to disputes over access to services.

Many people object to these clauses, because plan members are forced to accept binding arbitration when they sign up. Yet in doing so, they relinquish their rights to sue the plan or its providers. In practice, however, some patients have sued in spite of arbitration clauses, and in a few cases, they have won.

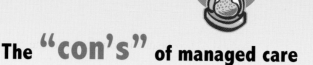

The "con's" of managed care

- Limits patient choices of providers and services.

- Incentives may prompt doctors or nurses to deny specialized care.

- Complex, changeable plan policies can be confusing.

- Patients' ability to change doctors may be limited.

- Appeals can be difficult and time-consuming.

- Services of a plan may be tied to a geographic region.

- Plan contracts rarely favor providers of indigent care.

- Contracts may exclude research or teaching hospitals.

Legislation to regulate managed care

The ongoing public debate over managed care has spurred many state legislatures to consider or to pass regulatory laws. Many legislatures, for example, passed laws mandating some form of an appeal process in managed-care plans, and Congress considered a variety of bills to improve and expedite appeal processes.

High on many states' agendas were *patient protection acts,* consumer-protection bills for patients in managed-care health plans. Typically these acts ban gag rules, protect patients' choice of doctor, and limit questionable financial incentives for providers. As of August 1, 1996, 26 state legislatures had passed some form of patient protection act.

Other bills before state legislatures and Congress addressed patients' rights issues such as health-plan members' ability to use hospital emergency facilities, better access to specialists, and easier appeal processes. More than 1,000 managed-care bills were submitted in state legislatures in 1996. By August 1996, every state except Hawaii and Michigan had passed at least one such bill.

By August 1996, 27 states had passed laws to protect the right of women to stay overnight in the hospital after giving birth. In

September 1996, Congress passed a similar law, which also guaranteed a hospital stay of up to 96 hours for women who undergo Caesarean section. This law was set to take effect in 1998. At the same time, pressure was being brought to bear on Congress and the states to mandate minimal hospital stays for mastectomy patients.

Some health-care professionals have tried to take managed-care issues directly to voters in initiatives. An *initiative* is a constitutional method in some states by which voters can approve laws by voting for them directly on the ballot. In the November 1996 general election, one ballot initiative in Oregon and two in California—all developed by health-care professionals—proposed laws that would have limited the ability of managed-care plans to do business. All three efforts failed at the polls, but they contributed to the overall debate.

Of particular concern to health-care professionals, especially doctors, has been an erosion of their ability to make a living under managed care. Again, cost-cutting is the central issue. Most managed-care plans achieve cost savings by paying doctors and hospitals less than they would get from fee-for-service payment and by payment arrangements such as *capitation* (prepayment for health services over a period of time). Indeed, in 1996 the American Medical Association reported that overall physician income was declining by 4 percent a year. Doctors in many specialties were experiencing even steeper reductions in income because of the decline in referrals to specialists. In fact, the shift to managed care was redistributing income in health care. Physicians, hospitals, and other providers were earning less income, while health plans, investors, managers, and executives were earning more.

In response to these concerns, physicians and hospitals began to form their own health plans. Such plans are called provider-sponsored organizations (PSO's). In a PSO, a group of physicians, hospitals, and/or other providers run their own health-care operation, accepting premiums directly and managing care themselves without the involvement of an insurer.

A work in progress

In the rapidly changing environment of health-care financing, it is often difficult to separate fact from fiction, truth from anecdote, and consumer issue from special interest. Moreover, managed-care plans differ widely by ownership, structure, and many other measures. Thus, drawing any clear-cut conclusions about managed care can be daunting. Some observers said that the chaotic, frequently changing health-care marketplace represents American free enterprise at its best. Others claimed that this marketplace represents the worst of free enterprise. The rhetoric is likely to heat up even more as managed care enters new markets and becomes more widespread. As with most innovations in health care, managed care in America remains a work in progress. **•••**

People can take
steps to improve
their chances of
receiving quality
medical care

Getting the Most
Out of Your
HEALTH PLAN

By Jeanne Finberg

IN THE 1990's, MILLIONS OF PEOPLE SHIFTED from traditional fee-for-service health plans to the managed-care system. The sudden change—mainly caused by employers hoping to cut the cost of providing insurance to workers—left many people confused about the new system and about how they could make managed care work best for their health-care needs.

Managed care keeps medical costs to a minimum by maintaining a close watch on the services and treatments offered to patients. Managed-care providers routinely deny tests and procedures that are deemed medically "unnecessary" or not cost-effective. The plans also limit the numbers of doctors and hospitals available to plan members. As a result, a patient may feel as if the system has placed restrictions on his or her right to choose high-quality health care and may feel helpless to challenge decisions made by managed-care providers.

According to health-care experts, however, people in managed-care programs can take steps to improve their chances of receiving satisfactory medical care under managed care. Individuals can make informed choices on choosing a health plan and a doctor; get to know the benefits in their health plan and use those benefits to their best advantage; learn about their rights; and become assertive about their health-care needs. Not everyone has the luxury of choosing from a selection of plans. Some employers offer only one health-care plan, but other employers offer two or more. And people who are self-employed can choose from a wide variety of plans.

Make a personal medical inventory

People who are able to select their own plan should first take an inventory of their own and their family's medical needs, according to health-care experts. They suggest using the following questions as a starting point:
- How often do you go to the doctor?
- What types of doctors or specialists do you or your family go to? For example, a woman might regularly see a gynecologist, and a child may see a pediatrician.
- Do you have a chronic medical condition that requires regular treatment, perhaps from a specialist? Examples of such conditions are diabetes, arthritis, asthma, or allergies.
- Have you had a medical condition such as cancer or heart disease that might require extensive treatment in the future?
- Do you require mental health care?
- Do you take any prescription drugs regularly?

Research health plans

Health-care experts also advise that people research the health plans they are considering. They should obtain a listing of the doctors, hospitals, and services included in the plan's network. Also

The author:

Jeanne Finberg is a senior attorney, policy analyst, and head of the health group for the West Coast office of Consumers Union, publisher of *Consumer Reports*. This article expresses the views of the author, not Consumers Union.

request a copy of the *policy* (the written description of the plan). Most information on any health-care plan is available from representatives of the managed-care company or from the benefits manager at the individual's place of employment.

Friends, family, and coworkers enrolled in the plan are another good source of information about the plan. They can be asked if they have encountered any unexpected costs or limitations of coverage and if the plan provides high-quality health care.

Health-care professionals also suggest that individuals research specific services and coverage provided in the plan, such as:

Choice of doctors. If you regularly see a doctor, check to see if he or she is included in the plan's list of available doctors. Make sure that the list is current and call your doctor to ensure that he or she is still in the plan's network of doctors. If you do not already have a doctor, call a number of the doctors in the plan's network and ask if they are accepting new patients. Some health-care advocates have criticized managed-care providers for including the names of doctors who are not members of the plan or are not ac-

Guidelines for choosing a managed-care health plan

For each plan, perform the following checks:

- If you know someone in the plan, ask for their opinion of the health services.

- Request a directory of doctors and hospitals. If you have selected a doctor, check whether that doctor participates in the plan.

- Try to determine if most of the services you expect to use are located nearby.

- Request a list of excluded or limited services. Check for services that are of concern to you.

- Ask the plan representative what percentage of doctors are board-certified.

- Try to determine if the plan is overcrowded. A way to check is to select doctors from the directory and ask their staff about appointments.

- Ask what referrals require *precertification* (advance approval that is required for certain costly procedures).

- Obtain cost information, including monthly fees and copayments. Calculate how much your last year's medical care would have cost under this plan.

- Request a quality "report card" from a plan representative. You can also obtain accreditation information from the National Committee for Quality Assurance (NCQA), which evaluates health providers:
  Phone contact: 1-800-839-6487
  Internet address: http://www.ncqa.org
                                (Select "Accreditation.")

- Check with your state's Department of Insurance or Department of Health. Some states maintain a list of complaints and grievances concerning health-care providers.

Sources: National Committee for Quality Assurance (NCQA); Agency for Health Care Policy and Research (AHCPR) of the U.S. Department of Health and Human Services; the Health Insurance Association of America.

cepting new patients. Also, check the rules of the plan to determine if it will cover the costs of consulting a medical specialist.

Location of services. Determine whether the doctors, hospitals, and pharmacies in the plan's network are located in convenient locations.

Coverage of preexisiting conditions. Check the plan's policy on *preexisting conditions*, medical conditions diagnosed before enrollment in the plan. Some plans cover preexisting conditions, such as heart disease, cancer, and diabetes, and some do not. The exclusions and limitations of coverage of preexisting conditions are often buried in the fine print of the plan.

Services offered. Determine which services are covered by the plan. Managed care encourages the use of some services, such as regular checkups with the primary-care physician, by making them inexpensive to plan members. Other services, such as those that are not considered to be preventive care, may not be covered by the plan.

Restrictions on diagnosis and treatment. Managed-care plans rarely pay for experimental treatments and also closely regulate treatments and surgeries recommended by primary-care physicians. Ask if certain diagnostic tests and treatments, such as mammograms or corrective surgery, require *precertification* (advanced approval from the plan's administrators). In many plans, costly tests such as *magnetic resonance imaging* (a medical technique that uses powerful magnets to view tissues inside the body) require precertification. Some plans also require precertification for visits to a specialist or for prescription renewals.

Second opinion option. Find out if the plan allows patients to consult with another doctor about a condition diagnosed by the primary-care physician.

Point-of-service (POS) option. Some managed-care plans offer a POS option, which allows plan members to consult doctors outside of their plan for an extra—often substantial—fee.

Changing doctors. Ask if the plan imposes any restrictions on changing primary-care doctors. Some plans require that patients keep the same primary-care physician for entire term of their contract, which can be a year or more.

Emergency care. Find out how the plan covers emergency care. In an emergency, a patient may need to go to a doctor or hospital that is not in the plan's network of providers. Some plans will cover the cost of emergencies regardless of which hospital the individual visits or which doctor treats the condition. However, many plans have strict definitions on what is an emergency condition and what is not. If the administrator of such a plan decides that an

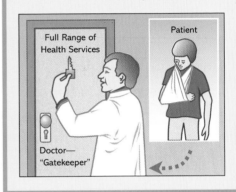

Doctor as gatekeeper

In managed-care plans such as HMO's, the primary-care doctor controls patients' access to medical services such as diagnostic tests or the services of medical specialists.

Full Range of Health Services

Patient

Doctor— "Gatekeeper"

Guidelines for choosing a primary-care doctor

- Request the directory of doctors and hospitals for your health plan.

- Try to obtain a recommendation from one of the following: a plan member; a health-care practitioner; a local medical society.

- Contact the state medical licensing board for information about a doctor's credentials.

- Look up doctor names in the *Directory of Medical Specialists,* a frequently updated reference on practicing physicians that is available at many public libraries.

- Use the "AMA Physician Select," the American Medical Association's free Internet service for information about physicians. Internet address: http://www.ama-assn.org.

- Find out whether the doctor is board-certified in her or his specialty. *Board-certified* means that the doctor has passed a standard qualifying medical test. *Board-eligible* means that the doctor has been qualified to take the test but has not passed it. For this information, phone

the American Board of Medical Specialties at 1-800-776-2378.

- Ask plan administrators if they require board certification of specialists.

- Interview the office staff. Ask how long patients usually wait for a routine appointment. (The wait shouldn't be longer than one week.)

- Ask to have a personal interview with the doctor. Assess the doctor-patient relationship and explain any of your special medical needs and conditions.

- Ask the doctor if he or she expects to leave the plan any time soon.

- Ask the doctor if he or she has experience in treating medical problems that you have or have had in the past.

- Use your own "people instincts" to decide if you and the doctor would be compatible.

Sources: National Committee for Quality Assurance (NCQA); Agency for Health Care Policy and Research (AHCPR) of the U.S. Department of Health and Human Services; the Health Insurance Association of America.

Asserting your rights: making an appeal

When choosing a plan, it is important to obtain information on its appeals process, which is used by a plan member to contest a decision, such as denial of a treatment, made by a primary-care physician or the plan's administrator.

Ask the managed-care plan's administrator if the plan specifies a time limit for responding to an appeal and if it provides published accounts on outcomes of patient appeals. Most importantly, find out if the policy contains an arbitration clause, a provision that forces plan members to settle disputes outside of a courtroom.

Taking the time to file an appeal often pays off. For example, according to the Health Care Financing Administration (HCFA), the federal agency that administers Medicare and Medicaid, about one-third of Medicare appeals in 1995 resulted in partial or total reversal of a health plan's decision.

According to health-care advocates, the following tips may help an individual file a successful appeal:
• If your doctor is on your side, request a written statement in support of your claim.
• Do not display anger. You will accomplish more by being courteous, yet firm and assertive.
• Make careful written records at every step of the process, and keep all records together in a file.
• Obtain and record the name of everyone you

speak to during the process of appealing a decision.
• If a plan representative is uncooperative, ask to speak to the supervisor.
• Be persistent, don't give up until every option has been tried.

If an individual's appeal is rejected, he or she can request a hearing with the health-plan's administrators. If the hearing does not resolve the dispute, an individual can seek the help of agencies outside of the health plan.

A good place to start is the benefits office at the individual's place of employment. A company's benefits manager is answerable to superiors in the company, not to the health plan. Furthermore, this manager may be sensitive to employee opinion within the company. He or she may be strongly motivated to support an appeal that seems reasonable.

Another option is to file a complaint with the state's department of insurance or the department of health. Complaints about Medicaid or Medicare can be filed with HCFA. Although state laws vary, most states have a grievance process regarding health-care providers. The support of a consumer-oriented state agency can make a difference.

If all else fails, an individual may pursue legal action against the health-plan company or arbitration.

An overview of the appeals process in an HMO

An appeal of an unfavorable decision starts on the inside of the HMO. The patient first contacts the plan representative and then the plan's administrator. If the appeal is rejected, the patient can then appeal outside the HMO by first contacting the benefits manager at the place of work. Another option is to contact a state agency, such as the state department of health or insurance commission. A last resort is to bring the appeal to the court system.

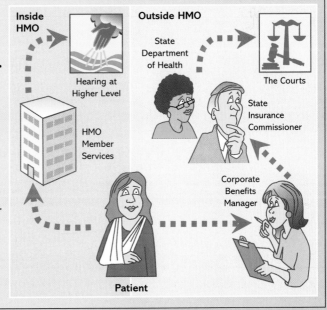

Inside HMO

Hearing at Higher Level

HMO Member Services

Outside HMO

State Department of Health

The Courts

State Insurance Commissioner

Corporate Benefits Manager

Patient

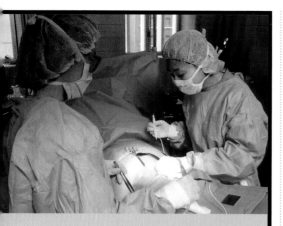

individual sought unneeded emergency care at a hospital or with a doctor outside of the plan's network, the cost of care will not be covered and the patient will have to pay.

Cost of Plan. Health plans vary greatly in the cost of premiums and coverage. Before choosing a plan, health-care advocates advise that individuals calculate the amount of the monthly premium as well as the cost of *copayment,* the out-of-pocket costs for checkups, tests, and treatments.

Check plan quality

Once an individual has determined the services provided and the tests and treatments covered by the plan, health-care experts say that it is important to analyze the quality of the plans. They suggest, for example, contacting The National Committee for Quality Assurance (NCQA) for information on the plan. The NCQA is a private organization set up by large corporations and health-care plans to accredit managed-care plans. Individuals can also request information about managed-care health plans from the state insurance department.

Take advantage of the plan's features

After choosing a plan and a doctor, the best way to get the most out of a managed-care plan is to take advantage of the system's greatest benefit—its practice of preventive medicine. Most plans offer annual physicals and regular screening tests for cancer, heart disease, and other serious illnesses at little or no cost to the patient. Moreover, many plans offer programs such as those that help people quit smoking. Although managed-care plans offer a full range of preventive programs, these benefits are useless if plan holders do not make themselves aware of the offerings and use them to their greatest benefit.

Health-care experts agree that the individuals who get the most out of their health plans are those who take an active role in their health care. Individuals must become partners with their doctors and informed about their health care and health status. If an individual does not manage his or her own health care, it may be mismanaged by the managed-care system. **• • •**

Your rights as a patient in a managed-care plan

• Your health provider must clearly itemize any exclusions or limitations to full medical coverage. For example, its policy of coverage for preexisting conditions should be spelled out.

• You should be able to obtain a current directory of doctors and medical services in your health plan.

• Your plan should provide a reasonable pool of doctors from which to choose your primary-care physician.

• You have a right to change your doctor assignment upon request.

• A full range of standard medical services, including physicians in major specialties, should be available in your plan.

• Emergency and urgent care should be available around the clock.

• You are entitled to a prompt explanation for denial of a request for any medical service.

• Your plan should provide a well-defined, easy-to-use appeals process as well as a process for patient feedback and quality improvement.

• You have the right to obtain any of your medical records upon request.

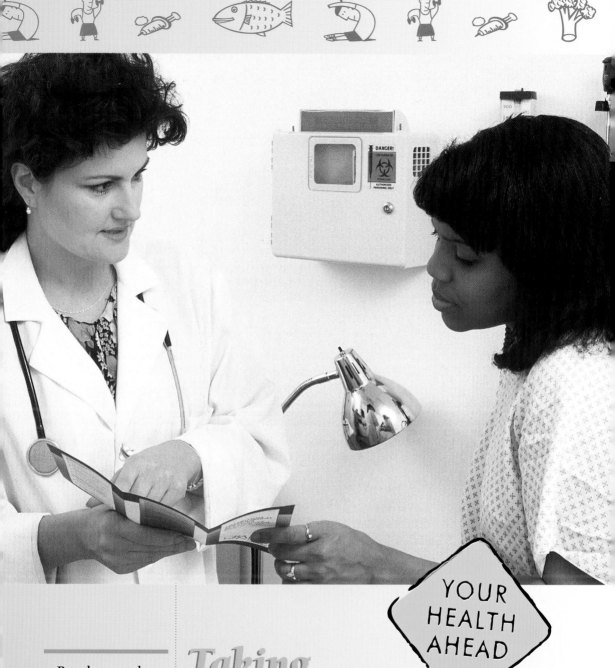

YOUR
HEALTH
AHEAD

Taking
Charge of
YOUR HEALTH

People can take
charge of their own
health by adopting
healthful behaviors
and practicing
prevention.

By Jeanne Finberg

I N TODAY'S CLIMATE OF MEDICAL COST-CUTTING AND MANAGED CARE, the watchword in health care is prevention. Health planners, analysts, and health-care professionals know that the financial and human costs associated with preventing illness are far less than the costs of treating illness. For this reason, many managed-care programs strongly emphasize preventive care.

You can take charge of your own health with your doctor as a partner by practicing preventive health maintenance in your daily life. You can adopt behaviors that maintain or improve good health while rejecting those behaviors that may harm your health. If you belong to a managed-care health plan, such as an HMO, the task is made a little easier, because some plans provide incentives and opportunities for prevention and health maintenance.

Statistically, people who eat right, stay fit, and avoid smoking live longer, healthier lives than people who do not do these things. Although good health habits do not guarantee a long, healthy life, and bad habits do not ensure that you will die young, you can stack the odds on your side by practicing healthy behaviors.

Smoking and its hazards to health

The one action that will benefit health most is to refrain from smoking. The hazards of smoking are well documented by a large body of scientific research. Smokers are about 10 times more likely to develop lung cancer, and they are at least 10 times more likely to develop *emphysema* (a disabling chronic lung disease) than nonsmokers. Smokers are also more likely to die from cancers of the lung, throat, and mouth. They have significantly higher rates of heart disease than nonsmokers as well. Moreover, researchers have documented the dangers of *second-hand smoke* (smoke breathed in by nonsmokers). More and more evidence shows that second-hand smoke increases the risk of heart and lung disease and cancer for people who are exposed to smokers' smoke.

Quitting smoking will benefit a person no matter how long they have been a smoker, and it will contribute to the health of those around them. Smokers often find, however, that they need help in quitting the habit. Fortunately, many managed-care health plans offer programs that help people quit smoking. Employers may also offer such programs or some reimbursement for them.

The benefits of a healthy diet

Another important way to reduce the chance of illness is to pay attention to diet. Healthy eating greatly reduces the risk of heart disease, the number-one killer in the United States. The most important contributing factor to most heart disease is the buildup of a fatty substance called *cholesterol* in the bloodstream. Deposits of cholesterol in arteries can reduce blood flow to the heart and cause a heart attack. Because diet affects the level of cholesterol in the

The author:

Jeanne Finberg is a senior attorney, policy analyst, and head of the health group for the West Coast office of Consumers Union, publisher of *Consumer Reports*. This article expresses the views of the author, not Consumers Union.

Common screening tests

Regular screening for common killers, such as cancer, is crucial to disease prevention. The following screening tests are recommended by medical professionals.

Type of test	Description	Frequency
Blood pressure reading	Inflation of rubber cuff around upper arm	Every 1 to 2 years in adulthood.
Cholesterol reading	Small blood sample taken for analysis	Every 5 years in adulthood if readings are in normal range.
Colorectal cancer exam	Digital rectal examination	Every year after age 40.
	Sigmoidoscopy (lower colon exam with instrument)	Every 5 years after age 50.
	Blood stool test	Every year after age 50.
Dental exam	Teeth cleaning and examination for gum disease, oral cancer, and other mouth and tooth problems	At least once a year in adulthood.
Eye exam	Vision test; checks for glaucoma and cataracts	Every 2 or 3 years after age 40; yearly after age 65.
Mammogram	X ray to screen for breast cancer in women	Every year after age 40.
Prostate cancer tests	Rectal exam and blood test (PSA) to search for prostate cancer in men	Every year for men over 50 who have at least a 10-year life expectancy.
Pelvic exam and pap smear	Physical examination of cervix, ovaries, and uterus to look for cancer and other abnormalities; cell sample to check for microscopic cancerous changes	Every year for sexually active women and women over age 18.

Sources: American Cancer Society; National Heart, Lung, and Blood Institute; and other health organizations. Note that the cancer screening recommendations presented here are for people with average risk of cancer.

bloodstream, the best way to reduce cholesterol is to avoid or reduce saturated fats in your diet. Saturated fats are the fats in meat, dairy products, and tropical oils, such as coconut or palm oil.

It is not a good idea to eliminate dietary fat completely, however. Fat produces energy and is an essential part of cells. Some fat acts as *high-density lipoprotein*, or *HDL*, a substance that helps rid the blood of harmful cholesterol.

A healthy diet consists of plenty of fruits, vegetables, and grains, and small quantities of meat and dairy products. The U.S. Department of Agriculture offers a food pyramid as a guide for eating healthy. The items at the pyramid's narrow top—fats and sugars—are to be used sparingly, while those at the broad base—whole grains—should be eaten in larger quantities. The food pyramid also contains information about the number of daily servings that nutritionists recommend eating from each group. Your doctor, a nurse, or a nutritionist can provide help in understanding and using the food pyramid as a guide to a healthy diet.

The food pyramid

The U.S. Department of Agriculture offers a food pyramid as a guide for healthy eating. Foods, such as fats and sweets, at the upper levels of the pyramid should be eaten less often than breads and pastas, at the lower levels.

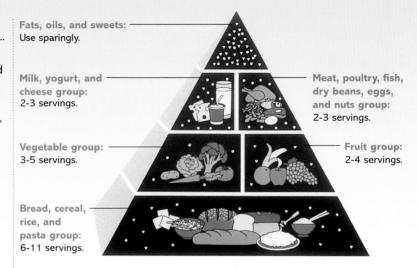

Fats, oils, and sweets: Use sparingly.

Milk, yogurt, and cheese group: 2-3 servings.

Meat, poultry, fish, dry beans, eggs, and nuts group: 2-3 servings.

Vegetable group: 3-5 servings.

Fruit group: 2-4 servings.

Bread, cereal, rice, and pasta group: 6-11 servings.

For good health eating, plenty of fiber is also important. *Fiber* is the portion of some vegetables, fruits, and grains that pass through the body undigested. Some studies have shown that fiber may help reduce cholesterol and prevent high blood pressure. A high-fiber diet helps protect against colon cancer and possibly other kinds of cancer, too. Nutritionists recommend eating 20 to 35 grams of fiber daily. High-fiber foods include fresh fruits, vegetables, and whole grains such as whole-wheat bread and brown rice.

Nutritionists also recommend a diet rich in *antioxidants* (nutrients that may protect against cancer). An antioxidant diet should include foods rich in vitamins C and E and beta-carotene. Some examples of such foods are broccoli, carrots, and tomatoes.

Maintaining a healthy weight is another way to reduce the risk of illness. Being overweight dramatically increases your risk of heart disease. It can also cause many other health problems, including higher risk for diabetes and some types of cancer.

According to the U.S. Centers for Disease Control and Prevention in Atlanta, Georgia, about one-fourth of all Americans are overweight. Overweight is loosely defined as being heavier than the recommended weight for your height. Other factors affect an evaluation of appropriate weight, however. A muscular, big-boned individual, for example, can weigh more than the recommended weight for his or her height and still not be considered overweight. A doctor can help you calculate your ideal weight and plan a diet that will allow you to lose weight effectively and safely.

Other prevention tips

Regular exercise is another component of a healthy lifestyle. Many studies have shown that regular *aerobic exercise* (which increases the use of oxygen by the body) can prevent high blood pressure and heart disease or reduce the severity of these life-threatening problems. Cycling, jogging, skating, swimming, and fast walking are forms of aerobic exercise.

Aerobic exercise does not have to be strenuous or complicated. Simple exercises such as walking for 20 minutes three times a week may benefit health. In fact, studies have shown that moderate exercise is almost as beneficial to the heart as strenuous exercise. Your physician can help you choose a regular routine of aerobic activity that is appropriate for your age, weight, and fitness.

The sun is another threat to maintaining good health. The sun's ultraviolet rays are a major cause of skin cancer. According to the American Cancer Society, more than 800,000 Americans are diagnosed with some form of skin cancer each year. Although most skin cancers are not life-threatening, a few types are fatal. *Melanoma* (cancer of dark-pigmented cells) is one of the most dangerous types of cancer.

The best protection against all forms of skin cancer is to avoid direct sun exposure or to cover exposed skin with sunscreen. This protection is especially important to fair-skinned or red-headed people, who have a higher risk of skin cancer.

Regular checkups and screenings

No matter how much you cultivate healthy habits, you still need regular checkups by a physician. Moreover, as people age, they should have regular screening tests for common killers such as cancer, high blood pressure, and heart disease. Early detection of disease is often the best defense against serious illness.

In fact, according to the American Cancer Society, early detection of breast, tongue, mouth, colon, rectum, cervix, prostate, testis, and melanoma cancers would save about 115,000 lives annually. About 67 percent of people with these forms of cancer survive at least five years after diagnosis. However, the survival rate jumps to 95 percent for people who are diagnosed and treated during the earliest stages of illness.

Most managed-care plans promote regular checkups and screenings by offering these services at little or no out-of-pocket cost. This emphasis on keeping costs low through prevention is one of the great strengths of managed care. If you belong to a managed-care health plan, you can use this strength to stay in charge of your own health and well-being. ● ● ●

For further reading:
The United States Department of Agriculture (USDA). Nutrition and *Your Health: Dietary Guidelines for Americans/4th Edition, USDA* Home and Garden Bulletin No. 232. You can obtain information about this document by phoning the USDA Center for Nutrition Policy and Promotion at 202-418-2312; or you can view the document on the USDA's website at http://www.usda.gov/fcs/cnpp.htm.

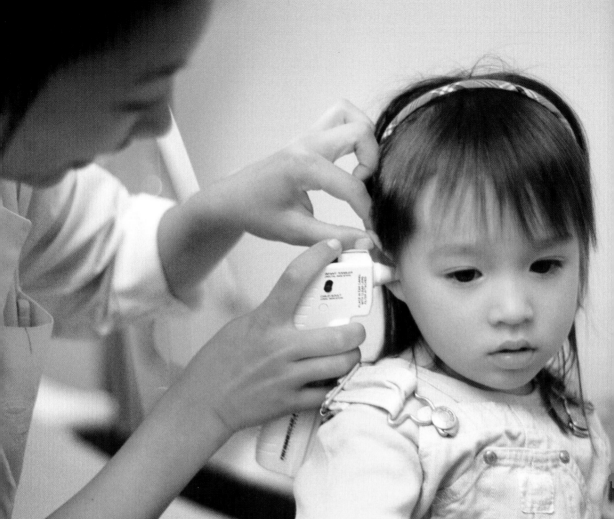

Managed care's
cost cuts have
affected research,
education, and
the uninsured.

MANAGED CARE

and Society

By Jennifer Parello

IN THE 1990'S, MILLIONS OF AMERICANS WERE SHIFTED from traditional fee-for-service insurance plans into managed health-care programs, which has dramatically altered the financing and delivery of health care in the United States. Managed-care programs—first developed by medical professionals attempting to extend quality health care to all members of a community regardless of income—have evolved into enterprises that put a special emphasis on managing costs associated with health care.

Although managed care has been successful in cutting costs, critics of the system have claimed that certain cost controls may, in fact, endanger the health of society as a whole. Some medical experts, including former U.S. Surgeon General C. Everett Koop, have sharply criticized funding cuts to academic hospitals and research facilities and have raised concerns about the role managed care plays in the growing number of uninsured Americans.

Managed care aims to restrain health-care costs by stressing the importance of preventive care, by standardizing medical practices to produce better outcomes, by restricting freedom to choose a physician, by limiting hospital stays and treatment options, and by eliminating unnecessary procedures. By the late 1990's, however, cost cuts were threatening the financial stability of many academic medical centers and research facilities. Many doctors feared that the lack of financing to hospitals and researchers might jeopardize future medical advancements and new treatments.

Hospitals, educators, researchers feel the pinch

Hospitals, which used to receive large subsidies from insurance providers and government agencies, were especially hard hit by managed-care cost cuts. To make matters worse, the federal government was at the same time slashing funds for *Medicaid* (the federal program that covers health-care costs of the poor). Hospitals receive fewer dollars from managed-care companies than from fee-for-service plans. In 1996, California hospitals for example received nearly 50 percent less money from insurance reimbursements than in 1991, when many patients were still in fee-for-service plans. The loss of funds forced more than 40 private hospitals in the six-county southern California region to close and several teaching hospitals to cut staff and training positions.

Teaching hospitals play a crucial role in the U.S. medical system. There patients find specialized care that is unavailable elsewhere, and young doctors receive training. Teaching hospitals are more costly to run than other hospitals, because they staff more people, use more expensive diagnostic tests, and care for a greater number of patients suffering from rare, difficult-to-treat disorders.

These hospitals have traditionally charged insurance companies high fees for routine procedures in order to cover training and research costs. Cost-conscious managed-care plans, however, refuse to pay those prices and often reject experimental treatments.

The author:

Jennifer Parello is managing editor of the *Health & Medical Annual.*

A doctor reviews a medical procedure with residents undergoing on-the-job training in a teaching hospital. Teaching hospitals have been hit hard by the cost-cutting practices of health-care companies in the era of managed care.

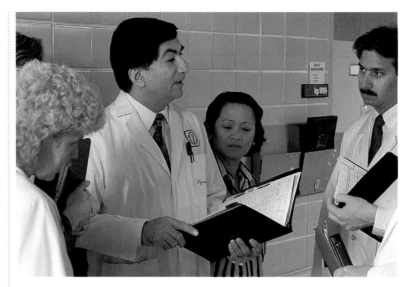

In response to dwindling funding, University of California Los Angeles (UCLA) Medical Center, for example, was forced to trim its staff from 4,200 in 1990 to 3,200 in 1996. It also shortened patient hospital stays and hired unlicensed technicians to take over some of the duties of higher-paid registered nurses. The hospital, a world famous training facility for medical specialists such as *cardiologists* (doctors who specialize in diseases of the heart), also instituted the less expensive practice of training medical generalists, such as primary-care doctors, greatly limiting the number of specialists accepted into its training program.

Managed care has also resulted in funding cuts to medical researchers, who study treatments for diseases and develop the equipment and techniques that save lives. Until managed-care cost-tightening measures took hold, insurers were often partners with research institutions in funding *clinical trials* (tests performed on humans) that tested new treatments for diseases.

While a few managed-care companies agree to pay for treatment in such clinical trials, many refuse to cover the treatments because their effectiveness is unproved. Without these experimental clinical studies, however, scientists say they would be unable to develop successful new treatments for diseases such as cancer and AIDS.

The plight of the uninsured

Dwindling funds paid by managed-care organizations have also limited hospitals' ability to care for the growing number Americans without health insurance. In 1997, more than 40 million Americans—many of whom were children—had no health insurance, according to the U.S. Census Bureau. In addition, about 33 percent of the population under age 65 who had insurance were underinsured. These people risked huge, out-of-pocket expenses if they got sick because of the limitations of their health plans.

In the days before managed care, most hospitals used income made from treating insured patients to cover the costs of caring for the uninsured. However, because managed-care plans refuse to pay for many costly tests, treatments, and procedures, there is far less profit to make up for the shortfall.

The uninsured, on the whole, are in poorer health and are more costly to treat than the insured because they are less likely to get preventive exams and treatment services and to have diseases diagnosed, according to a 1996 report by the Health Insurance Policy Program performed by researchers at UCLA. The uninsured often seek medical help only in emergency situations, which is much more costly than preventive medicine. The cost of treating these people is passed on to the insured through rising hospital and insurance premium costs.

Critics also claim that managed care has contributed to the escalating number of uninsured by denying coverage to those people suffering from preexisting conditions or expensive diseases, such as AIDS. In fact, some managed-care companies routinely find ways to deny coverage to people with costly illnesses, according to Linda Peeno, chair of the ethics committee at University Hospital in Louisville, Kentucky. Peeno worked for three managed-care companies as part of a team of doctors whose job was to grant approval of tests and hospitalization recommended by a primary-care physician.

The managed-care system has been effective in reducing the expense of medical care, say health-care experts, but not without exacting a toll from society. According to an essay written by C. Everett Koop in 1996, managed care will not be judged a success until it goes beyond cutting costs. Health-care experts say that the system must also recognize the need for medical education and research funding and not neglect the growing number of Americans without health insurance—a number that may reach 60 million by the year 2000.　●●●

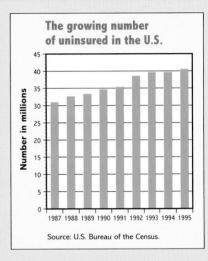

The growing number of uninsured in the U.S.

Number in millions

1987 1988 1989 1990 1991 1992 1993 1994 1995

Source: U.S. Bureau of the Census.

Outside the medical safety net

The trend toward larger numbers of uninsured people promises future trouble for individuals and for society. In 1987, about 32 million Americans were uninsured, and in 1995, the number of uninsured rose to nearly 42 million. People without insurance have difficulty getting health care, and paying for it may impoverish them.

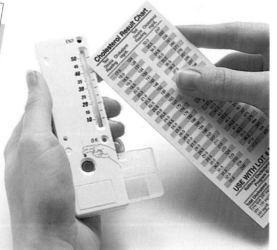

A HEALTHY YOU

Self-test Kits Bring Medicine Closer to Home

By Lauren Love

Over-the-counter kits allow consumers to take an active role in monitoring their own health care

IN THE DAYS BEFORE HOME MEDICAL TESTING KITS APPEARED on store shelves, all medical tests were performed in either a hospital or a doctor's office. People had to wait days or weeks before test results were available. Taking tests for a number of conditions out of the laboratory and bringing them into the home has cut time and expense involved in diagnosing and monitoring many common medical conditions.

Pharmacies carry two basic types of tests: diagnostic tests and monitoring tests. A diagnostic test determines whether a certain condition is present. Diagnostic tests check for conditions such as pregnancy, urinary tract infection, fecal blood, and human immunodeficiency virus (HIV). A monitoring test checks a known condition, such as blood glucose levels, blood pressure, cholesterol, and ovulation.

The first home test, which enabled diabetics to check glucose levels in their urine, was introduced in 1941. By 1997, over-the-counter products tested several basic conditions. The newest test on the market was one that detected HIV, the virus that causes AIDS. It was approved for sale in 1996 by the FDA (Food and Drug Administration). Home medical tests must receive approval from the FDA before tests can be sold over-the-counter in drugstores.

Home medical tests are inexpensive and easy to use. Most home tests provide results within minutes of testing, and some tests are as accurate as those performed in a doctor's office. And studies have shown that many home tests have improved rates of early detection of illness.

The author:

Lauren Love is a freelance writer.

BLOOD GLUCOSE MONITORS

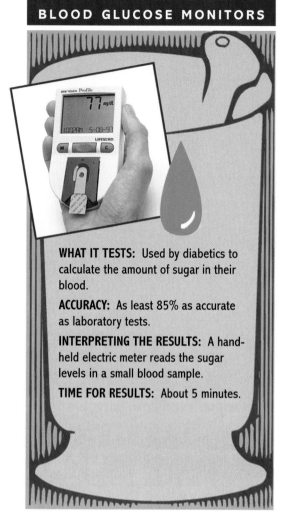

WHAT IT TESTS: Used by diabetics to calculate the amount of sugar in their blood.

ACCURACY: As least 85% as accurate as laboratory tests.

INTERPRETING THE RESULTS: A hand-held electric meter reads the sugar levels in a small blood sample.

TIME FOR RESULTS: About 5 minutes.

Diabetes—the third leading cause of death in the United States—afflicts more than 15 million Americans. Diabetics whose blood sugar is not carefully controlled are at increased risk of heart disease, stroke, kidney disease, blindness, and circulatory and nerve problems. Blood-glucose monitors have made the management of the disease much easier for patients who must keep a close eye on their blood-sugar levels and adjust their insulin in accordance with the test results.

Blood-glucose monitors are electronic meters that are compact, easy to operate, and provide almost instant readings of blood-sugar levels. The monitors have made a significant impact on the treatment of dia-betes, making it possible for patients to adjust medication, diet, or exercise in direct response to their latest blood-sugar reading.

How it works

Blood-glucose meters read blood-sugar levels by analyzing a blood sample placed on a test strip. Diabetics provide the sample by pricking their finger with a lancet included in the monitoring kit. Monitor kits also provide a supply of test strips that must be purchased separately once the original supply runs out.

Interpreting the results

Most monitors provide a digital display of a blood-glucose level minutes after a patient deposits a blood sample. Patients using monitors that are not equipped with digital displays must compare the test strip with a colored-bar chart. Diabetics whose vision has been impaired by the disease may find it difficult to read these results.

Most monitors provide patients with a log to chart their blood-sugar levels. Some electronic monitors log the data into their memory banks. Data can also be transferred to a computer program for long-term storage.

Accuracy

Blood-glucose monitors are at least 85 percent as accurate as tests performed in a laboratory. The American Diabetes Association accepts this standard of accuracy.

To get the most accurate reading, it is important to keep each test sample free of dirt or blood from a previous test. The design of some monitors require that they be cleaned frequently to ensure accurate readings.

Cautions

Patients should consult their physician before attempting to treat or monitor diabetes.

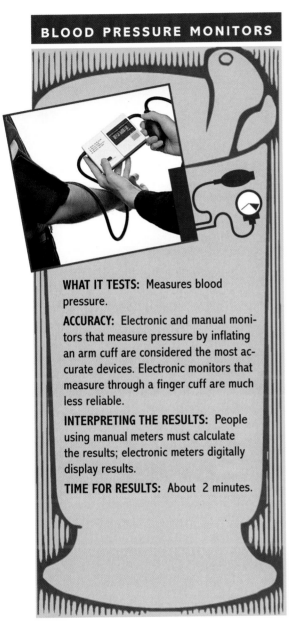

WHAT IT TESTS: Measures blood pressure.

ACCURACY: Electronic and manual monitors that measure pressure by inflating an arm cuff are considered the most accurate devices. Electronic monitors that measure through a finger cuff are much less reliable.

INTERPRETING THE RESULTS: People using manual meters must calculate the results; electronic meters digitally display results.

TIME FOR RESULTS: About 2 minutes.

Hypertension (high blood pressure) affects more than 50 million Americans. If left untreated, hypertension can cause stroke, heart disease, or kidney disease. Doctors consider it important to carefully monitor a patient's blood pressure. Patients who want to keep tabs on their own condition can do so through the use of a home blood pressure monitor.

Two components make up the force known as blood pressure—systolic (pumping) pressure and diastolic (resting) pressure. Blood pressure monitors provide readings of both these pressures.

Pressure against artery walls peaks when the heart contracts and pumps blood through the arteries. This is the systolic pressure. Blood pressure is lowest between heartbeats, when the heart is at rest. This is the diastolic pressure. Doctors consider a systolic pressure of more than 150 or a diastolic pressure of more than 90 serious enough to require treatment.

How it works

All meters measure blood pressure in a similar fashion. A person places a cuff around their upper arm, wrist, or finger. The cuff is then inflated either manually or electronically. As the cuff inflates, it compresses an artery, momentarily interrupting blood flow. As the cuff pressure is gradually released, blood flow resumes.

Interpreting the results

There are two basic types of blood pressure meters—manually operated meters and electronic devices. Manual meters require an individual to place a stethoscope over a brachial (main) artery, and listen for the distinct sounds blood makes as it starts to flow again through the artery as the cuff deflates.

The first sound a self-tester must identify is the systolic pressure—the hollow thumping sound that signals that the flow of blood through the brachial artery has resumed. As the arm cuff deflates, the thumping increases and then sharply decreases—a sound that signals diastolic pressure. As an individual hears the cues for systolic and diastolic pressure, they refer to an attached circular dial, which translates each of the pressures into a number—120 (systolic)/80 (diastolic), for example.

Electronic devices do not require a stethoscope. People using electronic meters need only strap on the inflatable cuff and wait for the device to provide a digital readout of the test results.

Accuracy

When used correctly, manually operated monitors are generally more accurate than electronic devices. However, electronic monitors are easier to use. Doctors consider electronic devices that automatically inflate cuffs around the upper arm to be nearly as accurate as manual monitors. Other electronic models, especially those that measure blood pressure by inflating a cuff around a finger, are much less reliable, according to the American Heart Association. People who use in-home blood pressure monitors should periodically take the device to a doctor's office to calibrate the monitor and check its accuracy.

Cautions

Several factors can affect a blood pressure reading. Physical activity and emotional state can cause great fluctuation in blood pressure. Doctors recommend that several readings be taken consecutively and averaged to obtain an accurate blood pressure measurement.

People should not change their treatment for hypertension based on a home blood pressure reading. Patients should always consult a physician before making any changes in their diet, exercise, or medication.

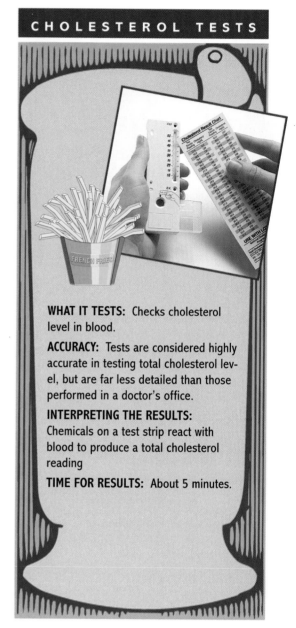

CHOLESTEROL TESTS

WHAT IT TESTS: Checks cholesterol level in blood.

ACCURACY: Tests are considered highly accurate in testing total cholesterol level, but are far less detailed than those performed in a doctor's office.

INTERPRETING THE RESULTS: Chemicals on a test strip react with blood to produce a total cholesterol reading

TIME FOR RESULTS: About 5 minutes.

Cholesterol is a fatty substance that makes up an important part of the membrane of each cell in the human body. Certain foods, such as eggs, dairy products, and red meat, contain high levels of cholesterol. When eaten in excess, these foods can raise blood cholesterol to an unhealthy level.

About 52 million Americans have high cholesterol, according to the Federal National Cholesterol Education Program, which increases risk of serious illness. When an individual's blood cholesterol rises above a desirable level, cholesterol builds up in the arteries, blocking the flow of blood, and puts the person at risk for heart attack or stroke.

According to the Federal National Cholesterol Education Program, adults should have their cholesterol checked at least once every five years. Since 1994, people have been able to test their total cholesterol level through the use of a home kit.

How it works

Most home cholesterol kits require that an individual prick a finger and deposit a drop of blood on a test strip. Other tests require that several drops of blood be deposited on a test strip. Chemicals on the strip react with cholesterol in the blood.

Interpreting the results

Shortly after blood is deposited, a colored bar appears on the test strip. An individual then compares the colored bar to a chart that translates the color into a total blood cholesterol reading.

Cholesterol levels below 200 are generally considered within the healthy range. People with cholesterol levels between 200 and 239 are considered to be at an increased risk for developing heart disease, and people with levels above 240 are considered to be at high risk.

Accuracy

Home cholesterol tests are considered highly accurate in reading total blood cholesterol levels. The total cholesterol level is not the most important measure of blood cholesterol, though if it is high, that is a signal for a person to get further testing. Tests performed by doctors that check levels of HDL (high density lipoprotein) and LDL (low density lipoprotein) give patients a more accurate diagnosis of their condition.

HDL and LDL transport cholesterol from the liver through the bloodstream to cells throughout the body. According to doctors, an increased concentration of HDL is helpful in preventing heart disease while an increased concentration of LDL is considered a contributor to heart disease.

Cautions

Several factors, such as weight loss, illness, and stress, can change cholesterol levels from day to day. For this reason, medical experts recommend that several tests be taken and their results averaged to provide the most accurate reading. Inaccurate results can also be produced if an individual has taken vitamin C or a nonaspirin painkiller, such as Tylenol, within four hours of testing.

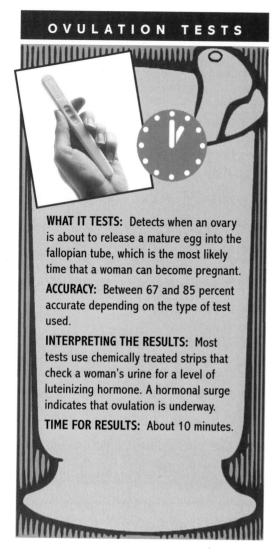

OVULATION TESTS

WHAT IT TESTS: Detects when an ovary is about to release a mature egg into the fallopian tube, which is the most likely time that a woman can become pregnant.

ACCURACY: Between 67 and 85 percent accurate depending on the type of test used.

INTERPRETING THE RESULTS: Most tests use chemically treated strips that check a woman's urine for a level of luteinizing hormone. A hormonal surge indicates that ovulation is underway.

TIME FOR RESULTS: About 10 minutes.

Ovulation tests help women predict when they are most likely to get pregnant. Before the advent of these tests, women had to chart their temperature daily to calculate when they were ovulating—an imprecise measurement at best. Ovulation tests have removed some of the guess work from the process by detecting the hormone surges that indicate ovulation is about to begin.

Ovulation occurs when an egg is released from a woman's ovary, usually at the midpoint of her menstrual cycle. During ovulation, an egg is in its best position to become fertilized by a man's sperm.

How it works

Ovulation tests check a woman's urine sample for a sharp increase in luteinizing hormone (LH). A surge in LH signals that the ovary is preparing to release a mature egg into the fallopian tube for fertilization.

A woman using an in-home ovulation test holds a wandlike device in her urine stream for several seconds. Chemicals in the wand detect the levels of LH in the urine.

Interpreting the results

The wand displays test results in either a color or symbol form about 10 minutes after a woman takes the test. Instructions provided with the test explain what the different colors or symbols indicate.

If a woman's body is experiencing a surge in LH, the following one to three days are considered to be her most fertile time of the month. Intercourse during this time will most likely result in pregnancy.

Accuracy

The most sensitive brands of ovulation tests can detect LH surges in about 85 percent of women. However, even the most sensitive tests may fail to detect LH if the hormone surge is not very strong or did not occur at all during the testing period.

Some medication may skew test results. Fertility medications containing LH and human Chorionic Gonadotropin (HCG), a hormone produced by pregnant women, may make results falsely high. Most kits provide at least five tests so a woman can test herself several times over a one- to two- day period.

Cautions

If testing repeatedly fails to detect an LH surge, the woman being tested may be producing amounts of the hormone that are too small to be detected. Women who have this problem may need to undergo blood tests to determine when or whether they are ovulating.

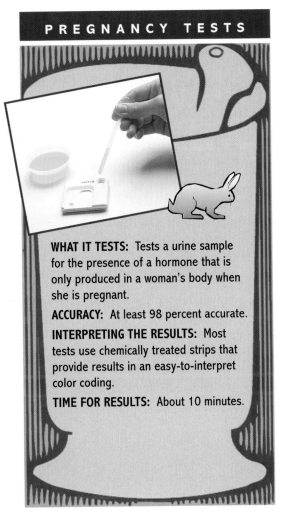

How it works

Home pregnancy tests check a urine sample for the presence of human Chorionic Gonadotropin (HCG), a hormone that is only produced in a woman's body when she is carrying a fertilized egg in her uterus. HCG reacts with chemicals in a testing wand provided in most pregnancy kits. A woman dips the wand into her urine stream for about 10 seconds. The tip of the wand collects a urine sample.

Interpreting the results

Wands provided in many tests have two windows. One window changes color to show that the test is working properly. The second window displays results of the test. If the chemicals in the wand detect the presence of HCG, a color or sign will appear in the window about 10 minutes after the test has been performed.

Accuracy

When directions are followed properly and the woman being tested has no unusual medical condition present—such as a recent miscarriage or ovarian tumor—home pregnancy tests are 98 percent accurate. Doctors consider the home tests to be as accurate as the tests performed in laboratories. False-positive results may be caused by fertility drugs that contain HCG (Pregnyl and Profasi), but other fertility drugs, such as Clomid and Serophene, will not interfere with test results.

Cautions

A woman taking the test must carefully follow directions—if she waits even 10 minutes too long to read the results, chemicals may transform a negative reading into a positive one, which could lead the woman to believe that she is pregnant when she is not.

Home pregnancy tests have been available since the 1960's. The first tests carried by drugstores were time consuming and complicated to use. Women had to wait nine days after their first missed menstrual cycle before they could perform the test, which involved mixing a messy potion of chemicals and urine.

By 1997, home pregnancy tests had become a fast and easy alternative to a trip to the doctor's office. The tests allowed women to detect if they were pregnant the day after a missed menstrual period by simply dipping a chemically treated stick into their urine stream.

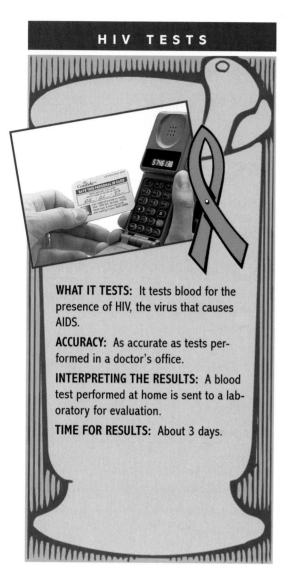

HIV TESTS

WHAT IT TESTS: It tests blood for the presence of HIV, the virus that causes AIDS.

ACCURACY: As accurate as tests performed in a doctor's office.

INTERPRETING THE RESULTS: A blood test performed at home is sent to a laboratory for evaluation.

TIME FOR RESULTS: About 3 days.

According to a study by the Centers for Disease Control (CDC), in 1996 fewer than 18 percent of adults in the United States had been tested for HIV, a virus that infects about 40,000 Americans annually. An HIV infection can develop into full-blown AIDS, a disease that cripples the body's immune system, leaving the body vulnerable to all kinds of infection. The virus is spread mainly through the sharing of HIV-contaminated needles by drug abusers and unprotected sexual intercourse with an HIV-infected person.

Many people at risk of contracting HIV re-fused to get tested because they feared the results of their test would not be kept private, according to the CDC study. The CDC expected the number of people tested to triple after the FDA approved the sale of anonymous home testing kits.

How it works

The HIV home test checks for the presence of the HIV antibody (a substance produced by the body in response to an infection) in the bloodstream. After the HIV virus has infected the body, the antibody that fights the virus can be detected in a blood sample.

When using the test, an individual draws a small amount of blood from their fingertip and rubs it on a piece of paper. Both the lancet used for pricking the finger and the paper used to blot the sample are provided in the kit.

After completing the test, the individual sends the blood sample to a laboratory. A special mailing envelope that meets postal regulations for delivery of medical specimens is provided in the kit. The laboratory analyzes the blood sample and reports the test results over the phone. Because anonymity is highly valued by users of home HIV tests, each blood sample is identified only by a special code number that is included in the kit—a patient's name is never connected to the sample.

Interpreting the results

About a week after sending the sample to a laboratory, the user of the self-test calls a toll-free phone number to get results of the test. The individual identifies himself or herself by the code number attached to the sample. If a person's test result is negative (they are not infected with the HIV virus), a recorded message reports the result. Individuals whose results are positive (they are infected with HIV) are automatically connected with a trained counselor who explains the test result and refers them to medical professionals and services.

Test manufacturers offer counseling for all people who take the test. Pretest counseling is offered to people who are nervous about taking the test. Counseling is also offered to people who test negative for HIV.

Accuracy

According to a CDC report, home HIV tests are 99.9 percent accurate, which makes them as accurate as those performed in a doctor's office. Only 1 in every 1,000 people who carefully follow testing directions test false-positive (they are HIV-negative but the test indicates that they are infected with the virus). Also, because the body sometimes does not produce HIV antibodies until several months after it has become infected with the virus, individuals may test negative when they are, in fact, infected. For this reason, people who are at risk of contracting HIV should be tested every six months.

Cautions

Many doctors have been critical about the way in which in-home HIV tests results are reported. Doctors have raised concerns that phone-based counseling may not provide the support needed by individuals who have just learned that they suffer from a potentially fatal illness.

People who test positive for HIV should consult a doctor immediately for treatment options. According to doctors, drug treatments are most effective when the virus is detected in its early stages.

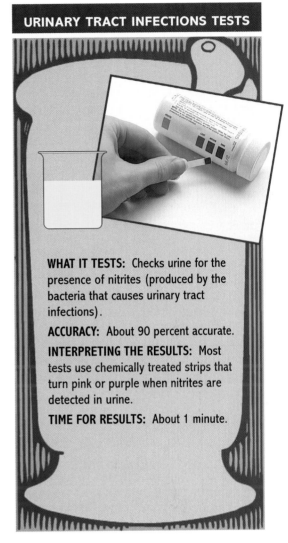

URINARY TRACT INFECTIONS TESTS

WHAT IT TESTS: Checks urine for the presence of nitrites (produced by the bacteria that causes urinary tract infections).

ACCURACY: About 90 percent accurate.

INTERPRETING THE RESULTS: Most tests use chemically treated strips that turn pink or purple when nitrites are detected in urine.

TIME FOR RESULTS: About 1 minute.

A urinary tract infection is an infection of one or more parts of the urinary system usually caused by bacteria. Home tests check for the presence of bacteria in the urine.

About 8 million people suffer from urinary tract infections (UTI's) every year. Young girls, pregnant women, diabetics, and men over age 50 are most at risk for contracting these infections. Symptoms include frequent urination, painful urination, and in, severe cases, blood and pus in the urine. If left untreated, these infections can lead to serious kidney damage.

How it works

When using an in-home urinary tract infection test, an individual immerses a chemically treated strip into the urine. The chemicals in the strip detect the presence of nitrites in the urine. Nitrites are produced by the bacteria that cause urinary tract infections.

Interpreting the results

Most strips turn pink or purple when they detect nitrites in the urine. Results appear about a minute after testing has been completed.

Accuracy

According to the National Institutes of Health, home urinary tract infection kits are about 90 percent accurate. Test strips can detect nitrites in the urine even when no physical symptoms are present. According to doctors, these tests can improve the possibility for early detection and treatment.

Cautions

Individuals should confirm test results with a doctor, who can then provide treatment for the illness.

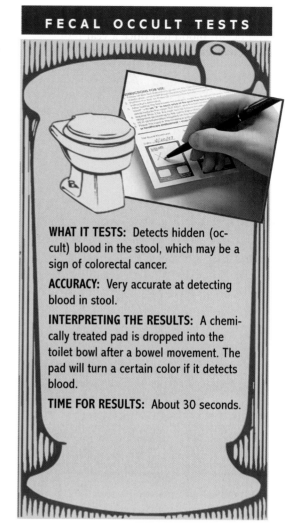

FECAL OCCULT TESTS

WHAT IT TESTS: Detects hidden (occult) blood in the stool, which may be a sign of colorectal cancer.

ACCURACY: Very accurate at detecting blood in stool.

INTERPRETING THE RESULTS: A chemically treated pad is dropped into the toilet bowl after a bowel movement. The pad will turn a certain color if it detects blood.

TIME FOR RESULTS: About 30 seconds.

According to the American Cancer Society, more than 55,000 people every year die from colorectal cancer—the second deadliest type of cancer in the United States next to lung cancer. After age 50 the chance that a person will acquire the disease doubles every 10 years. Doctors advise that everyone over the age of 40 test for fecal occult (hidden) blood at least once a year. Fecal blood is a symptom of colorectal cancer, though it can be a symptom of other conditions as well.

About 90 percent of all cases of colorectal cancer can be cured if a patient receives treatment in the early stages of the disease. A study by the University of Minnesota in

Minneapolis found that people using a home fecal occult blood test once a year reduce their chances of death by at least 33 percent.

How it works

An individual drops a chemically treated pad into the toilet bowl after a bowel movement. In about 30 seconds, the pad will display results of the test. The test pad can then be flushed away.

Interpreting the results

The test pad changes color (usually blue or green) if any blood is detected in the stool. The pad remains its original color if it does not detect blood in the stool.

Anyone experiencing diarrhea, constipation, or unexplained weight loss for more than two weeks should contact a doctor.

Accuracy

Doctors rate home fecal occult blood tests as highly accurate in detecting blood in the stool. However, test results can be skewed by certain chemicals used in toilet bowl cleaners. Certain foods, such as red meat, broccoli, cauliflower, horseradish, and cantaloupe, can produce false-positive results. People are also advised to avoid taking vitamin C and aspirin for two days before testing.

Cautions

Over-the-counter tests allow people to check for blood in their stool. However, these tests do not detect cancer. Blood in the stool can be caused by any number of things—hemorrhoids, rectal tears, or even heavy exercise. If a fecal occult blood test indicates that there is blood in the stool, an individual should contact a doctor immediately for further testing.

The future of home testing

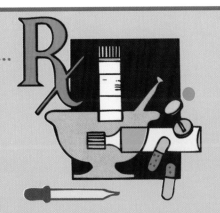

In 1997, manufacturers of home medical tests were developing faster, more accurate, and less invasive products. Some tests that were being prepared for home use included:

- A blood-glucose monitor that uses infrared beams to read blood-sugar levels. The technology would eliminate the need for diabetics to draw blood from test-worn fingertips.

- An HIV test that detects the antibody orally. A pad placed between a person's cheek and gums would eliminate the need for a blood test.

- A test that parents can use to detect if their children are taking illegal drugs was approved for home use by the FDA in early 1997.

- A monitor that measures blood levels of theophylline, a drug taken by asthma patients to control their illness.

Doctors expressed some concern over the growing reliance on home testing. They feared that many people mistake home testing as a diagnostic tool, and after reviewing test results they attempt to treat themselves without the aid of a doctor. Medical professionals warned that home tests can not substitute for the care of a physician. Doctors make diagnoses based on the patient's medical history, regular examinations, other tests, and professional expertise and consultation with other doctors. Developing treatment plans depends on many factors as well. Home testing devices are useful supplements to a physician's care.

Taking a trip abroad involves planning.
And people traveling to exotic locales
should also have a plan for staying well.

How to
Travel Well

By Richard Trubo

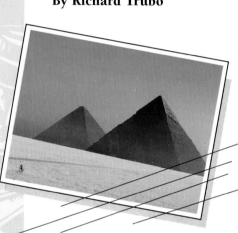

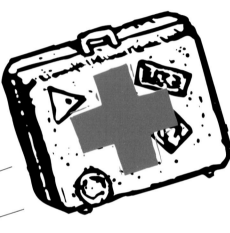

I MAGINE THIS: You are just a day or two into a dream vacation.
After months of planning, preparing, and saving, finally there is
nothing left to do but enjoy yourself. But suddenly you just do
not feel right. Your stomach is rumbling, you feel nauseated, and
you are running a fever. So instead of hopping a tour bus to Egypt's
ancient pyramids at Giza or stretching out on the beach in
Acapulco, you wind up crawling into your hotel room bed, pulling
the covers over your head, and trying to sleep.

It probably would not be much comfort in a situation like this
to know that you are not alone. Every year the media report unset-
tling stories of travelers who encounter more than tourist attractions
on their vacations. In January 1997, for example, doctors from the
United States Centers for Disease Control and Prevention (CDC) in
Atlanta and the California Department of Health published the case
of a California woman who became violently ill with severe diarrhea
and vomiting. Tests showed that the woman had cholera, which she
contracted by eating a meal containing raw seaweed that a friend

had brought back from the Philippines. And in August 1996, a Tennessean returning home after a fishing excursion in South America died of yellow fever—the first confirmed yellow fever death in the United States since the 1920's.

Fortunately, cases like these are extremely rare—the vast majority of people who take trips abroad experience nothing more serious than a bit of jet lag or a sunburn. As the popularity of traveling abroad increases, however, people are beginning to discover that a number of health hazards may be waiting for them when they travel, many with the potential to ruin their vacations—or worse.

However, there are a number of simple things you can do to greatly increase your chances of an illness-free holiday. These include learning about and planning for any special risks associated with the areas you plan to visit, getting the proper immunizations before your departure, and choosing carefully what you eat and drink while you are away.

Travel-related illnesses are generally linked to the primitive sanitation and disease-control measures practiced in some parts of the world. Problems often arise, for example, in the developing countries of Central and South America, Eastern and Central Europe, Africa, Asia, and the former republics of the Soviet Union. Poor food-handling practices and inadequate sewage and water-treatment systems in these parts of the world are most often responsible for the spread of disease.

Although people traveling abroad can develop the same kinds of illnesses they contract at home—such as the common cold, the flu, or problems related to asthma or diabetes—certain infectious diseases are associated with travel to foreign countries. Some of these illnesses are mild, but others can be deadly if not treated promptly.

Diseases spread by bacteria

The illness most often encountered by tourists is travelers' diarrhea (TD)—also known by such colorful names as "turista" or "Montezuma's revenge." TD affects 40 to 60 percent of individuals who visit developing countries. It often strikes people visiting parts of Latin America, the Middle East, and Africa. Although TD is rarely life-

threatening, it forces many tourists to cut back on activities or suspend them altogether. Symptoms of TD—loose, watery stools, often accompanied by nausea, vomiting, bloating, fatigue, and headache—usually persist for three to four days. The majority of TD cases are caused by food or water contaminated by bacteria, most commonly *Escherichia coli,* which infects the small intestines, causing *dehydration* (the extreme loss of bodily fluids).

Bacteria-tainted food or water can also cause more serious illnesses, such as cholera. Cholera is transmitted through contaminated water and food. A cholera infection, caused by a bacterium called *Vibrio cholerae,* can be mild, but it also can be fatal if it is not treated properly. An infected individual may begin to experience severe diarrhea, vomiting, leg cramps, and nausea within about three days after consuming tainted food. Severe cases of cholera can cause dehydration and shock, which can lead to death within hours.

The number of Americans infected with this potentially life-threatening disease rose sharply in the 1990's. Between 1992 and 1994, the CDC documented that nearly 20 percent more American tourists were infected with cholera than during the entire period from 1965 to 1991. Cholera epidemics were rampant in some parts of the world in 1997. In fact, a 1997 CDC report identified areas in 63 countries as cholera-infected. And in Africa, a cholera epidemic that appeared in the 1970's was still active in 1997.

Diseases spread by parasites

Parasites, such as *Giardia* or *Entamoeba,* can invade the body through food and water and cause illness in travelers. These parasites take longer than a bacterium to become active in the body, so symptoms usually do not appear until later in the trip or after the infected person has returned home. Symptoms of these parasitic infections include diarrhea, fever, cramps, and blood or mucus in the stool. These symptoms can last for two weeks or more without medical treatment. A doctor should be called if a fever exceeds 101 °F (38 °C) or lasts for more than two days; if diarrhea continues without improvement for more than four days (one day if a child is infected); or if vomiting persists for more than 12 hours.

A deadlier parasite, called *Plasmodium,* causes malaria, a disease

The author:

Richard Trubo is a free-lance medical writer.

that is spread by mosquitoes in the tropics and subtropics. Malaria infects about 30,000 American and European travelers each year. Between 300 to 1,500 of these cases result in death. In the early stages of malaria, the infection may be mistaken for the flu, because the illnesses share similar symptoms—fever, muscle aches, fatigue, chills, and headaches. As the parasites multiply within the body, however, red blood cells can rupture, creating the more serious symptoms of severe chills and fever, mental confusion, shortness of breath, and blood in the urine. Recognizing the symptoms of malaria and seeking immediate treatment can save a person's life. Delaying treatment just 24 hours raises the average mortality rate from 2 percent to 5 percent.

Diseases spread by viruses

Mosquitoes are also responsible for spreading two killer viruses, one that causes yellow fever and another that causes dengue fever. Yellow fever was once widespread in tropical areas of the world, but mosquito-control measures developed in the early 1900's have reduced the threat, especially in urban areas. Occasional outbreaks occur in jungle areas, especially in South America. The yellow fever virus is especially damaging to the liver. Early symptoms of yellow fever—headache, fever, and dizziness—usually appear three to six days after a person is bitten by an infected mosquito. In many cases, symptoms linger for a few days and then disappear. But in more severe cases the fever breaks for a day or two and then rises sharply. The infected person then develops *jaundice* (yellowing of the skin and eyes), and the gums and stomach lining begin to bleed. Many people recover from this stage of the disease, but some may slip into a coma and die.

Dengue fever is a risk in tropical and subtropical regions, such as Southeast Asia. Symptoms include fever, fatigue, severe headache, loss of appetite, and joint and muscle pain. These symptoms are sometimes accompanied by a sore throat, runny nose, or skin rash. Dengue fever is seldom fatal, but it can lead to a more severe condition, dengue hemorrhagic fever, which can be fatal, especially to children. This disease is widespread in Southeast Asia.

Traveler's first-aid kit

Preparing a traveler's first-aid kit is a good idea whenever you plan a trip. The higher the level of risk associated with the area you plan to visit, the better prepared you should be. A well-stocked kit might include the following essentials:

- Nonprescription, anti-inflammatory pain relievers, such as aspirin or ibuprofen.

- Over-the-counter antacid medication for stomach ailments.

- Antidiarrheal medications.

- A topical antibiotic to self-treat minor abrasions and wounds.

- Medications for motion sickness.

- Nasal-spray decongestants to ease ear pain during airplane flights.

- A supply of the prescription medications you take regularly to last the duration of your trip.

- A brief written summary of your medical history and conditions.

- Water purification tablets.

- Bandages, gauze, tape, small scissors, tweezers, and an elastic bandage for sprains.

- Sunscreen with a sun protective factor (SPF) of 15 or greater.

- Insect repellent containing the compound DEET (diethyltoluamide) at concentrations of 30 to 35 percent. (This repellent is particularly important when traveling in mosquito-infested regions.)

- A spare pair of glasses or contact lenses, along with your eyeglass prescription.

Diseases a traveler might encounter

Infectious travel-related diseases pose a greater risk to travelers in some areas than in other regions.

Disease	Areas of great risk	How it is transmitted
Yellow fever	• Certain parts of Africa and South America.	• Viral infection transmitted by mosquitoes.
Hepatitis A	• All areas except Western and northern Europe, Japan, Australia, New Zealand, and North America (excluding Mexico).	• Viral illness transmitted through contaminated food and water supplies.
Typhoid fever	• Many developing countries of Latin America, Asia, and Africa.	• Bacterial illness transmitted in contaminated food and water.
Polio	• Developing countries of Asia, Africa, the Middle East, the Indian subcontinent, and many parts of the former Soviet Union.	• Viral infection spread by contaminated water and food.
Japanese B encephalitis	• Many Asian countries.	• Viral infection transmitted by mosquitoes.

Bacteria or parasites in the local water supply are a major source of illness to travelers. In high-risk areas, it is best to avoid water unless it has been boiled or chemically treated.

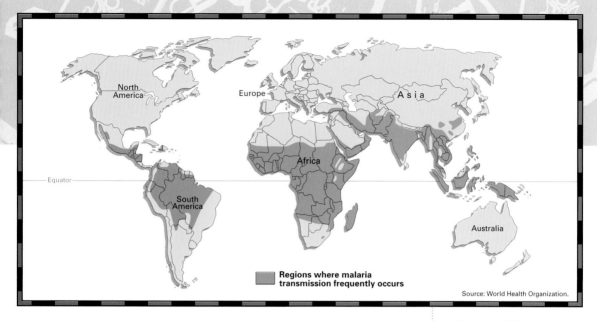

Regions where malaria transmission frequently occurs

Source: World Health Organization.

Vaccines for travelers

Doctors can treat and cure many travel-related illnesses. Well-prepared travelers, however, can take steps to avoid getting sick in the first place. Long before you board a plane, ship, or train for a trip to a developing country, you should consult your physician. Discuss any chronic health conditions you have—asthma, diabetes, or heart disease, for example—and how you should care for them while you are gone. If you have insulin-dependent diabetes and plan to fly from New York to Hong Kong, ask your physician when to take your insulin, considering the time zones you will be crossing. Also make sure that your routine immunizations are up to date before you travel. According to the CDC, these include vaccines for measles, mumps, rubella, diphtheria, tetanus, pertussis, polio, and haemophilus influenza B.

It is equally important to be immunized against any infectious diseases that may be on the attack at your destination. Travelers can be vaccinated for yellow fever, cholera, typhoid, hepatitis A, and other, less common diseases. Visitors planning to travel in rural areas of developing countries are routinely advised to get a hepatitis A shot. The traditional vaccine against hepatitis A has been a gamma globulin injection. However, the immunity offered by gamma globulin lasts only about five months. A newer vaccine, called Havrix, lasts much longer.

Hepatitis A is caused by a virus that contaminates water systems, but it can also be spread by seafood—often raw oysters that have been harvested in sewage-contaminated water—and fruits and

Malaria, which is spread by mosquitoes, is widespread in certain regions of developing countries. The shaded areas of the map indicate regions where malaria transmission frequently occurs.

vegetables. The hepatitis A virus can cause a liver infection, which produces symptoms of nausea, vomiting, loss of appetite, fever, and jaundice. The infection usually lasts about one or two weeks, but severe cases can last longer. About 1 in 1,000 people infected with hepatitis A dies from the illness.

In addition to vaccines, some medications taken before a trip may prepare the body to battle with infectious diseases it encounters during the trip. If you are going to visit a region where malaria is a risk, for example, your doctor may prescribe antimalarial medications, such as mefloquine (often sold as Lariam). Travelers take this medication one week before a trip, and continue taking it during the trip and for four weeks after returning.

Your family physician may recommend that you visit a traveler immunization center. A number of hospitals and other health organizations in the United States operate these centers, which specialize in helping people prepare for international trips. Traveler immunization centers use data from the CDC and the World Health Organization to provide up-to-date information on the immunizations necessary for travelers to various regions of most countries. A traveler immunization center should be able to tell you about the specific health risks that are present in the areas you plan to visit, how best to avoid those risks, and how to seek help in a particular foreign country if you do become sick.

The traveler's first-aid kit

Sometimes it is difficult to find medical care in a foreign land, so it is important to pack a traveler's first-aid kit. A well-stocked kit might include the following essentials: a nonprescription, anti-inflammatory pain reliever, such as aspirin or ibuprofen; antidiarrheal medication, such as loperamide (sold as Imodium A-D) or bismuth subsalicylate (sold as Pepto-Bismol); adhesive bandages and a topical antibiotic to treat minor abrasions and wounds; insect repellent containing the compound diethyltoluamide (DEET) at concentrations of 30 to 35 percent; sunscreen with a sun protective factor (SPF) of 15 or greater; medications, such as Dramamine, for motion sickness; a nasal-spray decongestant to ease ear pain during airplane flights; a spare pair of glasses or contact lenses, along with your eyeglass prescription; an adequate supply of the prescription medications you take regularly, such as insulin for diabetes, and inhalers for asthma, to last the duration of your trip; and, in high-risk areas, water purification

Travelers' diarrhea

Travelers' diarrhea is the most common illness experienced by tourists, affecting 40 to 60 percent of individuals who visit developing countries, most often in parts of Latin America, the Middle East, and Africa. Most cases are caused by food or water contaminated by bacteria.

Symptoms: Loose, watery stools, nausea, vomiting, bloating, fatigue, headache. Cases caused by a parasite may also include fever, cramps, or blood or mucus in stool. Symptoms usually persist for about three to four days, but parasitic cases can persist for two weeks or more without medical treatment.

Treatment: Rest and drink enough fluids to replace those lost to diarrhea. A doctor should be called promptly if the fever exceeds 101 °F (38.3 °C) or lasts for more than two days; the diarrhea continues without improvement for more than four days (one day if a child is affected); or vomiting persists for more than 12 hours.

Prevention: To protect against bacterial infection, the United States Centers for Disease Control and Prevention (CDC) recommends using over-the-counter medications, such as bismuth subsalicylate or loperamide. These can be taken safely for up to three weeks. According to one study, bismuth subsalicylate prevents 62 to 65 percent of cases of diarrhea when taken four times a day with meals.

tablets. In case of an emergency, you should also pack a brief written summary of your medical history and conditions and a list of the prescriptions you take.

Advance preparation can also greatly simplify matters should you require medical attention in a foreign country. Prior to your departure, check your health insurance policy. Does it cover you for treatment outside your home country—including emergency evacuation by air ambulance to a major medical center? If not, consider purchasing travel health insurance before your departure, which is sold by independent firms specializing in services for tourists. Ask your travel agent about them. Many travel insurance companies can refer you to a foreign doctor who can provide care that is covered by your insurance. If you need to see a physician while traveling abroad, go to the largest university hospital in the area—where you are likely to get better care—or ask the hotel concierge for a referral. United States embassies or consulates in other countries also can often recommend doctors.

Protecting yourself from disease

Once you reach your destination, there are other simple precautions you can take to protect yourself from travel-related diseases. For example, the best way to prevent travelers' diarrhea, cholera, hepatitis A, or any other food-borne infection, is to choose carefully the food and drink you consume on vacation. If you are traveling in a high-risk region, adhere to the adage "Boil it, peel it, cook it, or forget it." Avoid tap water, even in ice cubes. Do not brush your teeth with tap water and avoid opening your mouth in the shower. You can also disinfect water by boiling it for five minutes or by using tablets such as Potable-Aqua. Drink bottled beverages or hot drinks made with boiled or chemically disinfected water. Carbonated drinks are also generally safe. The food you eat should be fully cooked and served very hot. If the food is too hot to eat immediately, it is hot enough to kill any potentially harmful bacteria.

Avoid raw and undercooked seafood, including seafood salads, as well as unpeeled fruits and vegetables. Stay away from lettuce and other leafy vegetables and make sure that all vegetables have been washed with boiled water. Unpasteurized milk and other dairy products should also be avoided.

As an additional defense against travelers' diarrhea, the CDC recommends using over-the-counter medications containing bismuth subsalicylate for protection. According to one study, bismuth subsalicylate (including Pepto-Bismol and other brand names) prevents about 60 percent of cases of diarrhea when taken four times a day with meals. Most people can take these medications safely for up to three weeks. However, so many added doses of bismuth subsalicylate may be harmful to people who are already taking salicylates (usually aspirin) for arthritis or people with blood-clotting disorders, peptic ulcer disease, or an allergy to salicylates.

You can improve your chances of remaining free of malaria by avoiding mosquito bites. The best way to discourage mosquitoes is to wear long sleeves and long pants after sunset—the mosquitoes that spread malaria are active during the evening and night—and protect exposed skin with insect repellent. The CDC recommends using repellents that contain DEET as the active ingredient. Another repellent, called permethrin (sold as Permanone or Nix), repels mosquitoes and kills them on contact, and can be applied directly to clothing. The CDC also advises using a flying insect-killing spray in your living and sleeping areas from dusk until dawn, when the mosquitoes are

Who to call for further information

- The International Association for Medical Assistance to Travellers provides health information for travelers and a directory of English-speaking physicians in foreign cities. Write to 417 Center St., Lewiston, NY 14092; (telephone 716-754-4883).

- The U.S. Centers for Disease Control and Prevention (CDC) operates an international travelers' hotline with up-to-date information on the prevention and treatment of commonly acquired travel illnesses and a directory of local traveler immunization centers. Information is available in person, by audio recording or fax (telephone 639-3534).

- The International Society of Travel Medicine maintains a World Wide Web site (http://www.istm.org) that lists more than 250 travel medicine clinics in the United States (telephone 770-736-7060).

most active, and using mosquito netting over your bed—preferably netting that has been treated with permethrin.

The same preventions apply to lessening the risk of contracting dengue fever. However, since the mosquitoes that spread the dengue fever virus bite during the daytime, travelers must use these precautions in the morning and afternoon.

Treatment of travel-related illnesses

No matter how careful you are, an illness can break through your best defenses. By responding quickly, however, you can often minimize the problem and prevent an illness from becoming severe. If you are stricken with travelers' diarrhea, for example, and you drink plenty of clear liquids to replace lost fluids and get lots of rest, the illness should disappear in a few days. For faster relief, you can try an over-the-counter medication, such as Pepto-Bismol or Imodium A-D. A prepackaged powder mixture of sugar and salts, added to water, is used throughout the world to treat diarrhea. You can prepare a homemade version of the treatment by mixing 4 teaspoons of sugar and 5 grams of salt in 1 liter of water. Drink enough of the mixture to replace the amount of fluid lost to vomiting or diarrhea. The best sign that you have replaced enough fluid is that you begin urinating normal amounts every 2 to 4 hours. Seek a doctor's advice if the diarrhea is severe, contains blood or mucus, is accompanied by chills or fever, or has not started to improve after a couple of days.

You should also treat cholera and its accompanying diarrhea by replacing fluids and salts. A doctor may prescribe antibiotics to speed recovery and ease the severity of the illness, but replacing fluids remains the most important treatment.

By taking the proper preventive measures, adhering to guidelines, and tending to illnesses promptly before complications develop, you can help ensure that the roads you travel will be paved with good health. With a little preparation and precaution, your vacation memories will be captured in photographs, and not in a stack of doctor's bills.   •••

For further reading:

Dawood, Richard, M.D. *Travelers' Health: How to Stay Healthy All Over the World.* Random House, 1994.

Traveling Healthy, a bimonthly newsletter (108-48 70th Road, Forest Hills, NY 11375; telephone 718-268-7290).

Weinberg, Winkler G., M.D. *No Germs Allowed! How to Avoid Infectious Diseases at Home and on the Road.* Rutgers University Press, 1996.

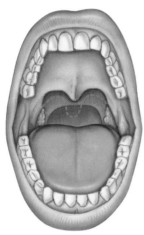

A HEALTHY FAMILY

Innovative new remedies are helping
snorers and their sleepy spouses
enjoy a more peaceful night's rest.

Quieting the Snores

By Dianne Hales

S NORING, A SOUND THAT PROVOKES FURY, shatters the silence
of the night with ear-piercing and immensely irritating blasts,
snorts, and roars. Eyes closed and mouth open, snorers may
buzz like chain saws, bellow like water buffaloes, or wheeze like
trains chugging up a mountainside. Sleep researchers have recorded
snores as loud as 80 decibels—equal to the sound level of a motor-
cycle revving up.

Who snores? At least on occasion, we all do, particularly if our
nasal passages are stuffed up. But about 25 percent of Americans—
40 million people—snore regularly, according to the American
Academy of Otolaryngology (AAO). (Otolaryngology is the medical
specialty dealing with disorders and treatment of the ear, nose, and
throat.) The likelihood of snoring increases with age. Although only
about 30 percent of men snore at age 30, 45 percent of men snore by
age 50, reports the National Sleep Foundation. Generally, twice as
many men as women snore, perhaps because of the effects different
sex hormones have on the muscles of the airway. However, snoring
among women increases dramatically after menopause, for reasons
still unclear.

Snoring certainly has been a rich source of material for stand-up
comics and cartoonists. But, in reality, snoring is no joke. Although
some snorers are so noisy they wake themselves, most slumber

The author:

·····················

Dianne Hales is a free-lance writer and frequent contributor to the Health & Medical Annual.

peacefully. More frequently, the cacophony disturbs spouses and may sabotage the sleep partners' daytime relationship. Snoring is also the most common symptom of a breathing disorder during sleep. The most serious of these disorders, obstructive sleep apnea, may be life-threatening.

"Snoring has graduated from being regarded as a hopeless nightly nuisance to the status of a legitimate medical problem—as respectable a symptom as back pain or headache," says otolaryngologist Derek S. Lipman, the author of several books on snoring. Advances in sleep studies, now considered a medical subspecialty, have improved researchers' understanding of the basics of breathing and sleep-related breathing disorders. As a result, though quack remedies for snoring still abound, innovative new treatments are helping snorers—and their long-suffering spouses—make it through the night without making a ruckus.

Causes of snoring

Snoring is, fundamentally, a problem with air turbulence. Think of your breath as a column of air moving through your nose and mouth, into your throat and lungs, and then out again. A blockage at any point in the airway will create mini air currents in the air column that cause the soft, floppy tissue in the mouth, throat, and neck to vibrate and make noise. The most common trouble site is the *pharynx*, the cavity where the back of the mouth meets the upper throat. Other problem areas are the back of the nose and base of the tongue. Snoring may occur when inhaling or exhaling.

The most frequent cause of occasional snoring is *postural* (the position of the body). If you lie on your back as you sleep, your lower jaw tends to fall forward and the base of your tongue may partially block the air column entering your throat. You're also likely to snore if you can't breathe properly through your nose, because of a cold, sinus problem, or allergies. Medical conditions that decrease overall muscle tone, such as *hypothyroidism* (low levels of thyroid hormones), also can contribute to snoring.

The most common causes of *chronic* snoring (frequently recurring over a long time) can be found inside the body. For example, an unusually long *uvula*, the fleshy tissue that looks like a tiny punching bag dangling from the roof of the mouth, may block the airway. Nasal deformities, such as a deviated *septum* (the partition separating the two sides of the nose), also increase the likelihood of snoring. Other anatomical causes include a larger-than-normal tongue or an unusually narrow throat. Some children and adults snore because their tonsils or *adenoids* (glandular tissues in the upper throat) are especially large or have become swollen because of infection. Cysts or polyps in the nasal passages may also trigger snoring.

But for most people—particularly those who have gained weight as they've gotten older—the culprit is sagging or excessive soft tissue in the throat and soft palate. The soft palate is the tissue at the back of the roof of the mouth that closes when you swallow so food does not rise into the nasal passages. Normally, as we sleep, the muscles in the pharynx and throat relax, and the upper airway collapses somewhat. If the soft palate and uvula are enlarged because of weight gain or are just showing the effects of gravity and loss of muscle tone over time, they may actually droop onto the back of the throat. In heavy snorers, the uvula and soft palate may be three times their normal size. In particular, the edges of the soft palate can flutter like a sail in the wind. The weight gain that often occurs in women around menopause may explain why more women begin snoring in middle age. Some researchers have speculated that hormonal changes also may be at fault, though no studies have provided evidence of this.

Certain behaviors increase the likelihood of snoring because they relax the muscles and tissue of the upper airway. If you're extremely tired when you fall asleep, for instance, you may plunge into the deepest stages of sleep, when your muscles, including those in your mouth and jaw, become most profoundly relaxed and your airway even narrower than usual. The heavy use of alcohol relaxes saggy

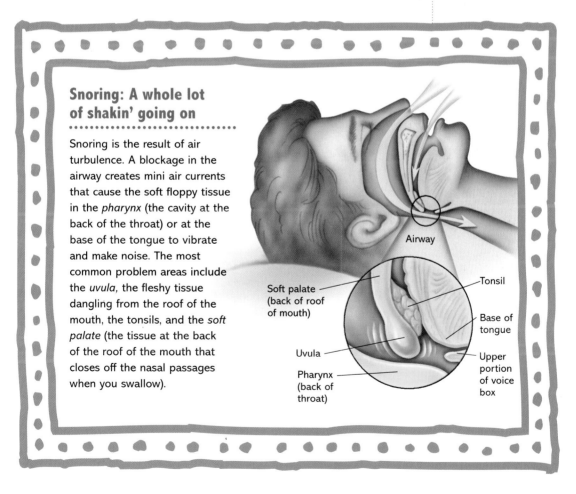

Snoring: A whole lot of shakin' going on

Snoring is the result of air turbulence. A blockage in the airway creates mini air currents that cause the soft floppy tissue in the *pharynx* (the cavity at the back of the throat) or at the base of the tongue to vibrate and make noise. The most common problem areas include the *uvula,* the fleshy tissue dangling from the roof of the mouth, the tonsils, and the *soft palate* (the tissue at the back of the roof of the mouth that closes off the nasal passages when you swallow).

Airway

Soft palate (back of roof of mouth)

Uvula

Pharynx (back of throat)

Tonsil

Base of tongue

Upper portion of voice box

tissue in the pharynx and upper throat and swells the *mucous membranes* (linings) of the nose and throat, so the airway is more likely to collapse. Smoking also irritates mucous membranes. Some medications, including sleeping pills, certain antidepressants, and antihistamines, also make you sleep more deeply and cause a slackening of the airway.

"Regular snoring needs to be listened to—literally," says sleep specialist Sonia Ancoli-Israel of the University of California at San Diego and the author of *All I Want Is a Good Night's Sleep*. She notes that the more often and more loudly a person snores, the greater the reason for concern. "Most people are one-room snorers; they disturb only the person sleeping next to them. But if you're a two-room snorer or if you snore so loudly that you wake up the entire household, there could be something seriously wrong."

Frequent snoring also may indicate that there is more to the problem than meets the ear. "If you snore intermittently—just one or two times a week—I wouldn't say that's a health problem," says Robert Nemeroff, chairman of the otolaryngology department at Cedars-Sinai Medical Center in Los Angeles. "But if you're what we call a heroic snorer, if your snoring is unremitting and occurs most nights, it definitely warrants investigation."

Effects of snoring

Snoring can cause a host of complications. Snorers may not sleep soundly themselves and so may suffer from excessive daytime sleepiness. And if their nighttime symphony doesn't jar them from sleep, a spouse's jab in the ribs or tap on the shoulder will. Sleepy people find it more difficult to concentrate, have less energy, and are more irritable and less creative than their brighter-eyed counterparts, according to research studies. In addition, they may be more prone to illness. More dangerous still, people who are sleep-deprived are more likely to injure themselves and others. Each year 200,000 sleep-related accidents claim more than 5,000 lives, cause hundreds of thousands of injuries, and incur billions of dollars in indirect costs, according to the United States Department of Transportation. In addition, sleep deprivation has contributed to major catastrophes, including train wrecks, mishaps in nuclear energy plants, and airplane crashes.

Chronic snoring can have other serious health effects. "Snorers are at higher risk of *ischemic heart disease* [an inadequate flow of blood to the heart] and stroke," notes Ancoli-Israel. Heavy snorers also tend to develop *hypertension* (high blood pressure) at a younger age than do nonsnorers, according to the AAO. Such complications may arise because snorers' narrowed airways fail to pro-

Why we snore

Common causes of snoring include:

- Sagging or excess tissue in the throat and mouth because of weight gain or aging.
- Lying on your back during sleep.
- Colds, allergic reactions, sinus attacks, and other conditions stuffing up nasal passages.
- Heavy use of alcohol.
- Smoking.
- Medications that relax the muscles of the airway.
- Medical conditions that decrease muscle tone.
- An unusually large uvula or tongue or an unusually narrow throat that blocks the airway.
- Inflamed tonsils or adenoids.
- Cysts or polyps in the nasal passages.

Restoring nighttime harmony

Laugh, and the world laughs with you;" British writer Anthony Burgess observed, "Snore, and you sleep alone." For millions of people and their sleep-starved partners, snoring is no laughing matter. Just as one partner slips into slumber, the other starts rattling and roaring. Soon, the aggrieved partner is poking and kicking at the offender. This scenario, played out night after night, can undermine even the most loving relationship.

In addition, fatigue, resulting from inadequate or disturbed sleep, can pose psychological and health risks for both the snorer and suffering spouse. These range from trouble concentrating to a greater susceptibility to colds and other infectious diseases to a greater likelihood of being involved in a car or workplace accident.

According to the National Sleep Foundation, 20 percent of all men over age 50 snore so loudly they disturb their bed partner. "Seventy percent of the male snoring patients I see are brought in by their spouses," said sleep specialist Robert Nemeroff of Cedars-Sinai Medical Center in Los Angeles. "Their wives often feel resentment, but they also feel guilty because they know their husbands can't help it. I've had patients who say that their snoring was responsible for their separations and divorces."

So what is a sleepy spouse to do—other than move out of the bedroom? First, you should familiarize yourself and your spouse with preventive strategies for snoring. For example, if your spouse is overweight, you should encourage him or her to diet and exercise. You can note the noisy effects of eating heavily or drinking alcohol before bed. If you notice that your spouse stops breathing temporarily during sleep—a sign of sleep apnea—you should urge him or her to consult an otolaryngologist or a sleep specialist.

You could also try to fall asleep first, so that by the time the snorer starts honking away, you are already in the deep stages of sleep and not easily roused. Another good option is a sound machine, a simple device that emits soothing sounds, such as the lap of waves on the shore, that can muffle the sounds of snoring. Some spouses try to block the buzzing by donning earphones and listening to a radio or personal stereo. But perhaps the most popular solution remains the simplest: the tried-and-true tactic of wearing earplugs.

vide adequate amounts of oxygen to the blood. When blood oxygen levels drop, the heart must work harder than normal to adequately nourish body tissue, especially the brain. This increased exertion strains the heart and the rest of the cardiovascular system.

These effects may be more dangerous, even life-threatening, in people whose loud snoring is a sign of obstructive sleep apnea (OSA), the total or almost total collapse of the airway. The word apnea comes from Greek words for *no* and *breath*. People with OSA briefly stop breathing tens or even hundreds of times a night, then awaken in order to resume breathing. Mild OSA is characterized by at least five episodes of interrupted breathing per hour of sleep, with each episode lasting at least 10 seconds. People with severe apnea may stop breathing 20 to 30 times per hour for periods lasting up to a minute.

As blood oxygen levels fall during these breathing pauses, rising carbon dioxide levels cause the brain to bring the sleeper to a higher, lighter level of sleep and to signal the muscles of the upper air-

Sleep apnea: The most serious side of snoring

Obstructive sleep apnea (OSA), a potentially life-threatening sleep disorder, occurs when the tissue in the airway collapses totally or almost totally, halting breathing. People with OSA may stop breathing tens or even hundreds of times per night. During the breathing pauses, falling oxygen levels and rising carbon dioxide levels alert the brain to rouse sleepers to a lighter level of sleep and signal airway muscles to open. As sleepers struggle for air, they erupt in ear-splitting gasps and snorts. These frequent arousals make adequate nighttime rest nearly impossible and may increase the risk of high blood pressure, abnormal heart rhythms, and heart attack.

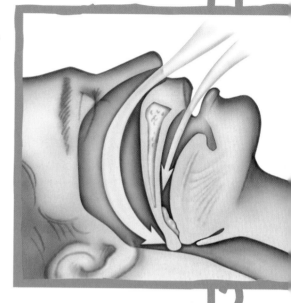

way to open. People with OSA may not awaken completely and, in fact, may even be unaware of their aroused state. As they wake and struggle for air, however, they erupt into ear-splitting gasps and sputters as loud as a jackhammer. In 1993, the National Commission on Sleep Disorders Research, a study panel established by Congress, estimated that nearly 18 million Americans suffer from OSA, with more than 3 million affected by moderate or severe versions of the condition.

The frequent arousals during episodes of apnea make it impossible to get an adequate night's rest. But excessive daytime sleepiness may be only one of the serious heath risks posed by untreated severe OSA. Sleep studies have revealed that blood oxygen levels in patients with severe OSA often fall more than 20 percent below normal during episodes of apnea. These serious drops in blood oxygen levels cause swings in blood pressure that, many sleep researchers believe, may contribute to or even cause hypertension and other damaging effects on the heart, blood vessels, and lungs. The commission noted that up to 50 percent of patients with untreated OSA also have hypertension. In addition, low oxygen levels may increase the risk of abnormal heart rhythms and contribute to a higher rate of heart attack among people with *cardiovascular diseases* (diseases of the heart and blood vessels). According to the commission, OSA may be responsible for as many as 38,000 U.S. deaths per year attributed to cardiovascular disease.

The link between OSA and cardiovascular problems is far from conclusive, however. Other factors and behaviors commonly found in patients with OSA, including smoking, lack of exercise, and, particularly, obesity, have complicated sleep researchers' efforts to study apnea's effects. In fact, researchers are still uncertain whether OSA causes cardiovascular disease, is a risk factor in its development, or is a coincidental condition.

Some researchers argue that the threat posed by even severe OSA has been grossly overstated. In March 1997, British researchers led by John Wright of Bradford Royal Infirmary in West Yorkshire reported that their review of 54 studies of apnea and health problems published between 1966 and 1995 revealed "conflicting and inconclusive" evidence that apnea increases the risk or severity of cardiovascular disease or the likelihood of death from heart failure. In 1994, the National Center on Sleep Disorders Research, a branch of the National Institutes of Health, began a $14-million study of the relationship between OSA and hypertension, stroke, heart attack, and other cardiovascular diseases. The results, due in 1999, may provide more solid evidence of OSA's dangerous effects.

Turning down the noise

Snoring cures have abounded for as long as snoring has plagued sleepers. During the Revolutionary War in America, American soldiers reportedly stitched *snore balls* (small cannon balls) into a back pocket of their uniforms so they wouldn't sleep on their backs and sound off in the still of the night, possibly alerting their British enemies. In 1900, an inventor developed a leather brace that pushed a sharp multipronged object against a sleeper's shoulder blades if he turned onto his back. In all, the U.S. Office of Patents lists more than 300 antisnoring devices—most useless, some helpful, others downright hazardous.

"There aren't any scientific data on any of them," observes Ancoli-Israel, who cautioned against devices that disrupt sleep, such as alarms that awaken a sleeper whose snores reach a certain noise level. Other potentially dangerous antisnoring devices are machines that gag a snorer or straps that keep a sleeper's mouth tightly shut (and so may severely reduce his oxygen supply).

For occasional garden-variety snoring, the National Sleep Council recommends the following preventive strategies:

- Lose weight. "If snorers are overweight by more than 10 to 15 percent of their ideal body weight, weight loss makes a big difference," said Nemeroff. "Sixty to 80 percent of those who get down

Symptoms of sleep apnea

Sleep apnea is a potentially deadly sleep disorder in which a person temporarily stops breathing for periods lasting up to a minute. Symptoms include:

- Loud, irregular snoring or other unusual breathing sounds during sleep.
- Pauses in breathing during sleep.
- Feeling abnormally sleepy during the day or falling asleep at inappropriate times (at work or while driving).
- Difficulty concentrating and remaining alert.
- Chronic irritability.
- Impotence.
- Morning headaches.
- Bedwetting.

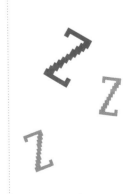

A technician at a sleep center monitors the brain activity, breathing patterns, oxygen levels, heart rate, and other body functions of a sleeping patient to determine whether he has a sleep disorder.

to their ideal weight really reduce their snoring."

- Exercise. Shaping up will help you lose weight.
- Avoid overexhaustion. When sleep-deprived people finally fall into bed, they plunge into the deepest stages of sleep, when they are most likely to snore.
- Humidify your bedroom. Swollen mucous membranes in the nasal passage—the result of a too-dry environment—may block air passages.
- Do not drink heavily, especially before bed.
- Quit smoking. Smoking irritates mucous membranes, reduces lung capacity, and generally makes breathing more difficult.
- Sleep on your side rather than on your back. To keep from rolling over, fasten a small pillow to your back with a belt or put a marble or golf ball in a sock pinned to the back of your pajamas. If you roll over onto your back, the ball will remind you to turn onto your side.
- Avoid antihistamines, tranquilizers, and sleeping pills. These medications relax the muscles of the soft palate and increase the likelihood of a blocked airway.
- Raise the head of your bed about 4 inches (10 centimeters) higher than the foot of your bed by putting boards or a brick under the headboard. Or try stacking up pillows to keep your head raised. A raised airway stays open more easily.
- If you wear dentures during the day, leave them in at night to prevent slack tissues in the mouth from vibrating.
- Check with your doctor to see if you are allergic to house dust, the feathers in your pillow, pollen, or other common substances. Such allergens also can swell mucous membranes.

If these measures fail to curtail your snoring, a consultation with your doctor may be in order. Your doctor will question you about your sleep and dietary habits, your intake of caffeine and alcohol, and any drugs you may be taking, and examine your mouth and throat for enlarged or inflamed tissue. Depending on the results of the examination, your doctor may refer you to an otolaryngologist or sleep specialist.

If an otolaryngologist decides that the cause of your snoring is an obstruction in or narrowing of the nasal passages, an external nasal dilator that pulls open the upper nostrils may help. These adhesive strips, approved by the Food and Drug Administration, have been shown to increase air flow through the nasal passages and lower the volume among heavy snorers. If polyps are the problem, nasal surgery may be needed. A 1993 study reported that among 126 people who complained of heavy snoring and blocked nasal passages, surgery eliminated snoring in 31 percent and reduced it in another 57 percent.

Another option for opening an airway partially blocked by excess tissue in the mouth or throat is a custom-made prosthesis that resembles the mouthguards boxers wear. These devices, which are molded by a dentist or oral surgeon from an impression of the mouth, pull the lower jaw forward, tightening the muscles of the throat and preventing the tongue from slipping back into the throat. "The main drawback is that after six to eight weeks, many people find it too uncomfortable," says Nemeroff. "They complain about jaw pain and other problems."

Surgical solutions

Before 1990, the final option for severe snoring was a surgical procedure called a uvulopalatopharyngoplasty (UPPP). In this procedure, a surgeon tightens the muscles of the airway, removes the tonsils, and cuts away excess tissue in the soft palate, uvula, and the back of the throat. The operation, which is performed under general anesthesia, requires a hospital stay and about two weeks of recovery.

In 1990, French surgeon Yves-Victor Kamami developed an alternative surgical procedure called laser-assisted uvulopalatopharyngoplasty (LAUP). In this procedure, a trained otolaryngologist uses a beam from a carbon dioxide laser to vaporize excess tissue in the throat and reshape the uvula and palate. "With treatment, the palate rises like the curtain in a theater," says Nemeroff. "In effect, a LAUP is like a face-lift for the palate. It tightens and restores tissues to where they were when the patient was young or before snoring was a problem."

A LAUP typically requires three to five 30-minute sessions, with a four-week recovery period between each session. Because only local anesthesia is used, a LAUP can be performed in a physician's office or an outpatient clinic rather than in a hospital. There is no bleeding and speech is normally unaffected. The biggest drawback is pain, which some patients equate to that of a tonsillectomy.

Although doctors do not yet know the long-term results of the

Questions for snorers

A sleep specialist or otolaryngologist attempting to determine the cause of your snoring would ask the following questions:

- How often do you snore?
- How loudly do you snore? Can your snoring be heard outside your bedroom?
- Do you stop breathing temporarily during sleep?
- Do you snort or gasp in your sleep?
- Do you feel excessively sleepy during the day? Have you ever fallen asleep at work or while driving?
- How many hours do you usually sleep?
- How do you feel when you wake in the morning?
- Are you overweight?
- Do you usually sleep on your back?
- Do you smoke?
- How much caffeine do you drink? What time of day do you drink caffeine?
- How much alcohol do you drink? Do you drink in the evening?
- What medications do you take? Do you take antihistamines, sleeping pills, or sedatives?
- Do you have problems breathing through your nose?

Turning down the volume

Some antisnoring devices can safely quiet sleepers who snore because of a narrowing of the nasal passages or obstruction in the airway. However, sleep experts warn against devices that awaken snorers or block their breathing.

Adhesive breathing strips, fitted across the bridge of the nose, open the upper nostrils and increase air flow through the nasal passages. Other nasal dilators are inserted inside nostrils to widen nasal passages.

Continuous positive airway pressure (CPAP) is the most commonly recommended treatment for people with severe sleep apnea, though it does not cure the condition. A CPAP device consists of a nose mask attached to an air compressor that pumps a stream of pressurized air into the airway. The air stream forces the airway open. Some people find sleeping with the device difficult.

surgery, many LAUP patients and their relieved spouses report better sleep and quieter nights. But the results of the surgery may depend on the reason for the snoring. One study found that the surgery reduced or eliminated snoring in 86 percent of patients whose saggy soft palate was the culprit. Only 18 percent of patients whose problem lay elsewhere in the airway benefited from the procedure.

In Canada, some surgeons have begun performing a one-step LAUP procedure using a new type of "cold" laser, not yet approved in the United States, that causes less damage to the surrounding tissue. The new laser allows surgeons to cut away more tissue in a single session. In addition, the procedure involves the use of a different type of anesthesia that numbs the throat and mouth more thoroughly. According to a 1996 report on 220 patients who underwent the one-step procedure, 85 percent reported a 75- to 100-percent reduction in snoring.

Undergoing a sleep evaluation

If your physician suspects that your snoring is a symptom of OSA, you will likely be referred for a sleep evaluation. This test involves monitoring—in an accredited sleep laboratory or hospital or at home—a number of body functions during sleep. The all-night evaluation involves no injections, anesthetics, incisions, X rays or discomfort—other than the slight irritation of having *electrodes* (conductors of electrical current) attached to your skin. In fact, the idea is for you to sleep right through it. Using the data from the test, a sleep specialist can confirm a diagnosis of obstructive sleep apnea and determine its severity.

For an evaluation at a sleep center, you will be asked to prepare for bed as you usually do. But before you settle down for the night, a technician will attach electrodes to your skin at several places on your face and body. Usually, an ointment is first dabbed on the skin to form a better seal. All the electrodes are arranged in pairs so that if one falls off during sleep, the other serves as a backup.

Two electrodes on the chin monitor muscle tension. Two at the corner of the eyes measure eye movement. Two on the scalp detect brain waves. Other electrodes on the upper right and lower left of the chest monitor heartbeats. One electrode on each leg records movements of those limbs. A temperature-sensitive device, taped under the nostrils, assesses breath rate and volume of inhaled air. A beltlike device worn around the lower chest monitors the movements of the diaphragm. An oximeter, a small device attached to one finger, measures blood oxygen levels.

Through the night, the electrodes send signals to a sleep-monitoring machine known as a polysomnograph. These signals are converted into electrical impulses that appear as wavy lines on continuous sheets of paper, which may be a mile long by morning. By evaluating these patterns, sleep specialists can detect even subtle signs of sleep apnea and other disorders.

As a cost-saving alternative to a nightlong sleep laboratory session, some physicians suggest ambulatory or "unattended" sleep monitoring in an individual's home. A technician delivers a microcomputer, demonstrates how to hook up the various electrodes, and returns in the morning to collect the data and equipment. Although less complete than a traditional sleep assessment, this method can determine if an overnight sleep study is necessary and can detect even mild OSA.

As with regular snoring, weight loss often helps improve mild to moderate sleep apnea. Some people benefit from an oral prosthesis. LAUP surgery has produced mixed results. Only about half of OSA patients undergoing LAUP surgery experience improvement in their snoring.

For severe sleep apnea, the most commonly recommended treatment is continuous positive airway pressure (CPAP). This treatment involves the nighttime use of a nose mask attached to a bedside air compressor, about the size of a humidifier. The compressor pumps into the throat a steady stream of air under pressure greater than that of the atmosphere. Although CPAP does not cure OSA, it eliminates snoring in almost 100 percent of OSA patients who can learn to tolerate sleeping with the equipment, which isn't always easy. Some users complain of skin irritation, sore eyes, dryness in the nose, and headaches.

A newer form of positive airway pressure called BiPap (bilevel positive airway pressure) uses nostril plugs rather than a mask. The BiPap device maintains high air pressure in the air column when the

A surgical solution to snoring

Severe snorers who fail to respond to other preventive strategies may benefit from surgical procedures to remove excess tissue in the pharynx and tighten muscles in the airway.

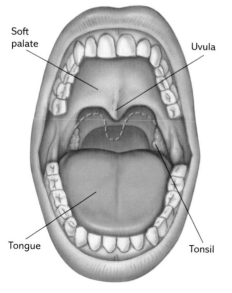

Soft palate

Uvula

Tongue

Tonsil

A uvulopalatopharyngoplasty (UPPP) involves removing the tonsils, trimming the soft palate, and shortening the uvula. The surgery is performed under general anesthesia and requires a hospital stay and about two weeks of recovery. In a laser-assisted uvulopalatopharyngoplasty (LAUP), a laser beam is used to vaporize excess tissue in the throat and reshape the uvula and soft palate. LAUP surgery involves three to five 30-minute sessions, with a four-week recovery period between sessions. It requires only local anesthesia and can be done in a physician's office. LAUP surgery may be most effective for patients whose snoring is the result of a saggy soft palate.

sleeper inhales but cuts the pressure when the sleeper exhales. Some people find this easier to adjust to than conventional CPAP.

CPAP effectively reduces daytime drowsiness, sleep studies have found. But researchers have yet to determine whether the treatment improves the health of OSA patients with cardiovascular disease or reduces the risk of developing cardiovascular disease or dying of its effects.

If your snoring is disturbing your household, making your spouse cranky and your days fatigued, don't despair. "There are safe and effective remedies for snoring," says Ancoli-Israel. "The most important step is finding out the true cause of the problem and curing it, rather than just treating the symptom."   ● ● ●

For further reading:

Ancoli-Israel, Sonia. *All I want Is a Good Night's Sleep.* Mosby-Year Book, 1996.

Johnson, T. Scott, et al. *Phantom of the Night: Overcoming Sleep Apnea Syndrome and Snoring.* New Technology Publishers, 1996.

Linde, Shirley, and Peter Hauri. *No More Sleepless Nights.* John Wiley & Sons, 1996.

Lipman, Derek. *Snoring from A to ZZZZ: Proven Cures for the Night's Worst Nuisance.* Spencer Press, 1996.

Lipman, Derek. *Stop Your Husband from Snoring: A Medically Proven Program to Cure the Night's Worst Nuisance.* Smithmark, 1993.

For more information:

The American Sleep Apnea Association, 2025 Pennsylvania Ave., Suite 905, Washington, D.C. 20006. Telephone: (202) 293-3650.

The Better Sleep Council, 333 Commerce Street, Alexandria, Va. 22314. Telephone: (703) 683-8371.

National Sleep Foundation, 1367 Connecticut Ave. NW, Suite 200, Washington, D.C. 20036. Telephone: (202) 785-2300.

New Options in Elder Care

By Donna Cohen

A growing array of home-based
services and residential care are
helping seniors and caregivers.

THE AGE OF AGING IS UPON US. By 1997, about 12 percent of Americans had passed their 65th birthday, triple the number who were over that age in 1900. By 2040, the ranks of older Americans, swollen by the 76-million-strong baby boom generation (those born between 1946 and 1964) will make up 21 percent of the population.

These statistics framed the challenges American society and American families faced in 1997 in caring for the elderly. Nearly 22.5 million American households—one in four nationwide—provided care for an elderly relative or friend, according to a 1997 survey by the nonprofit National Alliance for Caregiving (NAC) in Bethesda, Maryland. Such care included help with household chores, transportation, or personal needs.

Most of the caregivers surveyed consider their experience rewarding. But caring for a senior, especially one with chronic illnesses, can create stressful—even impossible—demands on family members. Moreover, caregivers for the elderly are often women who also hold jobs outside the home and have dependent children. These multiple demands can put caregivers at risk of depression and other serious mental health problems, physical illness, lost work productivity, job loss, and even premature death.

In 1997, fortunately, seniors and their families never had a greater number of elder-care options available to them. Among these were innovative models of residential care for the frail elderly, private long-term-care insurance, more affordable adult communities, and a wide range of home-based services that helped seniors maintain some level of independence and eased the burden on family caregivers.

The need for long-term care

Americans who reached age 65 in 1997 could expect, on average, to live another 17 years. Indeed, since 1980, the over-85 crowd has been the fastest growing age group in the United States. Between 1997 and 2030, the number of people over age 85 will grow from 8 million to 11 million, according to the U.S. Bureau of the Census. During the same period, the number of people age 100 or older is expected to increase from 49,000 to 477,000.

In the first half of the 1900's, the increase in life expectancy resulted largely from better sanitation and nutrition, vaccines, and drugs against infection. In the last part of the century, however, medical advances that made conditions such as diabetes and heart and kidney ailments treatable were responsible for prolonging the lives of millions of older people.

People who live longer, however, may develop *chronic conditions*— that is conditions that persist over time and affect the ability to live independently. Arthritis, osteoporosis, Alzheimer's disease, general memory loss, vision and hearing loss, and loss of muscle mass that results in frailty and weakness are conditions that frequently make life more difficult for older people. Although the severity of such

The author:
....

Donna Cohen is professor and chair of the Department of Aging and Mental Health at the University of South Florida in Tampa.

Baby boomers move on

By 2020, aging Baby Boomers—those born between 1946 and 1964—were expected to boost the number of Americans age 65 and older to more than 50 million. In 1990, there were only about 30 million Americans age 65 and older.

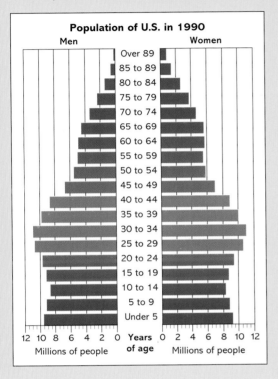

Population of U.S. in 1990

Men — Women

Over 89 / 85 to 89 / 80 to 84 / 75 to 79 / 70 to 74 / 65 to 69 / 60 to 64 / 55 to 59 / 50 to 54 / 45 to 49 / 40 to 44 / 35 to 39 / 30 to 34 / 25 to 29 / 20 to 24 / 15 to 19 / 10 to 14 / 5 to 9 / Under 5

12 10 8 6 4 2 0 **Years of age** 0 2 4 6 8 10 12
Millions of people — Millions of people

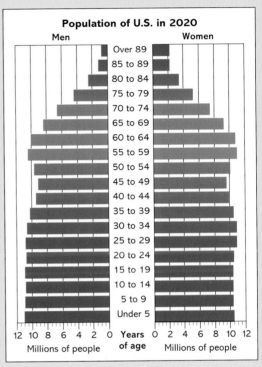

Population of U.S. in 2020

Men — Women

Over 89 / 85 to 89 / 80 to 84 / 75 to 79 / 70 to 74 / 65 to 69 / 60 to 64 / 55 to 59 / 50 to 54 / 45 to 49 / 40 to 44 / 35 to 39 / 30 to 34 / 25 to 29 / 20 to 24 / 15 to 19 / 10 to 14 / 5 to 9 / Under 5

12 10 8 6 4 2 0 **Years of age** 0 2 4 6 8 10 12
Millions of people — Millions of people

conditions may stabilize or even lessen, patients with such conditions require ongoing monitoring by health professionals and may need to take medication and make changes in their eating habits, exercise patterns, and other aspects of their lifestyle.

In 1997, people age 65 or older represented nearly half of the almost 50 million Americans disabled by chronic conditions. A 1996 survey by researchers from Harvard University in Cambridge, Massachusetts, and pollsters Louis Harris & Associates found that one in five Americans over age 50 and one in three over age 75 were likely to need long-term care because of chronic illness within any 12-month period. And as the population ages, the demand for elder care is likely to increase among seniors who are mildly or moderately disabled as well as those who need nursing home care.

For seniors with chronic conditions, social, community, and family supports are at least as important as medical care. As a result, many voices, including the voices of seniors themselves, will be determining where the increasing number of seniors will live; who will

Preparing for long-term living

- Decide how to distribute your property and whom to name as executor of your will. Have a lawyer create or review the will to avoid errors that could invalidate it.

- Have a lawyer draw up a power of attorney to name someone you trust to act on your behalf if you are unable to manage your own affairs.

- Create an advance directive, such as a living will or health-care power of attorney, that spells out your preferences for medical treat-

ment if you are unable to make your own decisions.

- Discuss estate planning with a financial planner or lawyer if you would like to set up trusts, establish joint ownership of some assets, or make gifts to lower estate taxes.

- Obtain and verify your earnings record from the Social Security Administration.

- Assess your financial status to determine which services you can afford.

care for them; and how will society provide the help they need while promoting independence, vitality, and satisfaction with life.

Elder care encompasses an almost endless variety of arrangements designed to provide varying levels of medical care as well as help with the ordinary activities of daily living. Generally, however, elder care falls into four categories: home care, assisted living facilities, nursing homes, and adult living communities. Living at home ranks first among housing options, but a chronic condition may make it impossible for seniors to live safely and comfortably at home.

Home care

Home care encompasses *home health care*—skilled nursing and other medically necessary care provided by nurses—and *personal care*—assistance with dressing, bathing, and other ordinary activities of daily life, often provided by a home health aide. Home care also includes housekeeping assistance, transportation, and services that promote well-being.

Home care is the most common form of elder care. In 1997, about 60 percent of seniors receiving long-term elder care obtained that help in their home, with families providing most of the care. Some 15 percent of full-time U.S. employees provided some care for elderly relatives or friends. The typical caregiver was a middle-aged woman who spent 18 hours per week caring for her mother, the NAC found. But more than 4 million family caregivers spent at least 40 hours per week caring for a senior, and at least 35 percent of caregivers were over age 65 themselves, according to the nonprofit Older Women's League.

Home-care services enable impaired seniors to remain in familiar surroundings and retain more control over their lives. These services also provide much-needed help for family caregivers.

Home-care financing

Medicare, the government health insurance program for seniors and the disabled, paid for about $1.3 billion in home-care services in 1994, up 657 percent over spending in 1985. Most of the Medicare funds went for skilled nursing services and for physical, occupational, and speech therapy.

In order to qualify for Medicare's home health-care benefits, seniors must be confined to their homes and meet certain financial eligibility requirements. Care is limited to 35 hours per week or 8 hours per day. Medicare also funds some personal care, housekeeping, and respite care for seniors who qualify for home health care. However, the individual's doctor must prescribe these additional benefits and continue to certify their need.

State Medicaid programs, which fund medical care for the poor, also pay for a range of home-care services, including home health care and housekeeping, for seniors entitled to nursing home services. In the years 1993-1994, Medicaid paid for about $7 billion in such services. However, eligibility requirements vary greatly by state. In addition, states may limit their total expenditure on these services, the types of services covered, or the number of people served. Money also may be available under the Older Americans Act, which funds some home care, regardless of the individual's income. Waiting lines may be lengthy for the services, which are provided by local Area Agencies on Aging (AAA's), federal agencies that administer funds and provide referrals for senior services. Some states also finance home-care services.

Long-term-care insurance policies were an emerging source of funding in 1997 for some home-care services. Such policies generally cover the total cost of home health care and about half the cost of personal care, but pay nothing for housekeeping services. Premiums, which in 1997 could cost as much as $12,000 annually, depend on

Health-care services

Skilled nursing and other services provided by health-care professionals enable many seniors to remain at home despite disabilities.

Home care includes health care, personal care, housekeeping assistance, transportation, and services that promote mental well-being.

Home health care includes skilled nursing services performed or supervised by a registered nurse. These services include monitoring intravenous lines, administering chemotherapy, and caring for bedsores. Home health care also includes physical therapy, occupational therapy, speech therapy, nutritional counseling, foot care, and mental health counseling. In addition to caring for individuals, home health-care professionals educate patients and family members on patient care. For example, they may instruct seniors on the use of a walker or teach a family caregiver to administer injections.

Personal care services provide assistance with the ordinary activities of daily life. Such services are often provided by home health aides who are trained to assist with bathing, dressing, and other aspects of personal care. These aides, who generally come into the home for several hours several days a week, also may help with light housekeeping and meal preparation.

Personal emergency response services monitor seniors' safety through notification devices connected to the telephone system. The devices can be worn by an individual or placed in a convenient location in the home. The push of a button after a fall or during a medical emergency automatically summons paramedics or the police. Many hospitals lease the equipment, or you may be able to obtain one free through local Area Agencies on Aging, community agencies that develop and administer programs for older Americans. Personal emergency response services also sell the devices, but users must pay a monthly service fee.

Nutrition services, such as Meals on Wheels, deliver prepared meals to private homes as well as to churches, housing projects, senior centers, and other group settings. In most cases, these meals are low cost or free to people whose disability prevents them from shopping or preparing their own meals. Some services provide only five meals per week, while others supply lunch and dinner in addition to weekend meals. Generally, meals are delivered once daily.

Chore or housekeeping services provide homemakers who will clean house, cook, shop, do laundry, make minor home repairs, and maintain a yard. Home maintenance services may provide this type of help as well. Homemakers generally do not provide personal care.

Home maintenance and repair services provide workers to make minor repairs and maintain gardens and lawns. Such services also modify homes to make them safe and comfortable for seniors, for whom falls are the major cause of injuries. For example, maintenance services install handrails, tub or shower seats, and special door handles that can be used easily by people with arthritis. These modifications also may be made by community or church volunteer groups. Home adaptation may be covered by insurance or be tax-deductible.

Transportation and escort services are often available through senior centers and public transportation systems. Some services also provide physical assistance to disabled seniors who wish to travel to medical appointments or shopping.

Companion care provides day-time or full-time companionship, assistance with housekeeping, meal preparation, and personal care. Companions generally do not provide medical or nursing care.

Friendly visitor services can make living alone less lonely. Such services typically are staffed by volunteers who make regular visits to home-bound seniors.

Telephone reassurance services, also usually staffed by volunteers, call people daily or even more frequently, when necessary.

Protective services provide financial and legal guidance to seniors who cannot manage their own affairs.

Respite care programs include day-care facilities and nursing homes that relieve family care-givers of their responsibilities for a limited period.

Adult day-care centers offer a planned program of health, recreational, rehabilitative, and social services. In addition to providing seniors with a secure, pleasant, stimulating environment, day-care centers work to restore or retain seniors' ability to care for themselves. Seniors may attend for several hours or the entire day.

Although the first elder-care centers appeared in the 1970's, in 1997 they were still relatively uncommon. Only about 50,000 seniors, most of whom have Alzheimer's disease or other forms of dementia, attend the estimated 1,500 centers in the United States.

Elder-care centers are run by hospitals, nursing homes, and religious organizations. Many centers provide transportation to and from the center, while some also offer transportation to health-care providers.

Homemakers from chore or housekeeping services may help mobile seniors shop or such workers may shop for homebound seniors.

the age and health of the individual, the extent of coverage—from one year or until the individual dies—and the waiting period until benefits begin. Although such policies were expensive in 1997, premiums still trailed the average annual cost of long-term care.

Working with home-care providers

Families who hire a home-care worker are inviting a stranger into their home. Health-care experts recommend that families seeking professional caregivers:

- Use only home-care agencies that are bonded and insured. Ask if the agency is a member of the local Better Business Bureau.
- Ask the agency for references. Check them out. Request references for any recommended home-health aides.
- Make sure that aides have been trained for the duties and responsibilities they will be performing in the home.
- Before an aide begins, settle all payment arrangements, including Social Security payments.
- Prepare a schedule of tasks as well as working hours and make sure the aide understands what is expected of him or her.
- Prepare a list of phone numbers of people who can be called in an emergency.

Assisted living facilities and adult living communities often offer residents a program of staff-organized social activities.

- If the aide comes from an agency, request that the aide's supervisor visit the home on a regular basis.
- If an aide fails to perform satisfactorily, request another aide from the agency.

Assisted living

Assisted living facilities (ALF's) offer housing, limited nursing care, social services, and personal care to seniors who are too ill or frail to live independently but who are not sick enough be admitted to a nursing home. ALF's provide a homelike environment where social and personal services are specialized and health care is designed to keep seniors functioning at their best. The involvement of family and friends is encouraged. ALF's are also known as personal care, domiciliary, or board-and-care homes.

Although some nonprofit groups have been providing such services for more than 100 years, in the 1990's, ALF's became a multibillion-dollar business that was one of the fastest growing housing markets for seniors, though some nonprofit groups have been providing such services for more than 100 years. In 1997, an estimated 1 million older Americans lived in about 40,000 ALF's. Most ALF's are small-scale operations, housed in converted private homes or small hotels. However, in the late 1990's, large corporate chains operating in several states were beginning to dominate the industry. State regulations governing ALF's vary. Some states require larger facilities to be licensed, but smaller facilities often fall outside regulations.

Assisted living financing

ALF's may charge more than $1,000 per month for basic services, in addition to a substantial entry fee or deposit, according to 1997 figures. Basic services usually include daily meals, a private or semiprivate unit, staff-run social activities, and transportation to medical appointments and shopping. Residents who require additional services, such as help with dressing or taking medication, pay substantially higher assessments.

Generally, ALF residents qualify for Medicare benefits only if they are receiving skilled nursing services provided by one of the few Medicare-certified ALF's. In some states, Medicaid pays for certain ALF services for poor seniors. In addition, some long-term-care insurance policies pay assisted living benefits in place of nursing home care, though the number of such policies in 1997 was still small.

Nursing homes

About 1.6 million Americans over age 65 were residing in nursing homes in 1996, according to the National Center for Health Statistics. More than half of new residents transferred from hospitals; the rest moved from their homes or the home of a family member.

How to find help

Seniors and their families attempting to locate elder care services and programs in their community have many resources. However, no one resource will have all the information needed to identify all the services in the community. Finding long-term care service takes patience, time, and a lot of detective work.

The best starting point is your local Area Agency on Aging (AAA). These agencies, established in 1974 under the Older Americans Act, administer funds and provide referrals for senior services. For the office nearest you, call 1-800-235-5503. Be prepared to provide the city and county where your senior lives. Nearly all states have at least one AAA office and those that don't disseminate information through a state office of aging. This agency also may be called a department, agency, or a division of seniors, senior citizens, or elder affairs.

A local senior center, public library, or college library may have two important directories: A Directory of State and Area Agencies on Aging and the National Directory for Eldercare Information and Referral.

Another important resource is the toll-free Eldercare Locator, which refers callers to information, resources, and services. It is supported by the U.S. Administration on Aging and two organizations: the National Association of Area Agencies and the National Association of State Units on Aging, both in Washington, D.C. Call 1-800-677-1116 between 9:00 a.m. and 11:00 p.m. EST on weekdays. Be prepared to give the address and zip code of the older person who needs assistance and a short description of the assistance being sought.

Selected Readings on Elder Care

Cohen, Donna and Eisdorfer, Carl. *Caring for Your Aging Parents*. New York: Tarcher/Putnam, 1994.

Cohen, Donna and Eisdorfer, Carl. *The Loss of Self: A Family Resource for the Care of Alzheimer's Disease and Related Disorders*. New York: Plume/Penguin, 1987.

Strauss, Peter and Lederman, Nancy. *The Elder Law Handbook*. New York: Facts On File, Inc., 1996.

Computer resources

- Senior centers and organizations and university librarians have created many Internet and e-mail resources on aging. Start with key words such as "eldercare," "aging," or "senior services" to locate general sites. The key words "health" and "health care" will lead to information on specific disease conditions, such as Alzheimer's disease, stroke, or Parkinson disease. Information on long-term care insurance may be found using "health care" or "health insurance." Other key words include "elder law," "assisted living," and specific health problems.

- The U.S. Administration on Aging has a home page with information on the agency's programs and information, (URL: http:/www.aoa.dhhs.gov).

- The Directory of Web and Gopher Aging Sites lists all Area Agencies on Aging and other Internet aging sites, (URL: http://www.aoa.dhhs.gov/aoa/webres/craig.htm).

- Senior Living Alternatives magazine provides information on senior care options at (http://www.senioralternatves.com).

- Caregivers Resources Guide, (http://www.sfgate.com/examiner/caregivers/resources/national.html).

- National Association for Home Care, (http://www.nahc.org).

- Senior Housing (http://www.seniorsites.com)

- Guide to Choosing a Nursing Home, (gopher://gopher.gsa.gov:70/00/staff/pa/cic/health/nursehme.txt)

Information on home-care services

- Local AAA's will either offer a free assessment or refer you to an agency that does. That is, a social worker will determine a senior's needs and provide a list of service providers. Some communities also have private geriatric service agencies that make assessments, contact service providers, and then coordinate and oversee the delivery of the services.

- Approximately 8,600 U.S. agencies have been certified to provide skilled nursing and other home-health-care services by the U.S. Health Care Financing Administration, which administers Medicare. Federal law requires each state to maintain a toll-free hotline to collect complaints on home-health-care agencies and to share that information with the public. Your local AAA can provide you with the number in your state.

- Another 9,000 agencies provide housekeeping and companion services and other types of home care. These agencies are not certified by Medicare, though they may be licensed by the state. Some agencies have undergone voluntary accreditation by a professional organization, such as the Community Health Accreditation Program in New York City. The program's hotline (1-800-669-1656, ext. 242) distributes a checklist for assessing the quality of home care and its cost.

- Home-care workers also may also be found through registries that provide lists of available workers. Registries typically are not licensed or certified, and workers may not be screened or even trained.

- Not all communities have a full range of home-based services and resources. When paid services are not available, seniors and their families should talk with clergy, physicians, and the staff at hospitals and senior centers to find volunteers, students, or others who might be willing to provide help with housekeeping, lawn care, and transportation. Other resources include religious groups, civic organizations, the Red Cross, and the Visiting Nurses Association.

- Call the National Meals on Wheels Foundation (1-800-999-6262) to find out if there is a program in your community.

- For information on assistive devices, equipment, and furniture, call ABLE DATA, the National Rehabilitation Information Center in Washington, D.C., at 1-800-346-2742.

Selected Readings on Home Care

- "Consumer Guide to Home Health Care," free from the National Consumers League, 815 Fifteenth Street, NW, Suite 928, Washington, D.C. 20002.

- "Home Care: Is It A Better Answer?" Consumer Reports, October 1995, p. 660–662.

- "How To Choose a Home Care Agency: A Consumer's Guide," free from the National Association for Home Care, 519 C Street, NE Stanton Park, Washington, D.C. 20002.

- "Staying at Home," published by the American Association of Retired Persons, 601 East Street, NW, Washington, D.C. 20041.

Information on assisted living communities

- "The Promise and the Pitfalls of Assisted Living'," Consumer Reports, October 1995, p. 656–659.

Information on nursing homes

- More than 800 state and local ombudsmen across the United States provide helpful information on locating a good nursing home. Almost all state ombudsmen are located in state agencies on aging in that state's capital. State officials can give you the number of your local ombudsman.

- A Practical Guide to Nursing Home Advocacy, is an excellent consumer manual for understanding nursing home care, financing, the admission process, resident's rights, and quality of care. Write the American Association of Retired Persons at 601 East St., NW, Washington, D.C. 20045.

- Nursing Homes: Getting Good Care There. Burger, Sarah Greene, and others. San Luis Obispo, CA: American Source Books, 1996.

- "Nursing Homes: When a Loved One Needs Care," Consumer Reports, August 1995, p. 518–527.

- "Who Pays for the Nursing Home," Consumer Reports, September 1995, p. 591–597.

Information on adult living communities

- The report "How Continuing Care Retirement Communities Manage Services for the Elderly" is available free from the U.S. Government Accounting Office. Write U.S. GAO, P.O. Box 6015, Gaithersburg, MD 20884-6015.

- The booklet "The Continuing Care Retirement Community: A Guide for Consumers" a list of facilities accredited by the American Association of Homes and Service for the Aging may be obtained by calling 1-800-508-9442.

According to the National Center for Health Statistics, a woman age 65 or older in 1997 had a 25- to 35-percent chance of being admitted to a nursing home at some time in her life. For men, the likelihood was lower than 25 percent. About 60 percent of seniors admitted to nursing homes stay for several years, often until they die. Most of these long-term residents are affected by dementia and memory loss.

Nursing homes provide 24-hour medical and personal care for seriously disabled people and people recovering from strokes, surgery, or injuries. In general, nursing homes offer three levels of medical and personal care: custodial, intermediate, and skilled. Not all nursing homes provide all levels of care, however. Custodial care meets personal rather than medical needs. Intermediate care involves medical supervision and skilled nursing that is not intensive and continuous. For example, intermediate-care residents may need to have surgical bandages changed or help with medication. Skilled care is medically necessary inpatient care provided by nurses and supervised by a physician.

Nursing homes are licensed and regulated by state departments of public health. In 1997, about 75 percent of the 17,000 nursing homes in the United States were owned by individuals or private corporations. The other nursing homes were run by religious or charitable groups or by government agencies, such as the U.S. Veterans Administration.

The decision to move a parent or relative into a nursing home is often difficult and painful. But a good facility—one that feels like a

A senior is transported to a day-care center by a worker from an elder-care agency. Day-care centers for the elderly are increasingly popular alternatives to nursing home care.

home—with trained and caring nurses—often can provide a higher quality of care than the frail elderly can receive from family members at home.

Nursing home financing

Nursing homes are costly. In 1997, the national yearly average for a one-year stay was about $37,000, though some facilities charged $100,000 or more. Medicare pays only about 4 percent of the $70 billion spent annually on nursing home care in the United States. That figure is so low because Medicare covers only skilled nursing care.

To qualify for skilled nursing benefits, a senior must be admitted to a Medicare-certified facility within 30 days of a hospitalization that lasted at least three days for an acute illness or injury. Medicare pays only for 100 days of skilled nursing per spell of illness and completely covers only the first 20 days of care. For the remaining 80 days, the nursing home resident is assessed a copayment, which was $92 in 1996. For this reason, financial experts recommend that seniors buy Medicare-supplement insurance to cover the difference as soon as they turn age 65, even if they are still healthy.

Long-term-care insurance also helps defray the cost of nursing home care by paying a daily benefit of from $50 to $200. Coverage may be limited or last for the lifetime of the beneficiary.

Seniors who need nursing home care but have few financial resources may qualify for Medicaid benefits. In fact, Medicaid is the single largest financier of nursing home care, followed by families. Medicaid also covers more services than does Medicare. For example, eligible seniors are entitled to nursing home care for an unlimited number of days. Medicaid also pays for intermediate as well as skilled nursing care.

Adult living communities

Traditionally, adult living communities have been designed for independent seniors with few health problems or with problems that interfere little with daily activities. Adult living communities, a multibillion dollar business in the United States, are also known as retirement homes, congregate living facilities, and residential care facilities. They can be communities of rental apartments, condominiums, or townhouses.

Most adult living communities offer few, if any, medical services and few on-site personal care services. The services available are usually amenities, such as security, transportation, housekeeping, and laundry. Larger facilities may have tennis courts or other sports facilities, branch banks, and pharmacies. Adult living communities often have a common dining room where residents may eat prepared meals together. And the facilities often sponsor social activities.

Although the cost of adult living communities varies widely, most are for-profit enterprises. Residents are responsible for all fees.

The services available in adult living communities, also known as retirement homes, are usually amenities such as sports facilities, transportation, and housekeeping.

Continuing care retirement communities

An increasingly popular form of adult living community in the 1990's was the continuing care retirement community (CCRC). CCRC's offer a range of housing options from independent living in homes, cottages, or apartments to nursing homes. They are designed for healthy seniors who are able to live on their own but who want the security of knowing that more supportive medical and personal care or even skilled nursing care is available. The number of CCRC's is growing rapidly in the United States. In 1997, an estimated 350,000 people were living in about 1,200 CCRC's, up from an estimated 230,000 people in 800 such facilities in 1992.

About one-third of CCRC's provide lifetime care and require new residents to pay an endowment or entry fee ranging from $23,000 to more than $100,000 and then pay fees of from $800 to more than $2,500 per month, according to 1997 figures. These CCRC's, also known as all-inclusive or life-care communities, assume full financial risk for residents' long-term care. A slightly less expensive type of CCRC assumes partial risk for long-term care by limiting the types and extent of services.

CCRC's are no longer only for the wealthy, however. In the 1990's, some CCRC's began offering units on a rental basis without requiring an endowment or entry fee. As a result, these facilities became affordable for seniors who had an annual income of $25,000 to $35,000. Some CCRC's also operate on a fee-for-service basis. For example, a basic package may include only a living unit and dining privileges. Additional fees would be charged for housekeeping, personal care, or limited medical care.

Moving into a CCRC can be like buying both a home and an insurance policy for long-term care. Two major factors to consider are the financial health of the CCRC and the quality of services offered. Seniors and their families should review the conditions under which the endowment or entry fee may be refunded—for example, if a resident dies shortly after moving in. They should also determine who makes the final decision about transferring a resident to more supportive care. They should make certain the facility has an adequate number of assisted living units and nursing home beds and should understand which services require additional fees and under what conditions fees may be increased. Renters should clearly understand whether they can return to the same unit if they require hospitalization and know their rights for moving out. Obtaining the advice of a lawyer and financial expert is important before signing a CCRC contract.

Most people do not plan for the possibility of debilitating conditions and illnesses in later life. Planning for long-term care, however, is the best way to protect financial resources and to make sure your preferences for managing your health care are followed. ●●●

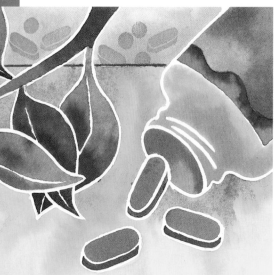

CONSUMER HEALTH

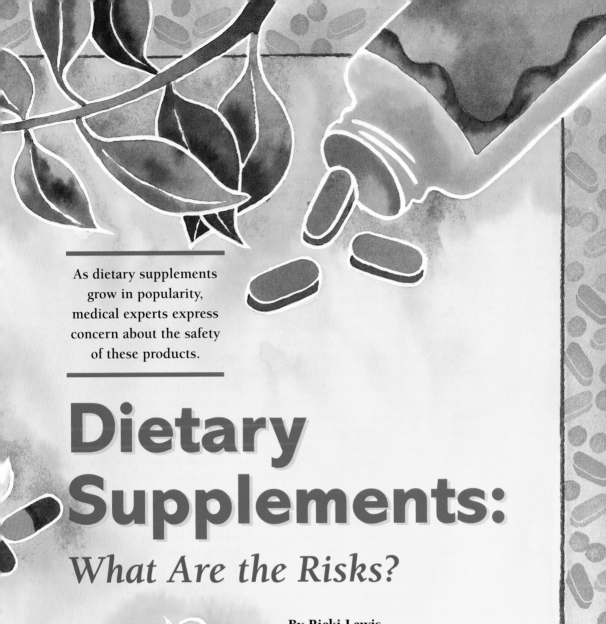

As dietary supplements grow in popularity, medical experts express concern about the safety of these products.

Dietary Supplements:

What Are the Risks?

By Ricki Lewis

The average health food store is likely to display many signs claiming the benefits of various natural remedies. One sign may claim that an all-natural compound can dramatically lower cholesterol levels. Another may promise a natural way to cure cancer and even reverse the aging process. Still another may advertise a "miracle weight-loss" pill. All of these products, like drugs, contain chemicals that affect the body, yet all of them are readily available because they fit into a special category of products called dietary supplements.

Consumers often assume that these natural remedies—extracts of plants or animals, including chemicals naturally produced in the human body—are more effective and safer than drugs made in the laboratory. However, a chemical is a chemical, and one that causes harm to the body will do so whether it comes from a vegetable or a test tube. As dietary supplements gained popularity in the 1990's, some medical experts came to believe that without careful regulations, consumers could not make informed judgments about the safety and value of these products.

Why is a dietary supplement not a "drug"?

Many drugs originally came from nature. Aspirin was derived from a chemical in willow tree bark; caffeine, from coffee beans. And flowers and bark have been the source of many modern cancer drugs. To develop drugs from a natural product, chemists isolate a single active ingredient in an organism that has a medicinal effect, or they improve upon the naturally occurring chemical by making a related one in the laboratory. The *synthetic,* or laboratory-created, versions of the chemical are often more effective or safer than the "natural product" itself, because they are more concentrated or purer. Whether the substances chemists use to make drugs are natural products or synthesized chemicals, the Food and Drug Administration (FDA) approves them for sale in pharmacies and regulates the drug company's manufacturing process.

Products known as dietary supplements, however, are less carefully regulated. The makers of dietary supplements do not need to conduct extensive research, meet specific production standards, or abide by other FDA regulations for drugs. Many dietary supplements, however, are promoted as herbal remedies and "natural drugs."

Dietary supplements are widely available in health food stores, on the Internet, in pharmacies, and from health-care practitioners. These products include vitamins, minerals, herbs, *botanicals* (plant products), certain hormones, amino acids, and products derived from these substances. According to the Dietary Supplement Health and Education Act of 1994, the difference between a dietary supplement and a drug depends largely on the intended use of the product. A product is considered a drug if the maker claims that the substance is intended to diagnose, prevent, treat, cure, or lessen the severity of a disease or condition of a disease. The makers of dietary supplements, on the other hand, cannot make any of these claims.

The author:

Ricki Lewis has a doctorate in genetics and is the author of several life science textbooks.

The difference between a drug and a dietary supplement

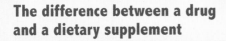

Drugs and dietary supplements both have active ingredients that can affect the body. Knowing the difference between these medicinal products can help consumers make more informed decisions.

Prescription drugs	The active ingredient in a prescription drug has an effect on a condition or symptom of a disease. A person can use this medication only when a physician prescribes it.
Over-the-counter drugs	Over-the-counter (OTC) drugs are intended to treat medical conditions that normally would go away even if untreated. OTC drugs are often versions of drugs that had once been available only by prescription.
Homeopathic drugs	Homeopathic drugs contain highly diluted chemicals. A large dose of an ingredient would cause an undesirable condition in a healthy person, but the diluted ingredient is claimed, but not proven, to cure the same condition in an ill person.
Dietary supplements	Dietary supplements include vitamins, minerals, herbs or other *botanicals* (plant products), amino acids, certain hormones, and products derived from these substances.

Instead, they can only say that the product is intended to supplement an individual's diet. The product's label can describe the effects of the supplement on a function of the body, but it cannot claim any medicinal effect. The label on saw palmetto, for example, states that it improves urinary flow, but it does not claim that saw palmetto treats an enlarged prostate, which is a disease condition.

This distinction between dietary supplements and drugs is important because the two categories have very different regulations. Pharmaceutical companies must conduct laboratory and animal tests on a prescription drug before it can be presented to the FDA for approval. The FDA then uses manufacturer's studies to determine whether the company can test the product in a series of *clinical trials* (studies with humans). Although the FDA regulates the process, it is the manufacturer's responsibility to prove that the drug is both effective and safe in treating certain conditions and that the benefit of taking the drug outweighs the risks of side effects. The FDA specifies the conditions for which a drug can be prescribed, its potency, the dosage schedule, the package labeling, a profile of the possible side effects, the method of production, and standards for purity.

In addition, the FDA closely regulates *over-the-counter* (OTC) *drugs,* drugs that can be purchased without a physician's prescription. The agency has approved about 700 active ingredients that can be used in OTC drugs, established guidelines for the recommended dosages, and issued warnings that must appear on the packages of products containing any of these ingredients. And the FDA has an extensive review process to ensure the effectiveness and safety of a product when a manufacturer wants to create an OTC version of a drug that had previously been approved only for prescription use.

The FDA also regulates homeopathic medicines, which are sold both as prescription and OTC drugs. Homeopathic treatment is based on "the law of similars." This theory, which dates to the late 1700's, suggests that the same substance that causes a disease symptom when taken in high doses will counteract this same symptom when taken in low doses. For example, poison ivy causes rashes. Homeopathic practitioners prescribe compounds with extremely low doses of poison ivy extracts to treat rashes caused by other factors. Most homeopathic remedies are so dilute, in fact, that the active in-

FDA-controlled drugs and dietary supplements

The Food and Drug Administration (FDA) regulates the production of prescription, over-the-counter, and homeopathic drugs. Regulations governing dietary supplements are not as strict and give the FDA little control over the products.

Product	Tests	Regulations
FDA-regulated drugs	The drug company must conduct tests to prove through a series of laboratory, animal, and human studies that a new drug is effective and that the benefit of the drug outweighs the risks of side effects.	The FDA determines what a drug can be used to treat and specifies the production standards, potency, dosage recommendations, profiles of side effects, and labeling requirements.
Dietary supplements	The kinds and number of tests needed to show the effectiveness of a dietary supplement have not been clearly defined. The FDA, not the manufacturer, must prove that a product is unsafe before it can be pulled off the market.	The FDA does not regulate the production, packaging, and dosage recommendations of most dietary supplements. The agency can issue warnings about the risks of a particular product.

gredient cannot be detected in the final product. According to the theory of homeopathic treatment, even if the active ingredient is diluted to near nothingness, its "imprint" remains and heals. There has never been any scientific proof that homeopathic treatments are effective. However, since homeopathic remedies are so dilute, FDA regulations for the manufacturing of these products are much less stringent than are those governing conventional drugs.

Limited regulations on dietary supplements

Dietary supplements are subject to even looser standards. The 1994 dietary supplement law established that manufacturers of dietary supplements do not have to prove the effectiveness of their products. Manufacturers must only have evidence of some "substantiation" for the claims that they make about their products, though the law does not clearly define the term "substantiation." The proof for the effectiveness of a dietary supplement, for example, can be based on the results of laboratory tests even if the effect has not been proven in clinical trials on human beings.

The makers of dietary supplements also do not need to prove the safety of a product, according to the 1994 law. Instead, they must show that there is a "reasonable assurance" that the ingredients in a product do not "present a significant or unreasonable risk of illness or injury." Consequently, many dietary supplements have not undergone thorough tests, especially for the long-term effects of products or for possible harmful interactions with other drugs. Therefore, even if a dietary supplement seems to have the desired effect, a consumer does not know whether the product could prove to be dangerous if taken over a long period of time or with a combination of other supplements or drugs.

The FDA must prove that a dietary supplement is unsafe before the product can be restricted or taken off the market. Furthermore, the FDA can intervene only after a number of people have reported that a supplement has caused harm. The FDA's Office of Special Nutritionals, which is responsible for monitoring complaints, does not have the resources to conduct the research itself. Consequently, the FDA must rely on the research of independent institutions to prove that the product causes a health risk. For example, the FDA began investigating the Chinese herb ma huang, or ephedra, in April 1996 after receiving reports that at least 15 people died after taking the supplement. (Ma huang is sold under brand names, such as Herbal Ecstasy, Ultimate Xphoria, and Cloud Nine, and in formulas marketed as exercise aids, such as Ripped Fuel.) Several factors complicated the process of proving the harm of the product. For instance, most of the deaths occurred after a person took more than the manufacturer's recommended dosage—a fact that makes it more difficult for the FDA to prove a significant health risk. In June 1997, the FDA issued proposed restrictions for ephedra products, and final recommendations were scheduled to be released after August.

Dietary supplements that may present health risks

According to the FDA and other public health organizations, some dietary supplements on the market present risks if taken in large quantities or over extended periods of time. Also the lack of long-term studies or the lack of information provided by the manufacturers of these products can present safety risks.

Dietary supplement	Source	Health claims	Risks or warnings
Chaparral	Extract from the twigs and leaves of the chaparral bush are used in tea and pills.	**Possible benefits:** acts as an antioxidant, a chemical compound that prevents certain cell damage. **Unproven claims:** slows aging process, cures cancer, cleanses the blood, and treats skin problems.	Chaparral has been linked to liver damage.
Chromium picolinate	Chromium is an essential mineral in a human diet. Picolinate is an organic molecule.	**Possible benefits:** Chromium is necessary for metabolism of some sugars and fats. **Unproven claims:** helps a person lose fat and keep muscle.	In laboratory tests, chromium picolinate was shown to cause damage to the chromosomes in cells.
Comfrey	All parts of this plant are used to make pills, teas, tinctures (prepared with alcohol), and ointments.	**Possible benefits:** may promote the growth of cells. **Unproven claims:** heals wounds, treats sore joints, and acts as a general cure-all.	Comfrey has been linked to liver damage, and animal studies suggest possible damage to other organs.
DHEA (dehydroepiandrosterone)	A hormone produced in the adrenal gland. Synthetic versions are used in dietary supplements.	**Possible benefits:** unknown. **Unproven claims:** slows aging, prevents cancer and heart disease, promotes weight loss, and treats Alzheimer's and AIDS-related conditions.	The long-term effects of taking DHEA are unknown. Some research suggests it may cause liver damage.
Ephedra (ma huang)	The twigs of ephedra are usually sold as a pill or tincture. It is often combined with caffeine.	**Possible benefits:** treats symptoms of some upper respiratory problems. **Unproven claims:** "safe high," promotes weight loss, and boosts energy.	High doses of ephedra products can cause liver failure, high blood pressure, heart attack, psychosis, stroke, and death.
Germander	An herb sold as a tea or tincture.	**Possible benefits:** may aid weight loss. **Unproven claims:** treats digestive disorders and liver problems.	Germander has been linked to liver damage.

Dietary supplement	Source	Health claims	Risks or warnings
Germanium	A metallic element that is nonessential in the human diet.	**Possible benefits:** unknown. **Unproven claims:** promotes general health and corrects toxicity from other metals.	Extended use of germanium may cause irreversible kidney damage and can cause death.
Jin bu huan	An herb sold in a tablet form.	**Possible benefits:** treatment for pain and insomnia (traditional Chinese remedy).	Jin bu huan has been linked to liver damage. Ingestion by children has resulted in life-threatening reactions.
Lobelia (Indian tobacco)	Dried parts of the plant are used in pills and teas.	**Possible benefits:** expands small air passages in the lungs when taken in low dosages.	High doses can slow breathing, lower blood pressure, increase the heart rate, and cause death.
Melatonin	A hormone produced in the human pineal gland in the brain. Synthetic versions are used in dietary supplements.	**Possible benefits:** helps to regulate the body's sleep-wake cycle. **Unproven claims:** treats numerous diseases, restores youthfulness, and prolongs life.	Nothing is known about the long-term effects of taking the supplement.
Phenylalanine	Phenylalanine is an essential amino acid in the human body. It is often an ingredient of supplements called "smart" drinks.	**Possible benefits:** Phenylalanine drugs are used to treat dementia and Parkinson's disease. **Unproven claims:** "Smart" drinks improve memory, intelligence, and energy.	In large doses, phenylalanine causes irritability and weight loss. Some people are not able to metabolize this amino acid.
Willow bark	The bark of white willow trees is sold as pills or tinctures.	**Possible benefits:** treats headaches and other pain. (A synthetic version of the bark's active ingredient, salicylic acid, is used to make aspirin.)	Most labels do not warn that salicylic acid can cause Reye's syndrome in a child who has just had chicken pox or the flu.
Yohimbe	Yohimbe is the bark from a West African tree that is sold as a tea or pill.	**Possible benefits:** none proven. **Unproven claims:** enhances male sexual and athletic performance.	Possible adverse effects include kidney failure, seizures, and death.

Sources: The U.S. Food and Drug Administration and *The Honest Herbal: A Sensible Guide to the Use of Herbs and Related Remedies*.

The 1994 law also does not allow the FDA to regulate the manufacturing process or to inspect the product to make sure that it contains the correct plant or plant part. The active ingredient might be in the leaf of the plant, but to save on production costs, a manufacturer may use the whole plant, thus creating an inferior product. In some cases, plants used in dietary supplements are not harvested by specially trained botanists. On occasion, untrained harvesters have reportedly tainted dietary supplements with harmful plants and substances. In 1996, for example, seven New Yorkers fell ill from drinking herbal tea contaminated with belladonna, a poisonous plant. Three of the people who drank the tea were hospitalized with racing heartbeats, fever, dilated pupils, and flushed skin.

"Natural" does not mean "safe"

Because the manufacturing of dietary supplements is not regulated, these products may not be *standardized,* meaning that the amount of the active ingredient may not be consistent from bottle to bottle. In 1996, the Center for Science in the Public Interest in Washington, D.C., examined garlic supplements sold at health food stores. The researchers found that the brand with the highest concentration of garlic in the pills had 40 times more than the brand with the least amount of garlic. Such discrepancies can occur because an individual plant can have a concentration of a medicinal chemical as much as 10,000 times greater than another plant of the same variety, according to botanist James A. Duke of the U.S. Department of Agriculture. Further complicating the picture, some manufacturers combine several different plants to make a "multi-herbal" product. Given this fact—and that many people take more than one supplement at a time—concerned doctors say it is almost impossible to determine which ingredient relieves which symptoms or causes which side effects.

The lack of regulations over the labeling of dietary supplements can also present risks to consumers, according to critics of the dietary supplement law. White willow bark, for example, contains an active ingredient called salicylic acid, the same active ingredient that is synthetically produced for aspirin. The label on a bottle of aspirin warns that when a child has just had a mild viral infection, such as influenza or chicken pox, aspirin may cause Reye's syndrome, a potentially fatal disease that affects the liver and central nervous system. Manufacturers of willow bark, however, do not have to put a similar warning on the product's label even though willow bark poses the same danger to children.

The absence of warning labels, as well as the assumption that "natural" always means "safe," may lead some people to assume that dietary supplements are safe in any dosage or combination. Even a product that has been used successfully to treat a particular condition can have toxic effects when taken in high dosages. One such product, which the FDA has identified as potentially dangerous, is

Indian tobacco or lobelia. A 55-milligram dose of dried lobelia—less than the usual amount in a single lobelia pill—can improve breathing by causing the *bronchioles* (small branches of air passages in the lungs) to expand. In higher doses, however, lobelia can slow breathing, lower blood pressure, increase the heartbeat, and cause death.

The makers of chaparral, an herb sold in tea or tablet form, advertise that the product slows aging, cleanses the blood, and heals skin problems. But it also can cause liver damage if taken in large doses or over an extended period of time. The FDA has linked chaparral to at least six cases of *acute nonviral hepatitis* (a liver disease not caused by an infection). Yohimbe, a pill made from tree bark, supposedly enhances male athletic and sexual performance. In large doses, however, it can cause kidney failure, paralysis, seizures, and even death.

Even if a natural drug is safe under all circumstances, some people have put themselves at risk by relying solely on the "natural cure" promised by proponents of dietary supplements rather than continuing a doctor-advised treatment. Michael Diaz, an *oncologist* and *hematologist* (cancer and blood disorder specialist) at Mt. Sinai Medical Center in New York City, reported in May 1996 that he treated a cancer patient who grew more ill after each chemotherapy session. The doctor discovered that instead of taking the prescribed medication between chemotherapy treatments, the patient was taking shark cartilage, a dietary supplement promoted as a cancer cure.

Consumers who want to avoid the possible risks associated with taking dietary supplements have a formidable task in choosing among the estimated 20,000 products on the market. Some products can be helpful and have few or no known side effects. *Pharmacognocists* (specialists in herbal and plant medicines) Varro Tyler of Purdue University in West Lafayette, Indiana, and Norman Farnsworth of the University of Illinois in Chicago have noted the benefits of several medicinal plants that are safe for most people. For example, echinacea, an herb in the daisy family, may boost immunity by stimulating production of white blood cells. And ginger and peppermint can prevent motion-sickness and treat some nausea.

Other so-called "natural drugs" may not have such a clean bill of health. Under scrutiny were some of the most popular dietary supplements in 1997, such as melatonin, dehydroepiandrosterone (DHEA), chromium picolinate, ma huang, and shark cartilage. All of these products meet the conditions of the Dietary Supplement and Health Education Act; however, medical professionals raised questions about each of the products' effectiveness, safety, the legitimacy of health claims, and the need for long-term studies.

Melatonin

Melatonin is a hormone produced in the human pineal gland, a tiny, pea-shaped gland located in the center of the brain. The natural cycle of darkness and daylight seems to trigger the production of this hormone. At night, levels of melatonin are high, and during the day

they are very low. Researchers believe that melatonin serves as a chemical messenger that tells the rest of the body that it's time to sleep. A 1993 study at the Massachusetts Institute of Technology in Cambridge, Massachusetts, suggested that small doses of melatonin could induce sleep. Further medical studies have shown that melatonin may ease the effects of *jet lag* (fatigue and irritability following long flights through several time zones). But no clinical studies have proved claims that melatonin helps with long-term *insomnia* (inability to fall asleep or remain asleep).

Although affecting short-term sleep problems is the only known benefit of the hormone, the proponents of the dietary supplement melatonin list many others. In 1996, consumers spent an estimated $200 million to $350 million on melatonin in hopes of treating cancer, heart disease, diabetes, cataracts, AIDS, Alzheimer's disease, depression, epilepsy, autism, schizophrenia, and influenza. Some of these hopes were based on inconclusive research on how melatonin functions in the body. Babies begin producing melatonin when they are about 3 months old. Production gradually increases throughout childhood and peaks just before puberty. Then it declines. By the time most people are 70 years old, melatonin production has almost ceased. Many proponents of the supplement concluded that if melatonin production decreases with age, then the dietary supplement could reverse the aging process and the cellular changes that lead to diseases such as cancer.

Miracles or myths of melatonin

The popularity of melatonin stemmed largely from claims made in books, such as *The Melatonin Miracle* by physicians Walter Pierpaoli and William Regelson. However, neurobiologist Fred Turek at Northwestern University in Evanston, Illinois, and other experts argued that the evidence presented in these books was based mostly on hearsay or insufficient laboratory tests. *The Melatonin Miracle*, for example, reported that researchers had proved that melatonin reverses the aging process in humans. However, the study on aging used to support this claim was performed on mice—not humans. When scientists switched the pineal glands of older mice with those of younger mice, the younger mice died prematurely and the older mice lived longer. Turek pointed out, however, that the pineal glands in the strain of mice used in the study do not produce melatonin. Whatever extended the lives of the mice, it was not melatonin.

Researchers at a meeting of the National Institutes of Health in August 1996 advised consumers to avoid using melatonin. They raised concerns about the long-term effects of the hormone, the proper dosage of the supplement, how the hormone interacts with other drugs, how different people react to the recommended dosage, what effects the hormone may have on reproduction, and what happens in the body when the level of one hormone is increased when the levels of other hormones are still changing with age. Also, studies have not proven that the body actually incorporates the supplement as it does the naturally produced hormone. Therefore, even if it does present no risks, it could be a waste of money.

DHEA

DHEA is a hormone produced by the adrenal glands that the body converts into the sex hormones estrogen and testosterone. Like melatonin, DHEA levels decrease as people age. Research published in 1986 by Elizabeth Barrett-Connor, an *epidemiologist* (disease-control specialist) at the University of California, San Diego, prompted further research about the hormone. She found that of the 143 men in the study, those with naturally high DHEA levels had half the incidence of heart disease as those with low DHEA levels.

Since Barrett-Connor's study, other research has offered some promising evidence for the benefits of DHEA. But many proponents of the dietary supplement DHEA have claimed that researchers have proved that it can slow the aging process, prevent cancer and heart disease, promote weight loss without dieting, and treat Alzheimer's disease and AIDS-related conditions. According to a March 1997 report from the Center for Science in the Public Interest, many of these claims have been supported with misinterpretations of published research about the hormone. Furthermore, proponents of DHEA supplements do not mention Barrett-Connor's 1996 follow-up study that showed high DHEA levels lowered the risk of heart disease in men by only 20 percent and had no noticeable effect on the heart disease incidence among women.

Although some researchers believed that further studies would reveal the benefits of DHEA, others expressed concern over its safety. Biochemist Arthur G. Schwartz of Temple University in Philadelphia reported in 1995 that DHEA could cause liver damage in rodents. He also noted that an increased level of testosterone in older men taking DHEA supplements could make them more susceptible to prostate cancer. Also, as with melatonin, researchers are not certain if the body actually incorporates DHEA supplements.

According to FDA regulations, a bottle of aspirin, *left*, must warn consumers of the various risks of the product. A willow bark label, *right*, which contains essentially the same active ingredient as aspirin, does not need to list those risks. The only stipulation is that the label does not claim that willow bark can treat a disease or disease condition.

Indications: Fast, safe, temporary relief of headache pain, muscular aches and pains, aches and fever due to colds and flu, and minor aches and pains of arthritis.

Directions: Adults, take 1 or 2 tablets with water every 4 hours, as needed, up to a maximum of 12 tablets per 24 hours.

Warnings: Children and teenagers should not use this medicine for chicken pox or flu symptoms before a doctor is consulted about Reye's syndrome, a rare but serious illness reported to be associated with aspirin. Do not take if: allergic to aspirin; have asthma; for pain more than 10 days or for fever for more than 3 days unless directed by a doctor. If pain or fever persists or gets worse, if new symptoms occur, or if redness or swelling is present, consult a doctor because these could be signs of a serious condition. Keep out of reach of children. In case of accidental overdose, contact a doctor immediately. As with any drug, if you are pregnant or nursing a baby, seek the advice of a health professional before using this product. It is especially important not to use aspirin during the last 3 months of pregnancy unless specifically directed to do so by a doctor because it may cause problems in the unborn child or complications during delivery.
Read carton for other warnings.
Active ingredient: 325 mg Aspirin per tablet.
Avoid excessive heat (over 104 °F or 40 °C)

White Willow bark was the basis for the synthesis of aspirin. It contains salicin and related compounds.

Recommendation: Take one or two capsules three times daily with water, as needed.

Chromium picolinate

Chromium picolinate was another popular dietary supplement that continued to cause concern among researchers in 1997. Chromium is an essential nutrient that helps bind insulin to cell membranes and is therefore important for the metabolism of some sugars and fats. Some cases of adult-onset diabetes mellitus have been linked to a deficiency of chromium in the diet. In 1995, researchers at the Louisiana State University Agricultural Center in Baton Rouge found in animal studies that when chromium is combined with a molecule called picolinate, it appears to cause fat loss. Manufacturers of the dietary supplement chromium picolinate used this study, as well as related research, to claim that the supplement helps regulate blood sugar levels and helps dieters "lose fat and keep muscle."

Despite claims by manufacturers that chromium picolinate is "exceptionally safe," a study published in December 1995 suggested that the supplement may cause cancer. Chemists at Dartmouth College in Hanover, New Hampshire, and George Washington University Medical Center in Washington, D.C., found that chromium picolinate damages the chromosomes of cells growing in laboratory cultures, which is a sign that it might cause cancer. Researcher Steven R. Patierno explained that when chromium enters the body on its own, it works outside of cells. However, when chromium is combined with picolinate, it enters cells and disrupts chromosomes. The researchers concluded that chromium picolinate needed further study before it could be classified as a safe diet pill.

Ma huang

Chinese herbalists have reportedly used ma huang, or ephedra, for at least 2,000 years to treat respiratory problems. In the body, ephedra is converted into ephedrine, a powerful stimulant to the heart and central nervous system. Ephedrine and the chemically related pseudoephedrine are used in cold remedies and some asthma medications. Most manufacturers of ephedra-based dietary supplements combine the herb with caffeine to boost the effect. This combination, however, creates a greater risk of adverse reactions.

Manufacturers of workout formulas containing ma huang and caffeine claim that the products promote weight control and boost energy. Other ephedra-based dietary supplements, such as Herbal Ecstasy, are promoted as a way to get a "natural high"—a legal alternative to an illegal and chemically unrelated drug called Ecstasy. The makers promise that the product can heighten energy, inspire inner visions, boost sexual sensations, and bring on cosmic consciousness.

Public health officials have criticized the safety of this "natural high," however. Medical researchers have linked Herbal Ecstasy and similar ephedra-based supplements to liver failure, skyrocketing blood pressure, heart attack, psychosis, stroke, and death in several young people. Many states outlawed ephedra-based supplements after the March 7, 1996, death of 20-year-old college student Peter

Herbal supplements that may help

Medical studies have shown that some dietary supplements based on plant products have beneficial effects. Although the evidence establishing the effectiveness of these plants is reasonably strong, many of the products can still cause problems in people allergic to the substances or when taken in high doses.

Echinacea seems to boost immunity by stimulating production of white blood cells, but continued use of the product may reduce its effectiveness. Also, since it is a member of the daisy family, it may cause allergic reactions in some people.

Garlic has been shown to help lower cholesterol levels in humans, and some garlic pills are made to dissolve in the intestines to avoid the unpleasant odor of the plant. Too much garlic, however, can hinder blood clotting. Also, the concentration of active ingredients in pills tends to vary widely.

Ginger can treat motion sickness and prevent some nausea. Although side effects are rare, studies have indicated that large doses may inhibit blood clotting and depress the central nervous system.

Valerian has a mild tranquilizing effect that can aid sleep. Although it has no known toxic side effects, its very unpleasant smell may discourage its use.

Saw palmetto berries are used to improve urinary flow in men with noncancerous, enlarged prostates. It may also have some anti-inflammatory effects. Until the 1950's, saw palmetto extracts were a prescription drug in the United States, but questions about its effectiveness caused it to fall out of use. Although some new evidence of its medicinal benefits exists, no pharmaceutical companies in the United States have pursued research on the plant.

Feverfew can be an effective treatment of migraine headaches. However, the tablet form of the herb often does not have a consistent potency. Also, studies have not determined all of the active ingredients contained in the plant.

Ginko biloba leaves have been shown in some studies to be effective in improving blood flow to the brain. In many European countries, the extract from the leaves is sold as a prescription drug. In high doses, however, it can inhibit blood clotting.

Chamomile is most often used as a tea to treat indigestion and inflammation in the digestive system. People allergic to ragweed can have adverse reactions to chamomile. Also, in high doses, the herb can be poisonous to children.

Sources: *The Honest Herbal: A Sensible Guide to the Use of Herbs and Related Remedies* and *Consumer Reports.*

113

Taking dietary supplements safely

There are dietary supplements on the market that are effective and safe for most people. Since these products are not carefully regulated, however, determining which products to use is a difficult task. The following tips are recommended by the U.S. Food and Drug Administration and *Consumer Reports* magazine.

- Check with your physician before taking a dietary supplement to avoid serious side effects or dangerous interactions with prescription medicine.

- Consult a pharmacist who specializes in the use of herbal remedies.

- Pregnant and nursing women or people with serious health problems should not take supplements without a physician's approval.

- Use single-ingredient products to avoid confusion about the effects.

- Seek out several independent sources for research on a dietary supplement rather than depending on the manufacturer's literature or other promotional material.

- Read packages carefully for warnings.

- Take small doses at first. Never take more than a recommended dosage.

- Buy products that at least claim to have standardized potency.

- Be alert to both possible benefits and negative effects of a supplement.

- If you experience any adverse effects, stop taking the supplement and call your physician.

Schlendorf in Panama City, Florida. Schlendorf's heart stopped after taking twice the suggested dose of Ultimate Xphoria, which contains ephedrine, pseudoephedrine, phenylpropanolamine (an appetite suppressant), and caffeine. In June 1997, the FDA reported at least 20 deaths and 800 adverse reactions linked to the ephedra-based supplements. The FDA restrictions, scheduled for final approval after August 1997, would limit the recommended dosages of the supplements and require warning labels explaining the various risks.

Shark cartilage

The Chinese have eaten shark fin soup for centuries as an *aphrodisiac* (a substance that arouses sexual desire), but in the 1990's sharks were touted as a "miracle" treatment for cancer. Oncologist Judah Folkman at Harvard Medical School in Boston and his colleagues published research in 1983 showing that shark cartilage could slow the growth of the blood vessels necessary for cancerous tumors to grow. Although Folkman and the other researchers did not pursue this research any further, their study was a part of the evidence used in the book *Sharks Don't Get Cancer,* published in 1992. The book became the focus of media attention for its claim that the dietary supplements made from shark cartilage could cure cancer.

A shark's skeleton is made entirely of cartilage, a flexible tissue that consists of protein, calcium, phosphorus, sticky substances called mucopolysaccharides, and some unknown chemicals. The primary author of *Sharks Don't Get Cancer,* nutritionist and biochemist William Lane, claimed that sharks do not get cancer and attributed this to some unknown property of the shark's skeleton. Lane also conducted research with shark cartilage at cancer clinics in Cuba and Mexico. After a 1993 broadcast of the television program *60 Minutes* that featured this research, sales of shark cartilage, which sells for $30 to $60 a bottle, increased rapidly in the United States.

Critics were quick to point out that, first, sharks can get cancer. Also, none of the research performed in Cuba and Mexico had been reviewed by other specialists, and no peer-reviewed research had isolated a chemical in shark cartilage that shrinks tumors. The American Cancer Society concluded that "there is no record in the medical literature of any benefit to ingesting shark cartilage." Scientists are not even sure if the body can absorb the cartilage in a pill form.

Taking chances with nature

Since the enactment of the 1994 dietary supplement law, sales of "natural drugs" rose an estimated 15 percent annually. Consumers bought millions of dollars worth of products whose long-term effects doctors, pharmacists, and other medical specialists knew little or nothing about.

Many medical professionals fear that the leniency of federal regulations, the widely held belief that any natural product is safe, and the lack of long-term clinical trials may create health risks that outweigh the potential benefits of some products. They advise that when shopping for health products, consumers should focus less on claims about the "natural" benefits of a dietary supplement and more on how rigorously each product has been tested. ● ● ●

For further reading:

Cornacchia, Harold J. and Stephen Barrett. *Consumer Health: A Guide to Intelligent Decisions.* Fifth edition. Times Mirror/Mosby College, 1993.

Farley, Dixie. "Making Sure Hype Doesn't Overwhelm Science." *FDA Consumer,* November 1993, pp. 9-13.

Tyler, Varro E. *The Honest Herbal: A Sensible Guide to the Use of Herbs and Related Remedies.* Third edition. Pharmaceutical Products Press, 1993.

U.S. Food and Drug Administration website: http://www.fda.gov/

Although some people rely on supplements to fulfill daily vitamin and mineral needs, research shows that nutrients found in whole foods provide the most health benefits.

FOOD:

The Best Source for Nutrients

By Jeanine Barone

COUNTLESS NUTRITIONAL STUDIES HAVE SHOWN that satisfying the body's demand for vitamins and minerals through a well-balanced diet is a key to good health. Many people, however, think that they can get the health benefits of these powerful nutrients by swallowing a daily dose of vitamin and mineral supplements. Yet, research indicates that the vitamins and minerals that help maintain health when eaten in whole foods do not have the same effect when isolated in pill form.

Vitamins and minerals are essential ingredients for the health, growth, and development of the human body. They work alongside other nutrients, such as proteins and carbohydrates, to promote chemical reactions that allow our bodies to grow and develop. Without the help of vitamins and minerals, bones would weaken and snap, blood would be unable to carry oxygen, and cells could not reproduce.

Compared with the need for carbohydrates, fats, and proteins, very small amounts of vitamins and minerals are needed in the diet. Carbohydrates, fats, and proteins, along with water, make up about 96 percent of body weight. The remaining 4 percent is made up of various vitamins and minerals. Yet vitamins and minerals play a weighty role in maintaining health.

A diet lacking in certain vitamins may lead to serious health problems. A deficiency in vitamin C, for example, may lead to *scurvy* (disruption of the normal production of connective tissues that may lead to internal bleeding and problems with wound healing), and a lack of vitamin D may cause *rickets* (bone deformation) or *osteomalacia* (softening of bones).

Water-soluble and fat-soluble vitamins

Scientists have identified 13 vitamins that perform essential functions in humans. These compounds fall into two groups—water soluble vitamins and fat-soluble vitamins. Water-soluble vitamins dissolve in blood, which carries them throughout the body. Excesses of these vitamins usually wash out of the body through urine and sweat. The water-soluble vitamins are vitamin B_1 (thiamine), vitamin B_2 (riboflavin), vitamin B_3 (niacin), vitamin B_6 (pyridoxine), vitamin B_{12} (cobalamin), vitamin C (ascorbic acid), biotin, folate, and pantothenic acid.

The remaining vitamins—A, D, E, and K—are fat-soluble. They are carried in the fats found in foods. Vitamin D, for example, can be found in the butterfat of milk. The body stores excesses of these vitamins in its fatty tissues.

● Vitamin A keeps the tissues in the mouth, stomach, lungs, and intestines healthy. It helps cells grow, allows eyes to adjust to changes in light intensity, and helps protect the body from infection. *Retinoids* are forms of vitamin A found in foods of animal origin. *Carotenoids* are pigments founds in foods of plant origin; the body can convert some carotenoids, such as beta-carotene,

The author:
....

Jeanine Barone is a nutritionist and an exercise physiologist. She is also an editor of the *University of California at Berkeley Wellness Letter*.

into vitamin A. beta-carotene is a powerful *antioxidant* (a chemical compound that prevents cell damage by blocking the effects of unstable molecules called free radicals). Scientists have linked free radicals to a number of diseases, including heart disease and cancer. A vitamin A deficiency may lead to dry skin, poor night vision, and stunted growth in children. Sources of vitamin A include liver, milk, carrots, and spinach.

- Thiamine helps the body obtain energy from carbohydrates and fats. A thiamine deficiency may result in nerve damage, muscle weakness, and fatigue. A severe deficiency can cause *beriberi* (a potentially fatal nerve disease). Sources of thiamine include dried peas, nuts, whole grains, and pork.
- Riboflavin obtains energy from food and helps the body form niacin, another vitamin. A riboflavin deficiency may lead to dry skin and eye disorders. Sources of riboflavin include cheese, fish, green vegetables, and poultry.
- Niacin works with thiamine and riboflavin to obtain energy from food. Though niacin deficiencies are rare, people who are deficient may suffer diarrhea and mental confusion. Sources of niacin include fish, liver, enriched breads, and whole grains.
- Vitamin B_6 helps the body use proteins, fats, and carbohydrates. It is also essential for the formation of red blood cells and for the functioning of the nervous and immune systems. A vitamin B_6 deficiency may lead to depression, nausea, dry skin, and *anemia* (a decreased level of red blood cells). Sources of vitamin B_6 include eggs, fish, nuts, and poultry.
- Vitamin B_{12} helps the body use fats and make red blood cells. Vitamin B_{12} deficiency, which is typically caused by an inability of the body to absorb the vitamin, may lead to *pernicious anemia* (a potentially fatal type of anemia that causes severe nerve damage). Sources of vitamin B_{12} include liver, fish, milk, and eggs.
- Biotin, a type of B vitamin, helps the body use proteins, fats, and carbohydrates. People rarely suffer from deficiencies in biotin because it is made by intestinal bacteria. A deficiency, however, can lead to heart abnormalities, depression, fatigue, and hair loss. Sources of biotin include egg yolk, kidney, liver, and nuts.
- Folate, also called folic acid and folacin, is a type of B vitamin that helps form red blood cells and DNA (genetic material). A folate deficiency may lead to anemia. If a pregnant woman does not get enough folate during the first three months of pregnancy, the baby is at an increased risk of developing a spinal-cord defect. Sources of folate include fruit, dried peas and beans, and green leafy vegetables.

A deficiency of vitamin A can lead to:

- Night blindness and other eye problems.
- Dry skin.
- Impaired bone growth and tooth formation.
- Increased susceptibility to infections.
- Loss of appetite.

An excess of vitamin A can lead to:

- Headaches.
- Vomiting.
- Double-vision.
- Loss of hair.
- Liver damage.
- Bone abnormalities.
- Menstrual irregularities.
- Birth defects, including skull and heart malformations.

RDA's and RDI's—guidelines for good eating

To make an informed decision about what foods to include in a daily diet, an individual needs to know the amount of nutrients that the body needs and how much of these nutrients can be found in particular foods. The United States government has established a number of nutritional guidelines to help people make these dietary decisions. Perhaps the best known of these guidelines—and the standard on which other guidelines are based—is the Recommended Dietary Allowance, or RDA.

RDA's are the levels of essential nutrients needed to meet the daily nutritional needs of almost all healthy people. These figures, set by the National Academy of Sciences Food and Nutrition Board, reflect the nutrients needed to replenish daily losses and deficiencies. RDA levels fluctuate to meet the nutritional needs that vary with age and gender. Also, RDA's are generally set about 30 to 50 percent higher than necessary to ensure that people meet the lowest recommended amount of a nutrient.

The Food and Nutrition Board uses several scientific studies to determine RDA's. For example, the board examines vitamin deficiencies in individuals in weight reduction programs as well as the effects of nutrients on molecular functions in the body. The board only sets RDA's for those nutrients that have undergone the required scientific studies.

Many nutritionists complained that because RDA's are based on the amount of nutrients needed to replenish daily losses, the guideline fails to take into account the amount of nutrients needed to maintain good health. Nutritionists also criticized the fact that RDA's have not been estab-

lished for certain nutrients, such as beta-carotene and fiber, and that they provide no information on the toxic levels of some nutrients.

The Food and Nutrition Board addressed these concerns in April 1997 when it announced that RDA's would be replaced with a new guideline called Dietary Reference Intakes, or DRI's. This new nutritional guideline will include:

- Estimated Average Requirements (EAR's)—the estimated amount of each nutrient required to maintain adequate health, based on the average for sex and age.
- Recommended Dietary Allowances—RDA's refigured to reflect the amounts of each nutrient desirable for optimum health and disease prevention.
- Maximum upper levels—the level at which a nutrient may become toxic.

Certain nutrients that are beneficial to health, but are not covered by RDA's, will also be included in DRI's.

The DRI's will be set by seven panels of scientists, with each panel responsible for a certain group of vitamins. The scientists planned to announce the new guidelines over a four-year period, beginning in mid-1997.

Yet another guideline—the Reference Daily Intake, or RDI—is used by the United States Food and Drug Administration (FDA) to provide nutritional information on food labels. RDI's were called the U.S. Recommended Daily Allowance when first established in 1973. The FDA changed the name in 1993.

The FDA uses RDA figures to calculate RDI's. Generally, an RDI equals the highest RDA level established for a particular nutrient. If the RDA of a nutrient is 10 milligrams per day for men and 18 milligrams per day for women, for example, the RDI would be set at 18 milligrams for both sexes.

Food labels list the percentage of RDI's found in the main nutrients in a single serving of the food. These percentages, called Percent Daily Values, provide guidelines for children over age 4 and for adults—with the exception of pregnant and lactating women, who have greater nutritional needs than other people.

Food labels also list Percent Daily Values for fat, cholesterol, sodium, and carbohydrates—nutrients that do not have RDA values. The Percent Daily Values of these nutrients are derived from Daily Reference Values, or DRV's—figures set by the FDA. The Percent Daily Values for fat, cholesterol, and sodium in the daily diet should each not exceed 100 percent.

Reading food labels

All packaged and processed foods sold in the United States must carry a label with the title Nutrition Facts. An example of a standard food label is illustrated below.

Serving size reflects the amount of the food that people typically eat as one portion.

The label includes information about those nutrients that the Food and Drug Administration considers to be of special importance to people. The nutrients are measured in grams (g) and milligrams (mg).

Daily Reference Values are provided for diets of 2,000 and 2,500 calories. The values for fat, cholesterol, and sodium are the maximum amounts a person should eat each day. The values for carbohydrates are the minimum amounts.

Nutrition Facts

Serving Size 1 cup (228g)
Serving Per Container 2

Amount Per Serving

Calories 260 Calories from Fat 120

	% Daily Value *
Total Fat 13g	**20%**
Saturated Fat 5g	**25%**
Cholesterol 30mg	**10%**
Sodium 660mg	**28%**
Total Carbohydrate 31g	**10%**
Dietary Fiber 0g	**0%**
Sugars 5g	
Protein 5g	

Vitamin A	4%	Vitamin C	2%
Calcium	15%	Iron	4%

*Percent Daily Values are based on a 2,000 calorie diet. Your daily values may be higher or lower depending on your calorie needs:

	Calories:	2,000	2,500
Total Fat	Less than	65g	80g
Sat Fat	Less than	20g	25g
Cholesterol	Less than	300mg	300mg
Sodium	Less than	2,400mg	2,400mg
Total Carbohydrate		300g	375g
Dietary Fiber		25g	30g

Calories per gram:
Fat 9 • Carbohydrate 4 • Protein 4

The label shows the number of calories per serving and the number from fat, helping consumers follow guidelines that no more than 30 percent of calories come from fat.

Percent Daily Value is the percentage of the Daily Reference Value (for fat, cholesterol, sodium, and carbohydrates) or Reference Daily Intake (for vitamins and minerals) that a person gets by eating one serving of the food. This percentage is based on a diet of 2,000 calories per day, the amount recommended for many adults.

The label shows the amount of calories per gram of fat, carbohydrate, and protein. These values apply to all foods.

- Vitamin C helps keep gums healthy, helps heal wounds, and aids in the absorption of iron and the formation of red blood cells and bones. It also helps maintain a healthy immune system. Vitamin C is also an antioxidant. A deficiency may result in scurvy. Sources of vitamin C include citrus fruits and green leafy and orange-yellow vegetables.
- Vitamin D helps the body absorb the minerals calcium and phosphorus. A vitamin D deficiency may lead to weakened bones and *osteoporosis* (decrease in bone mass). Sources of vitamin D include eggs, salmon, tuna, and fortified milk. The body, when it is exposed to sunlight, also produces vitamin D.
- Vitamin E helps maintain healthy red blood cells and muscles. It is an antioxidant and may reduce the risk of heart disease and cancer, according to a 1996 study published in the *New England Journal of Medicine*. A study published in 1997 in this journal indicated that vitamin E slows the progression of *Alzheimer's disease* (a brain disease characterized by decreasing mental abilities). Another study published in 1997 in the *Journal of the American Medical Association* indicated that the vitamin strengthens the immune system of older people. Vitamin E deficiencies are rare. Sources of vitamin E include most fatty foods, especially margarine, olives, vegetable oils, nuts, and seeds.
- Vitamin K prevents hemorrhaging by helping blood to clot. People rarely suffer vitamin K deficiencies because bacteria in the intestines produce the vitamin. People who take antibiotics for long periods of time, however, may become vitamin K deficient. Sources of vitamin K include green leafy vegetables, soybeans, liver, and pork.

Major and trace minerals

Minerals differ from vitamins because they are *inorganic* (not produced by living things) and because they are indestructible. The body rids itself of minerals only through excretion. Minerals are part of the earth's crust. They dissolve in water and are taken up from the soil by plants, which may then be eaten by animals. Minerals help form tissues, regulate body fluids, and trigger important chemical reactions, such as the ones that regulate the beating of the heart and the transmission of nerve impulses throughout the body.

Minerals are classified into two groups: major minerals and trace minerals. Major minerals, which include calcium, magnesium, phosphorus, and potassium, are needed in large amounts—more than 250 milligrams per day. Trace minerals, which include chromium, copper, iron, selenium, and zinc, are needed in only small amounts—less than 20 milligrams per day.

- Calcium builds bones and teeth, helps contract muscles and clot blood, contributes to a healthy heart, and allows for normal nerve function. Some studies suggest that calcium reduces the risk of colon cancer. Calcium deficiencies affect bone structure and growth in children. Sources of calcium include milk, broccoli, spinach, and canned salmon.
- Chromium helps the body use the hormone insulin. A chromium deficiency may cause problems in regulating blood sugar—a process that is especially important for diabetics. Sources of chromium include liver, cheese, whole grains, and dried peas.
- Copper is needed to manufacture *hemoglobin* (the protein that carries oxygen in the blood). It also helps the body use other proteins and make hormones. High doses of zinc can reduce copper absorption, leading to anemia. Sources of copper include liver, seafood, nuts, and seeds.
- Iron is a vital ingredient in hemoglobin. An iron deficiency may lead to infections, fatigue, and anemia. Though many foods contain iron, the iron in certain foods is more easily absorbed by the body than the iron in other foods. Red meats, beans and lentils, and spinach are the best sources of easily absorbed iron.
- Magnesium is needed for the function of muscles, nerves, and bones. It helps the body obtain energy from food, manufacture proteins, and contract muscles. Some studies suggest that magnesium reduces the risk of heart disease. People rarely suffer magnesium deficiencies unless they consume large amounts of alcohol. Deficiencies can lead to an irregular heartbeat, nausea, and weakness. Sources of magnesium include green leafy vegetables, dried peas and beans, and nuts.
- Phosphorus is a major building block of bones and teeth, and it helps regulate cell growth and repair. A deficiency in phosphorus may weaken bones. Sources of phosphorus include milk, poultry, eggs, and nuts.
- Potassium helps the body maintain blood pressure, transmit nerve impulses, contract muscles, and regulate fluid balance. Diarrhea, vomiting, or kidney problems can cause a potassium deficiency, which may lead to fatigue and loss of appetite. Sources of potassium include bananas, orange juice, and dried beans and peas.
- Selenium helps blood carry out its functions and aids in cell growth. It is also an antioxidant. A deficiency in selenium may lead to heart problems. Sources of selenium include seafood, egg yolk, liver, kidney, and whole grain products.
- Zinc helps the body use carbohydrates,

A deficiency of folate can lead to:

- Anemia.
- Birth defects, including spinal-cord malformation.
- Weight loss.
- Headaches.
- Mental confusion.
- Tongue inflammation.
- Impaired nerve function.

An **excess** of folate can lead to:

- Seizures in epileptics.
- Allergic reactions.

Some good sources of vitamins

Vitamin A (RDI=875µg*)

Food	Serving Size	Amount
Beef (pan-fried liver)	3.5 ounces	10,728 µg
Sweet potato (baked)	1 whole	2,488 µg
Carrot (raw)	1 medium	2,025 µg
Spinach (canned)	½ cup	939 µg
Broccoli (frozen, boiled)	½ cup	174 µg

Niacin (RDI=20 mg*)

Food	Serving Size	Amount
Oatmeal (fortified)	1 ounce packet	21.6 mg
Cereal (fortified)	1 cup	20.0 mg
Beef (pan-fried liver)	3.5 ounces	14.4 mg
Chicken (fried breast)	½ breast	13.5 mg
Tuna (light, canned)	3 ounces	11.3 mg

Thiamine (RDI=1.5 mg)

Food	Serving Size	Amount
Oatmeal (fortified)	1 ounce packet	1.50 mg
Cereal (fortified)	¾ cup	1.50 mg
Pork (broiled center loin)	3.5 ounces	1.15 mg
Soybeans (stir-fried)	3.5 ounces	0.42 mg
Lentils (boiled)	1 cup	0.34 mg

Vitamin B$_6$ (RDI=2 mg)

Food	Serving Size	Amount
Cereal (fortified)	¾ cup	2.00 mg
Beef (pan-fried liver)	3.5 ounces	1.43 mg
Salmon (cooked by dry heat)	3 ounces	0.80 mg
Banana	1 medium	0.66 mg
Chicken (fried breast)	½ breast	0.57 mg

Riboflavin (RDI=1.7 mg)

Food	Serving Size	Amount
Beef (pan-fried liver)	3.5 ounces	4.14 mg
Cereal (fortified)	1 cup	1.68 mg
Yogurt (low fat)	8 fluid ounces	0.49 mg
Milk (2% fat)	8 fluid ounces	0.40 mg
Beef (roasted choice tenderloin)	3.5 ounces	0.33 mg

Vitamin B$_{12}$ (RDI=6 µg)

Food	Serving Size	Amount
Beef (pan-fried liver)	3.5 ounces	111.80 µg
Oysters (cooked by dry heat)	3 ounces	32.53 µg
Herring (cooked by dry heat)	3 ounces	11.17 µg
Beef (roasted choice tenderloin)	3.5 ounces	3.87 µg
Cottage cheese (2% fat)	1 cup	1.61 µg

Vitamin C (RDI=60 mg)

Food	Serving Size	Amount
Strawberries	1 cup	85 mg
Orange (navel)	1 medium	80 mg
Broccoli (boiled)	½ cup	58 mg
Cauliflower (boiled)	½ cup	34 mg
Sweet potato (baked)	1 whole	28 mg

Vitamin D (RDI=6.5 µg)

Food	Serving Size	Amount
Milk (fortified)	8 fluid ounces	1.6 µg
Margarine	1 tablespoon	1.0 µg
Pudding (instant mix)	½ cup	0.8 µg
Cod liver oil	1 tablespoon	0.5 µg
Egg	1 large	0.4 µg

Vitamin E (RDI=9 mg*)

Food	Serving Size	Amount
Sunflower seeds (dried)	1 ounce	14.18 mg
Margarine	1 tablespoon	8.00 mg
Almonds (dried)	1 ounce	6.72 mg
Sweet potato (raw)	1 medium	5.93 mg
Vegetable oil (cottonseed)	1 tablespoon	4.80 mg

µg=micrograms; mg=milligrams

*These amounts are equivalents. An equivalent is the composite of the nutrient in the food and the amount of the nutrient that the body can form from other substances in the food.

Source: *Bowes & Church's Food Values of Portions Commonly Used*, Sixteenth Edition, J.B. Lippincott Company

Biotin (RDI=0.3 mg)

Food	Serving Size	Amount
Instant breakfast (liquid pack)	8 fluid ounces	0.070 mg
Pudding (fortified)	½ cup	0.060 mg
Egg	1 large	0.010 mg
Cereal (oat bran)	⅓ cup	0.009 mg
Wheat germ	¼ cup	0.007 mg

Folate (RDI=0.4 mg)

Food	Serving Size	Amount
Cereal (fortified)	1 cup	0.400 mg
Lentils (boiled)	1 cup	0.358 mg
Kidney beans (boiled, red)	1 cup	0.229 mg
Beef (pan-fried liver)	3.5 ounces	0.220 mg
Spinach (boiled)	½ cup	0.131 mg

Pantothenic acid (RDI=10 mg)

Food	Serving Size	Amount
Beef (pan-fried liver)	3.5 ounces	5.92 mg
Salmon (cooked by dry heat)	3 ounces	1.63 mg
Chicken (fried leg)	1 leg	1.34 mg
Pork (broiled/ pan-fried cured bacon)	4.48 ounces	1.34 mg
Peanuts (dried)	1 ounce	0.79 mg

Some good sources of minerals

Calcium (RDI=1,000 mg)

Food	Serving Size	Amount
Yogurt (low fat)	8 fluid ounces	415 mg
Milk (2% fat)	8 fluid ounces	297 mg
Tofu (raw, firm)	½ cup	258 mg
Salmon (canned)	3 ounces	203 mg
Spinach (canned)	½ cup	135 mg

Copper (RDI=2 mg)

Food	Serving Size	Amount
Oysters (cooked by moist heat)	3 ounces	7.584 mg
Beef (pan-fried liver)	3.5 ounces	2.822 mg
Almonds (dry roasted)	1 ounce	1.300 mg
Crab (Alaskan King, cooked by moist heat)	3 ounces	1.010 mg
Cashews (dry roasted)	1 ounce	0.630 mg

Iron (RDI=18 mg)

Food	Serving Size	Amount
Pork (braised liver)	3.5 ounces	17.92 mg
Lentils (boiled)	1 cup	6.59 mg
Kidney beans (boiled, red)	1 cup	5.20 mg
Beef (roasted choice tenderloin)	3.5 ounces	3.69 mg
Spinach (boiled)	½ cup	3.21 mg

Magnesium (RDI=400 mg)

Food	Serving Size	Amount
Soybeans (boiled)	1 cup	148 mg
Navy beans (canned)	1 cup	122 mg
Sunflower seeds (dried)	1 ounce	100 mg
Almond (dried)	1 ounce	84 mg
Spinach (canned)	½ cup	81 mg

Phosphorous (RDI=1,000 mg)

Food	Serving Size	Amount
Beef (pan-fried liver)	3.5 ounces	461 mg
Soybeans (boiled)	1 cup	421 mg
Yogurt (low fat)	8 fluid ounces	326 mg
Salmon (canned)	3 ounces	277 mg
Milk (2% fat)	8 fluid ounces	232 mg

Zinc (RDI=15 mg)

Food	Serving Size	Amount
Oysters (cooked by moist heat)	3 ounces	154.62 mg
Beef (chuck blade roast)	3.5 ounces	10.27 mg
Pork (braised liver)	3.5 ounces	6.72 mg
Crab (Alaskan King, cooked by moist heat)	3 ounces	6.48 mg
Navy beans (canned)	1 cup	2.02 mg

µg=micrograms; mg=milligrams

Source: *Bowes & Church's Food Values of Portions Commonly Used*, Sixteenth Edition, J.B. Lippincott Company

proteins, and fats, and it is needed for cell growth and repair. A deficiency in zinc may weaken the immune system and cause loss of appetite and birth defects. Sources of zinc include seafood, red meats, and eggs.

Whole foods versus supplements

The National Academy of Science's Food and Nutrition Board recommends that people meet their daily nutritional needs through a diet consisting of a wide variety of foods rather than through vitamin and mineral supplements. Vitamin and mineral supplements—even those with 100 percent of the Recommended Dietary Allowances (RDA's) for vitamins and minerals—cannot provide all of the other nutrients that the body gets from a well-balanced diet. A vitamin C supplement, for example, does not contain the folate, potassium, and fiber present in an orange.

The U.S. Department of Agriculture reported in 1996 that a person would need to take a huge number of supplements to equal the health benefits of a few pieces of fruits or vegetables. However, taking handfuls of supplements could put a person at risk of serious illness or death. Megadosing on zinc can reduce the concentration of protective HDL cholesterol in the blood; too much niacin can damage the liver; excess vitamin A can damage the liver, nerves, and bones; large amounts of vitamin B6 can lead to nerve damage; and excess vitamin D can weaken bones and muscles, damage the kidneys, and cause deafness. An overdose of iron supplements—the leading cause of overdoses in U.S. children, according to the Centers for Disease Control and Prevention in Atlanta—can cause damage to the heart, liver, lungs, and pancreas, and even death.

By contrast, it is almost impossible to overdose on vitamins and minerals by eating too much food. A person would have to drink several gallons of orange juice in one sitting to reach toxic levels of potassium or several quarts of milk to be put at risk of vitamin D poisoning.

Many studies show that the nutrients that prevent disease when eaten as food lose their effectiveness when taken in supplement form. For example, more than 120 published studies on the health benefits of fruits and vegetables reported that the vitamin C, vitamin E, and beta-carotene contained in those foods lowered the risk of cancer. However, a number of other studies found that, when these nutrients came from a supplement instead of a food source, they did not lower cancer risk. A study published in the November 1996 *Journal of the National Cancer Institute,* in fact, suggested that beta-carotene

A deficiency of calcium can lead to:
••••••••••••••••••••
- Osteoporosis, a disease resulting in softening of bones.
- Rickets, a disease resulting in bone deformation.

An excess of calcium can lead to:
••••••••••••••••••••
- Kidney and urinary stones.
- Poor absorption of minerals, including iron and zinc.
- Muscle weakness.
- Fatigue.
- Constipation.
- Nausea.
- Depression.

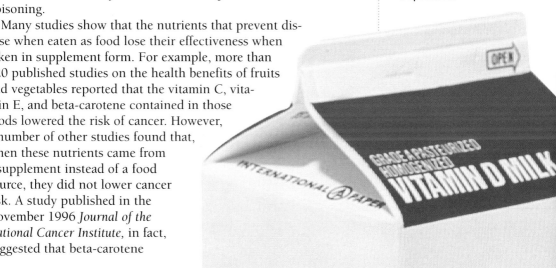

supplements may do more harm than good when taken by certain people.

The study, performed by researchers at the National Cancer Institute, reported that beta-carotene supplements may become cancer-causing agents when taken by heavy smokers. The researchers examined the effects of beta-carotene and vitamin A supplements on more than 18,000 individuals, many of whom were heavy tobacco smokers. The researchers stopped the study 21 months earlier than expected because none of the people taking the supplements became healthier and some became ill. The researchers found that people taking the supplements had a 28 percent greater rate of lung cancer and a 17 percent greater rate of death from cancer than those not taking the supplements.

The researchers attributed the increased cancer rate partly to the fact that the body absorbs beta-carotene more efficiently from whole foods than from supplements. The researchers also found that beta-carotene supplements have difficulty combating free radicals, which exist in great numbers in the bodies of heavy smokers. beta-carotene from a supplement may even convert into a free radical itself after an encounter with the harmful molecule, the researchers reported.

Beta-carotene damaged by free radicals needs the help of other nutrients to return it to its natural state, according to a study published in the January 1997 Journal of the American Chemical Society. Researchers in this study found that beta-carotene works with vitamin C and vitamin E and other antioxidants to protect the body from free radicals. The researchers also found that vitamin E and vitamin C repairs beta-carotene damaged in battles with free radicals.

This study suggested that, because smokers tend to be vitamin C deficient, the smokers in the National Cancer Institute study who developed lung cancer may not have had enough vitamin C in their bodies to repair the beta-carotene damaged by free radicals. If these individuals had eaten beta-carotene in fruits and vegetables instead of as supplements, they also would have increased their vitamin C levels and might have reduced their risk of cancer.

A deficiency of iron can lead to:

- Anemia.
- Fatigue.
- Poor concentration.
- Increased susceptibility to infections.
- Difficulty swallowing.
- Poor weight gain in children.

An **excess** of iron can lead to:

- Death in children.
- Impaired functioning of various organs, including the liver, heart, and pancreas.

Food nutrients fight disease

Many important ingredients not found in vitamin and mineral supplements help food nutrients battle disease and promote health. Fruits and vegetables, for example, contain hundreds of compounds called *phytochemicals* (plant chemicals). Some phytochemicals act as antioxidants. Others fight toxic substances in the bloodstream. Still others strengthen the immune system or lower levels of blood cholesterol.

Most vitamin and mineral supplements contain few, if any, phytochemicals. And research has shown that the phytochemicals found in supplements may not have the same health benefits as those found in food. Phytochemicals, like many other nutrients beneficial to health, often work only in combination with other ingredients found in whole foods.

Nutrients work together

The nutrients in foods work in so many complex combinations, in fact, that scientists often have a difficult task in determining which substance—or combination of substances—is responsible for a particular health benefit. A 25-year study by Finnish researchers published in the March 1996 issue of the *British Journal of Cancer,* for example, found that women who drink milk significantly lower their risk of breast cancer. Scientists suspected that the calcium and vitamin D in milk reduced cancer risk, but these nutrients do not reduce cancer risk when isolated in supplement form.

In a report published in the May 1996 issue of the journal *Epidemiology,* scientists studying the diets of 1,500 women over a three-year period found that those who regularly ate baked or broiled fish significantly reduced their risk of developing rheumatoid arthritis. And in a study published in the March 1996 issue of the *Archives of Internal Medicine,* researchers for the U.S. National Health and Nutrition Examination Survey reported that nutrients in fish cut the risk of stroke. The researchers examined the diets of more than 5,000 Americans for 12 years. The study found that white women who ate fish more than once per week cut their risk of stroke by 45 percent, compared with those women who ate no fish. And black men and black women who ate fish cut their risk of stroke by 49 percent.

Researchers speculated that certain fatty substances found in fish—called omega-3 fatty acids—thin the blood, preventing the blood clots that can cause a stroke. Omega-3 fatty acids may also be responsible for strengthening the immune system and thus lessening the risk of rheumatoid arthritis. When isolated in supplement form, however, omega-3 fatty acids may not provide these health benefits.

There are so many studies making health claims about certain nutrients that it's easy to become overwhelmed and confused by all of the information—especially when the findings of one study seem to contradict the findings of another. There is one nutritional standard, however, that research has proved consistently over the years: There is no substitute for a balanced diet—made up of grains, fruits, vegetables, lean meat, and low-fat dairy products—to help you maintain your health. ●●●

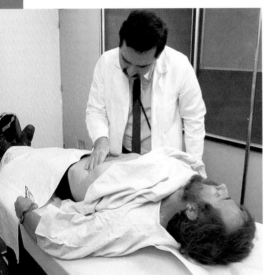

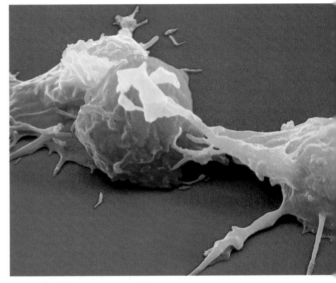

ON THE
MEDICAL FRONTIER

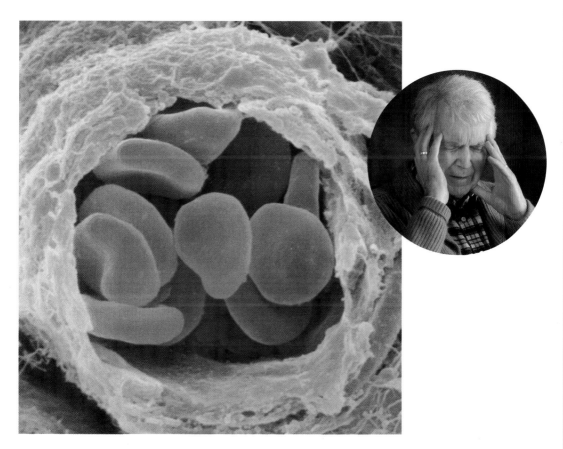

Inflammatory Bowel Disease

Inflammatory bowel disease affects the health and productivity of 2 million Americans while exacting a toll on the mental health of families and friends.

By James Regan and Jay Goldstein

I T AFFECTS AS MANY AS 2 MILLION AMERICANS, yet its origins remain a mystery. It strikes members of certain ethnic groups, for example, Jewish Americans of Eastern European ancestry, more often than others. And researchers are exploring a variety of factors for clues to its origin. The condition is called inflammatory bowel disease (IBD), a term used to describe two disorders of the digestive tract—ulcerative colitis and Crohn's disease.

Both ulcerative colitis and Crohn's disease result in *chronic* (long lasting) or recurring inflammation, ulceration, and bleeding in the *digestive tract* (the system of organs, from mouth to anus, that breaks food down into substances the body can use). Digestive tract inflammation is marked by swelling and redness of the tissues.

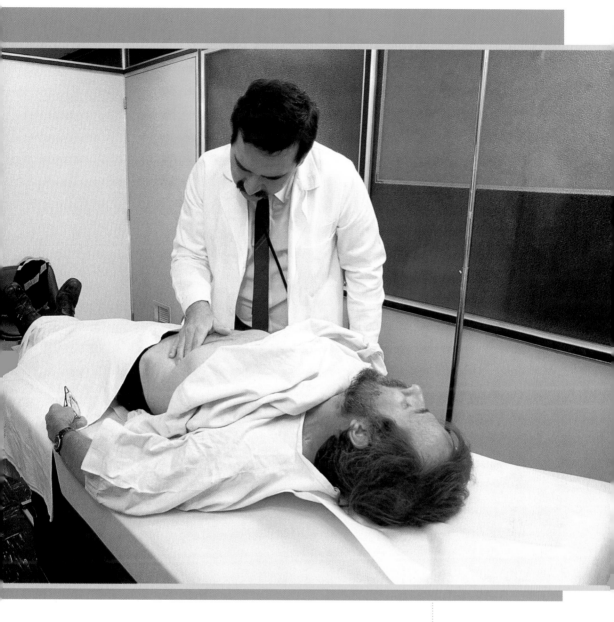

Ulceration is characterized by open sores on the intestinal lining.

Ulcerative colitis and Crohn's disease share many of the same symptoms. The fundamental difference between the two is the location of the inflammation in the digestive tract. Ulcerative colitis involves the *colon* (large intestine) and the rectum. Crohn's disease can involve the entire gastrointestinal (GI) tract, from the mouth to the anus, but typically is localized in portions of the small and large intestines. Because the symptoms of Crohn's disease and ulcerative colitis can be similar and overlap, it can be difficult to differentiate between the two without medical testing. If physicians are unable to reliably distinguish between the two, the condition may be labeled indeterminate colitis or simply inflammatory bowel disease.

Symptoms of ulcerative colitis

The major symptoms of ulcerative colitis are abdominal cramps and bloody diarrhea, which typically occur together. When the inflammation is severe, ulcerative colitis may be accompanied by fever and results in weight loss, severe blood loss, *anemia* (fewer than normal red blood cells), and dehydration. The inflammation, which always includes the rectum, may be limited to the rectum, or it may involve portions of the colon or even the entire large intestine.

Ulcerative colitis attacks generally come in cycles. While there are patients who undergo a single attack of *acute* (short-term) ulcerative colitis, most people experience a series of recurrent attacks. Between episodes, the patient with no symptoms and no active inflammation is said to be in remission. Effective medical treatment can control an attack of acute ulcerative colitis and bring about remission. However, most patients who discontinue treatment experience another acute episode within one year. Very few ulcerative colitis patients experience continuous symptoms of inflammation.

Symptoms of Crohn's disease

When Crohn's disease is localized in the large intestine, its symptoms can be similar to those of ulcerative colitis: abdominal cramps and diarrhea with or without bleeding. When the inflammation of Crohn's disease is located in the small intestine, the diarrhea, which is usually without visible bleeding, may be accompanied by abdominal pain, fever, nausea, vomiting, anemia, and weight loss. When the inflammation is severe, Crohn's disease in the small intestine may mimic the high fever and tender abdomen of appendicitis. It is not uncommon for Crohn's disease patients to undergo emergency surgery for suspected appendicitis.

While the inflammation associated with ulcerative colitis extends continuously over large segments of the colon, the inflammation characteristic of Crohn's disease is usually patchy, with areas of normal bowel existing between inflamed areas. Inflammation associated with Crohn's disease is characteristically deep and penetrates into the bowel wall. In contrast, the inflammation of ulcerative colitis is limited to the *mucosa*, the most superficial layer of the colon wall.

The authors:

James Regan, M.D., is a Fellow in Gastroenterology at the University of Illinois at Chicago. Jay Goldstein, M.D., is Associate Professor of Medicine at the University of Illinois at Chicago.

Incidence of IBD

Of the estimated 2 million people in the United States who have IBD, roughly half have ulcerative colitis and half have Crohn's disease, but ulcerative colitis is slightly more common. An estimated 2 to 10 new cases of ulcerative colitis are diagnosed annually per every 100,000 people in the U.S. population. One to six new cases of Crohn's disease are diagnosed annually per 100,000 people.

IBD does not occur equally in all age or ethnic groups in the population. While new cases can occur at any age, the highest number of new IBD cases occurs among people between the ages of 15 and

35. Americans over the age of 50 experience the second highest rate of new IBD cases, particularly of Crohn's disease.

Caucasians are more likely than African Americans or Asian Americans to develop IBD. Jewish Americans of *Ashkenazi* (Eastern European) backgrounds are three to six times more likely to develop ulcerative colitis or Crohn's disease than the population as a whole. Sex does not appear to be a factor in IBD. Men and women are equally likely to develop IBD.

What causes IBD?

The exact causes of ulcerative colitis and Crohn's disease are unknown. Scientists have investigated a variety of factors, including infectious agents, such as viruses and bacteria, environmental factors, and the genetic backgrounds and immune systems of patients. Many researchers currently theorize that inflammatory bowel disease is generated by a combination of such factors, rather than from any single one.

A series of studies published in 1996 gave further evidence that Crohn's disease runs in families. As previous studies indicated, a person with a parent, sibling, or child with IBD is approximately 15 times more likely to develop the disease than a person without a family history of the disease. Genetic predisposition appears to be even stronger among identical twins. When one twin develops ulcerative colitis, there is a 20 percent chance that his or her twin will also develop the disease. If one twin develops Crohn's disease, the chance that the other twin will develop Crohn's jumps to 50 percent.

Not all researchers investigating IBD agree that there is a hereditary link. IBD does not follow established rules of inheritance exhibited by such genetic diseases as hemophilia or cystic fibrosis. Many researchers are careful to note that a genetic predisposition does not rule out additional environmental or infectious causes.

For many years, researchers looked for an infectious cause for IBD. They noted that there were similarities between the inflammation characteristic of IBD and the inflammation characteristic of intestinal tract infections from microorganisms such as shigella, salmonella, or *Entamoeba histolytica*. However, all attempts to identify these and other bacteria—as well as viruses and other organisms in the intestines of IBD patients—failed.

While studies of the 1990's provided little proof that IBD is triggered by an infectious agent, such studies did lead researchers to form a theory that would explain the origin of IBD. The theory, which combines infectious, genetic, and immune system factors, has gained widespread acceptance among researchers and physicians as the most accurate description of the origin of IBD.

According to the comprehensive theory, IBD may result from an abnormal response by the immune system to an infectious or toxic agent, for example, to certain bacteria, viruses, or environmental

Inflammatory Bowel Disease

Inflammatory bowel disease consists of two distinct conditions—ulcerative colitis and Crohn's disease—that share similar symptoms and complications. The two conditions differ by the location of the inflammation produced in the bowel.

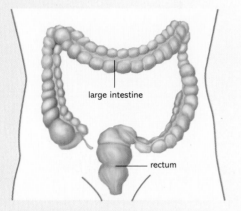

Ulcerative colitis attacks the colon or large intestine, causing abdominal cramps and bloody diarrhea.

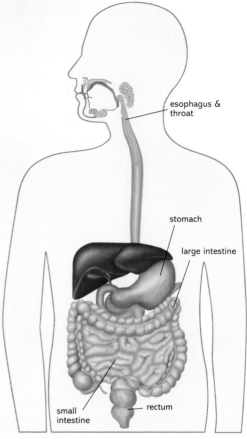

Crohn's disease can involve the entire gastrointestinal tract, from mouth to rectum, and may include the large and small intestines.

toxins. A genetic abnormality in certain individuals predisposes their immune systems to respond to these agents in a unique or abnormal way, triggering IBD. The genetic abnormality can cause the immune system to overreact to "foreign" invaders or even to certain bacteria normally found in the intestinal tract. The excessive response and the attack on the "foreign" invader leads to the damage of healthy cells, such as those lining the intestine.

The immune response continues this attack long after the offending agent has been wiped out, according to the theory. This continued attack, in effect, wages war with and may even be directed against healthy cells lining the intestine. This attack on healthy cells, according to the theory, explains the recurrent inflammation, ulceration, and bleeding characteristic of inflammatory bowel disease.

How is IBD diagnosed?

Physicians generally diagnose ulcerative colitis or Crohn's disease through the use of X ray, colonoscopy, or both.

If a patient's symptoms suggest involvement of the colon, the physician may examine the colon with a flexible instrument called a colonoscope, which allows the examining physician to see directly inside the colon. Areas of inflammation often appear as red, ulcerated regions. The physician may take a *biopsy* (a small tissue sample of these areas) through the instrument. The tissue sample is sent to a laboratory for microscopic examination. If the *pathologist* (physician who studies diseases of tissue) finds features typical of IBD and if the patient's physician rules out other causes for bowel inflammation, for example, bacterial or parasitic infection, IBD may be diagnosed. Physicians may also be able to distinguish between ulcerative colitis and Crohn's disease based upon the location, microscopic appearance, pattern, and distribution of inflammation.

While the colon is 5 feet (152 centimeters) long and can be examined directly with a colonoscope, the small intestine can be over 25 feet (7.5 meters) in length, making it very difficult to examine directly. The narrowing and scarring of the small intestine that is characteristic of Crohn's disease are clearly visible on X-ray films. Therefore, X rays are useful in the diagnosis of small bowel Crohn's disease.

Treatment of IBD

Physicians treat IBD with drugs, through nutrition, or with surgery. They turn to surgery only after other treatments have proved to be ineffective or if bleeding becomes life-threatening.

The drugs used to treat inflammatory bowel disease fall into three categories: aminosalicylates, corticosteroids, and immunomodulatory agents. The drugs in these categories are of different potencies and are designed to act on different regions of the GI tract. So physicians base their drug choice on the severity of the IBD episode and on the location of the inflammation. Inflammation of the rectum, for example, is generally treated with suppositories or enemas. Widespread inflammation of the small intestine is treated without oral

Colonoscopy allows physicians to view the interior of the colon via a television monitor. Inflammation and ulceration of the colon wall are characteristic of both ulcerative colitis and Crohn's disease, *below*. Location, appearance, pattern, and distribution of inflammation provide clues that allow physicians to differentiate between the two conditions.

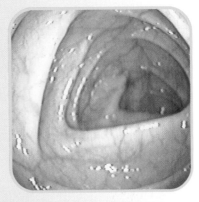

Normal colon

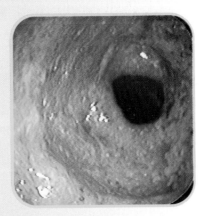

Crohn's disease

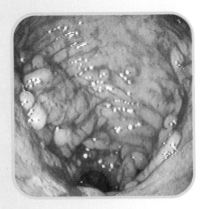

Ulcerative colitis

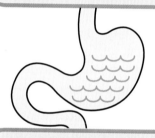

medications. But, if it is severe enough, physicians may treat IBD with *intravenous* (inserting drugs directly into a vein) medications, which often require hospitalization.

The majority of IBD patients suffer a recurrence within a year of the first attack. Because of the relapsing nature of the disease, researchers are challenged to find effective treatments for both the acute phase of the disease and to prevent recurrence. However, with proper medication and monitoring, up to 85 percent of patients experience fewer relapses and hospital stays than do patients who go off medication.

Aminosalicylate medications

Aminosalicylates, which are related to aspirin, are considered the first line of defense in the effective treatment of IBD, particularly in mild to moderate phases of the disease. Aminosalicylates are also effective in preventive therapy.

The active ingredient in aminosalicylates, salicylic acid, is available in many products, which differ in how the drug is delivered and absorbed. The most commonly prescribed aminosalicylate drugs include sulfasalazine (Azulfadine), mesalamine (Rowasa, Asacol, Pentasa), and olsalazine (Dipentum). Aminosalicylates are administered either orally or rectally. How the drug is administered depends on the specific drug and location and severity of the disease.

When aminosalicylates reach the inflamed area of the intestine, the active ingredient concentrates there to reduce inflammation. This allows the body an opportunity to heal, much the same way as aspirin reduces pain and inflammation in muscles and joints.

Corticosteroids

The corticosteroid group of drugs are extremely effective in treating moderate to severe flare-ups of IBD. They quickly reduce inflammation by directly interfering with the body's immune system. Corticosteroids reduce the immune response and suppress immune activity. The corticosteroid class of drugs can be administered orally, rectally, and intravenously.

Long-term use of corticosteroids can result in

What IBD is not: Irritable bowel syndrome

People often confuse inflammatory bowel disease with irritable bowel syndrome. The two conditions, however, differ in a number of ways, including severity.

Irritable bowel syndrome, which affects approximately 15 percent of the adult population, is one of the most common of all human maladies. It is also one of the least understood. While the cause remains unknown, onset of irritable bowel syndrome episodes appears to be related to elevated levels of emotional stress.

Irritable bowel symptoms—abdominal cramps and bloating, irregular bowel movements, excessive gas, passage of mucus, and abnormal "gurgling" from the abdomen—can be similar to inflammatory bowel disease symptoms. However, irritable bowel syndrome is less serious than inflammatory bowel disease. The symptoms of irritable bowel syndrome rarely grow more severe over time or lead to serious complications.

The irregular bowel movements that are symptomatic of irritable bowel syndrome can vary from severe diarrhea to constipation. Symptoms of the condition often wax and wane in intensity and can disappear for long periods of time. However, people who are subject to irritable bowel syndrome can experience symptoms throughout their lives.

While irritable bowel syndrome is treated with a variety of drugs, physicians normally suggest that patients attempt to control the condition through diet. Spicy, fatty, and fried foods should be avoided as well as foods that appear to upset the individual's digestion. Physicians often prescribe fiber preparations and stool softeners. Episodes of stress associated with the onset of irritable bowel syndrome are sometimes treated with tranquilizers and antidepressants.

significant side effects. These can include unusual infections, fractures, *cataracts* (a disease of the eye in which the lens becomes cloudy, making a person partly or entirely blind), and *osteoporosis* (a disease in which bones become weak and brittle, causing them to break easily and heal slowly). As a result of such side effects, physicians try to reduce or eliminate the longer-term use of corticosteroids as a preventive therapy.

Prednisone is the corticosteroid most often prescribed for IBD. In 1997, a new, highly potent steroid, budesonide, appeared to hold promise for long-term use. When given either orally or rectally, it appears to be as effective as other steroids in reducing local inflammation of the GI tract. However, it is poorly absorbed by the bloodstream and, thus, has fewer side effects than other corticosteroid drugs. This feature of budesonide may prove highly effective for long-term treatment to prevent recurrences of IBD. In 1997, budesonide had not been completely evaluated and approved by the U.S. Food and Drug Administration.

Immunomodulatory agents

In the 1990's, researchers investigated the use of various medications called *immunomodulatory* (drugs that modulate or decrease immune response) agents. This drug group exhibits greater potency against certain phases of IBD than either aminosalicylates or corticosteroids. Immunomodulatory agents reduce inflammatory response in a way that is similar to how corticosteroids limit inflammation. While immunomodulatory agents are effective during moderate to severe IBD episodes, they do not act as quickly as corticosteroids in treating acute flare-ups. Because they are associated with significant side effects, physicians generally save these medications for difficult or uncontrolled episodes of the disease. Immunomodulatory agents do appear to effectively prevent relapses without steroid side effects and may prove most valuable as a preventive therapy in severe cases. Specific drugs include azathioprine (Imuran), 6-mercaptopurine (Purinethol), and cyclosporine (Neoral, Sandimmune).

Treating IBD through nutrition

Certain aspects of severe ulcerative colitis and Crohn's disease—protein and fluid loss through diarrhea and poor absorption of nutrients from the intestinal tract—can make adequate nutritional balance difficult to maintain. In severe cases, complete rest of the bowel is essential for healing to occur. So patients are fed intravenously, by a process called total parenteral nutrition (TPN). Alternatively, patients with less severe symptoms may be given easily digestible, liquid food containing precise amounts of simple carbohydrates, fats, and proteins along with vitamins, minerals, and other essential nutrients.

Surgical treatment of IBD

Surgical treatment may be required when medications fail in treating ulcerative colitis, when there are such complications as infection, or when bleeding threatens the life of the patient. The operation most frequently performed is the removal of the colon, called a colectomy. As ulcerative colitis involves only the colon, its removal prevents ulcerative colitis from recurring. No further preventive medication is necessary.

The drawback to surgery is the loss of the colon. While not essential for life, the colon stores waste and absorbs fluid. Consequently, patients who have undergone colectomy will have more frequent and more liquid bowel movements, which can limit lifestyle. Fortunately, there are surgical techniques to control this problem, making incapacitating diarrhea rare for most people who have undergone the procedure.

Crohn's disease cannot be cured by surgery in the same way that ulcerative colitis can. While surgery is sometimes performed on a Crohn's patient to remove a diseased segment of intestine, the disease can recur in any other digestive tract segment at any time. Physicians are more conservative in recommending surgery to Crohn's disease patients, because the amount of intestine that can be removed is limited. The small intestine removes nutrients from digested food and sends them to the bloodstream. If too much intestine is removed, serious nutritional deficiencies can result.

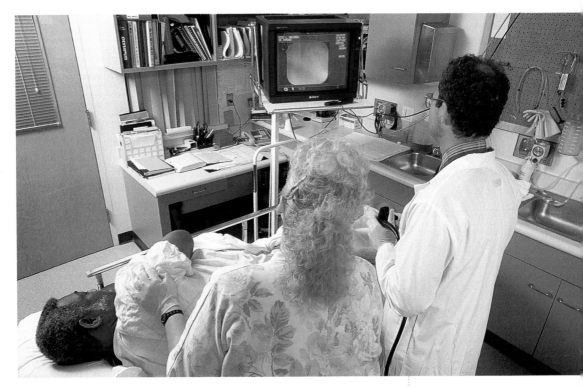

A physician examines the interior of the colon via a television monitor connected to a camera attached to a flexible instrument called a colonoscope. Colonoscopy is generally employed in the diagnosis of inflammatory bowel disease.

Complication of ulcerative colitis

Ulcerative colitis patients can experience a variety of uncommon conditions associated with the disease. Less than 5 percent of ulcerative colitis patients develop conditions involving organs other than the digestive tract. One serious complication is primary sclerosing cholangitis, a liver disease that can result in *cirrhosis of the liver* (scarring of the tissue with loss of liver function). Patients with a severe form of cirrhosis may develop *jaundice* (a condition in which the skin and whites of the eyes take on a yellow cast), severe itching, and even liver cancer.

Some people who suffer from ulcerative colitis develop inflammatory arthritis, which causes the small joints in the hands and wrists to swell and become stiff and painful. Additionally, ulcerative colitis can be complicated by another form of arthritis involving the sacroiliac joint in the low back, resulting in loss of flexibility.

People with ulcerative colitis can develop skin conditions, such as unusual ulcers, called pyoderma gangrenosum, on their legs. Some of the skin conditions associated with ulcerative colitis may become more or less severe when the intestinal inflammation flares up or improves. For example, erythema nodosum, a rash characterized by painful, red nodules on the legs, closely follows the severity of the bowel disease. When the inflammation occurs, the red nodules appear. They disappear when the inflammation clears up. Some researchers regard this effect as evidence of a abnormal immune response, an hypothesis that supports the theory that an imbalanced immune system plays a role in inflammatory bowel disease.

Preventive or maintenance therapy for patients with inflammatory bowel disease may include:

- Drug therapy

- Monitoring by a physician

Antiinflammatory drug types most often prescribed for preventive maintenance include:

- Aminosalicylates

- Corticosteroids

- Immunomodulatory agents

No evidence links inflammatory bowel disease with diet. However, maintaining a sensible diet has been found to:

- Reduce IBD symptoms

- Replace nutrients lost through diarrhea

Colon cancer is the most severe long-term complication of ulcerative colitis. Risk of colon cancer is particularly high among patients who have had *pancolitis* (ulcerative colitis involving the entire colon) or a long history of continuous symptoms. Patients who have had pancolitis for 15 years have a 12 percent risk of developing colon cancer. Those who have had the disease for 24 years run a 42 percent risk of colon cancer. Physicians recommend that patients who experience ulcerative colitis for 10 years or longer be screened annually for cancer. The screening process involves colonoscopy, the same procedure typically employed during IBD diagnosis.

Complications of Crohn's disease

Patients with Crohn's disease run only a slightly higher risk of developing colon cancer than does the general population. Examination for cancer, therefore, is not performed as commonly as it is with ulcerative colitis patients.

Complications of Crohn's disease that differ from those of ulcerative colitis appear to be due to the deep, penetrating nature of the inflammation associated with Crohn's. Bowel obstruction is a serious complication that results from a diseased segment of intestine. The obstruction can be caused by inflammation and swelling of the intestine or from scarring and narrowing of the diseased segment after the inflammation is in remission. The obstruction can cause nausea, vomiting, and abdominal distension.

Crohn's disease patients can also develop fistulas or perforations of the bowel, which result from chronic and severe inflammations involving the entire bowel wall. If inflammation develops in an area where two segments of bowel are folded next to each other, a *fistula* (a tube or passage) can form between them and cause intestinal contents to spill from one part of the bowel into another. This "short cut" can result in diarrhea and malabsorption of nutrients. Fistulas can also form from the bowel to other abdominal organs, such as the bladder, and from bowel to skin, for example, the skin around the anus.

Fistulas can lead to serious nonhealing wounds and perforations that allow intestinal contents to spill out of the intestine. The result can be the formation of abscesses or *peritonitis* (inflammation of the thin membrane that lines the walls of the abdomen).

Studies published in the 1990's indicate that ulcerative colitis does not affect female fertility. Whether Crohn's disease affects female fertility remains unknown. Physicians do know that IBD often grows worse during pregnancy, and miscarriages occur at higher rates

among women with active IBD. An operation to treat IBD during pregnancy also carries a high risk of spontaneous abortion. Physicians and patients need to work toward achieving remission during pregnancy. Fortunately, neither aminosalicylates nor corticosteroid drugs are associated with birth defects and appear to be safe medications during pregnancy. The effects of immunomodulatory agents on pregnant women are unknown. Aminosalicylates and corticosteroids are the only medications that are safe during breast feeding.

Groups of IBD patients meet regularly to provide members with information about their condition as well as emotional support and understanding of the psychological strain exacted by the disease.

Living with IBD

While most IBD patients live full and productive lives, the illnesses can be challenging for some patients and their families. Both ulcerative colitis and Crohn's disease generally begin between the ages of 15 and 35, a period during which personal identity, self-esteem, and psychological growth can be devastated by illness. The pain, suffering, and loss of productivity can take a toll on the mental well-being of patients, families, and friends. Patients often suffer psychological strain and depression and require education and counseling. The Crohn's and Colitis Foundation of America, in New York City, is a valuable resource that offers educational materials and information on local chapters and support groups. •••

New drugs and therapies are ushering in a quiet revolution in the battle against "brain attacks."

Combating the Effects of Stroke

By Steven I. Benowitz

FOR YEARS, PHYSICIANS COULD DO LITTLE for some-one who was suffering a brain-damaging stroke. Stroke, the result of a blood clot or a burst blood vessel, can steal the ability to think, talk, or move. Brain tissue dies, causing paralysis, memory loss, speech loss, and blindness, depending on the area of the brain affected. These devastating effects may even be permanent, because brain cells cannot be replaced.

Until recently, there was no treatment for stroke. Nothing could stop or even limit its destruction of brain cells. But by the mid-1990's, doctors and researchers were ushering in a quiet revolution in the treatment of stroke. Thanks to new drugs and therapies, a growing under-standing of how stroke affects the brain, and improved methods of rehabilitation, stroke sufferers lead better, healthier lives. And because there are now ways to treat a stroke in progress—as there are ways to treat a heart at-tack—physicians have taken to calling stroke a "brain at-tack" to stress the urgency of emergency treatment. Many major medical centers have developed brain attack teams —groups of neurologists, nurses, and other specialists

Two types of stroke

Strokes generally fall into two categories, called ischemic strokes and hemorrhagic strokes.

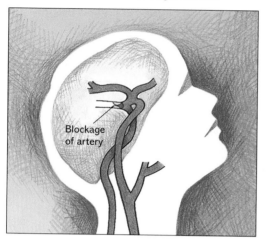

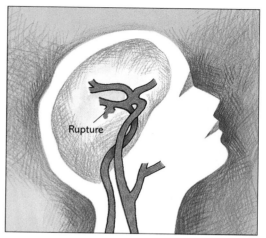

An ischemic stroke is caused by a blood clot that blocks an artery in or leading to the brain. The blockage deprives brain cells of oxygen and nutrients carried by the blood. As a result, brain cells served by the blocked blood vessel die.

A hemorrhagic stroke occurs when one or more blood vessels in the head rupture. The pressure caused by blood pooling in brain tissue damages or kills brain cells near the ruptured blood vessel.

ready at a moment's notice to treat someone suffering a stroke.

Yet stroke is far from a vanquished foe. Some 500,000 Americans suffer strokes each year, according to the American Heart Association (AHA). It remains the number-one cause of disability and the third leading cause of death in the United States (behind heart disease and cancer), taking some 150,000 lives annually.

What is stroke?

There are two types of stroke, those caused by *ischemia* (a cutoff in blood flow), and those caused by *hemorrhage* (bleeding). Ischemic stroke, which is caused by a blocked artery in the brain, is the more common of the two types. And the most common kind of ischemic stroke is a cerebral thrombosis, which occurs when a blood clot forms in—and obstructs—a brain artery already narrowed by *atherosclerosis* (a condition in which fatty substances in the blood build up inside arteries). About 70 to 80 percent of all strokes are cerebral thromboses.

About 10 percent of all cerebral thromboses are preceded by "little strokes" called transient ischemic attacks (TIA's), according to the AHA. TIA's have symptoms similar to strokes, but their effects are temporary. Experts believe that most TIA's are caused by clumps of

The author:

Steven I. Benowitz is a free-lance science and medical writer.

platelets (a blood component important in clotting) that form in blood vessels roughened by atherosclerotic build-up. The lumps may then break off and travel downstream, where they may temporarily plug a small vessel. More than 35 percent of people who experience TIA's will later have a stroke, and individuals who have one or more TIA's are almost 10 times more likely to have a stroke.

The symptoms of cerebral thrombosis and TIA are similar. The person may develop impaired vision and weakness, numbness, tingling, or paralysis on one side of the body. *Aphasia*, an inability to speak, read, or associate words with their meanings, is another common symptom. With TIA, normal function returns in 24 hours, but with cerebral thrombosis, the impairment may be permanent.

Cerebral embolism is a second, and less common, type of ischemic stroke, accounting for 5 to 14 percent of all strokes. It occurs when a blood clot forms in another part of the body (typically in a large blood vessel or in one of the chambers of the heart) and travels through the bloodstream to the brain. When the blood clot reaches a narrower artery in the brain, it creates a plug that instantly cuts off blood flow. About 15 percent of cerebral embolisms are the result of *atrial fibrillation* (a heart rhythm disturbance). Atrial fibrillation increases the risk of a blood clot's forming in the heart and breaking free. The symptoms of a cerebral embolism are virtually identical to those of cerebral thrombosis.

Hemorrhagic strokes are caused by the rupture of one or more of the brain's blood vessels. The most common hemorrhagic stroke is cerebral hemorrhage, in which the ruptured vessels are located deep within the brain. This type of stroke is often the result of high blood pressure, which can eventually weaken small arteries in the brain so much that they burst. When they burst, the blood supply to certain regions of the brain is diminished and oxygen-deprived cells in those regions die. As blood pools within the brain, it presses on nearby brain cells, disrupting their function. Cerebral hemorrhage accounts for about 10 percent of all strokes.

Another kind of hemorrhagic stroke is subarachnoid hemorrhage, which occurs when blood vessels on the surface of the brain rupture. These vessels bleed into the space between the membranes surrounding the brain, putting pressure on brain cells and depriving other cells of blood. About 7 percent of strokes are caused by subarachnoid hemorrhages.

This type of hemorrhagic stroke is usually caused by the rupture of an aneurysm, an abnormal, balloonlike distention of an artery caused by a weakness in the artery wall. Aneurysms are usually defects present since birth, but they can also be caused by an infection in the wall of an artery.

The effects of stroke

- Paralysis.
- Loss of feeling in an arm or leg.
- *Dysarthria* (slurred speech).
- Loss or impairment of vision.
- Loss of depth perception.
- *Aphasia* (loss of ability to speak and write and/or the ability to comprehend and read).
- Confusion.

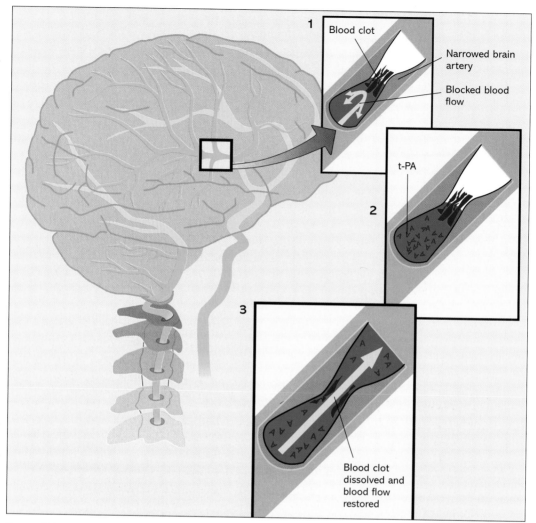

1 Blood clot
Narrowed brain artery
Blocked blood flow

2 t-PA

3 Blood clot dissolved and blood flow restored

How t-PA works

A drug called t-PA can be injected into the bloodstream to break up a blood clot that is causing an ischemic stroke. The drug travels to the narrowed part of the artery where the blood clot is lodged and chemically dissolves it, restoring blood flow to the brain.

Types of treatment and rehabilitation

- Carotid endarterectomy (a surgery that cleans clogged arteries).
- Preventative treatment with blood-thinning drugs.
- Clot-busting drug treatment with t-PA.
- Range-of-motion exercises (gently bending arms, legs, fingers, and toes).
- Stimulating blood circulation by lifting or stretching limbs.
- Walking.
- Psychological counseling.

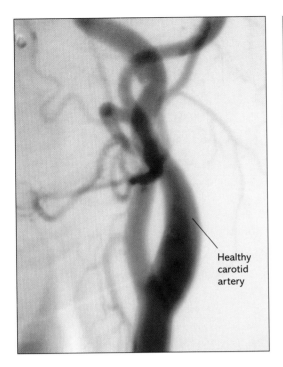

Healthy
carotid
artery

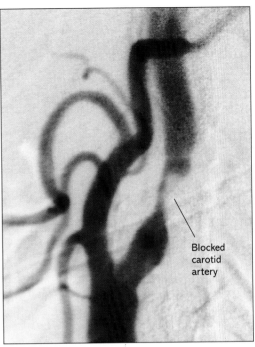

Blocked
carotid
artery

How clogged arteries cause stroke

A healthy carotid artery, *left,* which carries blood from the heart to the brain, becomes clogged, *right,* when *plaque* (deposits of fat and other substances) builds up within it. A blood clot that forms in a narrowed carotid artery can travel to the brain and clog a smaller vessel there, cutting off blood flow and causing stroke.

The symptoms of subarachnoid and cerebral hemorrhages are generally the same as those of ischemic stroke—paralysis, loss of vision or speech, and perhaps loss of consciousness. Because blood may leak slowly during these kinds of strokes, mild symptoms such as headache and vomiting may begin an hour or two before the person having the stroke begins to suffer its major effects. If an aneurysm in the brain bursts, the effect is akin to being shot in the head. The person typically feels a sudden, violent flash of pain and loses consciousness.

Doctors consider hemorrhagic strokes deadlier than ischemic strokes. According to the AHA, 50 percent of patients who suffer hemorrhagic stroke die within 30 days—most of them succumbing to increased pressure on the brain. Those who survive usually recover more fully than victims of ischemic stroke, however, because the pressure of accumulated blood causes less destruction of brain cells than does a complete cutoff in blood flow.

Most strokes occur suddenly and without warning. However, strokes can be prevented. In fact, according to the AHA, at least one-half of all strokes are preventable through changes in lifestyle and diet. Smokers and people with high blood pressure, for example, have a higher than average risk of stroke. Under a physician's supervision, however, people with these risk factors may be able to lower their blood pressure by losing weight and taking medication. They can reduce other risk factors by quitting smoking and maintaining a diet low in fat and sodium.

There are some risk factors, however, that cannot be eliminated or

A physical therapist assists stroke sufferers with exercises or activities to strengthen a patient's muscles and increase coordination and endurance.

minimized, such as a family or personal history of stroke. Researchers also have found that the stroke rate for men is 30 percent higher than for women and 60 percent higher for blacks than for whites. These differences may be explained by the fact that men are more prone to atherosclerosis and that blacks are more prone to high blood pressure.

Old age, which brings with it an increased risk of atherosclerosis, also increases risk of stroke. Although nearly 30 percent of all stroke victims are younger than 65, the rate of stroke doubles every 10 years after age 55. People with diabetes, who have an increased risk of atherosclerosis, also have an increased risk of stroke.

Treating stroke

Doctors can surgically clean the clogged arteries of some people at high risk of stroke. Since the 1970's, surgeons routinely performed a procedure called *carotid endarterectomy* (artery cleaning) on patients who had fatty blockages in the *carotid arteries* (the two main arteries in the neck supplying blood to the brain).

This type of surgery gained further acceptance after researchers at the Bowman Gray School of Medicine in Winston-Salem, North Carolina, in May 1995 announced the results of a seven-year clinical trial called the Asymptomatic Carotid Atherosclerosis Study. Researchers at 39 medical centers in the United States and Canada evaluated the health of 1,662 men and women with neck arteries that were at least 60 percent blocked. About half the patients underwent carotid endarterectomy, in which the surgeon made an incision in the neck and extracted the blockage—usually fatty deposits—from a carotid artery. Researchers said that the surgery cut patients' risk of stroke by 53 percent.

Despite the reported success of the surgery, some studies showed that not all doctors approve of this prevention method. In September 1996, Duke University's Stroke Patient Outcomes Research Team reported that 1 in 4 family doctors and 1 in 5 internists said that they would "seldom" or "never" recommend surgery on patients whose arteries were more than 70 percent blocked. These doctors said they were concerned about the risks involved with the surgery and preferred treating artery blockage with blood thinning medication.

Doctors use the blood thinning drug warfarin to cut the risk of stroke caused by atrial fibrillation. According to a study published in the December 1996 issue of Archives of Internal Medicine, researchers at Massachusetts General Hospital in Boston found that warfarin cut the risk of stroke by atrial fibrillation by 67 percent.

Doctors also use aspirin to treat people at risk of stroke. The Food and Drug Administration (FDA) approved aspirin's use as a stroke medication in 1980 after studies proved that aspirin thins the blood and significantly reduces risk of stroke. A 1990 study involving 15 U.S. medical centers noted that an aspirin a day cut stroke risk in half for people with atrial fibrillation.

Before 1996, physicians could prescribe drugs to prevent strokes, but they had no medications with which to treat a stroke in progress. Often physicians could only wait for natural chemicals in the bloodstream to dissolve the clot and then they assessed the damage to the brain. In 1996, however, the FDA approved a clot-dissolving drug called tissue plasminogen activator (t-PA). The genetically engineered t-PA is the same as the body's clot-dissolving chemicals, but the large dose used in treatment restores blood flow sooner and, therefore, minimizes the damage to the brain.

T-PA has long been used to treat heart attack patients. Scientists at the National Institutes of Health in Bethesda, Maryland, announced in December 1995 that t-PA may also reduce brain damage caused by stroke if a patient takes it within three hours of the onset of symptoms. A five-year study of 600 patients conducted by the National Institute of Neurological Disorders and Strokes in Bethesda, Maryland, concluded that patients who received t-PA at the onset of symptoms were 30 percent less likely to have a disability after three

As part of stroke rehabilitation, a speech therapist works with patients at home or in a rehabilitation facility to help them recover the ability to express thoughts and ideas.

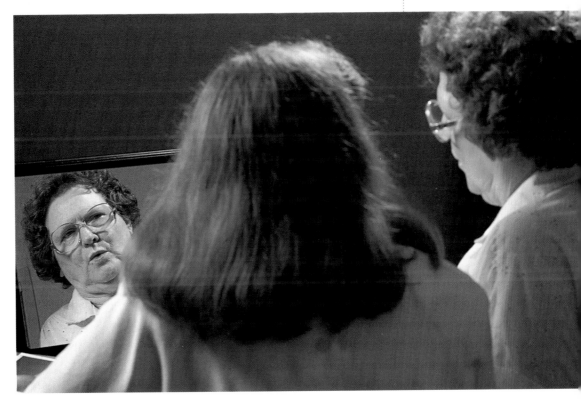

Warning signs of stroke

- Sudden weakness or numbness of the face, arm, or leg on one side of the body.
- Sudden dimness or loss of vision, particularly in only one eye.
- Loss of speech or trouble talking or understanding speech.
- Sudden, severe headaches with no known cause.
- Unexplained dizziness, unsteadiness, or sudden falls particularly in combination with other symptoms.

TIA warning signs

- Temporary weakness, clumsiness, or loss of feeling in an arm, leg, or the side of the face on one side of the body.
- Temporary dimness or loss of vision, particularly in one eye and often in combination with other symptoms.
- Temporary loss of speech, difficulty in speaking, or difficulty in understanding speech, particularly with a weakness on the right side.
- Dizziness, double vision, and staggering.

months when compared with those who did not receive the drug.

Although doctors were optimistic about the success of t-PA, some researchers cautioned that more study needed to be done on the treatment. In fact, according to Larry Goldstein, a neurologist at Duke University Medical Center, studies have shown that t-PA is effective in only about 10 percent of all cases.

T-PA treatment does involve risks, especially if the patient does not recognize symptoms of a stroke and seek immediate help. Although t-PA can treat ischemic stroke, it could worsen a stroke caused by a cerebral hemorrhage by increasing the flow of blood into the damaged area of the brain. Therefore, physicians must determine the cause of a stroke before administering t-PA. Another risk involves the timing of t-PA treatment. If more than three hours elapse between the onset of stroke and t-PA treatment, t-PA can cause hemorrhaging in the brain.

Diagnosing stroke

Before administering these medications, doctors must first determine if the patient is suffering a stroke, and then identify what type of stroke it is. Symptoms of stroke can be similar to those of other ailments. A brain tumor, for example, produces similar symptoms.

When a patient experiences symptoms of stroke, a doctor typically uses different techniques to determine the kind of stroke a patient is suffering. One technique, a computerized axial tomographic scan (CT), uses a large number of X rays to provide detailed cross-sectional images of the brain. Pools of blood are readily detectable on CT scans, making it possible to diagnose a cerebral hemorrhage soon after it occurs. Magnetic resonance imaging (MRI), a diagnostic technique that uses magnetic energy and radio waves rather than X rays, also helps physicians obtain a visual image of the brain. Doctors using a third imaging test, radionuclide angiography (nuclear brain scan), inject radioactive compounds into a vein in the arm. A machine tracks the compound, creating a map of the compound's movements through different parts of the brain. This technique can detect blocked blood vessels and areas where the brain is damaged.

After the patient's condition has stabilized, a doctor will examine the patient to determine the extent of brain damage. If the patient is alert, he or she will be given a detailed neurological examination to determine the size and location of the damaged area. If a patient is comatose, physicians can determine how much brain function is left by making an electroencephalogram (EEG)—a recording of the electrical activity of the brain. *Electrodes* (small, metal disks) placed on a patient's scalp pick up electrical impulses transmitted and received by brain cells. The doctor may also perform an evoked-response test to measure how the brain responds to such stimuli as flashing lights, sounds, and mild electrical shocks to the arms and legs.

There are also several types of tests that measure blood flow to the brain and detect blockages in arteries. A Doppler ultrasound produces pictures by bouncing sound waves off the artery walls. A technique called carotid phonoangiography detects a *bruit* (the sound created by turbulent blood flow as it passes through a partially blocked artery). Ocular plethysmography measures blood pulses and pressure in the eyes. And digital subtraction angiography tracks a trail of dye injected into the patient and then produces an image of the major blood vessels leading to the brain.

According to the AHA, about one-third of people who suffer strokes are severely disabled. The remainder of stroke patients usually suffer from some moderate disability—a limp or difficulty handling certain objects. They may have problems with their vision or difficulty in simple functions such as driving a car. They may have trouble remembering things or finding the right words to describe everyday objects. However, rehabilitation helps many stroke patients cope with disabilities and speeds recovery so they can return home to live relatively normal lives.

The recovery process

After a stroke, most people achieve the bulk of their recovery in the month following a stroke, according to the AHA. For this reason, doctors urge patients to begin the rehabilitation process soon after suffering a stroke. After the patient is well enough to leave the hospital bed, help can be provided by rehabilitation centers in hospitals or at special rehabilitation facilities. In these centers, nurses, physical therapists, speech therapists, and occupational therapists help patients regain lost functions and learn skills to compensate for those that cannot be regained.

Exercises are important for a stroke patient. They prevent muscles in the body from getting tight, and help patients regain strength. If a patient can still move an arm or leg, it is possible to strengthen different groups of muscles in that limb. In some cases, the patient may use weights to build strength in parts of the body weakened by stroke. Even walking with a cane can provide exercise, according to doctors.

Since stroke affects different patients in different ways, no single exercise program will work for all people.

Doctors are studying new types of physical therapy and other rehabilitation methods to help people recover from stroke. In 1995, researchers at Texas Woman's University in Dallas and the University of Texas Southwestern Medical Center in Dallas, experimented with using amphetamines to speed the recovery process. The drug dextroamphetamine appeared to increase recovery of motor functions of 10 partially paralyzed stroke patients, according to the study published in the December 1995 issue of the AHA journal *Stroke*.

Some drugs, however, can hamper recovery. Sleeping pills, known as benzodiazepines, and *antihypertension* (blood pressure) drugs, including clonidine, can interfere with the recovery process. Therefore, it is important for the rehabilitation team to be aware of all over-the-counter and prescription medicine the patient is taking.

Risk factors that can be reduced

- High blood pressure.
- Smoking.
- Elevated blood cholesterol.
- Physical inactivity.
- Obesity.

New hope for patients

While doctors were treating strokes with the drugs and methods available at the time, medical researchers were also investigating new drugs that might limit the damage stroke causes to the brain. The most promising of these drugs are thrombolytics, or neuroprotectants, which shield brain cells from chemical damage. When blood is blocked from reaching the brain, brain cells are damaged or killed. Dying brain cells may release harmful chemicals, which in turn damage other brain cells. Neuroprotectants shield brain cells by interfering with the series of chemicals released as a result of a stroke, according to James C. Grotta, professor of neurology at the University of Texas Medical School at Houston.

According to Grotta, a new neuroprotectant, called lubeluzole, has saved lives and has prevented brain damage. Grotta planned to pair lubeluzole with clot-busting t-PA and test their effectiveness on treating patients suffering ischemic stroke. Grotta was also studying the inner workings of the brain cells that cause damage during a stroke. In this study he hoped to target new protective drugs that may slow or prevent brain damage.

Researchers in 1997 were also studying a neuroprotective drug called citicoline, which may help repair damaged cell membranes after a stroke. In a study at Oregon Health Sciences University, expected to be published in late 1997, researchers found that patients who began citicoline therapy within 24 hours of stroke were twice as likely to recover completely as those who didn't take the drug. The drug appeared to limit brain damage, speed recovery, and improve mental functioning.

Researchers were also looking for drugs that could break dangerous clots but that, unlike t-PA, do not cause internal bleeding. In 1997, they were studying two such drugs—ancrod and pro-urokinase.

While experts maintain that drug and surgical treatments may lessen brain damage, researchers agree that medical science remains far from being able to repair the effects of stroke. Despite the efforts of physicians and rehabilitation teams and advances in medication, prevention remains the best hope for people at risk of stroke. • • •

Risk factors that cannot be reduced

- Age.
- Gender.
- Race.
- Prior stroke.
- Heredity.
- Heart defects.
- Diabetes mellitus.

Resources:

For more information about stroke, readers may contact a number of organizations.

American Heart Association National Center
7272 Greenville Avenue
Dallas, TX 75231-4596
Public Relations/214-706-1490

National Institute of Neurological Disorders and Stroke
National Institutes of Health
Building 31, room 8A06
Bethesda, MD 20892
301-496-5751

National Stroke Association
300 East Hampden Avenue, suite 240
Englewood, CO 80110
800-367-1990

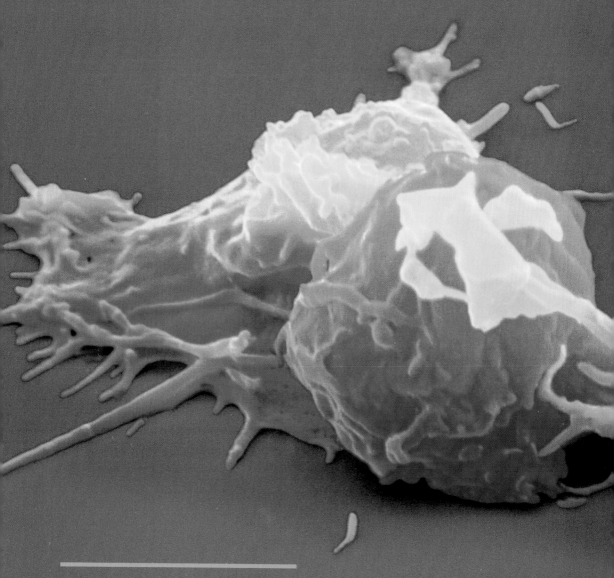

Powerful microscopes have allowed
scientists to take an up-close look at
the form and function of human cells.

Cells at Work

The attackers within

Two natural killer cells, *left*, white blood cells that are part of the human immune system, attack an invading leukemia cell. Another type of white blood cell, a lymphocyte, engulfs a yeast cell, *right*. White blood cells are the body's first line of defense against infection. (The images were magnified several thousand times by an electronic microscope.)

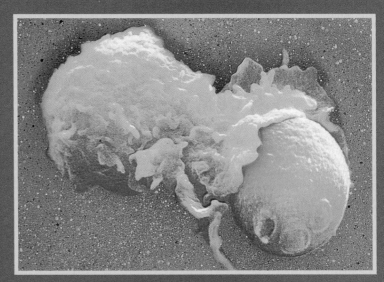

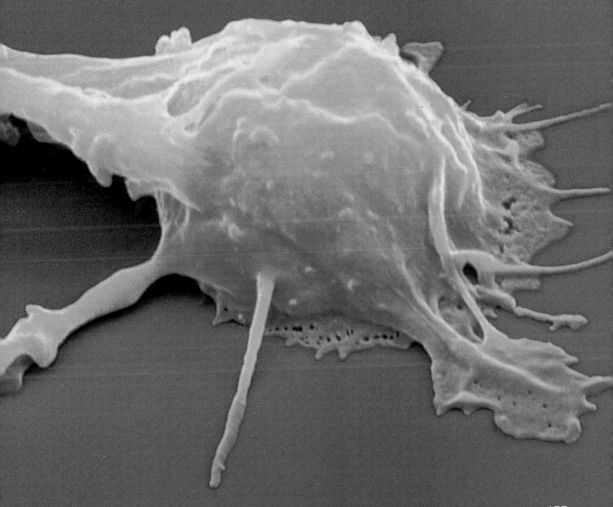

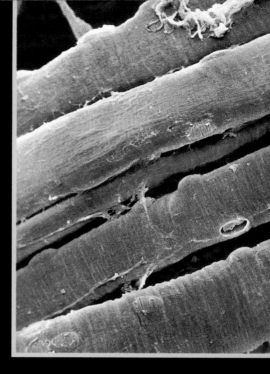

T HE MODERN MICROSCOPE has revealed an astonishing diversity in both the structure and the function of the cell, the building block of all living things. Most cells are about 1/1000 of an inch (0.0025 centimeters) in diameter. About 500 of these average-sized cells would fit within the period at the end of this sentence. Powerful microscopes, however, have allowed scientists to peek into the tiny world of the cell. An optical microscope can magnify a cell up to 2,000 times and an electronic microscope can magnify a cell by 1 million times.

To study cells, scientists first stain parts of a cell with certain dyes so that the various parts stand out clearly under a microscope. Scientists can then study each part's chemical content and activity.

Through the use of microscopes, scientists have learned much about how human cells reproduce, receive nourishment, die, and perform specialized functions such as fighting infection, carrying oxygen, building muscle and bone, transmitting messages, and packaging the genetic codes that make each individual unique. •••

The specialized structure of human cells

• •

Cells can be shaped like boxes, coils, corkscrews, octopuses, stars, or blobs of jelly. The greatest variety in cell shapes occur in human beings and other multicellular animals. A cell's shape is related to its needs or to the job it does. Human skin is made up of armorlike epithelial cells that capture invader cells such as bacteria, *left*, on pedestal formations, preventing the foreign cells from entering the body. Muscle cells, *above*, are long, thin cylinders, a shape that allows them to contract when they receive a signal from a motor nerve. Nerve cells, *right*, have long, spindly extensions to speed the transmission of electrical messages throughout the body.

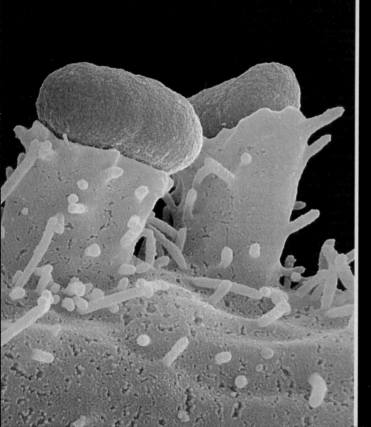

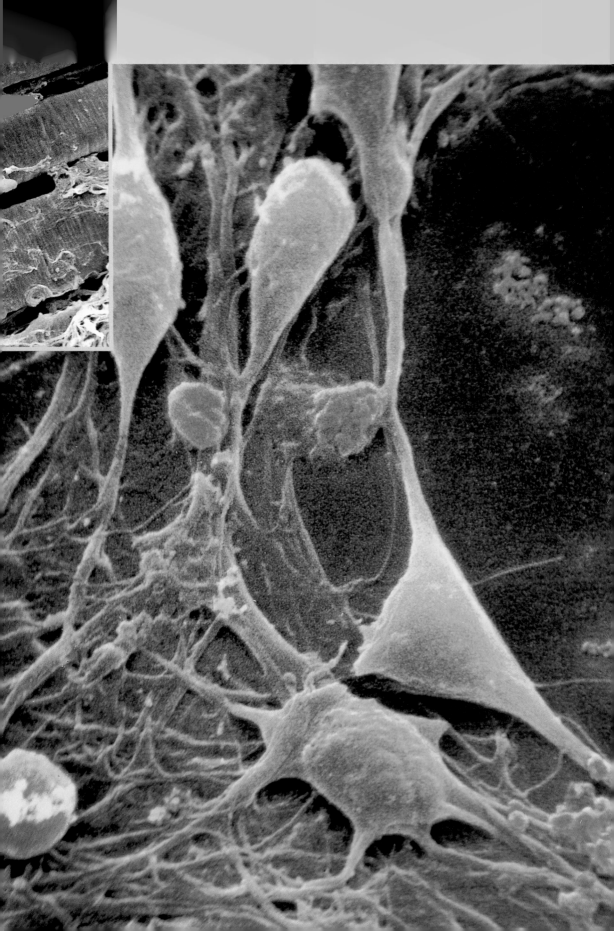

The production and action of blood cells

The bone marrow, a tissue rich in fats, contains plenty of nourishment for the production, *below*, of the different blood cells: white cells for the immune system, blood platelets for clotting, and red cells for the transport of oxygen. Red blood cells, traveling through a small branch of an artery, *right*, transport oxygen from the lungs to the tissues.

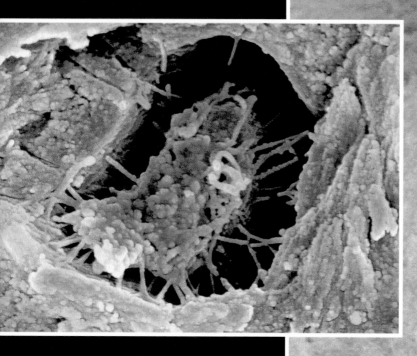

Building blocks
of the human body
• •

Cells in the human body, such as the
bone cell or osteocyte, *above*, are *differ-
entiated* (specialized) to perform specific
tasks. The function of osteocytes is to
group together to form bone, *right*.

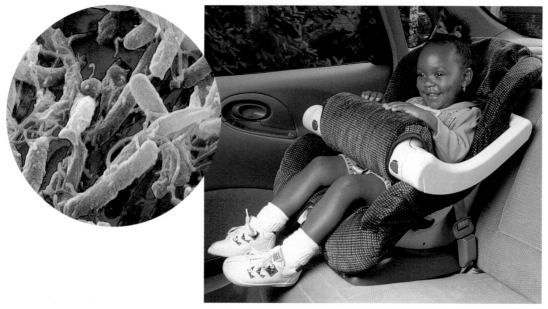

MEDICAL AND SAFETY ALERTS

Airbags:
An Exploding
Controversy

By Victoria Peters

Airbags save thousands of lives every year, but they can also cause fatal injury—especially to children.

MANY MEDICAL AND SAFETY AIDS DEVELOPED TO SAVE LIVES also can cause injury or death. Penicillin, for example, protects millions of people at risk of bacterial infection, but causes a fatal allergic reaction in a few people every year. The polio vaccine, which reduced polio cases in the United States from about 18,000 in 1954 to almost none in 1997, also causes paralytic polio in rare instances. And it was reported in 1996 that automobile airbags—once called the greatest road-safety device since the invention of the seat belt—could be dangerous, especially to children.

A 1996 study by the National Highway Traffic Safety Administration (NHTSA) on deaths caused by airbags stirred public debate about the safety of the device. The study concluded that airbags increased the risk of fatality to children sitting in the front passenger-side seat by 30 percent. Although airbags had saved more than 1,500 lives in America since 1986, public attention focused on the fact that more than 50 people—including some 30 children—had been killed by airbags in low-speed crashes that otherwise might have been survivable.

The debate about airbag safety centered on who was to blame for the tragedies: automakers who knew that the force of airbags could kill children, or drivers and passengers who were not aware of the proper ways to guard against injury. Injuries occurred not because the bags failed to restrain the passengers, but because the force of airbag inflation injured or killed the people it contacted. However, the NHTSA study found that almost all of the people killed by airbags either were not wearing seat belts or were children who should never have been in the front seat at all.

While the airbag safety debate raged on, the U.S. Congress gave the devices a vote of confidence by ruling that all passenger cars must have *dual* (airbags that protect the driver and front-seat passenger) airbags by 1998. At the same time, however, Congress also considered several proposals for making airbags safer and better at the job of saving lives.

Three collisions occur during a crash

Motor vehicle crashes are the leading cause of death in the United States for people aged 1 to 35 years old. Each year more than 50,000 people in the United States are killed in auto crashes—about 1 every 10 minutes. Another 3.5 million people are injured. According to NHTSA estimates, the average American has a one-in-three chance of being injured in a vehicle collision at some time in their life.

People who drive cars equipped with airbags and who wear seat belts are about 50 percent less likely to be killed in an automobile accident than are unrestrained riders. Padding on the steering wheels, dashboards, and door panels may make it seem that a collision with these soft surfaces could not result in serious injury. However, there is steel behind those pads. Some people believe they can brace themselves without the aid of a seat belt during a crash. But self restraint is nearly impossible.

Most serious injuries in automobile accidents occur when riders strike the interior surfaces of a vehicle after it comes to a sudden stop as the result of a crash. In fact, not one, but three distinct collisions occur during any automobile crash. The first collision occurs when the car hits an object—a wall for example—bringing the vehicle to a sudden stop. When a car traveling at 30 miles (48 kilometers) per hour crashes head-on into a wall, the car itself may slow from 30 to 0 miles per hour in about 1/10 of a second.

The second collision occurs inside the car. A passenger will continue to hurtle forward in the car at the speed at which the car was traveling, coming to an abrupt stop against the car's interior. That's about the speed at which a person would hit the ground if he or she jumped from the top of a three-story building. The knees ram into the dashboard; the head crashes into the windshield; and the driver's chest slams into the steering wheel.

As the second collision ends, the third begins. This collision takes place inside the body. After the body stops its forward motion, inter-

The author:

Victoria Peters is a freelance writer.

nal organs keep traveling forward. The internal organs collide with bones and other organs. The brain smashes against the skull. The heart crashes against the ribs and gets rammed from behind by the spinal column. The thigh bones snap from the force of the forward-moving hips. The massive injuries that occur in the third collision are the ones that kill and cripple.

Slowing the stop saves lives

During the fraction of a second that this crushing occurs, airbags and seat belts work together to protect people by allowing them to slow down with the car. The airbags help keep people's heads and chests from hitting the steering wheel, instrument panel, or windshield. If there is hard braking or other violent maneuvers before the crash, the seat belt also helps keep people in positions where there is still space for the airbags to create an energy-absorbing buffer between the person and the hard interior surfaces.

Since airbags and seat belts became standard features in cars, the percentage of deaths and injuries caused by auto accidents has dropped. The federal government first attempted to make cars safer in the mid-1960's, by requiring that cars be equipped with such items as shatterproof windshields, padded dashboards, and collapsible steering columns. In 1968, the government ordered automakers to equip the front seat of all passenger cars with lap and shoulder seat belts, often called three-point belts because they restrain the rider at three points: one near the shoulder and two on either side of the hips.

Three-point belts act almost like rubber bands, allowing riders to move some distance forward in their seat before their movement is halted. This is particularly true in head-on collisions. Seat belts are designed to stretch in order to reduce the force of the belts on the body. This means, however, that in accidents occurring at high speeds, the force exerted by the moving belted rider stretches the belt so far that the rider could still be thrown against the steering wheel, dashboard, or windshield.

Although standard seat belts are effective in reducing both injuries and deaths by slowing a person's movement inside a car during a crash, they have major limitations. Seat belts are *active re-*

The deadliest collision

A crash causes three collisions. The first damages the car. In the second collision, the forward-moving body strikes the car's internal surfaces. In the third collision, *below,* internal organs and bones, such as the pelvis, heart, and brain, collide with the outer frame of the body.

The pelvis rams into the thigh bone.

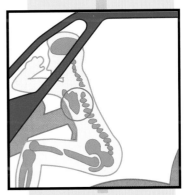

The heart crashes up against the chest and ribs.

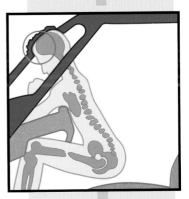

The brain slams into the skull.

How an airbag works

Automobile airbags protect properly restrained
drivers and passengers by rapidly inflating a bag to
further restrain the forward-moving body.

When the front of the
car strikes another ob-
ject, the sudden decel-
eration triggers an im-
pact sensor, which
sends an electric mes-
sage to the arming sen-
sor to deploy the bag.

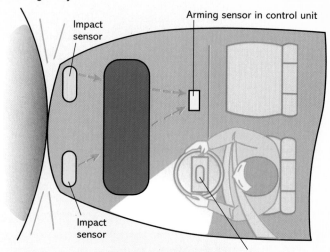

Impact
sensor

Arming sensor in control unit

Impact
sensor

Airbag deployment

Airbags were designed to
deploy into the chest of
an unbelted, 168-pound
(76 kilogram) man. They
inflate at speeds of up to
200 miles (322 kilome-
ters) per hour.

straints (drivers and passengers have to buckle them on if the belts
are to provide any protection), and many people dislike wearing or
forget to wear their seat belt. Even though most states have laws requiring seat belt use, in 1996 only 68 percent of Americans routinely
wore their seat belts while driving, according to the NHTSA.

Because of these limitations, in the late 1960's the federal government proposed requiring that all vehicles come equipped with *passive restraints* (devices that would protect motorists during collisions
even if they took no active steps for their own safety). Initially, auto
makers and safety officials considered the automated seat belt to be
the most effective passive restraint. These belts were designed to
strap drivers and passengers automatically into their seats once the
car was started. However, many people disconnected the belts, ren-

dering them useless. Automotive engineers developed airbags as an alternative to automated seat belts in the late 1960's, when only 12 percent of Americans wore seat belts.

How airbags work

Airbags are large, deflated balloons concealed in the steering-wheel *hub* (center), instrument panel, or other interior surface of a vehicle. Front airbags—the type that are in most U.S.-made vehicles—are designed for rapid inflation in a head-on crash, forming an air-cushion buffer between a rider and the dashboard and windshield. Front airbags deploy only in head-on collisions, which cause 50 percent of all crash deaths.

Airbag systems contain tiny devices called sensors that detect a sudden deceleration. During a crash, the sensors, which are connected to the car's battery, send an electric current to gas-generating pellets in the airbag. When the pellets ignite, they produce nitrogen gas that inflates the airbag.

The airbag pops out of its compartment and inflates at speeds of up to 200 mph (322 kph). The cushion first slows and then stops the passenger's forward movement. The whole operation—from impact to inflation—usually takes less than 1/10 of a second. That interval is short enough to ensure that the bag is fully inflated by the time the passenger hits it, even in high-speed collisions. Once the bag is inflated, the gas that deployed the bag escapes through vents, allowing the passenger to leave the vehicle.

In general, airbags are designed to deploy during collisions in which the car is moving at more than 11 mph (18 kph). The bag will not inflate if the car receives a hard bump. In addition, airbags will inflate only if the force of impact is within 30 degrees of either side of the centerline of the car. Front airbags do not provide protection in side- or rear-impact accidents or in rollovers, where the occupants can be ejected from the car.

Why airbags kill

Automobile airbags must inflate faster than the blink of an eye in order to save lives, yet such speed and force has resulted in the deaths of dozens of people. The device was designed to protect an unbelted, 168-pound (76 kilograms) man in a 30-mph crash. In order to protect adults who did not buckle up, airbags had to inflate at high rates of speed to catch unbuckled passengers hurtling toward the dashboard and steering column.

However, the speed can cause fatal injuries to people who are too short or weak to sustain the blow. Damage can be done to a short person's head, since the bags were designed to inflate into an adult's chest, which is better able to sustain an impact than is the head.

These two design elements were blamed for causing death and injury, especially to people under 5 feet (1.52 meters) tall who were

Danger from the dashboard

Airbags can be hazardous for children and short adults riding in the front seat. Infants in car seats and short adults and children should ride in the back seat.

Children and adults who are less than 5 feet (1.52 meters) tall, *below*, may be hit in the head by inflating airbags.

Infants in rear-facing safety seats, *below*, in the front seat may be slammed face-first into the backrest.

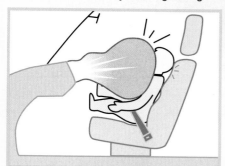
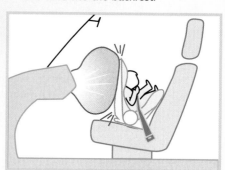

hit in the head instead of the chest. The NHTSA found that people killed by airbags suffered from massive head and neck injuries caused by the force and position of the blow.

Children are most at risk of airbag injury

Children—because of their size—are more likely than adults to be hit in the head by a deploying airbag and therefore are at increased risk for serious injury. Even children who are properly restrained in front car seats are in danger of being injured by an exploding passenger-side airbag. Children sitting in car seats are several inches closer to the intense forces of airbag deployment.

The majority of airbag injuries involving children occurred when infants were placed in the front seat of a car in a rear-facing child-safety-seat carrier, according to the NHTSA. These seats cannot be positioned far enough from the airbag to eliminate serious or fatal injury from the forces of the inflating airbag against the back of the restraint.

Virtually all of the older children killed by airbags were either unbelted or improperly belted in the front passenger seat, according to the NHTSA. Unbelted people are at risk because they are likely to move too close to the exploding airbag if there is hard braking or other violent maneuvers before a crash.

The airbag speed factor

Some experts say that the bags could explode at much slower speeds and still be as effective, but far less dangerous. According to automaker studies, even if the speed of deployment were reduced by 35 percent, airbags could still prevent injury and death. And according to an NHTSA study, automobile airbags that deploy at 135 mph (217 kph) are far less dangerous, yet they are fast enough to protect a belted adult in a 35 mph (56 kph) head-on collision.

Some safety experts, however, pointed out that it was not necessarily the force of the inflation that killed people, but the fact that the victims were not properly restrained or were not wearing seat belts at all. Seat belts not only restrain a person from having dangerous contact with an airbag, but also dramatically improve airbag effectiveness. When used without seat belts, airbags reduce crash fatalities by 18 percent. However, when used with a lap-shoulder belt, airbags reduce crash fatalities by nearly 50 percent.

Reducing risk of airbag injury

There are simple steps to take in reducing risk of injury from an airbag. Safety experts advise adults to learn the proper way to buckle up when riding in a vehicle and to take precautions when seating a child in a car.

To be worn correctly, a lap belt must be positioned snugly across the pelvis. If worn too high, it will impinge on the soft part of the abdomen. Incorrect use may result in harmful contact with an airbag as well as injury to the liver, spleen, intestines, bladder, kidney, and heart. *Submarining*, a phenomenon in which the pelvis sinks into the seat cushion and slips from beneath the lap belt during a collision, may occur because the occupant is slumping in the seat, the seat is in reclining position, the belt buckle lock is too high, or the belt is too loose.

The shoulder harness should be positioned over the *clavicle* (shoulder bone), sternum, and upper ribs. It should be snug, with less than 1 inch (2.54 centimeters) of slack. The harness can then provide good protection for the upper torso and ribs in a frontal impact and can prevent the body from lunging and smashing into an airbag. If

Safety tips

- Never place a child safety seat in the front seat, especially if you have a passenger-side air bag.

- Children should ride in the back seat, in proper safety seats or restraints, until they are old enough and big enough to use seat belts—usually after the age of 12.

- Children riding in the front seat should be at least 4 feet 11 inches tall.

- The safety belt should fit across the shoulder and chest, and shouldn't ride up on the neck and face.

- Infants and small children in the back seat should always ride in proper child safety seats. Older children (40 to 65 pounds) can use a booster seat and a seat belt.

- When driving, sit at least 12 inches away from the steering wheel (the deployment distance of an airbag).

- Avoid draping your hand over the top of the wheel. If you hold the wheel at the "9 and 3 o'clock" or "8 and 4 o'clock" position, your hands will be out of the way should the air bag deploy.

- If you have a passenger-side airbag, the front-seat passenger should push the seat back as far as possible.

- Never prop your feet on the dashboard.

- Don't hold packages or any items on your lap or in front of your face or chest.

Safeguarding against airbag injury

In 1997, the U.S. government and automakers proposed ways to reduce the risk of airbag injury. Until these safety measures are in place, experts advise that the best way to protect children against airbag injury is to buckle them into the backseat of the car. Infants and toddlers should always ride in car seats, *right,* in the back seat.

⚠ **WARNING**
DEATH OR SERIOUS INJURY CAN OCCUR
- CHILDREN 12 AND UNDER CAN BE KILLED BY THE AIR BAG
- THE **BACK SEAT** IS THE **SAFEST** PLACE FOR CHILDREN
- **NEVER** PUT A REAR-FACING CHILD SEAT IN THE FRONT
- SIT AS FAR BACK AS POSSIBLE FROM THE AIR BAG
- ALWAYS USE **SEAT BELTS** AND **CHILD RESTRAINTS**

The U.S. government proposed in 1996 that all new vehicles have bright interior labels warning parents that airbags can kill children.

Seat belts should fit snugly across the lap and over the shoulder of front-seat passengers, *left*. When worn properly, seat belts help restrain riders from dangerous contact with airbags.

the harness is incorrectly worn under the shoulder (often done to relieve neck irritation), the wearer is exposed to the risk of serious chest and abdominal injuries.

Children and adults under 5 feet tall should never be seated in the front passenger-seat of a car. According to the NHTSA, infants in rear-facing child-safety seats should never ride in the front seat of a vehicle equipped with a passenger-side airbag. Put rear-facing seats in the back seat facing the rear of the car. All children under 12 years old should be buckled up in the back seat. If a child or short adult must ride in the front, the seat should be adjusted as far back as possible from the dashboard.

Drivers should always buckle up and move their seat at least 10 inches back from the center of the steering wheel. The head of a driver who sits very close to the steering wheel could be in target range of an inflating airbag.

Airbag safety proposals

In 1997, the federal government and automakers were working on ways to reduce risk of airbag injury. NHTSA rolled out a five-part plan for airbags that, if adopted by Congress, would cover every passenger car and truck sold in the United States by the year 2000. The proposals ranged from allowing vehicle owners to disconnect airbags to requiring that a new generation of safer bags be phased in beginning with the 1999 model year.

The NHTSA proposal recommended that dealers or garages be allowed to unhook airbags at a customer's request; that bags deploy with 20 percent to 35 percent less power; that new vehicles have bright interior labels warning parents that airbags can kill children; that vehicles without rear seats be equipped with cutoff switches to disarm airbags; and that by 1999, automakers phase in systems with sensors that can cause airbags to inflate with a force that is appropriate and safe for a person's size and sitting position.

American automakers were working on solving the public's chief concern—airbag speed. Car manufacturers endorsed the NHTSA's proposal to power down airbags. Chrysler was developing a slower-speed airbag and expected to have it ready for the 1998 model year.

The auto industry was also developing sensors for airbags that could detect an occupant's size and adjust the speed and the size of a deployed bag accordingly. These so-called smart bags would automatically deactivate the passenger-side airbag if it sensed that a child-carrier seat was in the front seat. Airbags in 1998 Mercedes-Benz models were designed to deactivate when a child seat is placed in the front passenger seat.

The NHTSA cautioned that although technological advances could make airbags safer and more efficient, the best defense against injury rests in the hands of drivers and passengers. The agency stressed the need for a national campaign to educate people to the fact that, when used properly, airbags save—rather than destroy—lives. •••

While government agencies that help to protect the food supply revised safety regulations in 1997 agency officials cautioned the public to exercise precautions to minimize the risk of foodborne illness.

How Safe Is Our Food Supply?

By Joan Stephenson

IN MARCH 1997, MORE THAN 180 MICHIGAN SCHOOLCHILDREN and adults became ill with hepatitis A, a viral infection characterized by fever, fatigue, vomiting, and yellowing of the skin. The cause of the illness, the hepatitis A virus, was carried on frozen strawberries, later found to be imported from Mexico, that had been served as part of the national school lunch program.

The hepatitis A outbreak was only one of a number of episodes in 1996 and 1997 that focused public attention on foodborne illnesses. In the fall of 1996, a virulent strain of *Escherichia coli* bacteria—*E. coli O157:H7*—struck 66 people in the Western United States and Canada. The outbreak, in which one child died, was traced to unpasteurized apple juice.

In the summer of 1996, an exotic, tiny parasite, called cyclospora, caused some 1,000 people to develop diarrhea, which left some victims miserable for months. The foodborne *pathogen* (the microorganism that caused the disease) was eventually traced to raspberries imported from Guatemala.

In the United Kingdom, a troubling study made public in March 1996 inflamed fears that beef from cattle that had "mad cow disease" might be responsible for cases of Creutzfeldt–Jakob disease (CJD), a fatal brain disorder. CJD is a rare disease that usually affects people age 60 and older, because it develops very slowly after infection. The CJD cases in Britain, however, occurred among younger people.

Such outbreaks have heightened the concerns of public health experts and consumers alike. While the officials of government agencies that play a role in protecting the food supply began updating food safety regulations and methods in 1997, the same officials cautioned consumers to exercise precautions that will help to minimize the risk of illness. Many episodes of food poisoning are home-related—the result of improper handling, cooking, or storage of foods.

A higher incidence of food-related illnesses

As many as 9,000 people in the United States died in 1996 as a result of food-related illnesses, according to officials of the U.S. Department of Agriculture (USDA). Millions were stricken with nonfatal infections. The Council for Agricultural Science and Technology, a consortium of scientific and professional societies in Ames, Iowa, estimated that 6.5 million to 33 million food-related illnesses occur annually in the United States. The wide range of the estimate reflects uncertainty over how many people actually contract a foodborne illness. The vast majority of such illnesses are never reported to health authorities and so are never counted. Despite incomplete statistics, many health experts have come to believe that the risk of foodborne illness has increased for a variety of reasons.

One reason for the increase is easily explained. Many Americans have changed their diets and eat more fresh fruits and vegetables than they did in the past. Increased consumption of fruits and vegetables has led to increased imports of fresh produce. Some of the produce comes from developing countries where sanitary conditions and regulations are less stringent than in the United States.

Americans also consume fewer home-cooked meals than in past years. Restaurant patrons place themselves at an increased risk of exposure to pathogens transmitted by food handlers who do not practice proper sanitation and hygiene.

Mass production and processing techniques have also increased the opportunity for contaminating food. "Factory farms," in which livestock is raised in crowded conditions and antibiotics are increasingly used, foster the spread of microbes. The same conditions are suspected of promoting development of antibiotic-resistant bacteria.

The microbes themselves contribute to the problem by continually evolving, changing in ways that spell trouble at the dinner table. One relatively new threat is *E. coli O157:H7*, which was unknown before 1982. Another strain of bacteria—*Salmonella typhimurium DT104*—developed resistance to common antibiotics. An outbreak of this bacteria in the United Kingdom in 1994 resulted in the deaths of 10 people. The first outbreak of the same bacteria occurred in the United States in October 1996.

An increased incidence of food-related illnesses also may be tied to a rise in the number of people who are particularly vulnerable to infection. While anyone can be exposed to foodborne pathogens, certain groups—pregnant women, infants and young children, AIDS patients, and cancer and organ transplant patients receiving immunity-lowering treatments—are highly susceptible to infection.

The author:

Joan Stephenson is an associate editor with the *Journal of the American Medical Association*.

While the incidence of foodborne illness is believed to have increased, monitoring of the U.S. food supply by the federal government has decreased. The USDA Food Safety and Inspection Service had 12,000 inspectors on staff in 1978, compared with 7,500 in 1997. Rates of inspection of those imported foods for which the U.S. Food and Drug Administration (FDA) is responsible dropped from about 20 percent in the mid-1970's to between 1 and 2 percent in 1997. The decreases in food inspection are the result of a series of cuts made during the 1980's and 1990's to USDA and FDA budgets.

Uninvited dinner guests

Most foodborne illnesses are caused by bacteria, viruses, and parasites. While some foodborne pathogens are long-established foes of human beings—for example, species of salmonella and *campylobacter jejuni* bacteria—others are relatively new threats to the food supply—such as, *E. coli O157:H7* and cyclospora.

Symptoms of most foodborne illnesses are relatively mild, of short duration, and familiar—the vomiting and diarrhea associated with "food poisoning." Symptoms, depending on the microorganism responsible, can appear within hours after exposure or be delayed for weeks. Severity varies by degree of contamination and the state of health of the individual. Many mild infections are never diagnosed. However, a very small percentage of cases can be severe and lead to serious complications: miscarriage; reactive arthritis, a form of joint inflammation; Guillain-Barré syndrome, a paralyzing condition that is usually temporary; kidney failure; and death.

Foodborne bacteria

Bacteria are by far the most common cause of foodborne illness. Some bacteria infect otherwise healthy farm animals and remain in the meat after slaughter. Contamination also can result from tainted water used to irrigate crops, the use of tainted water or improperly maintained equipment during food processing, or the handling of food by an infected individual.

The bacteria most frequently linked to food poisoning are *campylobacter,* salmonella, shigella, and *E. coli O157:H7,* according to the Centers for Disease Control and Prevention (CDC), a federal agency in Atlanta, Georgia. Symptoms produced by these bacteria typically include nausea, vomiting, abdominal pain, and diarrhea, which in severe cases may be bloody or contain pus. Other symptoms include fever, weakness or fatigue, and headache.

Campylobacter, according to the CDC, is the most common cause of diarrheal diseases, causing 2.6 million illnesses in the United states in 1996. Researchers found the bacteria in 45 percent of human stool samples from patients with diarrhea. The most common source of *campylobacter* is contaminated poultry, but these bacteria also can be found in raw milk or untreated water or picked up from

Food inspection by sight, touch, and smell

The USDA method of inspection, called the "see-touch-smell" approach, remained unchanged from 1906—when food inspection was inaugurated—until 1996.

USDA inspectors in the early 1900's examine hog carcasses at the final point of processing before the meat is refrigerated.

A USDA meat inspector touches and smells carcasses for signs of disease or tainting, a method that is ineffective against microscopic pathogens.

infected dogs and cats. Two to four days after ingestion, *campylobacter* infection causes cramps, fever, and diarrhea, which can be bloody.

Salmonella infections, while less common than those caused by *campylobacter*, are deadlier, resulting in approximately 500 deaths annually in the United States. In addition to symptoms typical of food poisoning, salmonella infections can trigger reactive arthritis. These bacteria are commonly found in uncooked or undercooked poultry and are also present in meat and meat products, dairy products, and seafood. Eggs laid by infected hens can become tainted with a strain of salmonella even when uncracked. The bacteria have also been detected in fresh produce, such as cantaloupes, lettuce, tomatoes, and alfalfa sprouts.

Although *E. coli* is a normal resident of the human digestive tract, some strains produce a *toxin* (a substance that acts as a poison) that can be fatal, particularly in the very young and elderly. One such virulent strain, *E. coli O157:H7*, is responsible for about 25,000 cases of foodborne illness each year in the United States. In addition to producing typical gastrointestinal symptoms, including bloody diarrhea, infection can lead to the potentially fatal hemolytic uremic syn-

The HACCP food inspection system

The Pathogen Reduction and Hazard Analysis and Critical Control Points (HACCP) system of food inspection, put into effect in 1997, identifies various points in the processing procedure where microbes and other hazardous substances could be introduced into food.

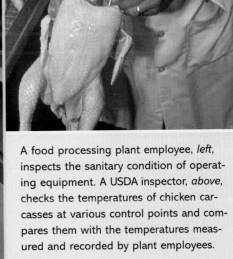

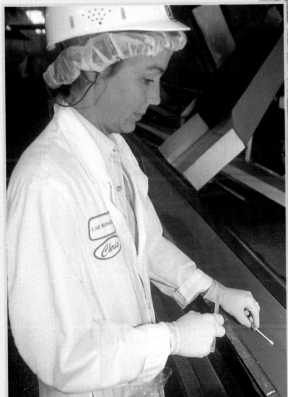

A food processing plant employee, *left,* inspects the sanitary condition of operating equipment. A USDA inspector, *above,* checks the temperatures of chicken carcasses at various control points and compares them with the temperatures measured and recorded by plant employees.

A USDA food inspector, *left,* verifies that a food processing plant temperature recorder is accurate and complies with HACCP procedures.

181

Common sources of infection

E. coli 0157:H7 bacteria

- *Sources of infection*
  Bacteria in cattle feces often contaminate meat or milk. The organism has also been detected in unpasteurized apple juice and cider, yogurt, green vegetables, and salami.

- *Symptoms of infection*
  Abdominal cramps, bloody diarrhea, possible kidney failure, and death.

- *Major outbreaks since 1990*
  United States, 1993: Four children died and 700 people in the Pacific Northwest were sickened from eating undercooked hamburgers containing *E. coli* bacteria.
  Japan, 1996: An outbreak of unknown origin left 11 people dead and more than 9,000 ill.
  United States, 1996: Forty people were poisoned and a child died from drinking unpasteurized apple juice contaminated with *E. coli* 0157:H7.

Salmonella bacteria

- *Sources of infection*
  The organism is most often found in raw poultry and meat, unpasteurized milk, and mollusk shellfish. It can be spread between humans through poor hygiene.

- *Symptoms of infection*
  Nausea, stomach pain, diarrhea, chills, fever, and headache that normally appear 6 to 48 hours after eating contaminated food.

- *Major outbreaks since 1990*
  United States 1994: Nearly 225,000 people nationwide were sickened after eating ice cream made from a premix that had been transported in a truck that also had carried liquid eggs.
  United States, 1995: Unpasteurized orange juice sickened more than 60 vacationers at Disney World in Orlando, Florida.
  United States, Canada, and Finland, 1995: Salmonella in alfalfa sprouts sickened more than 200 people.

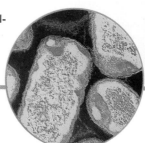

drome, which causes kidney failure. *E. coli 0157:H7* has been detected in ground beef, salami, mayonnaise-based salad dressings, raw milk, yogurt, lettuce, and fresh and unpasteurized fruit juices.

Shigella infections, while often mild, can cause serious illness and may be fatal to infants who are not diagnosed and treated. The bacteria are present in the feces of an infected person and can be spread when infected food handlers fail to wash their hands thoroughly after using the toilet or after changing diapers of infected children. Because shigella is introduced through handling, it is most commonly found in foods that are not subsequently cooked.

In some cases, foodborne bacteria inflict their damage by producing a toxin. The most notorious example is a fairly rare condition

Hepatitis A virus

- *Sources of infection*
  The virus is absorbed orally through contaminated food and water and transmitted through human waste.

- *Symptoms of infection*
  Fever, fatigue, loss of appetite, nausea, abdominal cramps, dark urine, inflammation of the liver, and yellowing of skin and eyes.

- *Major outbreaks since 1990*
  United States, 1997: More than 275 students in Michigan were infected after eating strawberries. The strawberries, which were raised in Mexico, were illegally purchased and processed for the U.S. school lunch program and served to children in six states.

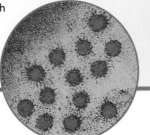

Cyclospora intestinal parasite

- *Sources of infection*
  The parasite is commonly absorbed orally through contaminated fruits and vegetables and transmitted via human waste allowed to pollute water.

- *Symptoms of infection*
  Diarrhea and abdominal cramps.

- *Major outbreaks since 1990*
  North America, 1996: Nearly 1,500 people in 15 U.S. states and in Canada were sickened by an outbreak traced to raspberries imported from Guatemala.

called botulism, caused by a deadly toxin of the common soil bacterium *Clostridium botulinum*. Tiny amounts of this substance, sometimes found in improperly canned food, can cause paralysis and death. A more common bacterial toxin, produced by *Staphylococcus aureus* (a bacterium that thrives naturally in the respiratory tract), typically causes nausea, vomiting, and diarrhea.

Foodborne viruses

Foodborne viruses, such as the hepatitis A virus and Norwalk virus, are less common than foodborne bacteria but can trigger very serious illnesses. In many developing countries, the hepatitis A virus is typically spread through unsanitary water supplies and by eating shellfish. In the United States, the virus is often spread by infected food handlers. Norwalk virus is the most frequent source of foodborne illness in the United States, causing an estimated 181,000 infections annually. Unlike hepatitis A infections, where symptoms appear two to six weeks after exposure, the effects of Norwalk virus (abdominal pain, nausea, vomiting, and diarrhea) usually appear within 12 to 48 hours. The most common source is shellfish, such as oysters.

Foodborne parasites

Parasites are a third significant cause of foodborne illness. Although cyclospora linked to contaminated raspberries from Guatemala captured headlines in 1996, outbreaks caused by this microbe have been rare in North America. A far greater problem is the parasitic, one-celled *Toxoplasma gondii*, which causes an estimated 1.4 million cases of disease and 300 deaths annually in the United States. Patients with weakened immune systems are particularly susceptible. People are usually infected by consuming tainted raw or undercooked meat or through contact with the feces of infected cats. Unwashed fruits and vegetables also may be a source of infection.

"Mad cow disease"

In March 1996, public health officials became concerned about a possible link between "mad cow disease"—bovine spongiform encephalopathy (BSE)—and certain cases of Creutzfeldt–Jakob disease. BSE is a disease that infects the brains of cattle, leaving the organ with a spongy appearance. The BSE epidemic that swept British cattle herds starting in 1986 was traced to animal feed containing protein supplements made from the remains of sheep infected with scrapie, a related disease. Although the infectious agent remains unknown, a widely accepted theory holds that it is a bizarre form of a normal cell protein, called a prion. British scientists have suggested that a small number of people may have contracted a variant form of CJD by eating beef from cattle infected with BSE. The variant form strikes people under the age of 30, an unusually young age for this disease.

   While this link remained unproven, the British government agreed in 1996 to destroy more than 100,000 cattle at risk for BSE. The United States, which has never detected BSE within its own borders, in 1989 banned the importation of processed beef or cattle from the United Kingdom. The United States imposed similar restrictions on imports from other countries where BSE has been found.

Government safeguards from farm to fork

The responsibility for ensuring the safety of America's food supply from farm to fork is shared by all levels of government—federal, state, and local—as well as by the food industry itself. Various federal agencies, along with state agricultural agencies, are concerned with the safety of the food supply from its origin on the American farm. The FDA oversees the use of drugs and feed in milk- and food-

Regulating the jungle

In 1906, Upton Sinclair, a writer for a socialist newspaper, published *The Jungle,* a novel about working conditions in the U.S. meat-packing industry at the turn of the century. The book described revolting conditions in the processing plants of Chicago's stockyards: filth and vermin on meat; standing water that could breed disease; the butchering of animals, diseased and even long dead. Characters recall scenes of workmen falling into tanks of animal parts and being ground up, then rendered into lard. Describing *The Jungle,* historian Stewart H. Holbrook wrote: "The grunts, the groans, the agonized squeals of animals being butchered, the rivers of blood, the steaming masses of intestines, the various stenches were displayed along with the corruption of government inspectors."

The Jungle, an immediate best seller, shocked the public, which demanded reform. While claiming the novel exaggerated working conditions, President Theodore Roosevelt and progressive politicians nevertheless quickly responded to the pressure. On June 30, 1906, the Pure Food & Drug Act was passed, prohibiting the sale of adulterated foods and drugs and demanding that product contents be honestly stated on labels. Later in 1906, Congress passed the Meat Inspection Act, which required that meat plants maintain sanitary conditions and mandated federal inspection of any plant involved in interstate commerce.

Ironically, Upton Sinclair had not written *The Jungle* intending to reform either the meat-packing industry or government. The novel was the author's revolutionary call to replace the existing capitalist system with a socialist state. "I aimed at the public's heart and by accident I hit it in the stomach," wrote Sinclair, who disliked both the Pure Food & Drug and Meat Inspection acts. They prolonged the existing social structure, which Sinclair regarded as too corrupt to fix.

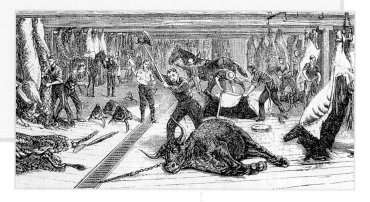

producing animals, and the USDA deals with the control of diseases of farm animals. Federal agencies also scrutinize activities on the nation's farms that could contaminate land or water through the discharge of solid wastes or wastewater.

The federal government plays a role in regulating food processing, as well. The USDA's Food Safety and Inspection Service (FSIS) has the responsibility of monitoring the country's commercial supply of meat, poultry, and egg products (as opposed to eggs in the shell). Inspectors from the FSIS examine nearly 6,000 slaughterhouses and processing plants to help ensure that these facilities are safe. The FSIS also inspects a wide range of processed products, such as hams, sausage, pizzas, stews, and frozen dinners.

In 1996, the USDA revised its inspection system, which had been in place for 90 years. The old system employed a "see-touch-smell" approach. Inspectors examined carcasses moving down processing lines for inflammation or other signs of disease. While the method kept food from visibly diseased animals or food tainted with dirt, in-

How consumers can protect themselves

Consumers need to carefully oversee how food in the home is stored, prepared, and cooked.

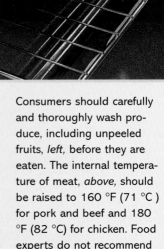

Consumers should carefully and thoroughly wash produce, including unpeeled fruits, *left,* before they are eaten. The internal temperature of meat, *above,* should be raised to 160 °F (71 °C) for pork and beef and 180 °F (82 °C) for chicken. Food experts do not recommend that meat be eaten rare.

Refrigerated meat, *left,* should be carefully covered or stored in containers so that juices do not drip onto lower shelves. Raw meat should be stored separately from other foods. Cooked foods should be stored separately from raw foods that could be infected. Refrigerate leftovers immediately.

sects, or animal droppings from reaching the consumer, it was ineffective against microscopic pathogens. The new system for food inspection, called the Pathogen Reduction and Hazard Analysis and Critical Control Points (HACCP) system, was partially put into effect in January 1997.

Tighter controls on food inspection

The FSIS formulated a plan to overhaul its traditional inspection system following a serious outbreak in 1993 of *E. coli O157:H7*, which was linked to undercooked hamburgers served at a fast-food chain in the Western United States. Under the agency's revised HACCP system, processors of meat, poultry, and seafood are required to take a more preventive approach. This system first involves identifying various points in the processing procedure where microbes and other hazardous substances could be introduced into food. The second step involves adopting strategies to prevent or eliminate contamination.

The regulations adopted in 1996 also require slaughterhouses to regularly test carcasses for bacteria levels. These plants, and others that process raw ground meat products, are expected to meet certain standards for controlling salmonella bacteria. Plants that fall short are required to correct the problem or face being closed down. Food safety experts expect that measures aimed at preventing and reducing salmonella contamination will also reduce contamination by other disease-causing bacteria. The new system also requires plants that process raw ground meat, such as hamburger, to conduct routine tests for *E. coli O157:H7*.

The FDA plays a role in regulating the safe processing of food and is charged with performing periodic spot inspections of more than 50,000 processing plants. With fewer than 700 inspectors and analysts devoted to this task in 1997, inspections were focused on foods and processing techniques that posed the greatest threat to the health of the public. State and local governments also play varying roles in inspecting food processors.

Like the USDA, the FDA has redesigned its food safety system and worked with the food processing industry to set up HACCP systems. Under

Store food safely

- Keep stored meat refrigerated or frozen.
- Keep raw meat separate from other foods.
- Keep cooked foods separate from raw foods that could possibly be infected.
- Do not allow meat juices to drip onto a refrigerator shelf where other food is stored.
- Refrigerate leftovers immediately or discard them.

Prepare food safely

- Thaw meat in a refrigerator or microwave.
- Wash cooking surfaces, utensils, and hands after touching raw meat, poultry, and eggs.
- Wash cutting boards after chopping raw meat and poultry parts.
- Wash counters and sinks with antibacterial cleanser and pour the antibacterial cleanser through the garbage disposal.
- Pour boiling water over pot scrubbers.
- Wash hands after going to the bathroom.
- Do not feed raw meat, such as unused turkey parts, to pets.

Cook food safely

- Cook meat thoroughly: 160 °F (71 °C) for pork and beef and 180 °F (82 °C) for poultry.
- Keep hot foods hot.
- Do not cook a stuffed bird in a microwave.
- Cover food to be cooked in a microwave with plastic wrap or a dish to allow bacteria-killing steam to heat up the surface of the food.

rules that went into effect in January 1996, an HACCP system was applied, for the first time, to seafood. The agency had previously relied primarily on unannounced spot inspections of seafood processors to uncover problems. The HACCP system required the nation's 5,000 seafood-processing plants to identify those factors—for example, failure to keep the catch cold during transportation—that could contribute to microbial contamination.

Businesses and institutions that sell food products or prepare and serve food to consumers are another link in the chain from farm and fishery to fork. State and local health authorities, under the guidance of the FDA, generally are charged with overseeing food safety in institutions, such as hospitals and nursing homes, as well as in restaurants, schools, and grocery stores.

Both the Food and Drug Administration and the Department of Agriculture's Food Safety and Inspection Service play a role in overseeing the safety of imported foods. If an imported item is suspected of being unsafe, these agencies can test it for contamination and bar its entry into the United States.

Tracking down pathogens

When safeguards fail and people become ill, local, state, and federal agencies may step in to investigate. Physicians who suspect a foodborne pathogen problem should alert health departments, which in turn can contact the CDC for help in identifying a pathogen, pinpointing the source of infection, and containing outbreaks. Containment is usually carried out by recalling any suspect food and warning the public. However, such investigations only occur in response to existing outbreaks.

In 1995, the CDC, the FSIS, and state and local health departments launched a surveillance network, dubbed "FoodNet," in parts of California, Connecticut, Georgia, Minnesota, and Oregon in an attempt to spot problems before they get out of hand. President Bill Clinton's January 1997 announcement that the 1998 budget included a $43-million initiative aimed at improving the safety of the nation's food supply brought hopes of additional improvements. The president asked the USDA, the Environmental Protection Agency, and the Department of Health and Human Services (of which the FDA and CDC are part), to provide recommendations to safeguard the food supply. One suggested improvement was the creation of a new "early warning system" (including an expansion of FoodNet) for prompt detection of outbreaks of foodborne disease, making it possible to curtail their spread. An innovation already underway at the time of the president's announcement was the creation of an electronic network that would allow state public health laboratories to compare the genetic material, or DNA fingerprints, of microbes causing illness across the country. Such a tool will enable laboratories to quickly establish if distant cases stem from the same food source.

Food safety at home

The final link in the farm-to-fork chain is the home, where many cases of foodborne illness can be traced to improper handling or storage of food. Food safety experts recommend certain precautions to reduce the risk of developing a foodborne illness: defrost meat in the refrigerator; thoroughly wash one's hands and kitchen counters before and during food preparation; thoroughly wash all produce; and thoroughly cook meat—160 °F (71 °C) for pork and beef and 180 °F (82 °C) for poultry.

If precautions involved in the safe handling of food fail, be aware that most cases of food poisoning can be treated at home. Experts advise drinking clear liquids, such as pasteurized apple juice, to replenish lost fluids. They also suggest a diet of bland foods, such as bananas, rice, applesauce, and toast, after vomiting and diarrhea subside. Most symptoms are gone within a day or two.

Infectious disease experts advise calling a doctor or making a trip to the emergency room if there are signs of a more serious foodborne infection, such as difficulty in keeping fluids down, repeated vomiting, severe or bloody diarrhea, or a fever that lasts more than 24 hours. Infants and children suffering from repeated bouts of vomiting or diarrhea become dehydrated especially quickly and should receive medical attention without delay.

In eating, as in life, it is impossible to avoid all risk. Experts believe that the new technologies and ongoing improvements by government agencies will improve the safety of the food supply. Consumers, however, must do their own part. Handwashing, practicing good kitchen hygiene, storing and preparing food properly reduces the chance of having what you sink your teeth into bite back.   • • •

For further information:

The USDA's Meat and Poultry Hotline provides information about the safe handling of meat and poultry, including storage, cooking times and temperatures, and other questions about food safety. The toll-free number is 1-800-535-4555

Web site: http://www.usda.gov/agency/fsis/consedu.htm

The FDA's Seafood Hotline answers questions about seafood safety and other food safety issues. The toll-free number is 1-800-332-4101.

Web site: http://vm.cfsan.fda.gov/list.html

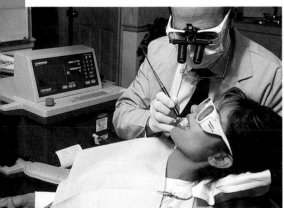

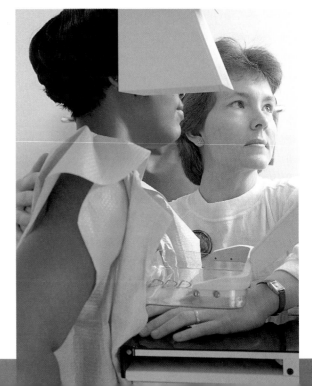

HEALTH UPDATES

- Estrogen and wrinkles
- Alendronate
  and bone fractures
- Fall-related hip fractures

Estrogen therapy, frequently used to help protect older women against bone loss and fractures, may prevent dry skin and wrinkling, according to a March 1997 report by scientists at the University of California at San Francisco and Los Angeles. Estrogen is a hormone produced mainly by the ovaries. While a woman is in her 30's, estrogen levels begin a gradual decline that accelerates when she reaches her 40's. Hormone levels continue to drop until they become so low that menstruation ceases, a condition that triggers menopause.

In an attempt to link estrogen use with skin wrinkling, dryness, and *atrophy* (the loss of thickness and elasticity in the skin), the researchers studied data on 3,875 women who had been enrolled in the First National Health and Nutrition Examination Survey (NHANES I). NHANES I, a study conducted by the National Center for Health Statistics in Hyattsville, Maryland, between 1971 and 1974, collected information on the health status of older Americans. The women in the NHANES I study were at least 40 years old and were past menopause.

Because information on the use of estrogen was not collected in NHANES I, the researchers obtained data on estrogen use on 3,403 women from follow-up surveys conducted between 1982 and 1986. The survey asked the women whether they

had taken female hormone pills for reasons related to menopause.

Of those women surveyed, 1,132 had dry skin; 499 had skin atrophy; and 880 had wrinkled skin. After adjusting for age, body weight, and lifestyle factors that cause skin damage, such as exposure to sunlight and smoking, the researchers discovered that estrogen therapy reduced the likelihood of developing dry skin by 25 percent and wrinkling by 30 percent. Estrogen did not have any impact on skin atrophy. The researchers concluded that estrogen therapy can combat some of the aspects of aging.

Alendronate and bone fractures.
Women who have postmenopausal *osteoporosis* (decreased bone density) and are treated with alendronate sodium, a nonhormonal drug that increases the strength of bones, can reduce the risk of wrist and hip fractures, according to an international research study published in April 1997. Alendronate sodium was approved by the U.S. Food and Drug Administration in 1995. The drug increases bone strength because it slows down the natural destruction of bone tissue, thereby allowing new bone formation to exceed bone loss.

Osteoporosis is a progressive disease that causes bones to become more prone to fracture. It affects more than 25 million Americans,

Four factors in maintaining mental agility

The results of a study by researchers at Harvard, Yale, and Duke Universities showed these four factors can help people maintain mental agility:

- Education, which appears to increase the number and strength of connections between brain cells.
- Strenuous activity, which improves blood flow to the brain.
- Lung function, which ensures that the blood is adequately oxygenated.
- The feeling that what you do makes a difference in your life.

Source: MacArthur Foundation Research Network on Successful Aging.

about 80 percent of whom are women. It occurs most commonly in women who have reached menopause. After menopause, a woman's body almost completely stops producing estrogen. Research has shown that this reduced level of estrogen after menopause causes the rate of new bone formation to decrease. In women with postmenopausal osteoporosis, the rate of natural bone loss significantly exceeds the rate of new bone formation.

An international group of researchers followed 1,602 women between the ages of 42 and 85 who had been diagnosed with osteoporosis and were past menopause for at least four years. The women, who were part of the Alendronate Osteoporosis Treatment Study Groups, were divided into two groups. One treatment group, consisting of 1,012 women, received alendronate sodium at a dose higher than 1 milligram per day. The control group, made up of the remaining 590 women, received a *placebo* (an inactive substance).

Researchers monitored the women's bone density and recorded all bone fractures over a period of two years. The researchers concluded that the rate of wrist and hip fracture in the group that received alendronate sodium was 9 percent, compared with a rate of 12.6 percent in the placebo group. The researchers concluded that alendronate sodium reduces the risk of wrist and hip fracture by increasing the strength of bones.

Fall-related hip fractures. Neurologic, muscular, and visual impairments place older women at risk for falls and, therefore, fractures of the hip, according to a study reported in July 1996 by researchers at the Epidemiologie de l' Osteoporose (EPIDOS) in France.

In the study, the scientists tested 7,575 women for muscle and bone strength, walking and balance ability, visual function, and use of medications. The women, who were 75 years of age or older and had no history of hip fracture, were then contacted by mail or telephone every four months for almost two years and asked whether they had experienced a fracture of the hip. During the fol-

Medic Alert celebrates 40th anniversary

Medic Alert, a nonprofit organization located in Turlock, California, that provides quickly accessible, vital personal medical information during emergency situations, marked its 40th anniversary in 1996. Vital medical facts are engraved on the backs of bracelets worn by members—information that has proved to save a patient's life if he or she is unconscious or unable to speak. The following are some facts about Medic Alert and its 40-year history:

- According to the company, the information on the bracelets has contributed to saving the lives of 80,000 members.

- An estimated 3.8 million people in 45 countries wear Medic Alert bracelets.

- A wide range of alerts to special conditions can be engraved on bracelets, including allergies; medications needed; diabetes; heart conditions; hepatitis; stroke condition; Alzheimer's disease; bleeding or clotting disorders; and hearing, vision, or speech impairment.

- The initial cost of a Medic Alert membership in 1997 was $35, with a $15 annual fee beginning in the second year. Records are updated as often as necessary at no charge for annual subscribers.

Source: Medic Alert.

low-up period, 154 women reported having had a hip fracture. The researchers compared the women who reported a fracture against those women who did not have a fracture.

Although increasing age and loss of bone strength are factors that can lead to fractures, the researchers reported four additional risk factors for hip fracture: slow walking speed; difficulty in heel-to-toe, or tandem, walking; weak lower-leg muscle strength; and reduced vision. The scientists concluded that some hip fractures might be prevented by identifying the presence of these problems as well as by finding new ways to increase bone strength.   • Rein Tideiksaar

See also NUTRITION. In WORLD BOOK, see AGING.

- U.S. AIDS deaths decrease
- International AIDS cases increase
- New drugs slow virus
- AIDS treatment guidelines
- *Time* magazine honoree
- Thalidomide and AIDS
- Gene linked to AIDS resistance
- HIV-infected pregnant women
- New treatment for Kaposi's sarcoma

The number of AIDS deaths decreased dramatically in the United States during the first half of 1996, according to a February 1997 report by the U.S. Centers for Disease Control and Prevention (CDC) in Atlanta, Georgia. Doctors credited improvements in AIDS treatments for the 13 percent drop—the first significant drop in deaths since the CDC began tracking the disease in 1981.

CDC statistics showed that an estimated 22,000 people died of AIDS in the first six months of 1996, compared with 24,900 deaths in the first six months of 1995. During that same period, however, the number of people newly diagnosed with AIDS continued to climb, though at a slower pace than in previous years. People who contracted the disease through heterosexual sex accounted for the greatest percentage of increase in new AIDS cases. According to the CDC, 573,800 Americans aged 13 and older were diagnosed with AIDS between 1981 and 1996. Men accounted for 85 percent of these cases, though the number of women diagnosed with AIDS was rising steadily.

International AIDS cases increase. The number of new AIDS cases continued to skyrocket in many developing countries, according to a statement issued by the Joint United

Nations Programme on HIV/AIDS (UNAIDS) on World AIDS Day, Dec. 1, 1996. Peter Piot, executive director of UNAIDS, reported that worldwide about 8,500 people per day—more than five people every minute—are newly infected with HIV (human immunodeficiency virus), the virus that causes AIDS. About 90 percent of people with HIV/AIDS live in developing countries. An estimated 8.4 million people had been diagnosed with AIDS since 1981. In 1996, about 1.5 million people (including 350,000 children) died from AIDS-related illnesses.

The UNAIDS report also stated that AIDS cases were rising in previously unaffected countries, such as China and Vietnam, and in many countries in central and eastern Europe. And in some hard-hit African countries, overall life expectancy had fallen by up to 10 years because of the AIDS crisis.

New drugs slow virus. Results from several studies showed that powerful new antiviral drugs called protease inhibitors slow the progression of AIDS and restore the function of the immune system when used in combination with older drugs, such as AZT (zidovudine) and 3TC (lamivudine). Protease inhibitors block the production of an enzyme called protease, a substance that HIV uses to *replicate* (reproduce) itself in the body.

AIDS deaths in the United States dropped significantly during the first half of 1996—the first such drop since the Centers for Disease Control and Prevention (CDC) in Atlanta, Georgia, began tracking the disease in 1981. According to the CDC, 22,000 people died of AIDS in the first six months of 1996. During that same period in 1995, 24,900 people died of AIDS. The CDC reported the drop in February 1997.

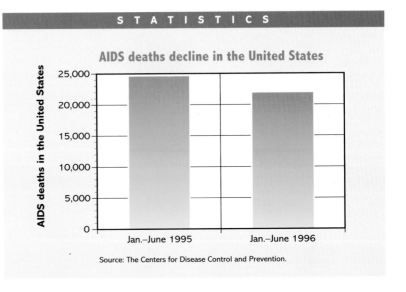

S T A T I S T I C S

AIDS deaths decline in the United States

AIDS deaths in the United States

25,000
20,000
15,000
10,000
5,000
0

Jan.–June 1995   Jan.–June 1996

Source: The Centers for Disease Control and Prevention.

In March 1997, the U.S. Food and Drug Administration (FDA) approved a new protease inhibitor called nelfinavir (marketed as Viracept). Other drugs in this class include ritonavir (Norvir), saquinavir (Invirase), and indinavir (Crixivan).

Studies showed that scientists had made remarkable progress in treating AIDS with the new combination drug therapy. Researchers at the Aaron Diamond AIDS Research Center in New York City gave ritonavir, AZT, and 3TC to nine patients who began the treatment within 90 days of acquiring an HIV infection. The researchers reported at the 11th International Conference on AIDS in July 1996 in Vancouver, British Columbia, that the AIDS virus was undetectable for as long as 300 days after the patients began taking the "drug cocktail."

In January 1997, researchers at University Hospitals of Cleveland and Case Western Reserve University reported that this same drug combination restored partial functioning of the immune system in patients with moderately advanced HIV infection. The study, presented at the Fourth Conference on Retroviruses and Opportunistic Infections in Washington, D.C., suggested that these drug treatments strengthen the immune system, which fights the so-called "opportunistic" infections (such as the cancer Kaposi's sarcoma) that often kill AIDS patients.

Although researchers called the drug combination therapy a major breakthrough in the treatment of HIV/AIDS, they cautioned that no studies had proved that the drugs cured the disease. The researchers also noted that there was no way to know how long the drugs' beneficial effects would last. In addition, in June 1997 the FDA warned doctors that a small number of patients taking protease inhibitors developed diabetes, and some patients who already had diabetes experienced a worsening of the condition. The FDA recommended that AIDS patients continue taking protease inhibitors, but that doctors monitor patients for signs of diabetes.

AIDS treatment guidelines. A panel of AIDS experts convened by the federal government announced guidelines in June 1997 for treating AIDS.

The panel was formed to help physicians determine when to begin treating people infected with HIV and which drugs—that can be used in more than 300 combinations—should be used.

According to the panel, AIDS treatment should be administered immediately to individuals with symptoms of the disease, regardless of the level of virus in their blood. Doctors should begin treatment with a "drug cocktail" consisting of one protease inhibitor and two additional medications, such as AZT and 3TC.

Time **magazine honoree.** *Time* magazine selected AIDS researcher David Ho as its "Man of the Year" in its Dec. 30, 1996-Jan. 6, 1997, is-

The AIDS Memorial Quilt, made up of more than 40,000 panels commemorating people who have died of AIDS, is spread over 11 city blocks in Washington, D.C., in October 1996. Although the number of people infected with AIDS continued to rise, the death rate from AIDS in the United States dropped dramatically in the first half of 1996. Doctors attributed the drop to improvements in AIDS treatment.

AIDS

AIDS "drug cocktail"

In June 1997, a panel of AIDS experts convened by the federal government recommended that people who have symptoms of AIDS begin immediate treatment with a new combination drug therapy, or "drug cocktail." The drug cocktail consists of one protease inhibitor (which blocks the production of an enzyme called protease) and two older AIDS drugs, such as AZT and 3TC.

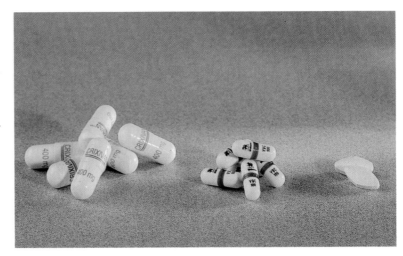

sue. Ho, director of the Aaron Diamond AIDS Research Center, pioneered in treating individuals in the earliest stages of infection with combination drug therapies. His drug treatment studies "fundamentally changed the way scientists looked at the AIDS virus," according to *Time.*

Thalidomide and AIDS. Researchers reported in May 1997 that thalidomide, a drug outlawed in the United States after it was found to cause severe birth defects, was effective in treating the aphthous mouth ulcers sometimes developed by people infected with HIV. The painful ulcers can destroy tissue in the mouths of

HIV-infected individuals whose weakened immune systems cannot fight infections and heal sores.

The research team, made up of doctors throughout the United States, gave daily doses of thalidomide to 29 HIV-infected individuals. The women participating in the study were carefully screened and monitored to ensure that they were not pregnant. Twenty-eight other participants with HIV were given a *placebo* (inactive substance). After four weeks, the mouth ulcers healed completely in 55 percent of the patients who had received thalidomide. The ulcers healed in only 7 percent of the patients who had received a placebo.

About 75 percent of people in the world infected with HIV acquired the virus through heterosexual sex, according to a United Nations Programme on HIV/-AIDS report in July 1996. The Centers for Disease Control and Prevention reported that homosexual sex was the most common method of transmission, accounting for 51 percent of all HIV infections in the United States. Blood transfusion was the least likely method of acquiring HIV, contributing to only 5 percent of AIDS cases worldwide and 1 percent of cases in the United States.

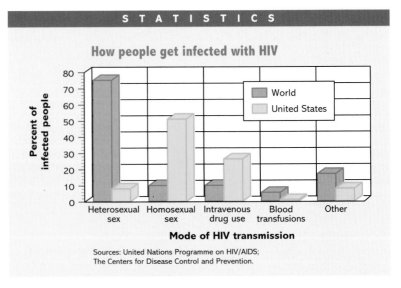

Sources: United Nations Programme on HIV/AIDS; The Centers for Disease Control and Prevention.

Gene linked to AIDS resistance.
Scientists reported in August 1996 that some people have genes that protect them from AIDS even if they are repeatedly exposed to the virus. Researchers at the Aaron Diamond AIDS Research Center found that people who inherit a copy of a defective gene called CCR5 (or CKR-5) from each parent are highly resistant to HIV. Those who inherit the gene from just one parent may have limited protection against the virus.

This finding, based on research involving 1,400 people, explained why about 1 in every 100 Caucasians is unaffected by exposure to HIV. Researchers hoped that by mimicking the activity of the mutated gene they could create a drug to prevent HIV infection. Mutated CCR5 seems to cause no other abnormalities.

HIV-infected pregnant women who receive regular obstetrical care and take oral antiviral medications can reduce the chances of transmitting the virus to their unborn baby, according to a study by Yale University School of Medicine researchers in New Haven, Connecticut. The researchers reported in April 1997 that this strategy cut the rate of HIV transmission from mother to child from 19 to 5 percent.

Yale obstetricians cared for 245 HIV-infected pregnant women who took the drug AZT throughout their pregnancies. The reduction in the incidence of HIV infections among the 267 infants born to the women was so dramatic that Yale doctors suggested that a test for the presence of HIV be made available to all women of child bearing age and that oral AZT be offered to all HIV-infected women during pregnancy.

New treatment for Kaposi's. Researchers at the University of Southern California in Los Angeles, the University of Maryland in Baltimore, and institutions in Paris and in Brussels, Belgium, discovered that the pregnancy hormone called human chorionic gonadotropin (HCG) attacks Kaposi's sarcoma, the purplish skin cancer responsible for about one-third of AIDS deaths. Injections of HCG destroyed the tumors in some patients, according to studies published in 1996.

The researchers injected varying doses of HCG into the skin lesions or tumors of 36 men with Kaposi's sarcoma. The higher the dosage of HCG administered, the more completely the tumor regressed. The tumors vanished in 10 of the 12 patients who received the highest dose of HCG. The researchers theorized that HCG attaches to receptors on the cancer cells and stimulates a natural form of cell death called apoptosis.

• Richard Trubo

In WORLD BOOK, see AIDS.

Two studies published in June 1997 reported that laboratory animals given large amounts of marijuana experienced changes in brain chemistry identical to those seen in people who abuse powerful drugs such as heroin and cocaine. These studies provided evidence that *chronic* (long-term) marijuana use may cause brain changes in people that could lead to the use of more potent drugs.

One of the studies, conducted by researchers at the University of Cagliari in Italy, examined the brain chemistry involved in producing a drug-induced "high." The researchers found that rats injected with a synthetic form of marijuana experienced a huge surge in the amounts of *dopamine* (the chemical that causes a high) produced in their brains. A similar surge occurred in rats given heroin. The researchers said that chronically elevated amounts of dopamine lead to a reduced ability of the brain to produce dopamine. A reduced ability to produce dopamine makes it increasingly difficult to achieve a drug-induced high, which may lead people to try more potent drugs, according to the researchers.

A second study, by researchers at Complutense University in Madrid, Spain, and Scripps Research Institute in La Jolla, California, examined the brain chemistry involved in *withdrawal* (a condition of extreme anxiety experienced by drug addicts who sud-

- Marijuana use may lead to stronger drugs
- Marijuana use on the rise
- The ease of getting marijuana
- "Speed" rises in popularity
- Drunk-driving laws get tougher
- Alcohol abuse among elderly
- Herbal stimulant regulated
- Drug treatment reduces crime

Alcohol and Drug Abuse

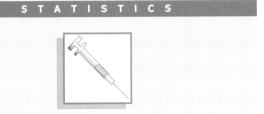

Heroin use on the rise

Research indicates that the use of heroin in the United States doubled between the mid-1980's and the mid-1990's. This increase was reflected in the number of emergency room cases related to overdoses of heroin or morphine (the drug that heroin is made from) and to the detoxification of heroin or morphine addicts. Detoxification is a process that eliminates drugs from the body.

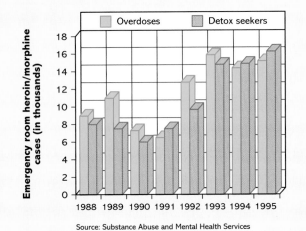

Source: Substance Abuse and Mental Health Services Administration, Drug Abuse Warning Network.

denly stop using drugs). The researchers found that when rats given regular injections of synthetic marijuana were given another drug to block the effects of the marijuana, their brains produced greatly elevated levels of a chemical called *corticotropin-releasing factor,* which causes the anxiety of withdrawal. The study provided evidence that marijuana can lead to symptoms of withdrawal similar to those caused by other drugs. The researchers said that, in order to prevent symptoms of withdrawal, marijuana users may feel compelled to keep using marijuana and, eventually, to turn to stronger drugs. The researchers said the findings of these studies apply to human beings, because there are a number of similari-

ties in the way in which human and rat brains respond to drugs.

Marijuana use on the rise. A nationwide survey reported in December 1996 that marijuana use continues to increase among American teen-agers. This finding was reported in the 1996 edition of the Monitoring the Future Survey, an annual study of the drug habits of United States youth conducted by the University of Michigan at Ann Arbor.

The survey revealed that the number of eighth-graders who used marijuana sometime during their lives increased from 19.9 percent in 1995 to 23.1 percent in 1996—continuing an upward trend seen throughout the 1990's. Among 10th-graders, the percentages increased from 34.1 in 1995 to 39.8 in 1996. The percentages of high school seniors who had used the drug increased from 41.7 in 1995 to 44.9 in 1996.

The ease of getting marijuana. A national telephone survey published in September 1996 found that about one-third of U.S. young people aged 12 to 17 think that marijuana is easier to buy than cigarettes or beer. The survey, sponsored by the National Center on Addiction and Substance Abuse at Columbia University in New York City, also indicated that the drug becomes easier to obtain as an individual gets older.

Of the 17-year-olds surveyed, 47 percent thought that marijuana was easier to buy than cigarettes or beer, and 68 percent of 17-year-olds said that they would be able to purchase marijuana within a day.

"Speed" rises in popularity. The number of U.S. high school seniors who had used methamphetamine (a drug also known as speed, ice, and crank) increased from 2.7 percent in 1990 to 4.4 percent in 1996. This finding was reported in the 1996 Monitoring the Future Survey. The survey was just one of many studies in 1996 and 1997 that reported a growing popularity of methamphetamine use among Americans.

Methamphetamine is a highly toxic stimulant that is smoked, snorted, injected, or taken as pills. It quickly produces feelings of joy, strength, and alertness, but excessive use of the drug can radically alter an individual's personality—making a person enraged, paranoid, homicidal, or suicidal. Permanent brain damage can result from the use of the drug.

Researchers traced the popularity of methamphetamine to its relatively low cost and the fact that it is easy to make. In addition, they said that the feelings produced by the drug last for a relatively long time.

States get tough on drunk drivers. Several states in 1997 considered lowering the limit of *blood-alcohol concentration* (the amount of alcohol in the blood) at which an automobile driver is considered to be intoxicated. In 1997, most states considered it illegal for drivers to have a blood-alcohol concentration of 0.10 percent or more. As of July 1997, however, 15 states had a blood-alcohol concentration limit of 0.08 percent—many of these states having lowered the limit from 0.10. The states hoped that the lower limit would help decrease the number of deaths caused by drunken drivers.

Organizations such as Mothers Against Drunk Driving (MADD), a group that works to reform laws and educate the public about drunk driving, launched a campaign in March 1997 to urge Congress to pass a law that would establish the national limit

for blood-alcohol concentration at 0.08 percent. Under this proposal, states that failed to enact the lower limit would lose federal highway funds. Other drunk-driving bills considered by Congress in 1997 proposed that the driver's license of a drunken driver be suspended for six months for a first offense, one year for a second offense, and permanently for a third offense.

Alcohol and the elderly. The consumption of excess alcohol is more common among elderly people than previously believed, according to a study published in December 1996. The researchers, from the Medical College of Wisconsin in Milwaukee and the University of Wisconsin in Madison, said that excess alcohol consumption is responsible for the health problems, hospitalization, and death of many elderly people.

Excess alcohol consumption can lead to high blood pressure, cancer, diabetes, and various injuries. The researchers recommended that primary care physicians screen elderly patients for alcohol abuse in order to help prevent such problems.

The study, which questioned more than 5,000 people over age 60 about their drinking habits, found that 15 percent of the men and 12 percent of the women regularly drank in excess of limits typically recommended by health authorities. These limits

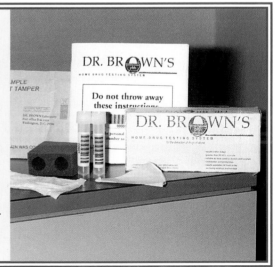

Home drug test available

In January 1997, the United States Food and Drug Administration approved the first over-the-counter test kit for detecting illegal drugs, including marijuana, heroin, and cocaine. The kit, called Dr. Brown's Home Drug Testing System (manufactured by Personal Health and Hygiene, Inc., of Silver Spring, Maryland), was developed for parents to check their children for illegal drug use. It includes vials for collecting urine samples, as well as directions for obtaining and interpreting test results. The user labels the samples with an identification number and sends them to a laboratory for analysis. Results are available over the telephone one to three days after the lab receives the samples.

Alcohol and Drug Abuse

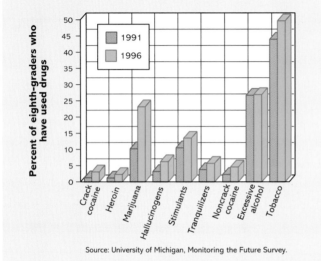

Drug use up among U.S. eighth-graders

Drug use among United States eighth-graders increased dramatically between 1991 and 1996, according to research by the University of Michigan in Ann Arbor. The percentages of eighth-graders who had used marijuana and crack (a form of cocaine) more than doubled during this period. The percentage of eighth-graders who had used heroin doubled, and the percentage who had used noncrack cocaine almost doubled.

Percent of eighth-graders who have used drugs

Legend:
■ 1991
■ 1996

Categories (left to right):
Crack cocaine, Heroin, Marijuana, Hallucinogens, Stimulants, Tranquilizers, Noncrack cocaine, Excessive alcohol, Tobacco

Source: University of Michigan, Monitoring the Future Survey.

are 14 drinks per week for men and 7 drinks per week for women. The heaviest elderly drinkers were found to be college graduates and married people—particularly men.

Herbal stimulant regulated. In June 1997, the U.S. Food and Drug Administration (FDA) announced regulations to limit the amount of ephedrine alkaloid that can be contained in herbal dietary supplements. Ephedrine alkaloid is a stimulant, also found in methamphetamine, that the FDA had warned could cause high blood pressure, heart attack, stroke, seizure, and death if taken in large doses or for long periods of time. Herbal supplements contain ingredients derived from plants and are largely unregulated by the FDA. The FDA, however, prevents manufacturers from using false health claims to market the supplements. The regulations announced in May prevent manufacturers from claiming that ephedrine alkaloid products can build muscles and burn calories. The regulations were expected to go into effect in late 1997 or in 1998.

In the 1990's, many Americans used herbal supplements containing ephedrine alkaloid to increase energy, build muscles, lose weight, and combat minor ailments such as the common cold. The FDA announcement came in response to reports of at least 20 deaths and 800 illnesses caused by the supplements, which were sold under various brand names—including Cloud 9, Herbal Ecstasy, Rave Energy, and Ultimate Xphoria. The FDA was unable to ban these products because a 1994 federal law declared them to be food supplements rather than drugs, thereby limiting the agency's regulatory authority over them. This law, however, did not affect the regulatory agencies in states, and Florida and New York banned all ephedrine alkaloid herbal products in 1996.

Drug treatment reduces crime.
Treatment for drug abuse helps prevent individuals from engaging in criminal activities. This finding was reported in September 1996 in a study by the Center for Substance Abuse Treatment at the University of Maryland in College Park.

The researchers studied more than 4,000 drug users and found that the number of people who sold illegal drugs dropped from 64 percent in the year before treatment to 14 percent in the year after treatment. A similar drop was seen in the number of people who shoplifted. The number of people who supported themselves primarily through illegal activities dropped from 17 percent before treatment to 9 percent after treatment, and the number of people who were arrested for any crime dropped from 49 percent before treatment to 17 percent after treatment.

• David C. Lewis

In WORLD BOOK, see ALCOHOLISM; DRUG ABUSE.

The use of inhaled steroids decreases asthma patients' risk of hospitalization by 50 percent, according to a study published in March 1997. A team of researchers from Brigham and Women's Hospital and the Harvard Medical School in Boston found those results after reviewing the records of 16,941 asthma patients belonging to the same health maintenance organization (HMO).

Inhaled steroids, which reduce inflammation in the lungs, are a key medication in treating moderate to severe asthma. Numerous clinical trials have demonstrated the effectiveness of inhaled steroids on improving the function of the lungs, but no studies investigated whether the medication reduced the risk of hospitalization, which would result in lowering the costs of treating asthma.

The Boston researchers reviewed the HMO's records to determine drug use, hospitalizations, the number and type of visits to a physician, the number of visits to an emergency room or urgent care center, and the age and sex of participants. Of the entire study group, 40 percent were given at least one prescription for inhaled steroids. The researchers expected that patients who use inhaled steroids—generally those patients with more severe cases of asthma—were more likely to be at a greater risk for hospitalization. The group that used

the steroids, however, had a 50 percent lower risk of hospitalization compared with the group that did not use the medication.

The authors noted that the study included no measure of the severity of asthma in each patient. By looking at the use of another asthma medication, however, they could determine to some degree the severity of each case. The researchers assumed that the greater number of prescriptions for beta-agonist, a drug used to expand air passages in the lungs, indicated a probable increase in the severity of the asthma. As the researchers expected, an increased use of beta-agonists was associated with a greater risk of hospitalization. But for those who took both medications, the inhaled steroids had a protective effect. The risk of hospitalization decreased by 70 percent for patients who received eight or more prescriptions of beta-agonist in one year and who also took inhaled steroids. Conversely, the hospitalization rate doubled for patients who received neither beta-agonist nor inhaled steroids.

Asthma therapy in 1997 emphasized regular use of anti-inflammatories. The researchers noted that their study supported the recommendations that individuals with moderate to severe asthma should include inhaled steroids as a part of their regular therapeutic regimen.

- Inhaled steroids and lowered risk of hospitalization
- Allergy medication and pregnancy
- Latex allergies
- Food and latex allergies

Dancing makes breathing a little easier for kids
Children with asthma participate in a dance therapy class at the National Jewish Medical and Research Center in Denver, Colorado. Dance and relaxation therapy is used along with medications to help children cope with the disease. In some cases, the alternative therapies have helped children become less dependent on asthma drugs.

Allergy medication and pregnancy.
Two common allergy medications, hydroxyzine and cetirizine, were found to present no risk to fetuses during the first trimester of pregnancy. Researchers led by Adrienne Einarson at the Hospital for Sick Children in Toronto, Canada, reported those conclusions in February 1997.

Doctors periodically question the safety of medications taken during pregnancy. The use of asthma and allergy drugs in pregnancy is a special concern, since allergies and asthma are *chronic* (long-term or permanent) conditions that sometimes get worse during pregnancy.

Hydroxyzine and cetirizine are both antihistamines, drugs that relieve the symptoms of allergic reactions. Of the 120 women in the Toronto study, 53 had taken hydroxyzine and 39 had taken cetirizine during the first trimester of pregnancy. In a follow-up analysis, the researchers found no significant difference between the group taking the medication and the control group in the number of birth defects, live births, spontaneous or induced abortions, or stillbirths. There was also no difference in the average birth weight, mode of delivery, length of pregnancy, or signs of distress in the newborn infants.

In an editorial commenting on the study of antihistamines, physicians Michael Schatz and Diana Petitti of the Southern California Permanente Medical Group and Kaiser Foundation Hospitals in San Diego addressed issues raised in the research. In general, they noted that studies in the use of any medications during pregnancy are difficult because it is unethical to expose pregnant women to unnecessary medications, especially if there is a threat to the developing fetus.

Schatz and Petitti added, however, that drugs that prevent *anaphylaxis* (severe allergic reactions) are important because they prevent life-threatening situations to the mother and fetus. Allergy medications are also important to prevent *maternal discomfort*—disturbance of the mother's eating, sleeping, or emotional well-being—which can adversely affect the fetus. In addition, uncontrolled allergic problems may make the mother more susceptible to sinus infections or make asthma conditions worse.

Latex allergies. Several studies addressing the growing concern about latex allergies were presented in February 1997 at a joint conference of the American Academy of Allergy, Asthma and Immunology; the American Association of Immunologists; and the Clinical Immunology Society. Latex is the sap of the Brazilian rubber tree, which is used to make numerous everyday products, such as rubber bands, balloons, and baby bottle nipples. In the health-care setting, the use of latex gloves increased greatly during the 1980's and 1990's to protect against viral

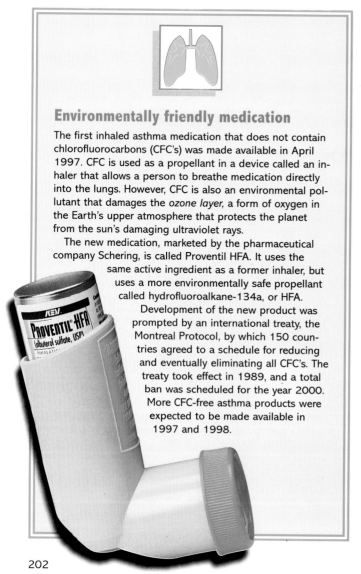

Environmentally friendly medication

The first inhaled asthma medication that does not contain chlorofluorocarbons (CFC's) was made available in April 1997. CFC is used as a propellant in a device called an inhaler that allows a person to breathe medication directly into the lungs. However, CFC is also an environmental pollutant that damages the *ozone layer,* a form of oxygen in the Earth's upper atmosphere that protects the planet from the sun's damaging ultraviolet rays.

The new medication, marketed by the pharmaceutical company Schering, is called Proventil HFA. It uses the same active ingredient as a former inhaler, but uses a more environmentally safe propellant called hydrofluoroalkane-134a, or HFA.

Development of the new product was prompted by an international treaty, the Montreal Protocol, by which 150 countries agreed to a schedule for reducing and eventually eliminating all CFC's. The treaty took effect in 1989, and a total ban was scheduled for the year 2000. More CFC-free asthma products were expected to be made available in 1997 and 1998.

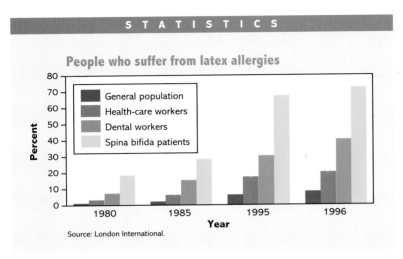

STATISTICS

People who suffer from latex allergies

■ General population
■ Health-care workers
■ Dental workers
□ Spina bifida patients

Percent

Year

Source: London International.

Allergies to latex, a product made from the Brazilian rubber tree, rose significantly from 1980 to 1996, according to London International, a maker of latex products used in hospitals and clinics. Latex gloves and other products provide an effective protection against infectious diseases, but they also create a health risk for medical professionals and patients such as those with spina bifida who are frequently exposed to latex products.

infections and other diseases. Latex is also used in anesthesia masks, blood pressure cuffs, catheters, and many other items. Latex allergy can result in skin symptoms such as rash, *dermatitis* (inflammation of the skin), *hives* (itchy lumps on the skin), asthma, and in very serious reactions, anaphylaxis and death.

A study at King Faisal Specialist Hospital and Research Centre in Riyadh, Saudi Arabia, showed that more than 33 percent of the staff members had allergic reactions to latex, but the prevalence of allergies varied by occupation. According to the self-administered survey of 1,526 employees, delivery room and intensive care personnel had the highest rates of latex allergies, with 53.3 percent and 45.9 percent respectively reporting latex sensitivity. About 36 percent of the nurses and technicians and about 22 percent of the physicians also reported latex allergies.

According to another report, rubber gloves vary significantly in the amount of detectable allergens from one product to the next. Researchers at the Mayo Clinic and Foundation in Rochester, Minnesota, reported those findings after conducting six different tests between 1993 and 1996 on rubber gloves from nine different distributors and manufacturers.

The researchers found that gloves purchased from distributors that did not manufacture the product varied the most in allergen content. Reportedly, those distributors often switched to different manufacturers of gloves. Consequently, according to the authors, the health-care facilities could not depend on getting the same product consistently from distributors.

Sensitivity to latex in many cases can be halted or decreased, however, according to a multicenter report. Researchers led by allergy specialist Anita Gewurz at Rush-Presbyterian-St. Luke's Medical Center in Chicago tested the changes in latex sensitivity of 10 health-care employees after using nonlatex gloves. After 12 months, seven of the employees showed a reduced sensitivity to latex allergens.

Food and latex allergies. People allergic to latex are also likely to be allergic to some foods, particularly avocados, bananas, and almonds. Those findings were also reported at the February 1997 joint conference by researchers at Vanderbilt University in Nashville, Tennessee.

The researchers tested 11 latex-sensitive patients for food allergies, and they interviewed the patients to determine a history of allergies. All of the patients reported increasing or worsening symptoms to latex over time. Nine patients showed allergic responses to avocado, nine to almond, six to chestnut, five to banana, and four to kiwi. The authors concluded that people sensitive to latex should be warned of possible reactions to foods. • Dominick A. Minotti

In World Book, see ALLERGY; ASTHMA.

An international team of researchers reported in February 1997 that the search for genes associated with systemic lupus erythematosus (SLE) was narrowed to a few specific regions of a particular *chromosome* (the structure within cells that carries genes). The researchers located the regions after comparing human chromosomes with the chromosomes of mice with a lupus-like disease.

SLE is an *autoimmune disease* (a disease in which the immune system attacks the body's own tissues). It can damage the skin, kidneys, joints, blood, and nervous system when abnormal *antibodies* (molecules produced by the immune system that normally protect people from disease) attack tissue and organ cells.

Scientists long suspected a genetic link for SLE because the disease occurs more commonly in people with a family history of SLE than in the rest of the population. Furthermore, certain strains of inbred mice develop an inherited disease that closely resembles lupus.

By early 1997, the researchers had identified several regions of chromosome 1 in mice that contain genes that may cause susceptibility to the lupus-like disease. The team suspected that chromosome 1 in humans may contain similar genes that contribute to the onset of SLE. The researchers analyzed blood samples from 43 families in which at least two siblings showed signs of SLE. They found that chromosome 1 in people with a family history of SLE carries genes that determine susceptibility to SLE just as chromosome 1 in mice with the lupus-like disease does.

The researchers planned to use the information gathered in this study to help identify the specific genes that make people susceptible to SLE. The discovery of the genes will give clues to the cause of the disease and allow doctors to develop new diagnosis and treatment methods for SLE.

A new drug treatment may lessen the signs and symptoms of rheumatoid arthritis (RA). Researchers at Leiden University Hospital in Leiden, the Netherlands, and at the Kennedy Institute of Rheumatology in London reported in July 1996 that a drug called anti-tumor necrosis factor (anti-TNF) reduces inflammation in joints.

RA is a form of inflammatory arthritis that causes pain, stiffness, and swelling in joints. It can destroy cartilage and bones and lead to crippling and deformity. Doctors generally treat RA by prescribing nonsteroidal anti-inflammatory drugs (NSAID's), such as aspirin and ibuprofen, and disease-modifying drugs, such as methotrexate and sulfasalazine. Researchers hoped that anti-TNF would be more effective than these other drugs in reducing inflammation. Anti-TNF, one of a class of drugs called biological

Reducing ulcer risk when using NSAID's

Doctors often recommend prescription or over-the-counter nonsteroidal anti-inflammatory drugs (NSAID's), such as aspirin and ibuprofen, to reduce the pain and swelling of inflammatory arthritis. But NSAID's can also cause stomach ulcers. The Arthritis Foundation recommends the following steps to reduce the risk of developing stomach ulcers:

- Never take more than the prescribed dose of NSAID's without consulting your doctor.
- Never combine prescription NSAID's with over-the-counter ones.
- Inform your doctor of other medications you are taking.
- Learn the symptoms of NSAID-induced ulcers, such as nausea, heartburn, and lightheadedness, and let your doctor know if you experience any of them.
- Don't smoke and don't drink more than two alcoholic beverages a day.

Exercises for arthritis sufferers

Many people with arthritis worry that exercise will only increase their aches, pains, and stiffness. But in October 1996, the American Academy of Orthopaedic Surgeons began a campaign encouraging arthritis sufferers to become more physically active. According to the academy, regular exercise strengthens bones, reduces joint and muscle pain, and improves mobility and balance. The following are some recommended exercises, but check with a doctor before you perform them.

While standing or sitting, lace your fingers and push your arms slightly back and up. Hold for 16 seconds.

Rest your head on the wall. Bend each leg, keeping the other leg straight. Slowly move your hips forward. Hold for 15 to 30 seconds.

Keeping the back of your head on the floor and the small of your back flat, pull each leg toward your chest. Hold for 30 seconds.

Flatten your lower back by tightening your hip and abdominal muscles at the same time. Hold for 5 to 8 seconds.

Source: American Academy of Orthopaedic Surgeons; critically reviewed by the Arthritis Foundation.

agents because they are similar to natural body proteins, reduces inflammation by blocking the actions of TNF, a hormone-like protein that causes inflammation. Patients with RA have high levels of TNF in their joints.

The researchers studied 14 people with RA, half of whom were given anti-TNF while the other half received a *placebo* (an inactive substance). The researchers found that the people who took anti-TNF showed a reduction of TNF in their joints while those who took the placebo did not. It was not clear how safe and effective anti-TNF would be in long-term treatment, but the researchers hoped that further studies would prove that the drug reduces inflammation and joint damage with few side effects.

Exercise and knee osteoarthritis.
Researchers reported in January 1997 that exercise is important in the treatment of osteoarthritis of the knee. Patients with the joint disease osteoarthritis who participated in aerobic exercise or resistance exercise programs experienced less disability and pain than those people who did not exercise.

Osteoarthritis commonly occurs in older people and results from the disintegration of *cartilage,* the smooth, resilient material at the ends of bones that helps lubricate joints. Healthy cartilage is smooth, but cartilage damaged by osteoarthritis becomes thinned, roughened, and frayed. Joints are less flexible and motion is painful. Osteoarthritis therapy includes drugs that relieve or reduce pain, such as acetaminophen (often sold as Tylenol), and anti-inflammatory drugs.

Doctors at the University of Tennessee in Memphis and at Wake Forest University in Winston-Salem, North Carolina, studied 365 patients aged 60 or older. In all of the patients, osteoarthritis caused pain and disability in one or both knees. The study found that those patients who participated in an 18-month aerobic exercise or resistance-training program had less disability and less pain than patients in a group that did not exercise.

The doctors also found that though abnormal stress on joints can increase the symptoms of osteoarthritis, the knee X rays of study participants who exercised showed no progression of the disease. The researchers noted that the effects of exercise on cartilage require further investigation. However, this study showed that moderate exercise does help people with osteoarthritis.

New approach for fibromyalgia.
Researchers reported in November 1996 that a new drug combination is more effective in treating fibromyalgia (FM) than medications used in the past. FM, a common condition of unknown origin, is considered an arthritic disease because it causes pain throughout the body. FM most often affects women and begins between the ages of 30 and 40.

Unlike osteoarthritis and rheumatoid arthritis, which primarily affect the joints, FM affects soft tissues and muscles. There is no inflammation associated with FM, but it causes persistent, intense, and sometimes debilitating pain. Patients with FM also have difficulty falling asleep and wake often during the night, causing them to feel fatigued throughout the day.

Doctors believe that an imbalance in brain chemistry may cause fibromyalgia. Therefore, they often prescribe tricyclic antidepressant drugs to correct the sleep disturbance and reduce pain. These drugs affect the metabolism of norepinephrine and serotonin, two nervous system chemicals that transmit nerve impulses. While these drugs decrease the symptoms of FM, they can cause such side effects as dry mouth and drowsiness.

Another class of antidepressants, selective serotonin reuptake inhibitors (SSRI's), specifically target the metabolism of serotonin. Researchers at the Newton-Wellesley Hospital in Newton and at the New England Medical Center in Boston studied 19 patients who were given either the tricyclic antidepressant amitryptyline, the SSRI fluoxitene (sold as Prozac), or both. The researchers found that the combination of the two drugs provided the greatest pain relief and corrected the sleep disturbance.

● David S. Pisetsky

In WORLD BOOK, see ARTHRITIS.

Birth Control

- "Morning-after" pills safe and effective
- Teen sex down, contraceptive use up
- Antiviral gel is also a contraceptive

The United States Food and Drug Administration (FDA) announced in February 1997 that ordinary birth control pills, or oral contraceptives, are a safe and effective means of preventing pregnancy when taken within 72 hours after unprotected intercourse. The announcement cleared the way for drug manufacturers to market these so-called "morning-after" pills.

The FDA also expected the announcement to lead to more physicians prescribing morning-after pills. Although many physicians were previously aware of the effectiveness of birth control pills when used after intercourse, they were reluctant to prescribe them for this purpose, because

they feared malpractice suits related to prescribing a drug for a purpose not approved by the FDA.

Studies examined by the FDA indicated that birth control pills reduce the likelihood of pregnancy by 75 percent when one pill is taken within 72 hours after intercourse, and another pill is taken within 12 hours of the first. The pills work by causing a release of hormones that prevents a fertilized egg from becoming implanted in the wall of the uterus. The studies indicated that the pills are a safe method of birth control

Teen contraceptive use. Results of the National Survey of Family Growth, announced in May 1997, indicated

Comparison of birth control methods

Contraceptives and contraceptive techniques vary in the degree
of their effectiveness, ease of use, and side effects.

Type	Effectiveness	Some Pros	Some Cons
Surgical Sterilization (female or male)	Over 99%	One-time surgical procedure.	Possible pain, bleeding, infection; difficult to reverse.
Oral Contraceptives (combined pill)	Over 99%	Some protection against infection and cancer of reproductive organs.	Possible nausea, weight gain, menstrual changes; increased risk of cardiovascular disease; must be taken daily.
Injection (Depo-Provera)	Over 99%	One injection every three months.	Possible bleeding, weight gain, breast tenderness, headaches.
Intrauterine Device (IUD)	98–99%	Can remain in place from 1 to 10 years.	Possible cramps, bleeding, infections, infertility, perforation of uterus; must be inserted by physician.
Male Condom (latex)	88%	Best protection against sexually transmitted diseases (STD's); nonprescription.	Possible irritation, allergic reactions.
Diaphragm (with spermicide)	82%	Protects against cervical infection, certain STD's.	Possible irritation, allergic reactions, urinary tract infection, toxic shock syndrome.
Female Condom	79%	Some protection against STD's; nonprescription.	Possible irritation, allergic reactions.
Spermicides	79%	Some protection against STD's, nonprescription.	Failure rate relatively high.
Abstinence	100%	No health risks.	

Sources: U.S. Food and Drug Administration; *Contraceptive Technology*, 16th edition, Irvington Publishers.

that fewer teen-agers were having sexual intercourse in the 1990's compared with the 1980's, and that more of those who were having intercourse were using contraceptives. The National Survey of Family Growth is a periodic survey conducted since 1970 by the U.S. Department of Health and Human Services (HHS). It is based on thousands of face-to-face interviews.

The survey found that in 1995, 50 percent of young women and 55 percent of young men aged 15 to 19 had ever had sexual intercourse. In 1988, the figures were 53 percent for young women and 60 percent for young men. The figures represented the first decrease in teen sexual activity ever recorded by the survey. Sev-

enty-six percent of the young women in the 1995 survey said they used some form of contraceptive the first time they had intercourse. In the late 1980's, the figure was 64 percent. An increase in contraceptive use was also reported for young men. The most common method of contraception among teen-agers was the use of condoms. The next most common method of contraception was the use of birth control pills.

HHS Secretary Donna Shalala said the decrease in sexual activity and the increase in contraceptive use may be responsible for a reported decline in the teen birth rate. The department reported in October 1996 that the teen birth rate declined 8 percent between 1991 and 1995.

Antiviral gel also a contraceptive.
Scientists at Procept, Incorporated, in Cambridge, Massachusetts, announced in May 1997 that tests on an antiviral gel developed by the company indicated that the gel also functions as a contraceptive. Other tests had previously indicated that the gel, named PRO 2000 Gel, could prevent infection by HIV, the virus that causes AIDS, and the herpes simplex virus. Procept is a developer of drugs that fight immune system disorders.

To test the gel's contraceptive properties, researchers applied it inside the vaginas of rabbits. The gel was found to be an effective contraceptive when it contained a concentration of 4 percent of the antiviral compound. This concentration was also effective against HIV. Tests indicated that a concentration of 0.4 percent would still be effective against HIV, but the compound would not be effective as a contraceptive.

In June 1997, Procept announced that clinical tests on women had demonstrated the safety of PRO 2000 for human use. The company planned additional clinical tests to demonstrate the effectiveness of the gel as both an anti-HIV drug and a contraceptive. Procept hoped that the gel would be ready for marketing within five years.   • Lauren Love
In WORLD BOOK, see BIRTH CONTROL.

Blood

• Abnormal gene and
  excess iron

• New hope for
  excessive bleeding

• More effective treatment
  for bone marrow cancer

Geneticists reported in August 1996 that they had discovered an abnormal gene associated with hemochromatosis, one of the most common genetic diseases among people of European descent. Hemochromatosis is caused by excess iron absorption.

Small amounts of iron are necessary for the proper functioning of all cells in the body. Iron is especially important to the health of red blood cells, which use the mineral to form *hemoglobin,* a substance that carries oxygen from the lungs to other tissues. The body normally excretes excess iron. The bodies of people with hemochromatosis, however, absorb iron too quickly, allowing high levels to build up in the heart, liver, and other organs. Excess iron can damage organs and lead to such conditions as heart disease and cirrhosis. Hemochromatosis is most damaging to older people whose bodies have accumulated a lifetime of excess iron.

The most common treatment for the disease is the ancient practice of *bloodletting,* the removal of blood on a regular basis that results in lower amounts of iron in the body. According to doctors, bloodletting can completely prevent complications of the disease if the condition is diagnosed and treated in its early stages.

**Tattoo or blood
donation?**

A tattoo artist uses a tattoo machine to apply a design to the shoulder of a client. The American Red Cross, concerned that blood-borne diseases such as AIDS and hepatitis can be transmitted through improperly sterilized equipment, will not accept a blood donation from anyone who has been tattooed within the 12 months preceding a donation.

Doctors have long hoped for a way to identify young people at risk for hemochromatosis, so that they can begin preventive treatment. Researchers led by Roger K. Wolff of Mercator Genetics in Menlo Park, California, discovered a gene that may allow for early diagnosis of the disease. The researchers studied 178 people with hemochromatosis and found that 85 percent had an abnormal gene called HLA-H. While the researchers were not certain what role HLA-H plays in iron regulation, they hoped that identifying the gene would lead to the development of a diagnostic blood test.

New hope for excessive bleeding.
In November 1996, researchers reported that a genetically engineered hormone called megakaryocyte growth factor can lower the risk of excessive bleeding in people undergoing chemotherapy or bone marrow transplantation. Such patients often experience a reduction in *platelets* (structures in blood that help it to clot). Platelets are made in the bone marrow by cells called megakaryocytes. The low platelet count increases the risk of severe bleeding.

Doctors use genetically engineered *growth factors* (hormones that the body produces naturally) to raise the level of some blood components, such as white blood cells. Currently available growth factors, however, are unable to consistently increase the number of platelets.

The researchers, led by C. J. O'Malley at the Centre for Developmental Cancer Therapeutics in Melbourne, Australia, administered a genetically engineered growth factor previously used to raise platelet counts in animals to patients with advanced cancers. This growth factor stimulated megakaryocytes to produce platelets. By day 16 of the treatment, the patients' platelet counts had risen. The effect lasted for up to three additional weeks, and the patients experienced no dangerous side effects. The study showed that megakaryocyte growth factor can help chemotherapy or bone marrow transplantation patients lower the risk of severe bleeding.

A more effective treatment for *multiple myeloma*, a cancer of the bone marrow, was tested by researchers led by Michel Attal at the Hôpital Purpan in Toulouse, France. The investigators compared the use of a high dose of chemotherapy followed by bone marrow transplantation with the use of a lower dose of chemotherapy, the standard treatment for myeloma. They reported in July 1996 that the high dose/bone marrow transplantation treatment significantly improved the patients' survival rate.

In patients with multiple myeloma, cancerous *plasma cells* (blood cells that normally make antibodies that fight infections) in the bone marrow produce abnormal antibodies that do not fight infection and block normal antibody production. Low levels of normal antibodies make people with myeloma very susceptible to life-threatening infections. In addition, otherwise normal cells called osteoclasts begin to destroy bone. The destruction results in severe bone pain or fractures.

Multiple myeloma is incurable, and most patients die within three years of diagnosis. Doctors have used high doses of chemotherapy followed by bone marrow transplantation to prolong the life of patients; but a randomized controlled study to compare new treatments performed on patients in one group with standard treatments performed on patients in a control group had never been done with a large group of patients.

The French researchers treated 200 multiple myeloma patients with either high-dose chemotherapy followed by bone marrow transplantation or with standard chemotherapy. The researchers found that 81 percent of the patients responded to the high-dose/bone marrow transplantation treatment, while only 57 percent responded to standard chemotherapy. Most importantly, 52 percent of patients in the high-dose/bone marrow transplantation group survived for at least five years, compared with 12 percent of patients who received standard chemotherapy. The study demonstrated that many patients with multiple myeloma benefit from high-dose chemotherapy and bone marrow transplantation.

• G. David Roodman

In WORLD BOOK, see BLOOD.

Bone Disorders

Bone Disorders

- Estrogen strengthens bones
- Duration key to therapy
- Chemical reduces risk of fracture

More than 1.5 million bone fractures occur every year in the United States. More than 50 percent of fractures in older people are fractures of the hip, often due to falls and *osteoporosis* (weakening of bones). More than 60 percent of fractures in younger people are of an arm or leg, often caused by recreational activities or accidents. Another common site of fractures in younger people is the skull.

Medical investigators made progress in 1996 and 1997 toward finding better treatments for *osteoporosis* (a disease in which bones become weak and brittle, causing them to break easily and heal slowly). Osteoporosis is common in women after *menopause* (the time in life when menstrual periods cease—typically between the ages of 45 and 55).

Estrogen strengthens bones. A study published in November 1996 found that postmenopausal women who were given *estrogen* (a female sex hormone) experienced an increase in *bone mineral density* (a measurement of bone strength), which decreases the risk of osteoporosis. The study was performed by researchers from several universities and institutions in the United States.

Estrogen helps the bones absorb calcium, a mineral that forms part of the framework in which bone cells are embedded. The production of estrogen nearly ceases after menopause, leading to the breakdown of the framework and the loss of bone.

The study examined the effects of 36 months of *estrogen replacement therapy* (a treatment in which estrogen is given to postmenopausal women) on the bone mineral density of hundreds of women. The researchers found that estrogen had the greatest bone-strengthening effect

on women who had low bone mineral density at the start of treatment and on women who had not taken estrogen previously.

Duration key to therapy. A study published in February 1997 found that the key to lowering a woman's risk of osteoporosis is to take estrogen for a long period of time after menopause. The study, performed by a group of researchers at the University of California in San Diego, examined hundreds of postmenopausal women aged 60 to 98.

The California researchers studied women who had never taken estrogen, women who had taken estrogen only for a short time soon after menopause, women who had continued to take estrogen since menopause, women who had begun taking estrogen after age 60 but had stopped taking it after a short time, and women who had begun taking estrogen after age 60 and had continued taking the hormone for a long period of time.

The researchers found that the women who had continued taking estrogen since menopause had the highest bone mineral density. However, bone mineral density was almost as high in the women who had begun taking estrogen after age 60 and had continued taking the hormone for a long period thereafter. The findings of

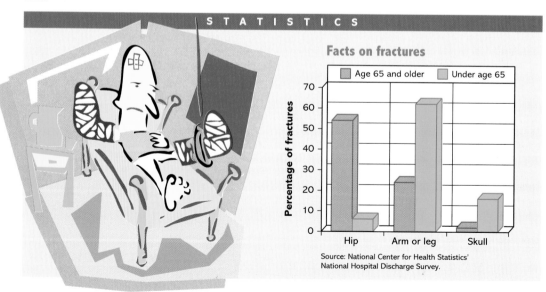

S T A T I S T I C S

Facts on fractures

Source: National Center for Health Statistics' National Hospital Discharge Survey.

this study contradicted a long-standing belief that estrogen replacement therapy is effective in reducing risk of osteoporosis only when begun immediately after menopause.

Chemical reduces risk of fracture. A study published in April 1997 examining the effects of a chemical compound called alendronate sodium found that the substance reduces the risk of fracture in women with osteoporosis. Alendronate sodium belongs to a class of chemical compounds called biphosphonates, which inhibit bone loss. Previous efforts to use biphosphonates against osteoporosis met with only limited success be-

cause the drugs often caused other bone-mineral problems.

The study, led by researchers at the Merck Research Laboratories in Rahway, New Jersey, examined more than 1,000 postmenopausal women with osteoporosis. The women took alendronate sodium for at least two years. The results showed that alendronate sodium reduced the risks of hip and wrist fractures in postmenopausal women without leading to other bone-mineral disorders. This study indicated that alendronate sodium may be very useful to women with osteoporosis.   • John J. Gartland

In WORLD BOOK, see BONE; OSTEO-POROSIS.

The following books on health and medicine topics were written for the general public. All were published in 1996 and 1997.

AIDS. *The Least of These My Brethren: A Doctor's Story of Hope and Miracles on an Inner-City AIDS Ward* by Daniel Baxter. Physician Baxter tells of the turmoils, triumphs, and joys he witnessed while treating patients dying of AIDS, and the lessons he learned from them. (Random House, 1997. 254 pp. $24.)

Working on a Miracle by Mahlon Johnson and Joseph Olshan. Neuropathologist Johnson became infected with HIV (human immunodeficiency virus), the virus that causes AIDS, when he cut himself during an autopsy. The authors describe Johnson's search for new treatments, some of which offer hope. (Bantam Books, 1997. 301 pp. $23.95.)

Allergies. *Jane Brody's Allergy Fighter* by Jane E. Brody. Brody, the personal health columnist for the *New York Times,* provides a guide that explains what causes allergies and what makes them worse. She also lists peak allergy seasons by geographic area and explores treatment options. (W. Norton, 1997. 127 pp. $12.95.)

Alzheimer's disease. *Alzheimer's: Answers to Hard Questions for Families* by James Lindemann Nelson and Hilde Lindemann Nelson. Two bioethi-

cists with extensive experience treating Alzheimer's disease examine common situations faced at every stage of the illness. They discuss the difficult moral and ethical decisions that caregivers must make and suggest ways to preserve the dignity of the patient while maintaining the caregiver's selfhood. (Doubleday, 1996. 224 pp. $21.95.)

Cancer. *Chicken Soup for the Surviving Soul* by Jack Canfield, Mark Victor Hansen, Patty Aubrey, and Nancy Mitchell. The authors group 101 stories about people who have survived cancer into seven sections: hope; courage and determination; attitude; faith; love; support; and insights and lessons. (Health Communications, 1996. 359 pp. $12.95.)

The American Cancer Society's Informed Decisions by Gerald Murphy, Lois B. Morris, and Dianne Lange. Murphy, a former chief medical officer of the American Cancer Society, with medical journalists Morris and Lange, explains the causes of cancer. The authors discuss such topics as cancer screening, diagnosis, treatments, pain relief, stress management, and quality of life. (Viking, 1997. 689 pp. $39.95.)

Man to Man: Surviving Prostate Cancer by Michael Korda. Korda, best-selling writer and editor-in-chief of the publishing company Simon & Schuster, provides information about prostate cancer as he tells the story

ALLERGY

JANE **BRODY'S**

FIGHTER

RELIEVE (AH-CHOO!) THE MISERY (SNIFF SNIFF) OF NASAL ALLERGIES WITH THE HELP (AHHH!) OF AMERICA'S MOST TRUSTED AUTHORITY ON PERSONAL HEALTH

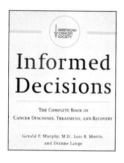

of his own experience with the disease. (Random House, 1996. 224 pp. $20.)

Chronic illness. *Essential Guide to Chronic Illness* by James W. Long. The author, a retired director of health service for the National Science Foundation and an internist, explains how patients can help their doctors diagnose and more effectively treat 47 chronic conditions. Entries include such subjects as acne, diabetes, migraine headaches, and psoriasis. Each entry discusses signs, causes, and treatments and lists institutions with expertise in particular conditions. (Harper-Perennial, 1997. 625 pp. $20.)

Health care systems. *Demand and Get the Best Health Care for You* by Curtis Prout. Prout, a physician and a lecturer at Harvard Medical School, offers an explanation of the U.S. health care system and outlines how patients can make the best use of it. The author discusses such issues as choosing a doctor, understanding health insurance coverage, and dealing with emergencies. (Faber & Faber, 1996. 244 pp. $24.95.)

Health Against Wealth: HMO's and the Breakdown of Medical Trust by George Anders. Anders, a *Wall Street Journal* reporter, explores why managed care is so attractive to employers and insurers, and why it is so often frustrating for patients and doctors. He offers examples of how HMO's have thwarted necessary, even life-saving, treatment under the guise of cost efficiency, and he proposes some corrective measures. (Houghton Mifflin, 1996. 299 pp. $24.95.)

Heart disease. *American Heart Association Guide to Heart Attack* by the staff of the American Heart Association. This book explains what happens during a heart attack and why. It also explores recovery from and prevention of heart attacks, including such aspects as the hospital experience, medications, surgery, nutrition, exercise, and coping with the emotional aspects of a heart attack. (Times Books, 1996. 300 pp. $23.)

History. *An Alarming History of Famous and Difficult Patients* by Richard

Gordon. Gordon, the author of the Doctor in the House series, presents the medical histories of 31 people, both real and fictional. Among those included are George Washington, Napoleon Bonaparte, Queen Victoria, Adolf Hitler, Vincent Van Gogh, and Sherlock Holmes. The author also highlights medical and dental practices of the 1600's and 1700's. (St. Martin's Press, 1997. 229 pp. $20.95.)

The People's Health by Robin M. Henig. In honor of the Harvard School of Public Health's 75th anniversary, Henig traces the growth of the public health field into a worldwide effort to create a healthy environment. He presents medical, social, historical, and behavioral perspectives, including such breakthroughs as the development of the *iron lung,* a type of respirator, for people with polio. (Joseph Henry Press, 1996. 244 pp. $29.95.)

Nursing. *Life Support* by Suzanne Gordon. Investigative reporter Gordon profiles three nurses in a variety of settings. Along with the nurses' experiences, Gordon examines nursing history, the role nurses play in patient care, and the changes in hospital policy that are affecting the quality of that care. (Little Brown, 1997. 328 pp. $23.95.)

Wellness. *Eight Weeks to Optimum Health* by Andrew Weil. Weil, a Harvard-trained holistic practitioner, outlines a preventive lifestyle approach to health. He explains how to make small changes in diet and exercise and includes recipes and information about dietary supplements. Weil also discusses the importance of deep-breathing techniques and taking the time to appreciate art and music. (Knopf, 1997. 276 pp. $23.)

Women's health. *Doctor Susan Love's Hormone Book: Making Informed Choices About Menopause* by Susan Love and Karen Lindsey. Love, a leading surgeon and breast cancer researcher, helped guide the largest study of postmenopausal women in the United States. Love and coauthor Lindsey explain the changes a woman's body undergoes during her lifetime, particularly during *perimenopause,* the three to six years before a woman's last menstrual period, and menopause. The authors discuss possible treatments, including hormone replacement, surgery, and lifestyle changes. (Random House, 1997. 362 pp. $25.)

Mental Wellness for Women by Rita Baron-Faust. Medical writer and broadcast journalist Baron-Faust collaborates with New York University Medical Center's Women's Health Service and Department of Psychiatry to offer advice and information on such issues as mood and eating disorders and addiction. (Morrow, 1997. 354 pp. $25.)

What Women Need to Know: From Headaches to Heart Disease and Everything in Between by Marianne Legato and Carol Colman. Women's health specialist Legato provides up-to-date, in-depth information on many important health questions and counsels readers on how to talk with their doctors. (Simon & Schuster, 1997. 239 pp. $23.)

Women's Symptoms by Ivan K. Strausz. Gynecologist Strausz provides an alphabetical list of 60 major symptoms and general information about each. He also lists 12 diseases along with their causes, treatments, and symptoms. (Dell, 1996. 510 pp. $13.95.) • Margaret E. Moore

---

Brain and Nervous System

- Animal model of Alzheimer's disease
- Hope for multiple sclerosis
- Gene linked to Parkinson disease
- Nerve cell protection
- Anxiety linked to gene
- Cocaine "high" explained

The first *animal model* (animals that share a condition or disease with humans) of Alzheimer's disease was developed by medical researchers from a number of institutions, including the University of Minnesota in Minneapolis and the University of Wales in Britain. The researchers announced in October 1996 that they had *genetically engineered,* or altered the genes of, mice to mimic the symptoms of Alzheimer's disease, in order to help them search for causes and treatments for the disease.

Alzheimer's disease—a devastating disorder in which brain cells degenerate and die, causing memory problems and, eventually, a complete loss of mental function—affects more than 50 percent of people over age 85, according to medical studies. The cause of the disease is not known, but genetic factors are believed to play a role in many cases. Identifying the cause of the disease has been difficult because Alzheimer's affects only humans and, therefore, scientists previously had been unable to study the disease in research animals.

To create the animal model of Alzheimer's disease, the researchers first made copies of a human gene known to increase the risk of the disease. The gene carries a *mutation* (a change in its structure) that results in the production of an abnormal form of a protein called amyloid. Scientists believe that this abnormal amyloid plays a role in a rare type of Alzheimer's disease that affects people who are 40 to 60 years old. However, the brain and behavioral changes the mutation is linked to are similar to those seen in other Alzheimer's patients.

The researchers inserted the gene into nerve cells in the brains of mice. The nerve cells carrying the gene produced large amounts of the abnormal amyloid, and the mice developed many of the changes in brain structure seen in humans who have Alzheimer's disease. For example, the brains of the mice developed *amyloid plaques,* tangled masses of cells and protein that are produced as brain cells die. The changes in brain structure were not seen in young mice but appeared gradually over time as the animals aged—a situation similar to that found in humans with Alzheimer's disease.

The researchers then examined the mice to determine if the changes in brain structure were associated with changes in ability to remember and perform complex tasks, such as navigating a maze. Although young mice with the abnormal amyloid gene performed these tasks as well as normal mice, by the time the mice were 9 to 10 months old (old age for a mouse), these same animals had great difficulties performing complex tasks. This increase in difficulty demonstrated that the mice experienced behavioral changes similar to those experienced by humans with Alzheimer's disease.

Healing spinal cord injuries

In July 1996, researchers at the Karolinska Institute in Sweden reported that they had repaired severed spinal cords in rats—the first evidence that damaged spinal cords can be repaired. Neuroscientists used chest nerves from the rats to build bridges from the white matter of one part of a severed cord to the gray matter of the other part. White matter consists of insulated nerve cells; gray matter, noninsulated. Nerve fibers from the white matter grew across the bridges to the gray matter, reestablishing nerve communication between the severed parts and allowing the rats to move their hind legs.

Source: New York University Medical Center.

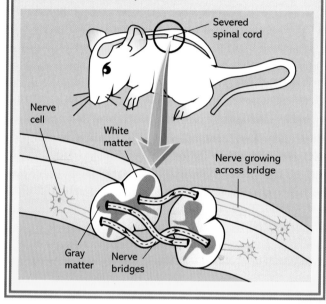

or blocking of nerve impulses through these regions. The blocking of nerve impulses results in such symptoms as weakness, tremor, fatigue, and loss of vision and balance. The cause of MS, which primarily strikes women in their 20's, is not known. Although several treatments slow the progression of MS, there are no treatments to reverse the loss of myelin in the central nervous system.

The researchers studied myelin in dogs that carried a mutated gene associated with myelin production. The mutated gene severely damaged the myelin in the animals, and these dogs exhibited symptoms similar to those found in people with MS. The researchers took myelin-producing cells from the spinal cords of animals that did not carry the mutated gene and injected the cells into the spinal cords of the dogs with damaged myelin. The transplanted cells were not attacked by the white blood cells in the immune system. Instead, the cells survived, multiplied, and formed normal myelin in the spinal cords of the dogs.

These experiments were the first to show that it is possible to repair myelin in the central nervous system of a large mammal by injecting myelin-producing cells. Although this research could ultimately prove beneficial to patients, the long-term effects of the treatment needed to be studied, because MS is a *chronic* (long term) illness in which myelin is continuously attacked. According to the researchers, the treatment would only be effective in humans if white blood cells could be prevented from destroying the new myelin made by the transplanted cells.

Hope for multiple sclerosis. In January 1997, medical researchers announced the discovery of a possible new treatment for multiple sclerosis (MS). Researchers from Emory University in Atlanta, Colorado State University in Fort Collins, and the University of Wisconsin in Madison, repaired damaged *myelin* (the fatty insulation that surrounds nerve fibers), a substance destroyed in multiple sclerosis and certain other diseases.

MS is a disease of the nervous system that occurs when large numbers of white blood cells in the immune system enter the brain and spinal cord and attack and destroy both myelin and the cells that produce myelin. Scars form in the areas of myelin destruction, causing a slowing

Gene linked to Parkinson disease. The first evidence that Parkinson disease has a genetic cause was reported in November 1996 by medical researchers from the National Institutes of Health in Bethesda, Maryland, and the Robert Wood Johnson Medical School in Piscataway, New Jersey. The researchers said that a gene for Parkinson disease could make a person susceptible to developing the illness when exposed to certain environmental factors, such as excessive quantities of carbon monoxide or the mineral manganese.

Parkinson disease is a degenerative disorder characterized by the death of nerve cells in a part of the brain called the corpus striatum. These cells normally produce a chemical called dopamine, which is essential for controlling body movements. As the cells die, the concentration of dopamine in the brain decreases, and the affected person develops tremors, muscle stiffness, and loss of balance.

The researchers studied more than 400 individuals in one extended family, many of whom had Parkinson disease. The researchers analyzed blood samples from the family members and found that all the individuals with Parkinson disease carried a *chromosome* (a structure made of genes) with a certain mutated region. Because the region is the site of many genes, it took the researchers several months to discover the exact gene containing the mutation. This discovery, which the researchers announced in June 1997, was expected to lead to better treatments for the disease.

Nerve cell protection. In March 1997, researchers announced the discovery of a possible treatment for degenerative diseases of the central nervous system, such as Huntington's disease, Alzheimer's disease, and Parkinson disease. Researchers from CytoTherapeutics, Incorporated, in Providence, Rhode Island, and various university and hospital research cen-

ters, reported that they had found a way to use *neurotrophic factors* (chemical substances that can protect nerve cells from injury) to protect brain cells from degeneration.

The researchers experimented using neurotrophic factors to treat Huntington's disease, a severe disorder of the nervous system that destroys brain cells and causes involuntary body movements, mental disturbances, and eventual death. A similar disorder can be produced in animals by injecting a chemical called quinolinic acid into the brain.

The researchers implanted genetically engineered, neurotrophic factor-producing cells into one hemisphere of the brain of monkeys. After one week, the researchers injected quinolinic acid into both hemispheres of the brain. Nerve cells survived in the hemisphere of the brain with the neurotrophic factor-producing cells, while nerve cells in the other hemisphere were destroyed by the quinolinic acid.

Because the implanted cells constantly produce the protective neurotrophic factors, the need for patients with degenerative diseases to regularly receive these factors in drugs could be diminished, according to the researchers. However, the researchers said that more studies need to be done, because the areas of the brain that can be exposed to neurotrophic factors by implants are relatively small.

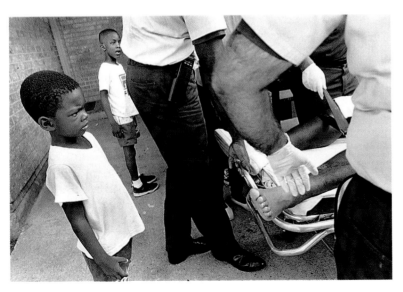

Trauma damages brain
A 1996 University of Minnesota study found that traumatized children, such as the two boys who have just witnessed a shooting, *left,* have excess amounts of *cortisol* (a hormone released in response to stress) in their brains. Cortisol can damage parts of the brain responsible for controlling emotions and attention. Such brain damage in children can result in psychiatric problems later in life, according to the researchers.

Anxiety linked to gene. Research published in November 1996 provided insight into the cause of anxiety-related personality disorders. Scientists from the National Institutes of Health in the United States and the University of Würzburg in Germany discovered a link between a gene regulating the function of a brain chemical called serotonin and people experiencing high levels of anxiety.

Serotonin helps transmit information from one brain cell to another. Individuals who are depressed often have low levels of serotonin and are prescribed drugs that boost serotonin levels to relieve the depression.

There are two forms of the gene that regulates serotonin. The presence of one form, called the long variant, leads to decreased levels of serotonin, while the presence of the other form, called the short variant, leads to increased levels. The researchers found the short variant in people experiencing much anxiety.

This research provided support to scientists' theory that serotonin levels are important in controlling emotions. According to the researchers, the discovery was expected to lead to tests to determine whether drugs that reduce the effects of serotonin help people disabled by anxiety.

Cocaine "high" explained. In April 1997, medical researchers from various institutions, including Brookhaven National Laboratory in Upton, New York, and the State University of New York at Stony Brook, announced that they had demonstrated for the first time how cocaine produces feelings of a "high." The information obtained from this demonstration was expected to help scientists design medications to prevent the pleasurable effects of cocaine—thus helping free addicts from the drug.

The researchers first administered cocaine *intravenously* (through the veins) to addicts in amounts sufficient to cause a "high." They then monitored the drug's effects in the brain using *positron emission tomography* (PET), a technique used to produce images of chemical activity in the brain. PET revealed that the drug rapidly binds to and blocks chemicals called dopamine transporters (DAT's), which normally transport dopamine from certain areas of the brain to other parts of the nervous system. The blockage results in a build-up of dopamine in the brain. Dopamine, important for the control of body movements, also produces feelings of reinforcement, which the brain can interpret as a "high." The researchers said that to prevent cocaine from causing a "high," a medication would need to prevent virtually all of the cocaine in the brain from binding to DAT. • Gary Birnbaum

See also MENTAL HEALTH. In WORLD BOOK, see BRAIN; NERVOUS SYSTEM.

Cancer

• Cancer deaths in decline
• Killing cancer with a virus
• Power lines and leukemia
• Assault on smoking

For the first time since about 1900, cancer researchers in 1996 reported that the *mortality* (death) rate from cancer in the United States appeared to be declining slightly. In a report published in the journal *Cancer* in November 1996, physicians Philip Cole and Brad Rodu of the University of Alabama at Birmingham reported that mortality rates for all types of cancer fell from a peak of 135 per 100,000 people in 1990 to 130 deaths per 100,000 in 1995. Although the decline was relatively small, the authors believed it signalled the beginning of a downward trend in cancer deaths, because the statistical effects of long-term reductions in smoking and of increased awareness of other cancer-causing risks, such as alcohol and ultraviolet sunlight, were only beginning to appear.

In May 1997, researchers from the University of Chicago reported a similar decrease in *The New England Journal of Medicine.* However, this report emphasized that the drop was not the result of better treatment but was due primarily to an increased public awareness of cancer risks and the wider use of screening techniques to detect cancer at early stages of development, including regular *mammogram screening* (special X-ray scans of breast tissue) to detect breast cancer, *PSA testing* (a special blood test to detect prostate cancer), and more sensitive tests to find hidden or microscopic traces of blood in stool samples for the early diagnosis of cancer of the colon and rectum.

The University of Chicago study also reported that mortality rates by race and sex decreased slightly or remained steady in the 1990's compared with the 1970's. The greatest decline in mortality was seen among African-American men, although the overall death rate was still about 40 percent higher in African-American men than in white men. Reduced death rates were also noted for breast, prostate, lung, and colorectal cancer, the forms of cancer that are most often fatal. The decline in lung cancer mortality, the researchers said, could be directly linked to a decline in smoking over the past 30 years in the United States.

But the most striking decrease in cancer mortality occurred among children. The University of Chicago study showed that the death rate for every major type of childhood cancer decreased by about 50 percent since the 1970's. This death rate was continuing to decrease, with the decline since the mid-1980's greater than that of the 10-year period immediately before. However, certain types of cancer, such as brain tumors, malignant melanoma, non-Hodgkin's lymphoma, and multiple myeloma, showed an increase in mortality since the 1970's.

John C. Bailar, lead author of the University of Chicago study, suggested that, despite notable progress in areas such as childhood cancers, testicular cancer, and Hodgkin's disease, the decreases in cancer mortality were the result of fewer occurrences of certain cancers (such as stomach cancer, which was declining worldwide) and more diagnoses of other cancers in their early stages. He challenged the notion that the decrease in cancer mortality could be attributed in any significant way to improvement in cancer therapy and argued for a shift in emphasis to efforts to prevent cancer.

In response, Cole disputed Bailar's assertion, saying that his study suggested that better treatments accounted for about half of the decline. However, Cole agreed that fewer deaths from lung cancer, due in large

part to less smoking, had played a major role in the decline.

Killing cancer with a virus. A mutant strain of *adenovirus* that produces symptoms of the common cold in humans may soon play an important role in cancer therapy. Researchers from ONYX Pharmaceuticals of Richmond, California, reported this finding in March 1997. Adenoviruses are a group of viruses that attack mucous tissue, especially in the respiratory tract. Scientists from ONYX produced a mutant strain of adenovirus, which they named ONYX-015, by deleting one of its genes, labeled E1B.

When a normal adenovirus invades a human cell, the E1B gene enables the virus to produce proteins that

The U.S. National Cancer Institute (NCI) in March 1997 revised its position on guidelines for breast cancer screening. Previously, the NCI did not recommend *mammogram screening* (X ray of breast tissue to detect cancer) for all women aged 40 to 49. However, many experts believed this position was inadequate. The new guidelines recommend mammogram screening every one to two years for all women in their 40's and every year for all women aged 50 and older. However, women at greater risk should be screened more often.

Talc may be linked to ovarian cancer

A study published in the *American Journal of Epidemiology* in March 1997 found that women who regularly applied talc to their genital area increased their risk of developing ovarian cancer by 60 percent. Ovarian cancer is the fourth deadliest cancer among women; about 14,000 Americans die from the disease each year.

Scientists have suspected a link between talc, a mineral related to asbestos, and ovarian cancer since the 1960's. However, in 1994 a U.S. Food and Drug Administration-sponsored workshop on the issue found insufficient evidence of a link to justify a warning to consumers. Many doctors, however, felt there was enough evidence of ovarian cancer risk to advise women to avoid using talc in the genital area.

suppress the activity of a gene in human cells known as p53. One function of the p53 gene is to prevent viruses from replicating in the human cells. Because the ONYX-015 virus lacks the E1B gene, it cannot overcome p53 activity in normal human cells and therefore cannot replicate inside them. However, about half of all human cancer cells do not have a functioning p53 gene, either because the gene *mutated* (changed) in some way or is missing altogether. Therefore, the ONYX-015 virus can invade these cancer cells, replicate inside them, and destroy them. In other words, the ONYX-015 virus can destroy about half of all tumor cells but

cannot harm noncancerous cells in the human body.

When an infected tumor cell is destroyed, it releases the viruses that have replicated inside it. These viruses can then spread to other tumor cells, and in this way continue and extend tumor cell destruction. When ONYX-015 was given to mice with p53-deficient human tumor grafts in preclinical trials, many of the tumors were destroyed. Moreover, ONYX-015, when taken together with anticancer drugs, produced greater tumor destruction than either ONYX-015 or chemotherapy alone.

These preliminary results have enormous implications for human

According to statistics published in 1997 by the American Cancer Society, the five-year survival rate for people with many types of cancer is quite high. If cancer is diagnosed early, before it has had a chance to spread to other parts of the body, the survival rate for people with many forms of the disease exceeds 90 percent. Some types of cancer, however, are rarely detected before they have spread.

STATISTICS			
The most survivable cancers			
Five-year survival rates for many types of cancer:			
Thyroid	100%	Kidney	88%
Testis	99%	Larynx	84%
Prostate	99%	Oral [mouth]	81%
Breast (female)	97%	Stomach	61%
Melanoma [skin]	95%	Lung	48%
Uterus	95%	Brain	34%
Urinary bladder	93%	Esophagus	22%
Ovary	92%	Liver	13%
Cervix	91%	Pancreas	13%
Colon & rectum	91%		

Source: *Cancer Facts & Figures 1997.*

cancer therapy. Mutation or deletion of p53 is the most common genetic abnormality in human cancer cells, but p53-deficient tumor cells are often resistant to standard cancer drugs and patients with p53-deficient cancers often have shorter survival times than other cancer patients. Trials of ONYX-015 therapy in humans were underway in mid-1997. Early reports showed that some tumors exposed to the virus had shrunk by 50 percent or more.

Power lines and leukemia. In July 1997 investigators from the National Cancer Institute (NCI) in Bethesda, Maryland, and other institutions published a definitive report showing that acute lymphoblastic leukemia (ALL) did not occur more frequently among children who lived close to high voltage power lines. ALL is the most common form of childhood leukemia,

In 1979, a limited study suggested that children living close to high voltage power lines had an increased risk of developing leukemia as a result of exposure to electromagnetic fields. This study included no direct measurement of electromagnetic exposure, but it triggered widespread concern among people who lived near power lines. The suspicion that electromagnetic fields caused cancer spread despite the fact that there was no biological basis for this association. Experimental animals exposed to electromagnetic fields did not develop cancer. In fact, electromagnetic fields had no consistently measurable biologic effect on the animals at all. Nevertheless, since 1979, a number of epidemiologic studies suggested weak associations between living close to high voltage power lines and the risk of developing cancer.

The NCI study compared 638 children with ALL to 620 children without leukemia. It involved the measurement of electromagnetic fields in the homes of these children by technicians who did not know the nature of the study or the health of the subjects being evaluated. In many cases, measurements were also conducted in the houses in which children's mothers had lived during their pregnancy. The study concluded that there was no proof power lines in-

crease the risk of childhood leukemia. In October 1996, the National Research Council of the United States similarly concluded that high voltage power lines do not represent a human health hazard.

Assault on smoking. In June 1997, the attorneys general of most states in the United States and the major American cigarette manufacturers agreed upon a proposal to provide billions of dollars in compensation to states and to change the way cigarettes are marketed. The settlement inspired hope that changes called for in the agreement would encourage more Americans to give up smoking

The wrath of grapes

A chemical substance found in grapes and wine may prevent or even reverse the development and spread of cancer, researchers at the University of Illinois College of Pharmacy announced in January 1997. The researchers said that the substance, resveratrol, may interfere with the development of cancer by blocking the action of cancer-causing agents, inhibiting the growth and spread of cancerous tumors, and reversing the transformation of individual cells from a cancerous to a normal state.

Although grapes are the leading source of resveratrol, the substance is also found in peanuts, lilies, and certain traditional Oriental medicines derived from roots. It may be part of a plant's natural chemical defense against disease. Resveratrol is a relatively simple chemical that could easily be synthesized to make a cancer-fighting drug.

and potentially lead to a further drop in the U.S. cancer death rate.

Under the terms of the proposal, which required congressional and presidential approval, cigarette manufacturers would admit for the first time that smoking is addictive and that it causes cancer. In addition, new, larger warning labels covering 25 percent of the front cover would appear on cigarette packages. These labels would state that cigarettes are addictive and that tobacco smoke causes fatal diseases in nonsmokers. In addition, tobacco marketing directed toward minors would be discontinued, and tobacco company profits amounting to billions of dollars would be turned over to the states over the next 25 years to help offset the cost at the state level of treating cigarette-related health problems.

According to doctors, no part of cancer prevention is more important than the effort to reduce cigarette smoking. Despite vigorous efforts by the government and medical professionals to educate the American public about the dangers of cigarette smoking, about 30 percent of all adult males and about 25 percent of adult females in the United States continued to smoke as of 1996, and about 3,000 people under the age of 20 began smoking every day in the United States. In 1996, 19 percent of all eighth-grade students smoked regularly—an increase over 14 per-

cent in 1991. By the 10th grade, about 25 percent of students were smoking regularly.

Reports from Europe linking cigarette smoking to lung cancer appeared in the scientific literature as early as the 1920's and 1930's. In 1950, a series of five scientific papers from researchers in Britain and the United States provided substantial scientific evidence for this linkage. In 1964, the surgeon general of the United States issued a statement on smoking and health, establishing the causal relationship between cigarette smoking and lung cancer. Since that time, a wealth of convincing scientific evidence has been published identifying cigarette smoke as a direct cause of approximately 30 percent of all cases of cancer diagnosed in the United States.

The cancers caused by cigarette smoking include cancers of the mouth, esophagus, stomach, pancreas, larynx, lung, bladder, kidney, and leukemia, especially acute myeloid leukemia. Cigarette smoke contains some 4,300 chemical compounds, of which 43 are known to cause cancer. Of these known substances, seven—2-naphthylamine, 4-aminobiphenyl, benzene, vinyl chloride, arsenic, chromium, and radioactive polonium—are known to cause cancer in humans.   • Jules E. Harris

See also SMOKING. In WORLD BOOK, see CANCER.

Child Development

- Children and day care
- The terrible 2's
- Bipolar/ADHD link
- Genetic link to social skills
- "Baby blues" and newborns
- Hepatitis B vaccination
- Risks of early puberty

Children in day care are more influenced by their family life than by the day-care setting. That was one of the findings reported in April 1997 by researchers conducting a study of the effects of day care upon children.

The study, conducted by the National Institute of Child Health and Human Development (NICHD—an agency of the National Institutes of Health in Bethesda, Maryland), began in 1991. Researchers observed the children at 6 months of age and planned to continue the study through the first grade.

In the portion of the study reported in 1997, investigators evaluated 1,364 children at 15 months, 2 years, and 3 years of age. The re-

searchers determined that 32 percent of the differences in the children's thinking and language skills were related to their experiences at home. Only 1 percent of the differences were a result of day care.

The study also explored other aspects of day care. Investigators reported that in high-quality day-care settings—those in which staff members were nurturing, supportive, and stimulating—children scored higher on tests measuring thinking and language development skills than children in less attentive day-care settings. The researchers also noted that mothers of children who were in day care full time (more than 30 hours per week) reacted slightly less sensitively to their child at 6 and 36 months of age than mothers of children in day care for short periods. Similarly, children who were in day care full time showed slightly less affection to their mothers at 24 months and 36 months of age. These effects were particularly noticeable in children who had been in day care full time before they were 6 months old.

The researchers concluded that children whose parents provide a warm, attentive family life usually develop good thinking and language skills and have a positive relationship with their mothers. The study also showed that the better the quality of day care, the better a child's thinking and language skills will be and the better the relationship between the child and his or her mother.

The terrible 2's. Parents' personality traits and parenting styles have a major influence on the cooperativeness and manageability of children who are 2 years old. That was the finding reported in July 1996 by researchers at Pennsylvania State University.

The researchers studied 69 families with firstborn sons. (Boys were chosen because they tend to be less cooperative and more aggressive than girls, according to the study authors.) The families were evaluated during home visits when the boys were between 1 and 3 years of age.

The investigators found that the most problematic 2-year-old boys were those whose parents used an authoritarian approach with their children. Authoritarian parents were likely to issue stern commands, such as "Get out of there!" when a child demonstrated curiosity about an object. Parents who used a so-called "control with guidance" approach—one in which they explained why something was not allowed or distracted the child with an appealing alternative— had more cooperative 2-year-olds.

Fathers played a critical role in behavior management, according to the study. The most defiant boys were those whose fathers were introverted, irritable, anxious, or depressed, as well as fathers with few friends or with stressful jobs. The researchers concluded that a child who was particularly defiant during the "terrible

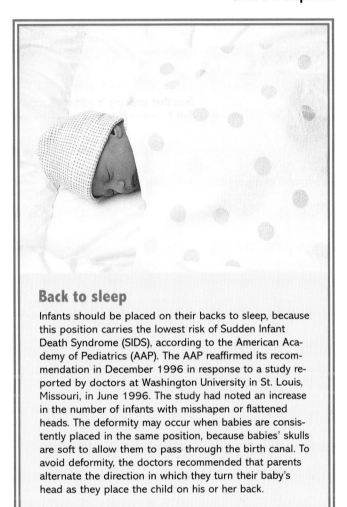

Back to sleep

Infants should be placed on their backs to sleep, because this position carries the lowest risk of Sudden Infant Death Syndrome (SIDS), according to the American Academy of Pediatrics (AAP). The AAP reaffirmed its recommendation in December 1996 in response to a study reported by doctors at Washington University in St. Louis, Missouri, in June 1996. The study had noted an increase in the number of infants with misshapen or flattened heads. The deformity may occur when babies are consistently placed in the same position, because babies' skulls are soft to allow them to pass through the birth canal. To avoid deformity, the doctors recommended that parents alternate the direction in which they turn their baby's head as they place the child on his or her back.

2's" was likely to be defiant later in childhood. However, skilled parenting can improve a child's behavior.

Bipolar/ADHD link. Children with attention-deficit hyperactivity disorder (ADHD) are more likely to develop *bipolar disorder* (manic depression). Researchers at Massachusetts General Hospital in Boston reported in August 1996 that nearly one in four boys with ADHD was also found to have bipolar disorder (BPD).

BPD is a mood disorder in which people experience extremes of depression and *mania* (a state of excessive joy and fast and confused speaking and thinking). ADHD has some of the same symptoms as BPD, including hyperactivity and talkativeness.

The Boston researchers conducted a four-year study of 140 boys with ADHD and 120 boys who did not have the disorder. The boys ranged in age from 6 years to 17 years at the beginning of the study. The researchers initially diagnosed BPD in 11 percent of the boys with ADHD. After four years, an additional 12 percent of the ADHD group had developed BPD. None of the boys in the group without ADHD had BPD at the beginning of the study, and only 2 percent had developed it after four years.

The study also found that boys with both BPD and ADHD were more likely to have a greater number of ADHD symptoms and a family history of mood disorders than boys with only ADHD. Boys with both conditions were more irritable—and more frequently violent—during manic episodes than boys with ADHD alone. The investigators hoped that, by being alert to characteristics such as a greater number of ADHD symptoms and a family history of mood disorders in boys with ADHD, doctors could identify boys with both conditions and treat them appropriately.

Genetic link to social skills. Researchers studying girls with Turner's syndrome at the Institute of Child Health in London reported in June 1997 that genes on the X chromosome may be linked with social skills. Turner's syndrome is a condition in which girls—who usually inherit two X chromosomes, one from each parent (unlike boys, who inherit an X chromosome from their mothers and a Y chromosome from their fathers)—are born missing an X chromosome, or part of one. Because of this deficiency, girls with Turner's syndrome are often short, have a thick neck, and are infertile. In addition, researchers noted that girls with Turner's syndrome usually have normal intelligence, but tend to have fewer social skills than other girls.

The British researchers analyzed the behavioral differences between school-age girls with Turner's syndrome who inherited the X chromosome from their fathers and girls who inherited the X chromosome from their mothers. The study showed that 40 percent of the girls who inherited the maternal chromosome had documented incidents of behavioral problems in school. Only 16 percent of the girls who inherited the X chromosome from their fathers had such problems. The researchers hoped that finding the gene that influences social skills would help not only girls with Turner's syndrome, but boys, who generally have more behavioral and learning disorders, as well.

"Baby blues" and newborns. New mothers who experience depression after childbirth—often called postpartum depression, or "baby blues"—

Wash those germs away
Children who wash their hands four or more times a day at school or day care are less likely to become sick with infectious diseases than children who wash less frequently. Doctors at Providence Hospital in Southfield, Michigan, reported in July 1996 that the children who frequently washed their hands lost 24 percent fewer days to colds and flu and 50 percent fewer days to stomach illnesses.

New polio vaccine recommendations

In January 1997, the Centers for Disease Control and Prevention, the American Academy of Family Physicians, and the American Academy of Pediatrics released a new childhood immunization schedule for polio. According to the organizations, any of the three polio vaccination schedules listed below is acceptable. Consult your doctor to determine which schedule is best for your child.

Form of Vaccine	When Administered	Risks and Benefits
Oral vaccine (OPV)	2 months 4 months 6 to 18 months 4 to 6 years	• Contains the live vaccine; slight risk of death or paralysis. • Inexpensive and easy to give; allows for greatest number of children to be immunized.
Inactivated vaccine (IPV)	2 months 4 months 12 to 18 months 4 to 6 years	• Because it must be injected, it is less convenient and more expensive than OPV; may result in fewer children being immunized. • Does not cause paralysis or other serious side effects.
Sequential IPV/OPV	IPV at 2 months IPV at 4 months OPV at 12 to 18 months OPV at 4 to 6 years	• Giving IPV first lessens the risk of paralysis and death from OPV. • Less expensive and easier to administer than the all-IPV schedule.

Source: Centers for Disease Control and Prevention, *Morbidity and Mortality Weekly Report,* Jan. 31, 1997.

can compensate for the effects of their depression on the baby by touching the child more often. Researchers at Florida International University and the University of Miami reported this finding in August 1996.

Mothers with postpartum depression may feel sad and anxious, cry often, and feel anger toward their infants. Such mothers tend not to smile at their babies and avoid eye contact with them, according to the study.

The researchers videotaped 48 new mothers—some of whom were depressed—and their 3-month-old babies. The mothers alternated activities in 90-second periods. First, each mother played with her baby in her normal manner. Then, the mother stared blankly and silently at her in-

fant without touching the baby. Next, while still showing no expression, the mother gently touched and stroked her baby's arms and legs. Finally, each mother played again with her baby in her normal manner.

The researchers noted that, when the babies of depressed mothers felt their mother's touch, they responded with smiles and sounds and often gazed at their mother's hands. The babies of nondepressed mothers— who were used to seeing their mothers smile—did not respond positively to a touch that was not accompanied by talking or smiling. The investigators concluded that mothers can make up for the negative impact of their post-partum depression by frequently touching their babies.

Hepatitis B vaccination. Researchers in Taipei, Taiwan, reported in June 1997 a dramatic drop in the number of children who developed hepatocellular carcinoma, the most common form of liver cancer. Taiwanese children are immunized against the hepatitis B virus, a virus that causes up to 80 percent of all hepatocellular cancers, as part of a nationwide program instituted in Taiwan in 1984.

The researchers studied data collected by the Taiwan National Cancer Registry on liver cancer in children. The investigators found that the average annual incidence of hepatocellular carcinoma in 6- to 14-year-olds dropped from 0.70 per 100,000 children between 1981 and 1986 to 0.36 per 100,000 between 1990 and 1994. Even more dramatic was the drop in hepatocellular carcinoma in 6- to 19-year-olds. Incidence of the liver cancer fell from 0.52 per 100,000 in children born between 1974 and 1984 to 0.13 in children born between 1984 and 1986.

The researchers concluded that a nationwide immunization program is an extremely effective method of controlling the spread of the hepatitis B virus and the resulting liver cancer. In 1997, universal immunization programs were in place in 85 countries, including the United States.

Risks of early puberty. Girls who enter puberty at younger ages are at greater risk for psychiatric problems than those who develop later. Researchers at Stanford University in California reported this finding in February 1997.

The Stanford team evaluated 1,463 sixth-, seventh-, and eighth-grade girls for signs of puberty and for the presence of so-called "internalizing" symptoms—those associated with depression, anxiety, panic attacks, and low self-image. After annual check-ups for up to six years, the researchers found that girls who had internalizing symptoms were an average of five months younger when they reached the midpoint of puberty than girls without such symptoms.

The Stanford findings were particularly timely in light of an April 1997 report by 225 pediatricians in the Pediatric Research in Office Settings network (a research group organized by the American Academy of Pediatrics). In their analysis of more than 17,000 girls between ages 3 and 12, the pediatricians concluded that girls are "developing pubertal characteristics at younger ages than suggested in standard pediatric textbooks and in earlier U.S. studies." The physicians hoped that awareness that puberty may begin earlier than previously thought would help physicians and other health-care professionals who educate and treat girls entering puberty.   • Richard Trubo

In WORLD BOOK, see CHILD.

Dentistry

- New laser treatment for cavities
- Dental sealants prevent decay
- Genetically engineered saliva cells for cancer patients

The first laser system for repairing cavities was approved by the U.S. Food and Drug Administration in May 1997. The system, developed by Premier Laser Systems, Incorporated, of Irvine, California, was marketed as a virtually painless alternative to conventional drilling.

Dentists fill 170 million cavities each year, usually by injecting a patient with local anesthetic and then drilling to remove the decayed portion of the tooth. The drill's noise and vibration can make the procedure painful and frightening for patients. Dentists had previously used less powerful lasers to treat gum disease and to whiten teeth. But early lasers powerful enough to cut through the hard tissue of teeth became so hot that they damaged the teeth.

The new laser, called the Erbium YAG, was tested by five dentists in more than 1,300 procedures. The tests showed that the Erbium YAG is safe for removing decayed tooth material. Most of the patients tested felt little discomfort, experienced no noise or vibration, and did not need anesthesia. The dentists were able to repair cavities more quickly—since they did not need to wait for anesthesia to take effect—and more precisely, allowing them to preserve more of the patient's healthy tooth.

Dental sealants are almost 100 percent effective in preventing decay on

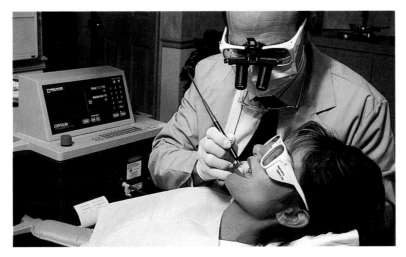

A new dental laser for treating cavities was approved by the U.S. Food and Drug Administration in May 1997. Unlike dental drills, the laser causes minimal discomfort, and most patients require no anesthesia. A beam of light, directed from a tabletop unit, travels through a cable and exits from a hand-held device. The dentist and the patient must wear special glasses to protect their eyes during the procedure.

the chewing surfaces of teeth, according to a report published in the *Journal of the American Dental Association* (JADA) in February 1997. Sealants are a plastic coating applied to the surfaces of *permanent molars*, the back teeth that begin to replace a child's "baby teeth" at about the age of 6 or 7. The coating forms a protective barrier over the natural pits and *fissures* (cracks) in which decay often begins.

The report, prepared by an ADA panel, stated that 82 percent of sealants remained intact five years after they were applied, providing almost complete protection against decay. Sealants not only prevent cavities from forming, they can also stop decay at an early stage by preventing oxygen and bacteria from coming into contact with a tooth.

Despite the proven effectiveness of sealants, less than 20 percent of American children had dental sealants on their permanent molars by 1996. One reason for the low usage of sealants, according to the panel, may be the fact that not all private health insurance plans and only 33 state Medicaid health insurance programs provided partial or complete payment for dental sealants.

Genetically engineered saliva cells could lead to a new treatment for thousands of people whose salivary glands are damaged during radiation treatment for head and neck cancer. In April 1997, scientists at the Na-

tional Institute of Dental Research (NIDR), an agency of the National Institutes of Health in Bethesda, Maryland, announced success in genetically engineering nonfluid-producing cells in the mouth into making saliva.

Radiation therapy sometimes kills *acinar cells*, cells in the salivary glands that produce saliva. Cancer patients develop *xerostomia* (dry mouth), which leads to such problems as difficulty swallowing, a higher risk of tooth decay, and frequent mouth infections.

NIDR researchers noted that radiation often does not kill *ductal cells,* cells in the salivary gland that do not secrete saliva. The researchers genetically altered ductal cells by transferring a gene into the cells that produce *aquaporin,* a protein that forms pores in cell membranes. Saliva can then pass through the pores.

The researchers inserted aquaporin genes into the ductal cells of one group of laboratory rats that had been exposed to radiation. Another group of rats, which had also been irradiated, did not get the gene. The researchers found that the rats that had been given the aquaporin genes produced substantially more saliva than rats that were not given the genes. Although the researchers said that it may be years before gene transfer can be used in people, they believed the experiment was a promising first step toward managing xerostomia.   • Michael Woods

In WORLD BOOK, see DENTISTRY.

Diabetes

In June 1997, an international panel of diabetes experts sponsored by the American Diabetes Association (ADA) issued guidelines recommending that doctors consider testing all their adult patients for diabetes by the age of 45. This testing would detect Type II diabetes (the most common type of diabetes) in an early stage—before such complications as heart, kidney, and eye problems develop. Early treatment is more effective in controlling the disease.

The panel also recommended changing the point at which a person is diagnosed as being diabetic. Diagnosis is typically performed with a test called the *fasting plasma glucose test,* which measures the level of sugar, or glucose, in a person's blood. Diabetics have elevated levels of glucose. The recommendations called for a diagnosis of diabetes to be made when glucose levels are 126 milligrams per deciliter of blood or higher—as opposed to the minimum level of 140 milligrams per deciliter of blood that is commonly used. This decreased level for diagnosis was recommended because studies have shown that complications from diabetes can occur at lower glucose levels than previously believed.

The new guidelines, which were endorsed by the United States National Institutes of Health, stated that people who test negative for diabetes should generally be retested every three years, and that people who are at high risk for diabetes would benefit from being tested more often. High-risk people include African Americans, American Indians, Hispanics, and individuals who are obese or have a family history of the disease.

The ADA said that many people with Type II diabetes have the disease several years before it is diagnosed. The association expected that the new guidelines would lead to the diagnosis and treatment of 2 million Americans who were previously unaware that they had the disease.

New class of diabetes drugs. A drug approved by the U.S. Food and Drug Administration in January 1997 allows some people with Type II diabetes to eliminate or reduce their reliance on insulin injections. Insulin is a hormone that converts glucose into energy. The cells of people with Type II diabetes are resistant to the activities of insulin and, as a result, glucose builds up in their bodies. Injections of insulin often help to control glucose levels. The drug troglitazone, which is taken orally, was approved for Type II diabetics who have poor control of their glucose levels.

Troglitazone (sold under the brand name of Rezulin) was the first of a new class of drugs called insulin sensitizers to be approved. Insulin sensi-

The number of Americans with diabetes increased from less than 5 per 1,000 people in the 1930's to more than 30 per 1,000 people in the 1990's. One of the main reasons for the increase in the diabetes rate was an increase in the obesity rate in the United States. Obesity is a major factor in increasing the risk of diabetes. In fact, 80 to 90 percent of people with Type II diabetes, the most common type of diabetes, are overweight.

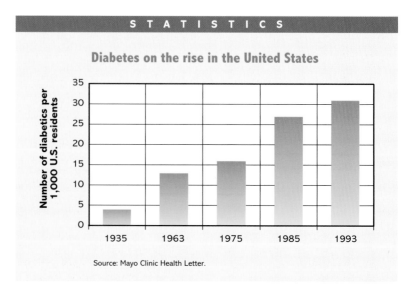

S T A T I S T I C S

Diabetes on the rise in the United States

Number of diabetics per 1,000 U.S. residents

Source: Mayo Clinic Health Letter.

tizers make cells less resistant to insulin. Because troglitazone enables diabetics to use insulin more efficiently, fewer insulin injections (and in some cases, no injections) are needed to control glucose levels.

Certain foods prevent diabetes.

Simple dietary changes, such as switching from white to whole-grain bread and from sugar-laden to high-fiber cereals, may reduce a woman's risk of developing Type II diabetes. A study of more than 65,000 women, published in February 1997, indicated that women who eat foods high in fiber and low in certain carbohydrates are less likely to develop diabetes than other women.

The study, which was part of the Nurses' Health Study at the Harvard School of Public Health in Boston, found a number of foods to be associated with a high risk of diabetes, including white bread, white rice, cooked potatoes, and cola drinks. These foods are all high in types of carbohydrates that are rapidly absorbed by the body. The researchers said that rapidly absorbed carbohydrates tend to trigger surges in glucose levels. Over time, high levels of glucose can lead to insulin resistance and diabetes.

In contrast to these foods, whole-grain breakfast cereals and other grain products that have been minimally processed contain carbohydrates that are absorbed gradually—and thus do not trigger glucose surges. This characteristic combined with the fact that such grain products are high in fiber (which reduces the need for insulin) makes them effective in preventing diabetes, according to the researchers. The study indicated that large amounts of cereal fiber can reduce the risk of developing Type II diabetes by 28 percent.

Diabetes and early menopause.

According to a study published in June 1997, women who developed diabetes in childhood are likely to enter *menopause* (the time in life when menstrual periods cease) at a younger age than other women. Early menopause is associated with an increased risk of *cardiovascular* (heart and blood vessel) disease.

New way to take insulin

A device making it easier for diabetics to take insulin was tested on patients in 1997. The user inserts a package of powdered insulin into the device's base, where it is punctured. When the pistol grip on the base is squeezed, compressed air carries the insulin as an aerosol into the clear chamber above the base. The insulin aerosol can be inhaled in a single breath through the mouthpiece at the top of the device, *right*. The particles of insulin are microscopic in size, *left*, enabling them to enter lung tissue and be absorbed into the bloodstream quickly. The device's developer, Inhale Therapeutic Systems of Palo Alto, California, expected the device to be marketed by the year 2001.

The study, by researchers at the University of Pittsburgh Graduate School of Public Health, compared women with Type I diabetes (the type of diabetes that typically strikes in childhood) with their sisters who were nondiabetic. Although the age at menopause varied widely among the women, the diabetic women reached menopause at an average age of 40.7 years—compared with 49.9 years for their sisters. The diabetic women who experienced early menopause developed diabetes at an average age of 8.6 years. The diabetic women who entered menopause at a normal time developed diabetes at an average age of 13.7 years.

The researchers recommended that women with diabetes try to manage the various risk factors for cardiovascular disease by not smoking and by adopting a low-fat diet, getting regular exercise, and avoiding obesity.

Is milk risky? A study published in August 1996 contradicted certain previous studies by finding that when babies with family histories of diabetes are given diets of cow's milk, their risk of developing diabetes does not increase.

The study, by researchers at the University of Colorado School of Medicine in Denver, looked for an association between the diets of 253 babies from diabetes-prone families and the presence of certain antibod-

ies known to be early indicators of diabetes. No association was found between diets of cow's milk and the presence of these antibodies.

Because a number of other studies had previously shown a relationship between diabetes and early exposure to cow's milk (and also to certain infant formulas), some physicians recommend that babies with family histories of diabetes be breastfed. However, other physicians believe that there is not enough evidence to justify the avoidance of cow's milk, which contains many essential nutrients valuable to a baby's health.

• Richard Trubo

In WORLD BOOK, see DIABETES.

Digestive System

• Bacterial infections and ulcers

• Ulcers and cancer risks

• Immunity in the small intestine

• Irritating bone medication

In September 1996, the U.S. Food and Drug Administration approved a breath test to diagnose infection by the bacterium *Helicobacter pylori,* a primary cause of *gastric* (stomach) and *duodenal* (small intestine) ulcers. Previously, diagnosis of *H. pylori* infection required a painful *biopsy* (sampling) of stomach tissue, a process in which a tube is inserted down the throat.

With the new test, a patient swallows a natural substance called urea, which includes carbon atoms that are slightly heavier than normal. The *H. pylori* bacteria produce an enzyme, called urease, that breaks down urea, releasing carbon dioxide that the patient then exhales into a bag. An instrument called a mass spectrometer detects the slightly heavier carbon dioxide present in the breath when bacteria break down urea.

Urease was also the basis of an experimental vaccine used to prevent *H. pylori* infection. A vaccine is a dead or weakened microorganism or a part of the microbe that stimulates an immune response without causing symptoms. Researchers from pharmaceutical companies in France and the United States reported findings of tests at a conference in Copenhagen, Denmark, in October 1996.

In the 1996 study, 24 people with confirmed *H. pylori* infection received either the urease vaccine with an *adjuvant* (helping substance), an adjuvant alone, or a *placebo* (inactive

substance). Only patients receiving the urease vaccine developed *antibodies* (disease-fighting proteins) against the bacterium. The presence of antibodies indicated the patients were developing an immunity to *H. pylori* bacteria.

Additional research, published in November 1996, revealed that *H. pylori* can be transmitted orally. At the James H. Quileen College of Medicine in Johnson City, Tennessee, gastroenterologist Eapen Thomas and his colleagues used a sophisticated biochemical test to look for genes specific to *H. pylori* in stomach biopsy samples, saliva, and feces of infected individuals.

In the Quileen College experiment, the test detected *H. pylori* genes in all of the stomach biopsies, but the telltale bacterial genes were also common in saliva. The genes were not, however, common in feces. The researchers concluded, therefore, that oral transmission of *H. pylori* is possible.

Ulcers and cancer risks. An international team of *oncologists* (cancer specialists), led by Lars-Erik Hansson of Uppsala University in Sweden, reported in July 1996 that people with gastric ulcers had twice the expected risk of developing stomach cancer as the general population. People with duodenal ulcers, however, showed a 40 percent reduction in the risk of stomach cancer.

The researchers based their findings on the medical histories of nearly 58,000 patients taken over an average period of about nine years. The researchers suggested that genetic background, the age at which infection begins, and other infections may be important factors in determining whether a person with the bacterial infection develops cancer. They also concluded that unidentified processes involved in duodenal ulcers may alter the cancer-causing ability of *H. pylori*.

Immunity in the small intestine. In March 1997, molecular biologists Jin Wang, Michael Whetsell, and John Klein of the University of Tulsa in Oklahoma reported findings on how immunity arises from the interaction between white blood cells and the cells in the lining of the small intestine. Researchers had known for years that the immune system protects the digestive tract, but they knew few details of how the system functioned in the small intestine.

The small intestine has a lining that is only one cell thick. While the lining provides extensive surface area for the bloodstream to absorb nutrients, the thin lining also makes it easy for disease-causing bacteria in foods to pass through to the body.

The Tulsa researchers discovered that specialized white blood cells in the small intestine secrete a biochemical called thyroid stimulating hormone (TSH) that was previously thought to originate in the brain. TSH causes nearby lining cells to produce protective antibody proteins. At the same time, the white blood cells secrete *cytokines,* another class of immune system biochemicals. The cytokines bind to the lining cells and activate the cells to resist infection caused by microbes in food.

The researchers hypothesized that disruptions in the immune control of the small intestine might cause digestive inflammatory disorders, because inflammation is part of the immune system response to infections.

Irritating bone medication. Three articles published in October 1996 examined contradictory follow-up studies of alendronate, a popular drug sold under the name Fosamax, and the drug's potentially harmful effects on the *esophagus*, the passageway between the mouth and the stomach. Fosamax, first introduced in 1995, is prescribed to treat bone disorders, such as osteoporosis and Paget's disease of bone. In more than 2 percent of cases, however, the drug has reportedly caused severe irritation of the esophagus.

Fosamax treats bone disorders by increasing the bone mass. Because the drug is known to irritate the esophagus, physicians and packaging labels warn patients to take the drug with a full glass of water before

**Breath test
for ulcer bug**

A new test to diagnose infection by *Helicobacter pylori,* the bacterium that causes most ulcers of the stomach and small intestine, is called the Meretek UBT Breath Test Collection Kit. A patient swallows a solution that causes a reaction with the bacteria, producing a gas that can be measured in the person's breath. The Food and Drug Administration approved the test in September 1996.

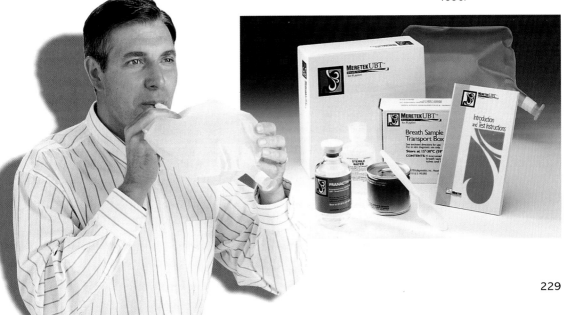

breakfast, to wait at least 30 minutes before eating, and not to lie down for 30 minutes after taking the drug.

Gastroenterologist (digestive system specialist) Piet C. de Groen at the Mayo Clinic and Foundation in Rochester, Minnesota, and colleagues evaluated effects of the drug on 199 patients. Fifty-one of the patients had esophageal disorders categorized as serious or severe, and 32 patients were hospitalized.

In contrast, researchers from Beilinson Medical Center in Petah-Tikva, Israel, and Merck Research Laboratories in Rahway, New Jersey, reported that they found no difference among people taking either a low, medium,

or high dose of Fosamax or a placebo in a drug evaluation that included 994 individuals. The difference in the two studies was that the participants in the second study had frequent medical checkups and were often reminded how to take the medication.

Donald Castell, a gastroenterologist at Graduate Hospital in Philadelphia, concluded in a review of the two articles that the difference in occurrence of esophageal side effects in the two studies underscored the importance of following instructions when taking medication.   • Ricki Lewis

In the section On the Medical Frontier, see INFLAMMATORY BOWEL DISEASE. In WORLD BOOK, see DIGESTIVE SYSTEM.

Drugs

- Continuing progress in the treatment of HIV infection
- Drug for interstitial cystitis
- New drugs for managing asthma
- An alternative to Seldane
- A second drug for Alzheimer's
- Protection against poison ivy

The U.S. Food and Drug Administration (FDA) approved nelfinavir mesylate in March 1997 and delavirdine mesylate in April 1997, increasing to 11 the number of drugs marketed in the United States for the treatment of infections caused by HIV, the virus that causes AIDS. Before December 1995, only 4 of these 11 drugs had been available.

Nelfinavir (sold as Viracept) was the fourth in a class of HIV drugs known as protease inhibitors to be approved, joining saquinavir (sold as Invirase), ritonavir (sold as Norvir), and indinavir (sold as Crixivan). Delavirdine (sold as Rescriptor) was the second HIV drug known as a nonnucleoside reverse transcriptase inhibitor to be approved, joining nevirapine (Viramune). Both of these classes of HIV drugs work by preventing the virus from *replicating* (reproducing). Nonnucleoside reverse transcriptase inhibitors attack HIV at the start of the replication cycle; protease inhibitors interfere with replication at the end of the cycle.

Although no single drug or combination of drugs will cure an HIV infection, the use of various combinations of drugs has yielded encouraging results, including significant reduction in the amount of the virus detectable in the blood, decreased death rate, and fewer instances of complications of HIV infections. In almost all HIV infections, two or three drugs are used together because the combination pro-

vides a greater action against HIV and may also reduce its ability to develop resistance to any one drug. Combination treatments may also reduce the risk of harmful side effects.

Drug for interstitial cystitis. In September 1996, the FDA approved pentosan polysulfate sodium (sold under the brand name Elmiron) as the first orally administered treatment for the relief of pain and discomfort associated with interstitial cystitis. Interstitial cystitis is a chronic disease of the urinary bladder that is characterized by severe pain in the bladder and pelvic area and a frequent need to urinate. It affects an estimated 100,000 to 500,000 people in the United States, primarily women. The symptoms often make it difficult for people with the disease to function in a work environment and also often prevent a person from sleeping.

Although the symptoms of interstitial cystitis are generally similar to those of a severe bladder infection, microorganisms are not detected in urinalysis and symptoms do not respond to antibiotics. Until recently, the only medication available in the United States to treat interstitial cystitis was dimethyl sulfoxide, but this drug has to be delivered directly into the bladder using a catheter inserted through the *urethra* (passage that carries urine from the bladder out of the body).

Pentosan will not cure the disorder,

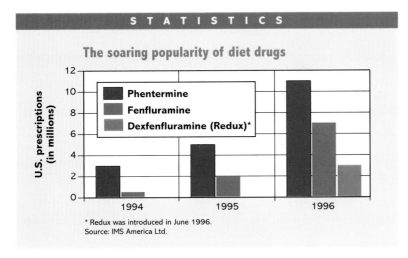

The soaring popularity of diet drugs

U.S. prescriptions (in millions)

- Phentermine
- Fenfluramine
- Dexfenfluramine (Redux)*

1994   1995   1996

* Redux was introduced in June 1996.
Source: IMS America Ltd.

Sales of prescription drugs that help people lose weight skyrocketed in the United States in 1996. The approval of dexfenfluramine (sold under the brand name Redux) helped fuel the popularity of these medications. These drugs were intended to treat people who were clinically obese—at least 20 to 30 percent over their ideal weight—but many people used the drugs in place of exercise or eating a healthy diet.

nor will it reduce symptoms in all patients for whom it is prescribed. In fact, though study results varied, only about one-third of patients who were treated with the new drug for at least three months experienced significant improvement in pain symptoms. However, pentosan was an important advance in the treatment of a condition for which so few treatment options were available.

One individual who benefited significantly from the use of pentosan was professional golfer Terry-Jo Myers. Prior to using pentosan, Myers experienced extreme pain and typically needed to use the bathroom 40 to 60 times a day, making an 18-hole round of golf almost impossible. After using the drug, her pain and frequent need to urinate subsided, and she was able to resume competing in golf tournaments. In February 1997, Myers won the Los Angeles Classic, her first victory since 1988.

New drugs for managing asthma. In 1996, two new medications, zafirlukast and zileuton, were approved for use in the United States for the prevention and treatment of asthma. Zafirlukast (sold as Accolate) was approved by the FDA in September, followed by zileuton (sold as Zyflo) in December. These were the first drugs created to treat asthma by inhibiting the action of *leukotrienes,* naturally occurring chemicals in the body that contribute to the inflammation of lung tissues. Inflammation causes the air-

ways to become constricted, making it difficult to breathe. Although both medications block the action of leukotrienes, they do so by different mechanisms—zafirlukast selectively blocks the action of leukotrienes at the receptors at which they act, whereas zileuton inhibits the formation of leukotrienes themselves.

Neither drug is intended to treat *acute* (severe, sudden onset) episodes of asthma, because they act much too slowly to be of value in such situations. There also has been no study comparing the effectiveness of zafirlukast or zileuton with corticosteroids, which have been used for many years to treat asthma.

An alternative to Seldane. In July 1996, the FDA approved fexofenadine (sold as Allegra), a derivative of terfenadine, for sale in the United States as a treatment for allergy symptoms. Introduced in 1985, terfenadine (sold as Seldane) was the first prescription antihistamine to relieve allergy symptoms without causing drowsiness. However, a number of serious and even fatal cardiovascular reactions to the drug, including irregular heartbeat, were reported.

Investigators discovered that people who used terfenadine at the same time that they were taking the antibiotic erythromycin or the antifungal drug ketoconazole risked raising the concentration of terfenadine in their bodies to toxic levels, causing potentially fatal *cardiac arrhythmia* (irregu-

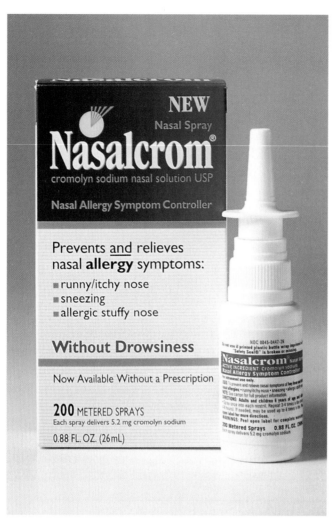

Relief for allergies

Cromolyn sodium nasal spray was approved for sale without a prescription in the United States in January 1997. Sold as Nasalcrom, it was the first over-the-counter medication that could both treat and prevent sneezing and nasal congestion associated with seasonal allergies. In addition, unlike other nonprescription allergy medicines, Nasalcrom did not cause drowsiness. However, the drug has to be taken three or four times a day to be effective.

lar heart rhythm). People with liver disease were also at increased risk.

Clinical studies showed that fexofenadine was as effective as terfenadine in reducing allergic symptoms such as runny nose, sneezing, itchy nose and throat, and itchy, watery, or red eyes, and was also unlikely to cause drowsiness. But fexofenadine, although it shares most of the properties of terfenadine, was not likely to cause cardiovascular reactions, even when taken in doses higher than recommended.

Several other effective antihistamines that do not cause drowsiness, such as Hismanal and Claritin, have also become available in the years since terfenadine was introduced. Therefore, the FDA announced

in January 1997 its intention to withdraw its approval of terfenadine. Manufacturers immediately appealed the FDA's decision, asserting that the drug was safe as long as it was taken in the proper dosage and the warnings on the product labeling were followed. The question of whether Seldane would remain on the market in the United States remained undecided in mid-1997.

A second drug for Alzheimer's. In November 1996, the FDA approved the marketing of donepezil hydrochloride (marketed as Aricept) for the treatment of patients with mild to moderate symptoms of Alzheimer's disease. It was the second drug in the United States to be approved for this condition. The first, tacrine (sold as Cognex), was introduced in 1993.

Alzheimer's disease generally affects older people. It causes the degeneration of brain cells, which leads to the loss of *cognitive* (mental) functions, such as memory, reasoning ability, and judgment. Neither tacrine nor donepezil could cure Alzheimer's disease, nor were they shown to prevent progression of the disease. However, both drugs have produced modest improvement in some areas of cognitive function and quality of life in people with less severe forms of the disease.

Although studies comparing donepezil and tacrine have not been conducted, the two drugs appeared to be about equally effective. However, donepezil has several advantages. For example, unlike tacrine, donepezil apparently does not cause harmful side effects involving the liver. In addition, donepezil may be taken just once a day; tacrine must be taken four times a day.

Protection against poison ivy. In August 1996, the FDA approved the over-the-counter sale of bentoquatam lotion (marketed as IvyBlock) to help protect people against *allergic dermatitis*—rashes, blisters, and swelling of the skin caused by contact with poison ivy, poison oak, or poison sumac plants.

The substance in poison ivy, poison oak, and poison sumac that causes an allergic reaction is called urushiol.

Roster of AIDS-fighting drugs

The following 11 drugs were available in the United States for the treatment of HIV infection as of June 1997.

Protease inhibitors	Nucleoside reverse transcriptase inhibitors	Nonnucleoside reverse transcriptase inhibitors
• Indinavir (sold as Crixivan)	• Didanosine (sold as Videx)	• Delavirdine mesylate (sold as Rescriptor)
• Nelfinavir mesylate (sold as Viracept)	• Stavudine (sold as Zerit)	• Nevirapine (sold as Viramune)
• Ritonavir (sold as Norvir)	• Lamivudine (sold as Epivir)	
• Saquinavir mesylate (sold as Invirase)	• Zalcitabine (sold as Hivid)	
	• Zidovudine (sold as Retrovir)	

The U.S. Food and Drug Administration approved nelfinavir mesylate and delavirdine mesylate in early 1997 for use in the treatment of HIV infections (HIV is the virus that causes AIDS). Seven new AIDS-fighting drugs have been introduced in the United States since November 1995. Therapies with various combinations of these and other drugs have yielded encouraging results in many AIDS patients.

Coming in contact with poisonous plants is the most common cause of allergic dermatitis in the United States. This is of particular concern for outdoor workers, such as park and highway maintenance workers, utility workers, farmers, and firefighters. In California, Oregon, and Washington, for example, approximately one-third of U.S. Forest Service firefighters typically are forced to leave during a fire because they develop rashes caused by poison oak. Exposure to burning poisonous plants can also cause allergic reactions, because urushiol droplets can stick to dust or smoke particles and be carried by the wind.

IvyBlock is prepared by combining bentoquatam, an organic compound, with bentonite, a natural clay that has been included in certain cosmetics and other products. When it is applied, the lotion formulation in which bentoquatam is used leaves a thin white coating on the skin, which acts as a barrier that helps prevent urushiol from reaching the skin, preventing or at least reducing the severity of the rash.
• Daniel A. Hussar

See also AIDS; RESPIRATORY SYSTEM. In WORLD BOOK, see DRUG.

Ear and Hearing

The number of children's ear infections is rising, according to researchers at the University of Rochester School of Medicine and Dentistry in New York. The researchers reported in March 1997 that children born in 1988 developed *otitis media* (middle ear disease) 44 percent more often than children born in 1981.

The researchers used data from the National Health Interview Survey, which gathered information from parents about the illnesses of their children under 6 years of age. The study showed that the number of ear infections rose in children from all regions of the United States and from all racial and ethnic groups. African American children, however, had fewer ear infections than white children, a result the researchers could not explain.

The investigators concluded that the rising number of children attending day care may play a role in the increase in ear infections. Children in day care and those with allergies had more ear infections than other children, according to the study.

Risk factors for ear infections. Researchers at the University of Pittsburgh School of Medicine in Pennsylvania confirmed a higher prevalence of ear infections. The Pittsburgh study, released in March 1997, also showed that African American children from low-income families develop just as many ear infections as

• Rise in ear infections
• Risk factors for ear infections
• Social skills and hearing loss
• Chewing gum and ear infections
• Cycles of ear growth

white children from low-income families. The researchers theorized that other studies found fewer ear infections in African American children because these children generally have less access to medical care than do white children and, thus, their ear infections may not be diagnosed.

The study also found that some children are at greater risk of ear infections than others. The researchers evaluated 2,253 children from 2 months to 2 years of age. The children had ear infections during an average of 20 percent of their first year of life and 17 percent of their second year. The study found that boys had more ear infections than girls, and that children who lived in urban areas, children who were in contact with many youngsters at home or in day care, and children with family members who smoked had ear infections more often than other children.

Social skills and hearing loss. The temporary hearing loss that children often develop during an ear infection may make the children more withdrawn in social situations. That was the finding reported in August 1996 by researchers at Pennsylvania State University and at the University of Michigan. Children develop ear infections when fluid builds up in the middle ear and becomes infected. The fluid causes hearing loss.

The researchers observed 36 children in day-care centers. The children were 1 year old when the two-year study began. Children with ear infections for at least 20 percent of the two-year period—about 2½ months per year—played alone more often and started conversations less often than children with fewer infections.

The researchers concluded that children with frequent hearing losses because of ear infections learn to withdraw from situations requiring many verbal interactions—such as in day-care settings—because such interactions are more difficult for them than for other children. The habit of withdrawing, noted the researchers, remains even when the children are older and have fewer ear infections.

Chewing gum and ear infections. Xylitol, a sweetener often found in chewing gum, cuts down the frequency of ear infections in children, ac-

---

Tune in for better hearing

Hearing aids are smaller, sleeker, and more versatile than those worn 20 years ago. Digital hearing aids, *left,* can be programmed for the specific hearing needs of the wearer.

Type	Description
Body-worn amplification	A box worn on a belt or under clothing, connected by a wire to an earpiece; most visible type, but also the most powerful.
Behind the ear (BTE)	A case worn behind the ear connected by a tube to an earpiece; more visible than ITE, ITC, or CIC, but also more versatile; can be digitally programmed.
In the ear (ITE)	Fits in the hollow of the ear; less visible than body-worn or BTE; more versatile than ITC or CIC; can be digitally programmed.
In the canal (ITC)	Barely noticeable; needs frequent battery changes and cleaning; can be digitally programmed.
Completely in the canal (CIC)	The least noticeable; needs frequent battery changes and cleaning; has more options than ITC, such as a telephone switch; can be digitally programmed.

Critically reviewed by Ellen Pfeffer Lafargue, M.A., C.C.C.A., Assistant Director of Audiology, League for the Hard of Hearing.

cording to a November 1996 report in the *British Medical Journal*. Researchers at the University of Oulu in Finland tested 306 children in day-care centers. About half of the children chewed gum containing sugar five times a day for two months while the others chewed gum with xylitol. Those chewing the xylitol-containing gum had 40 percent fewer ear infections than the sugar-gum group. The researchers theorized that xylitol minimizes the growth of bacteria called pneumococci, thus preventing ear infections caused by these organisms.

Cycles of ear growth. Researchers at the Louis Bolk Institute in the Neth-

erlands and at the University of Leuven in Belgium reported in December 1996 that men's ears grow in seven-year cycles. The investigators based their findings on data from a British study, which reported in 1995 that men's ears grow almost one-half inch over a period of 50 years.

The Dutch and Belgian researchers calculated the "mean ear length" of 206 men each year from the time the men were 30 years old until they reached 83 years of age. The investigators found that ear growth reaches a peak every seven years and then lapses into a rest period.

• Richard Trubo

In WORLD BOOK, see DEAFNESS; EAR.

Contaminated strawberries from Mexico, raspberries from Guatemala and Chile, and lettuce from Arizona and Peru caused several outbreaks of food poisoning in early 1997. In March, more than 180 children and adults in Michigan became sick after eating strawberries contaminated with the hepatitis A virus. The same shipment of strawberries may have also infected school children in California and Georgia with the virus.

Hepatitis A is a relatively mild form of the liver disease that causes fever, fatigue, loss of appetite, nausea, abdominal pain, and dark urine. It can also turn the eyes and skin yellow.

The hepatitis A virus often does not produce observable symptoms in young children, but it can lead to more serious illness in adults.

An estimated 9,000 school children in Los Angeles and 1,000 in Georgia, who may have eaten the contaminated berries in their school lunches, were immunized with gamma globulin as a protective measure, and none of the children developed hepatitis A. (Gamma globulin is a blood plasma protein that provides a temporary immunity to the disease.)

In June, the Centers for Disease Control and Prevention (CDC) in Atlanta, Georgia, reported that since

Environmental Health

• Food poisonings
• Nonsmokers at risk
• PCB's and intellect
• Effects of air pollution

Health hazards of floods
Grand Forks, North Dakota, was one of several U.S. cities hit by heavy flooding in the spring of 1997. To prevent diseases that often arise with flood conditions, the Centers for Disease Control and Prevention in Atlanta, Georgia recommends several precautions. These include discarding any food that has come in contact with flood water, getting necessary immunizations, and protecting against the increased number of mosquitoes.

mid-April at least 110 people had become ill after consuming raspberries contaminated with cyclospora parasites. The poisonings occurred in California, Maryland, Nevada, New York, Rhode Island, Texas, and Ontario, Canada. Cyclospora-contaminated lettuce also was responsible for illnesses in Florida.

Cyclospora parasites infect the small intestine and cause diarrhea, nausea, vomiting, and other symptoms. The condition is rarely fatal and can be cured with antibiotics.

Nonsmokers at risk. Nonsmokers who are exposed to cigarette smoke at work or home have nearly twice the risk of developing heart disease, according to a study released in May 1997. Researchers at the Harvard School of Public Health reported those results from a study of the health histories of 121,700 female nurses, aged 30 to 55 when the study began in 1976.

As many as 50,000 Americans die each year of heart attacks attributed to so-called passive smoking. Chemicals in the smoke can damage arteries, lower levels of a beneficial form of cholesterol called high-density lipoprotein, and increase the likelihood of blood clots. In the Harvard study, more than 32,000 of the women—who did not smoke and initially had no signs of heart disease—lived or worked with smokers. Those women were 91 percent more likely to suffer a heart attack than other nonsmokers.

PCB's and intellect. A mother's exposure to the environmental pollutant polychlorinated biphenyl (PCB) before or during pregnancy may cause fetal brain damage that hinders a child's intellectual development. Psychologists Joseph and Susan Jacobson at Wayne State University in Detroit, Michigan, reported those findings in September 1996.

PCB's were once routinely used as insulating fluids in electrical transformers and other industrial equipment. Although the product was banned in 1979, it still contaminates the environment.

The Jacobsons studied 212 children whose mothers had consumed fish from Lake Michigan, which has unusually high PCB contamination. The researchers determined the amount of each mother's exposure to the contaminant by testing the PCB level in the mother's breast milk at the time of each child's birth. When the children were 11 years old, the researchers then conducted a series of intelligence tests. They found that the 30 children with the highest prenatal exposure to the toxin had an average intelligent quotient (IQ) 6.2 points lower than the other children. Those same 30 children were also twice as likely to be at least two years behind in reading comprehension skills.

Whether the children were breastfed had no effect on the results.

What is that humming sound?

The World Health Organization's recommendation for the average nighttime noise level that allows for undisturbed sleep is 30 decibels (db's)—quieter than the hum of most refrigerators. Not sleeping in the kitchen may seem to be the solution to the problem; however, many sleepers must contend with other sources of everyday noise, such as street traffic, which can require people to sleep through noise levels between 40 and 60 db's.

Studies of the effect of everyday noise have changed many researchers' views about the health hazards of noise. Noise not only affects a person's hearing, but studies suggest that high levels of everyday noise can also raise blood pressure, disrupt the development of reading and thinking skills in children, and stimulate stress hormones. According to noise specialist Arline Bronzaft at the City University of New York, "Noise is a stress and eventually the body gives in some way."

Therefore, the researchers concluded that the effect of PCB occurred during fetal development.

Effects of air pollution. Exercising outdoors can damage the lungs, even when ozone levels are below legal limits, according to a study released in November 1996. Researchers at the Columbia University School of Public Health in New York City based those conclusions on a study of 15 volunteers who jogged outdoors on New York's Governor's Island.

The researchers reviewed ozone levels during summer and winter months when levels are generally at their highest and lowest. (Ozone is a gas produced by a chemical reaction between sunlight and other pollutants in the atmosphere, such as exhaust fumes.) The researchers also took tissue samples from the participants' lungs. They found inflammation of the lung tissues when ozone levels averaged only 58 parts per billion, well below the Environmental Protection Agency (EPA) standard of 80 parts per billion. Repeated inflammation can cause scarring of the lung, which can impair the ability to breathe.

Exposure to air pollution can also lower the lung's ability to fight off respiratory infections, according to an April 1997 report by scientists at the National Institute of Respiratory Diseases in Tlalpan, Mexico. The team studied five clinics in Mexico City and concluded that 10 to 16 percent of clinic visits for respiratory problems were related to air pollution.

When pollution levels were at their highest, the number of such visits increased by as much as 19 to 43 percent. Since clinic visits increased about five days after a rise in ozone levels, the researchers concluded that it may take time for pollution-related illness to develop or to become severe enough to warrant a clinic visit. Although Mexico City has high air pollution levels, at no time during the study did levels exceed acceptable U.S. air pollution limits.

Ozone may also be partly responsible for conditions such as dermatitis and psoriasis, which result in itchy, red, inflamed, and scaly skin. Researchers at the University of California in Berkeley reported in February 1997 that ozone strips away vitamin E, which is essential for the stability of skin-cell membranes.

In a study of mice, the researchers found that a two-hour exposure to ozone at levels twice those normally found in Los Angeles or Mexico City caused the loss of 25 percent of the vitamin E in the surface layer of the skin. After six days of two-hour exposures, 75 percent of the vitamin E was gone. • Thomas H. Maugh II

In the section Medical and Safety Alerts, see How Safe Is Our Food Supply? In World Book, see Environmental pollution.

Participating in a regular exercise routine may reduce the risk of breast cancer by more than 35 percent, according to a study released in May 1997 by researchers at the University of Tromso in Norway. The researchers studied the exercise habits of more than 25,000 women, who ranged in age from 20 to 54 when the study began in 1974. The women were all cancer-free at the start of the study; however, 351 of the participants had developed advanced breast cancer by the end of the 14-year study.

The researchers classified women who spent at least four hours a week exercising or participating in recreational athletics as being consistently physically active. Those women who exercised less than four hours a week were classified as being moderately active. Women who rarely or never exercised were classified as being consistently sedentary. The researchers took into account other factors that might be related to both the level of physical activity and the risk of breast cancer, including age, body weight, height, number of children, age at birth of first child, amount of food consumed daily, and location of residence.

The study concluded that women who exercised regularly were at less risk for breast cancer. The reduction in risk associated with regular exercise was particularly large among

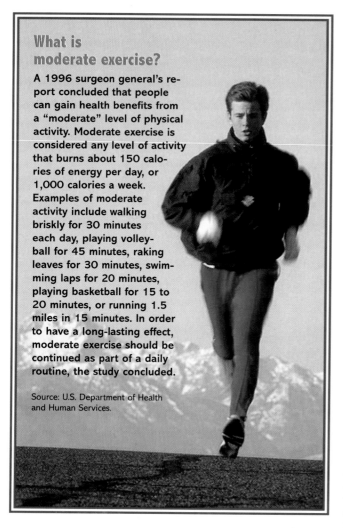

What is moderate exercise?

A 1996 surgeon general's report concluded that people can gain health benefits from a "moderate" level of physical activity. Moderate exercise is considered any level of activity that burns about 150 calories of energy per day, or 1,000 calories a week. Examples of moderate activity include walking briskly for 30 minutes each day, playing volleyball for 45 minutes, raking leaves for 30 minutes, swimming laps for 20 minutes, playing basketball for 15 to 20 minutes, or running 1.5 miles in 15 minutes. In order to have a long-lasting effect, moderate exercise should be continued as part of a daily routine, the study concluded.

Source: U.S. Department of Health and Human Services.

gen and progesterone. Previous studies linked these hormones to increasing the risk of breast cancer. In addition, women who exercise regularly are more likely to eat a healthier diet that is lower in fat and calories, which may also lower the risk of breast cancer, according to the researchers.

Benefits of intense exercise. Although nonstrenuous activity may reduce the risk of heart disease, strenuous exercise provides even greater health benefits. This finding was reported in June 1997 by researchers at the University of Washington in Seattle. The researchers studied the exercise habits of 2,274 people over the age of 65 who were free of any type of heart disease. The participants had no physical ailments. Prior to the study, the researchers conducted an examination of the participants to assess risk factors and any evidence of heart disease.

The individuals in the study completed a questionnaire detailing the various physical activities they had participated in two weeks prior to the study. The researchers ranked swimming, hiking, aerobics, tennis, jogging, racquetball, and walking at a brisk pace of at least 4 miles (6.4 kilometers) per hour as high-intensity activities; gardening, mowing, raking, golf, bowling, biking, dancing, calisthenics, cycling on a stationary bike, and walking between 2 miles and 4 miles (3.2 kilometers and 6.4 kilometers) per hour as moderate-intensity exercises; and walking at a pace less than 2 miles (3.2 kilometers) per hour or not exercising at all as low-intensity exercise.

The researchers took into account other factors that might be related both to the level of exercise and the risk of heart disease, including age, gender, education, hormone replacement therapy, smoking, and alcohol consumption. The researchers reported that the individuals who participated in moderately intense activity were at a lower risk of developing heart disease when compared with those who participated in low-intensity physical activity. Individuals who participated in high-intensity activities, however, showed an even lower risk of developing heart disease.

women who had not yet begun *menopause* (the time in life when menstrual periods cease), were younger than age 45, and were lean. Analysis revealed that lean women who exercised at least four hours a week during leisure time had a 37 percent reduction in the risk of breast cancer, according to the researchers.

The study also concluded that jobs requiring high levels of physical activity reduce the risk of breast cancer. The study participants whose jobs involved walking, lifting, or heavy manual labor were less likely to develop breast cancer than other women.

The researchers suggested that regular exercise may reduce risk of breast cancer by lowering the levels of certain hormones, such as estro-

The researchers concluded that though older people who participate in moderate exercise can lower their risk of heart disease, individuals who participate in higher-intensity exercises can achieve the greatest cardiovascular benefits. In mid-1997, the researchers planned to continue studying the effects of various types of moderate and intense regular exercise on older people.

Physical activity and longevity. Engaging in some type of exercise can lead to a longer life. That was the conclusion of a study reported in October 1996 by scientists at the Human Population Laboratory of the California Department of Health Services in Berkeley.

The researchers studied 6,928 adults who were between the ages of 16 and 94 when the study began in 1965. The individuals completed a survey in 1965, 1974, and 1983 detailing how many hours they spent participating in physical activities such as walking, swimming, or sports. The participants responded either "never," "sometimes," or "often" to each question. The researchers tracked the participants over the 28-year study period, during which time 1,226 participants died.

The researchers reported that the least active participants had the high-

Rubber band exercises

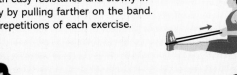

Health experts recommend using elastic exercise bands for simple and inexpensive strength training exercises. The bands provide the resistance needed to strengthen and tone muscle groups. Experts recommend that beginners start with easy resistance and slowly increase the difficulty by pulling farther on the band. Perform 10 to 15 repetitions of each exercise.

Biceps. Hold one end of band in one fist, palm up, the other end securely under arch of same foot. Slowly curl forearm toward shoulder, keeping elbow close to side. Switch sides.

Shoulders. Anchor band to fixed object. Stand with elbow at side, bent at 90 degrees. Grip band. Pull arm across body, keeping elbow at side, then return slowly. Switch sides.

Rhomboids and rear deltoids. Hold one end of band in each hand, with middle under arches of feet. Keep feet together, lean forward with back flat, and lift arms until parallel to floor. Lower arms.

Trapezius muscles. Sit on floor, loop band under arches of feet, and hold one end of band in each hand. With arms extended, back straight, and shoulders down, pull elbows back. Hold for 2 seconds.

Back and abdominal. Attach to object below knee level. Hold band against chest. Lean back 30 degrees. Keep pelvis stable, stomach muscles contracted, and back straight. Hold.

Buttocks and thigh muscles. Tie band around ankles, leaving a few inches of slack. Hold wall for support. Keeping legs straight, lift one leg back against resistance. Lower and switch.

Outer thigh muscles. Tie band around ankles, leaving some slack. Stand erect, hold chair for support. Keep legs straight, lift one leg sideways against resistance. Lower without letting band go slack.

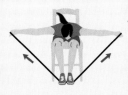

Exercise and sleep

A study at the Stanford University School of Medicine in Stanford, California, concluded that people over the age of 50 sleep better if they exercise regularly. Patients in the study participated in 30- to 40-minute exercise sessions four times a week. The exercises included brisk walking and stationary cycling. Compared with a control group of patients who received no exercise, the active group reported that they slept almost one hour longer and fell asleep in half the time, according to the study's results.

est *mortality* (death) rate, and the individuals who were most active had the lowest mortality rate. Although the researchers theorized that the impact of physical activity would have been better assessed had data been gathered more than once a decade, they concluded that higher levels of physical activity had a positive effect on a person's life and longevity.

Girls' weight on the rise. Studies conducted by the National Center for Health Statistics at the Centers for Disease Control and Prevention in Atlanta, Georgia, showed that the average weight of girls between the ages of 4 and 5 increased between 1971 and 1994. The results of the study were reported in April 1997.

Researchers studied more than 15,000 American preschoolers. The results revealed that more than 10 percent of 4- and 5-year-old girls surveyed between 1988 and 1994 were overweight. In studies conducted between 1971 and 1974, 5.8 percent of preschool age girls were overweight.

Consumption of both fat and calories were similar in both of the study groups, leading the scientists to theorize that inactivity was to blame for the increased percentage of obesity.

• David S. Siscovick
In WORLD BOOK, see PHYSICAL FITNESS.

Eye and Vision

- Laser surgery approved for astigmatism
- Glaucoma gene found
- Asthma drugs may increase glaucoma risk
- Smoking linked to eye disease
- New way to repair injured corneas

The United States Food and Drug Administration (FDA) in April 1997 approved a type of laser surgery called *photorefractive keratectomy* (PRK) for the treatment of *astigmatism* (a visual defect in which both nearby and distant objects appear blurred). PRK was previously approved by the FDA only to treat *myopia,* or *nearsightedness* (a visual defect that causes blurred distance vision).

Astigmatism is a condition shared by about 40 percent of adults who wear glasses or contact lenses. In most cases, it is caused by an abnormally shaped *cornea* (the transparent, outside layer of the eyeball). The cornea, which helps focus light rays on the *retina* (the light-sensitive layer of cells at the back of the eye), normally is evenly rounded. Astigmatism results when the cornea is curved like the back of a spoon—slightly steeper in one direction than the other—preventing light rays from focusing properly on the retina. PRK uses a laser to reshape the cornea, enabling the retina to produce sharp, clear images.

The FDA approved PRK to treat astigmatism after examining the results of the surgery performed in *clinical trials* (tests on humans). In 90 percent of the cases, PRK produced a vision ability of at least 20/40—a rating that, according to the laws of most states, would allow a person to drive a car without glasses. (Perfect vision has a rating of 20/20.)

Glaucoma gene found. Scientists at the University of Iowa College of Medicine in Iowa City and colleagues from six other institutions announced in January 1997 that they had identified a gene associated with some cases of *glaucoma* (an eye disease characterized by increased pressure of the fluid within the eye). The scientists said that the discovery of the gene could lead to a genetic test that would identify people at risk for developing this disease, which affects more than 2 million people in the United States—blinding about 12,000 of them every year. The test would enable glaucoma to be diagnosed and treated in its early stages, increasing the chance of saving a patient's vision.

The gene normally produces a protein called TIGR that helps fluid produced within the eye to circulate through tiny channels and nourish the tissues of the eye. The gene also helps TIGR drain from the eye. The scientists found that when this gene is *mutated* (altered in form), it produces an abnormal form of TIGR, which results in a blockage in the flow of fluid. The fluid then builds up within the eye, increasing the pressure on the *optic nerve* (the nerve that carries visual information from the retina to the brain). The pressure gradually increases until the optic

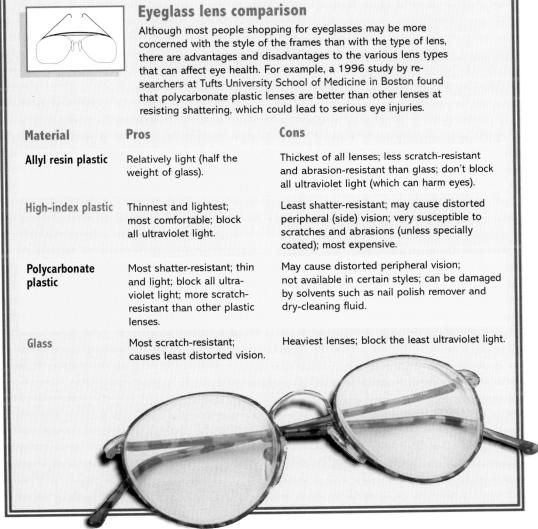

Eyeglass lens comparison

Although most people shopping for eyeglasses may be more concerned with the style of the frames than with the type of lens, there are advantages and disadvantages to the various lens types that can affect eye health. For example, a 1996 study by researchers at Tufts University School of Medicine in Boston found that polycarbonate plastic lenses are better than other lenses at resisting shattering, which could lead to serious eye injuries.

Material	Pros	Cons
Allyl resin plastic	Relatively light (half the weight of glass).	Thickest of all lenses; less scratch-resistant and abrasion-resistant than glass; don't block all ultraviolet light (which can harm eyes).
High-index plastic	Thinnest and lightest; most comfortable; block all ultraviolet light.	Least shatter-resistant; may cause distorted peripheral (side) vision; very susceptible to scratches and abrasions (unless specially coated); most expensive.
Polycarbonate plastic	Most shatter-resistant; thin and light; block all ultraviolet light; more scratch-resistant than other plastic lenses.	May cause distorted peripheral vision; not available in certain styles; can be damaged by solvents such as nail polish remover and dry-cleaning fluid.
Glass	Most scratch-resistant; causes least distorted vision.	Heaviest lenses; block the least ultraviolet light.

nerve is severely damaged and vision is lost. Because glaucoma worsens gradually, the disease can cause much serious damage before symptoms appear.

The researchers said that they linked the mutated gene to at least 3 percent of all cases of glaucoma, including both juvenile-onset glaucoma, which can occur as early as the teenage years, and adult-onset glaucoma, which typically occurs after age 40. The scientists estimated that the gene causes as many as 100,000 cases of glaucoma in the United States. Other researchers in 1997 were trying to identify additional genes that may cause glaucoma.

Eating for eyesight

Most people know that eating carrots is good for the eyes. Carrots owe their vision-saving properties to high levels of *carotenoids,* plant pigments that are converted by the body into vitamin A, which the eyes need in order to adjust to changes in light intensity. A diet deficient in vitamin A can lead to vision loss in dim light—a condition known as *night blindness.* Besides preventing night blindness, medical research indicates that certain carotenoids also help prevent *cataracts* (clouding of the lens of the eye) and *age-related macular degeneration* (an eye disorder that damages cells in the macula, an area inside the eye responsible for sharp vision). The most beneficial carotenoid is beta-carotene, which is a powerful *antioxidant* (a chemical compound that prevents cell damage by blocking the effects of certain harmful molecules in the body). Antioxidants, which also include vitamin C and vitamin E, have been linked to a number of health benefits in addition to eye protection—such as protection against heart disease and cancer. Other foods besides carrots that are rich in antioxidants and may help preserve healthy eyesight include sweet potatoes, spinach, broccoli, collard greens, cauliflower, pumpkin, strawberries, oranges, sunflower seeds, almonds, and liver.

Asthma drugs and eye disease.
Two studies reported in 1997 that people with asthma who use inhaled steroid drugs, a common form of asthma treatment, may face an increased risk of eye disease. One study, published in March and conducted by researchers from McGill University in Montreal, Canada, found a link between inhaled steroids and glaucoma. The other study, published in July and conducted by researchers from the University of Sydney in Australia, linked inhaled steroids with *cataracts* (a clouding of the lens of the eye that causes blurred vision). Both groups of researchers said it is important for people using inhaled steroids be checked periodically for eye disease, so that any disease can be diagnosed and treated early.

The Canadian researchers found that patients who used high doses of inhaled steroids for three months or more had a 44 percent greater risk of developing glaucoma or eye conditions that could lead to glaucoma than patients who did not use inhaled steroids. The Australian researchers found that inhaled-steroid users had a 50 percent greater-than-average risk of developing a cataract affecting the central part of the lens, and a 90 percent greater risk of developing a cataract affecting the back of the lens. The cataract risk increased the longer inhaled steroids were used.

Smoking linked to eye disease.
Researchers at the Harvard Medical School in Boston published two studies in October 1996 that found that heavy smokers have a greater risk of developing age-related macular degeneration (AMD) than do nonsmokers. AMD is an eye disorder that damages cells in the *macula* (the region of the retina that provides the sharp central vision used in reading and driving). AMD is the leading cause of blindness in people over age 65.

The studies found that men who smoked 20 or more cigarettes per day and women who smoked 25 or more cigarettes per day increased their risk of developing AMD by about 2½ times compared with non-smokers. The longer the people in the studies smoked, the greater was their risk of AMD.

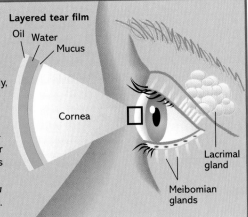

Importance of tears

Forty percent of Americans do not produce enough tears—a condition called dry eye—resulting in such symptoms as fatigue after short periods of reading and a frequent burning sensation in the eye. Normally, every time a person blinks, the eyelids spread a film of tears over the *cornea* (the transparent outer layer of the eye). The tear film—which lubricates the eye, washes foreign particles off of the eye, and kills bacteria—consists of an outer layer of oil, a middle layer of water, and an inner layer of mucus. The tear film is produced by the lacrimal gland above the eye, the meibomian glands in the eyelids, and the *conjunctiva* (a membrane lining the inside surface of the eyelids).

Although the researchers were unsure why smoking increases the risk of AMD, they speculated that smoking may decrease blood flow to the retina or interfere with *antioxidants* (chemicals that protect the body against certain harmful molecules).

New way to repair corneas. Italian researchers in April 1997 announced that they had developed a new transplantation technique to repair damaged corneas. The researchers said their technique had the potential to help many patients who fail to benefit from traditional cornea transplants, which usually involve transplanting tissue from a deceased human donor.

The donated tissue is sometimes attacked and destroyed by the patient's immune system.

The new technique, developed by scientists at the Instituto Dermopatico dell'Immacolata in Rome, used a tiny square of undamaged tissue taken from the patient's own eye. The tissue was grown in the laboratory until it was large enough to graft onto the damaged part of the cornea.

Two patients who were almost blinded by chemical burns were treated by the researchers. After treatment, the grafted tissue remained healthy, and both patients recovered nearly normal vision. • Michael Woods
In WORLD BOOK, see EYE.

Genetic Medicine

A team of scientists announced In May 1997 that they had isolated a region of human DNA (deoxyribonucleic acid) that might contain the genetic material associated with the learning defects of Down syndrome (DS). The researchers were from the Lawrence Berkeley National Laboratory in Berkeley, California; Tufts University School of Medicine and Veterinary Medicine in Boston; the Jackson Laboratory in Bar Harbor, Maine; and the University of California, Los Angeles School of Medicine.

Down syndrome is the most common cause of mental retardation. It occurs in about 1 in 800 births and affects more than 1 million individuals in the United States. The syndrome comprises a range of problems that affect almost all systems of the body, including the brain.

DS is caused by the presence of an extra chromosome. Usually, human chromosomes come in 23 pairs, with one of each pair coming from the mother and its matching partner coming from the father. Each chromosome contains one molecule of DNA, the information molecule that carries genes. Geneticists had known since 1959 that the presence of an extra chromosome 21 causes DS. The extra chromosome results from a mistake during the production of egg or sperm, or during the division of cells shortly after conception.

Although chromosome 21 is one

- Progress in understanding Down syndrome
- Human artificial chromosomes
- Genes and Alzheimer's disease

of the smallest human chromosomes, it still contains about 1,000 genes. (Humans probably have about 80,000 to 100,000 genes in total.) Geneticists do not know exactly which or how many genes are responsible for the broad range of symptoms in DS, but they identified a certain region of chromosome 21 associated with learning disabilities.

The researchers inserted large portions of human DNA from this region into fertilized mouse eggs. To transfer DNA from the cell of one creature to another, scientists use a *vector,* a molecule capable of carrying foreign genes. In the DS study, the scientists used vectors called yeast artificial chromosomes (YAC's). YAC's are a technology that allows the insertion of human DNA into easily manipulated, miniature versions of yeast chromosomes. YAC's can accommodate fairly large segments of DNA, so they were useful in the DS research. The scientists had to screen a region of chromosome 21 that encompasses about 2 million bases of DNA. Bases are four of the chemical subunits of DNA. It is the various sequences of these bases that determine the basic structure, and therefore the function, of proteins produced in a cell.

The team inserted YAC's containing different portions of the suspected region of DNA into mouse eggs, and some of the human DNA was taken up by the mouse chromo-

somes. The eggs were inserted into surrogate mothers, and the offspring were screened for the presence of the desired genetic material.

The researchers then tested the resulting "transgenic" mice to assess the effects of the new genetic material on their learning and memory. Through these tests, they isolated a portion of DNA from chromosome 21 that caused impairments of learning and memory in transgenic mice.

The researchers also noted that the 180,000 bases in the isolated portion of DNA contain the human version of a gene called minibrain, which is associated with nerve-cell development in fruit flies. Flies that have mutations in this gene also show learning defects, providing additional evidence that the DNA segment identified in the study of transgenic mice is associated with learning disabilities in DS. A gene that is present in species as distantly related as fruit flies and humans is most likely critical to normal development.

Human artificial chromosomes. A remarkable technological breakthrough for genetic research—the production of human artificial chromosomes (HAC's)—was reported in April 1997 by geneticist Huntington F. Willard and his colleagues at Case Western Reserve University School of Medicine and at Athersys, a biotechnology firm, both in Cleveland, Ohio.

Fruit flies—giants in genetic research

The tiny fruit fly, best known outside the scientific community as the pesky picnic creature hovering over fruit salads, plays a huge role in genetic research. Fruit flies, *Drosophila,* are ideal for laboratory studies because they mature within 10 to 14 days and produce numerous offspring. Consequently, researchers can follow genetic traits through several generations in a short amount of time. Also, changes in the appearance and behavior of flies due to genetic *mutations* (changes) are relatively easy to observe.

Genetic research on fruit flies is significant because genes involved in the development of a fruit fly are similar to those in other organisms, including humans. This phenomenon is known as "evolutionary conservation." Researchers studying fruit flies are learning about how and in what order genes work together for an organism to develop from an egg to an adult. This information can help researchers better understand both basic human development and the effects of genetic mutations in humans.

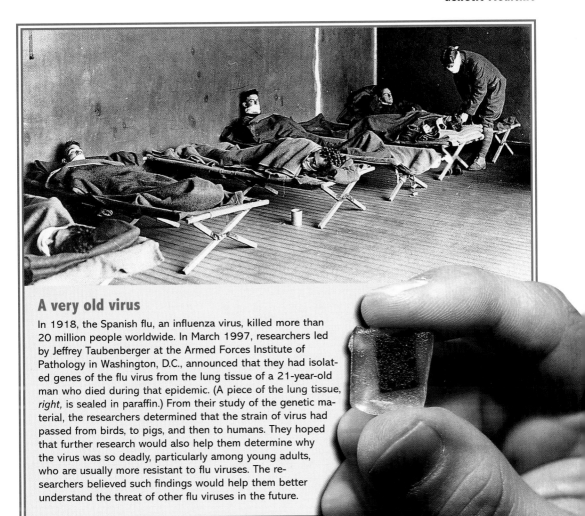

A very old virus

In 1918, the Spanish flu, an influenza virus, killed more than 20 million people worldwide. In March 1997, researchers led by Jeffrey Taubenberger at the Armed Forces Institute of Pathology in Washington, D.C., announced that they had isolated genes of the flu virus from the lung tissue of a 21-year-old man who died during that epidemic. (A piece of the lung tissue, *right,* is sealed in paraffin.) From their study of the genetic material, the researchers determined that the strain of virus had passed from birds, to pigs, and then to humans. They hoped that further research would also help them determine why the virus was so deadly, particularly among young adults, who are usually more resistant to flu viruses. The researchers believed such findings would help them better understand the threat of other flu viruses in the future.

HAC's, considered the next generation of vectors, were expected to improve understanding of basic cell biology and to serve as a new tool for *human gene therapy,* the insertion of properly functioning genes to replace genes that are defective.

The development of the technology was based on basic assumptions about how chromosomes function. Chromosomes are the central figures in the tightly choreographed steps of cell division, the process by which one cell becomes two, and of the special type of cell division that produces eggs and sperm. Although biologists know a great deal about both processes, much remains unknown, including the precise mechanisms that initiate cell division.

Prior work on yeast chromosomes had shown that three chromosomal components are necessary to produce an artificial chromosome that will survive cell division and be passed on to new cells. The *telomeres,* the regions at the ends of the chromosome, are the only component well understood in humans. The other components, well understood in the simpler yeast chromosomes, are the origins of replication and the centromere. The origins of replication are the multiple sites along the chromosome that stimulate the DNA to replicate prior to cell division. The centromere is the narrow region of the chromosome where fibers in a cell attach to the chromosome to pull apart the duplicated chromosome pair.

Willard's team inserted DNA associated with centromeres, telomeric DNA, and DNA from other parts of human chromosomes into cells in a laboratory culture. The cells assembled these components into small chromosomes that were retained for six months through 240 generations of cell reproduction. The successful replication of artificial chromosomes indicated that they had functional centromeres. These "microchromosomes" contained about 6 million to 10 million bases of DNA compared with 50 million to 250 million bases in natural human chromosomes.

Although much work remained to be done in 1997 in developing artificial chromosomes, Willard's group took a large step toward developing fully functional HAC's that could help explain basic biological processes such as cell division. In addition, scientists expected HAC's to improve the efficiency and feasibility of gene therapy. The vectors currently used for gene therapy generally are not big enough to carry large human genes and the sequences of DNA that turn the genes on and off at the right time. The HCA's, however, could be developed to serve as vectors for the insertion of normal genes into cells in which mutations have produced genetic disorders, such as cystic fibrosis or immune deficiency.

Genes and Alzheimer's disease.
A group of molecular biologists and neuroscientists reported in April 1997 that they had identified a link between Alzheimer's disease and a portion of the human genetic material called mitochondrial DNA. The research team was led by W. Davis Parker from the University of Virginia Medical School in Charlottesville and Robert Davis from MitoKor, a biotechnology firm in San Diego. Alzheimer's disease, which generally affects older people, causes the degeneration of brain cells, leading to the loss of mental function. Most specialists believe Alzheimer's is very likely caused by a complex combination of genetic and environmental factors.

Mitochondria are the power plants of the cell, using oxygen to produce energy-rich molecules from simple sugars. Cells contain multiple mito-chondria, and some types of cells contain more than others. Muscle cells, for example, contain many of these sausage-shaped structures because of the high energy requirements of those cells. Mitochondria contain their own, circular DNA molecules, which are separate from the DNA of chromosomes in the nucleus of the cell. Whereas the nuclear DNA includes about 3 billion base pairs, each mitochondrial DNA molecule contains 16,569 base pairs. Molecular biologists also know the complete sequence of bases that make up this molecule.

Some mitochondrial genes provide the code for proteins involved in energy production, and energy production in the brain cells of people with Alzheimer's is known to be lower than normal. The Parker-Davis team investigated the mitochondrial genes that contain the code for 3 of the 13 proteins that make up an enzyme called cytochrome *c* oxidase (CO). (Mitochondrial genes do not code for the other 10 proteins.)

Researchers had known that CO activity is abnormally low in the brains of Alzheimer's patients who first suffer symptoms after age 60. The researchers investigated those genes for possible mutations, because children of affected mothers are more likely to develop Alzheimer's than are children of affected fathers. (All mitochondria are inherited from mothers.)

Two of the three mitochondrial genes associated with CO showed mutations at significantly higher frequencies in Alzheimer's patients than in unaffected individuals. The scientists also demonstrated the impact of the mutations by inserting mitochondria from affected individuals into cells without the energy-producing structures. Those cells then showed defects in energy production.

The researchers were hopeful that the analysis of mutations in the mitochondrial CO genes would lead to a better understanding of the underlying mechanisms of Alzheimer's. Because the mutations are detectable in blood cells, they also could provide the basis for a diagnostic test for the disease.

• **Joseph D. McInerney**
See also MEDICAL ETHICS. In WORLD BOOK, see CELL; GENETICS.

A hormone called human calcitonin (hCT) can be used to diagnose a type of thyroid cancer according to an Austrian study reported in May 1997. *Palpable* (detectable by touch) thyroid nodules occur in 4 to 7 percent of the adult population, but only less than 5 percent of these nodules are malignant tumors. A type of cancerous tumor known as medullary carcinoma represents less than 10 percent of all malignant tumors, but it leads to the increased release of hCT in the blood. A large study conducted by investigators from the University of Vienna in Austria, an area of the world where cases of thyroid enlargement (sometimes called a goiter) are common, tested hCT measurement as a possible method to detect the presence of medullary carcinoma in people with palpable thyroid nodules.

The researchers measured blood hCT levels in 1,062 subjects with palpable thyroid nodules. They found that, of the subjects who had an hCT level of between less than 1 and 5 picograms per milliliter (pg/ml), none had a tumor. Of those with levels between 5 and 100 pg/ml, three had medullary carcinoma and six had a precancerous condition known as C-cell hyperplasia. All patients with a hCT level of more than 100 pg/ml had medullary carcinoma.

Thus, hCT measurement led to the diagnosis of 13 new cases of either medullary carcinoma or medullary C-cell hyperplasia. Twelve patients were later cured by surgery (one declined treatment). Even considering the cost per case discovered, the researchers concluded that hCT measurement should be considered in every patient with a palpable thyroid nodule.

Treating pituitary tumors. In March 1997, investigators from the University of Federico II in Naples, Italy, reported the results of a study in which they used a new drug to treat 27 patients with a particular type of pituitary tumor. The pituitary gland is a small organ located beneath the brain that regulates many aspects of the body's growth and development. In pregnant women, the gland secretes *prolactin,* a hormone that stimulates the breasts to produce milk. A *prolactinoma* is a tumor of the pituitary gland that also secretes prolactin, leading to excessive levels of this hormone in the body. Prolactinomas are therefore associated with *galactorrhea* (milk production in nonpregnant women or in men) and disorders of the *gonads* (sex glands).

The first line of treatment for prolactinoma is a class of drugs known as *dopamine receptor agonists,* substances that inhibit the effect of *dopamine,* an important chemical in brain cells. Studies have shown that these drugs normalize prolactin levels

Understanding BPH

Benign prostatic hyperplasia (BPH) is a noncancerous growth of the prostate gland, a chestnut-sized organ at the base of a man's bladder. The prostate commonly enlarges as a man ages and can block the *urethra* (passage that carries urine from the bladder out of the body), interfering with normal urination. Men with this condition may not seek treatment due to embarrassment or fear that they have prostate cancer. However, BPH is a treatable condition that often does not require surgery.

Doctors advise men over 40 years of age to have an annual prostate exam. A physician can check the size of the prostate and detect lumps or hard spots that may indicate cancer. A prostate specific antigen (PSA) test may be used to confirm the condition as BPH or prostate cancer. Physicians stress, however, that the two diseases are not related. If BPH is diagnosed, treatment options may include:

- Lifestyle changes (for mild to moderate BPH): Avoid caffeine and alcohol, which irritate the bladder. Certain hypertension drugs also may aggravate the problem.

- Drug therapy (for moderate BPH): Several drugs are available that relax prostate tissue or shrink the gland itself, reducing pressure on the urethra.

- Surgery (as a last resort): A common surgical procedure performed using a fiberoptic scope employs an electric current to cut away excess prostate tissue.

Source: *American Health*, March 1997.

in 90 percent of cases and shrink the prolactinoma in 60 percent of cases. Some patients, however, do not respond well to therapy with bromocriptine, the most widely used dopamine receptor agonist. Therefore, the researchers tested the effectiveness of cabergoline (sold as Dostinex), a new type of dopamine agonist.

The patients received 0.25 milligrams (mg) of cabergoline once a week for two weeks, 0.25 mg twice a week for the next two weeks, and 0.5 mg twice weekly thereafter for up to two years. The researchers reported that cabergoline therapy reduced prolactin to normal levels in 22 of the 27 patients. In addition, gonadal function returned to normal in 18 of the patients and galactorrhea disap-

peared in 5 of the 6 women who had it. Tumors shrank in 13 of the 27 patients. The researchers concluded that cabergoline might be a safe and well-tolerated alternative treatment for prolactinomas that do not respond to other dopamine agonists.

The pros and cons of estrogen. In June 1997, investigators at Brigham & Women's Hospital and Harvard Medical School in Boston reported the results of the most extensive study to date on the effects of hormone replacement therapy (HRT) in women who have reached menopause. Previous studies had shown that HRT can protect postmenopausal women from osteoporosis and heart disease, but HRT had also been linked to breast and uterine cancer. The new study indicated that, for some women, the risks of HRT might actually outweigh the benefits.

The researchers studied the relationship between hormone replacement and death rate in 3,637 postmenopausal women from 1976 to 1994. They found that the death rate among women taking HRT was 37 percent lower than among those not taking HRT. The most significant drop was in deaths due to heart disease. The women who benefited most from HRT were those with risk factors for heart disease, such as smoking, obesity, or high cholesterol. These women cut their risk of death by 49 percent. However, women taking HRT who had none of these risk factors experienced only an 11-percent reduction in death rate.

On the other hand, the researchers found that the risk of death due to breast cancer increased by 43 percent among women taking HRT for 10 years or more. Furthermore, the benefits of HRT declined among women taking hormones for 10 years or more. Therefore, the researchers said, the higher survival rate among HRT users was partially offset by the risk of breast cancer. On average, the researchers concluded, the survival benefits of HRT appeared to outweigh the risks, but the decision to begin such treatment should be carefully considered by every woman and her physician. • Andre J. Van Herle

In WORLD BOOK, see GLAND; HORMONE.

The United States Supreme Court ruled in June 1997 that individual states have the right to ban physician-assisted suicide. Laws making physician-assisted suicide illegal in New York and Washington state had been challenged in lawsuits.

The justices' ruling overturned two lower-court decisions that found terminally ill patients had a constitutional right to die. Citing tradition and the value of human life, Chief Justice William H. Rehnquist wrote that the country had a long record of opposing suicide in history, legal traditions, and practices. However, some justices said that they might find in a future case that there is constitutional protection for a dying patient to control his or her manner of death.

The Supreme Court's long-awaited decision was not expected to end national debate on the issue of physician-assisted suicide. Because the justices' decision did not bar individual states from legalizing the process, some experts predicted that the issue will be a more hotly debated topic in state legislatures. In 1997, about 35 states had laws banning physician-assisted suicide. Only one state—Oregon—allowed the practice under the 1994 Oregon Death with Dignity Act. However, that law was blocked by a December 1994 lawsuit, and residents were set to vote in November 1997 whether to repeal the act.

Dying "bill of rights." The American Medical Association (AMA) approved a "bill of rights" for dying patients at its annual meeting in June 1997. The AMA provision made it easier for terminally ill patients to stop "unwanted intervention" by health-care professionals. The guidelines were also designed to allow terminally ill patients to "die with dignity." The medical association is opposed to physician-assisted suicide and has criticized the assisted suicide activities of Michigan pathologist Jack Kevorkian, calling his methods "unethical."

Stating that the AMA believes patients should expect high-quality care at the end of life, the guidelines list "elements of quality care" for doctors. These elements include discussing end-of-life care with the patients and making certain that physicians are skilled in managing pain, fatigue, depression, and other problems associated with terminal illness, according to Linda Emanuel, the AMA's vice president for ethics. Under the guidelines, physicians should honor patients' preferences for treatment "in accordance with the legally and ethically established rights of patients."

Medicare age debated. The United States House of Representatives in July 1997 rejected a Senate-approved proposal to raise the Medicare eligibility age from 65 to 67.

• Physician-assisted suicide
• Dying "bill of rights"
• Medicare age debated
• Medical marijuana
• Controversy over managed care
• Expanding health-care coverage
• Organ transplant policy
• Organ transplants in Japan
• Apology for Tuskegee

Asking forgiveness
President Bill Clinton embraces a victim of the Tuskegee Syphilis Study, following a formal apology at the White House in May 1997. Beginning in 1932, government researchers began a 40-year study on the effects of *syphilis*, a sexually transmitted disease, on black men. The government told about 400 men that they were being treated for "bad blood." They were never told that they had syphilis and were never treated for the disease.

Nurses protest outpatient care

Nurses from Brigham & Women's Hospital in Boston, Massachusetts, and their supporters stage an informational picket outside the hospital in September 1996 to draw attention to hospital outpatient care policies. With a growing emphasis on outpatient care, some nurses have argued that many less-gravely ill patients are not admitted to a hospital or admitted for only a short stay. As a result, they said an ever sicker inpatient population requires more registered nurses. Some hospitals instead use unlicensed technicians at patients' bedsides.

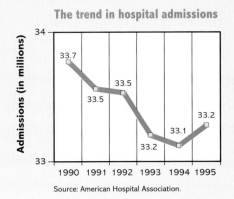

The trend in hospital admissions

Source: American Hospital Association.

Outpatient visits on the rise

Source: American Hospital Association.

The Medicare program, which covers the cost of many health-care services for Americans over the age of 65, is one of the largest sources of federal spending. Officials warned in June 1996 that Medicare will run a deficit in the year 2001 unless something is done. Both President Bill Clinton and Congress have agreed to slow the growth in Medicare costs by $115 billion through the year 2002.

However, the president expressed opposition to a June 1997 vote by the Senate that would have gradually increased the age of eligibility by two years between the years 2003 and 2027. The president had hinted that he might *veto* (reject) such legislation. Supporters said that raising the eligibility age was a sensible idea be-

cause Americans are living longer and *baby boomers* (people born between 1945 and 1964) will increase the number of retiring people early in the 21st century.

Medical marijuana. Two decisions by voters in November 1996 approving the use of marijuana and some other illegal substances for medicinal purposes set a new battlefield in the war on drugs. Although marijuana is classified as a dangerous drug by both state and federal authorities, voters in Arizona and California approved separate measures supporting its use to treat ailments such as AIDS and glaucoma.

In the referendum, 65 percent of Arizona voters approved Proposition

200, which allows physicians to prescribe marijuana, methamphetamine, heroin, LSD, and PCP to some patients. In California, Proposition 215, which decriminalizes possession of marijuana by patients and their caregivers if the drug is recommended by a physician, passed with a 56 percent majority.

Federal law still prohibited prescribing or providing marijuana and other illegal drugs by physicians to patients, so the issue of whether physicians could be prosecuted for doing so remained open in 1997. However, in April 1997, a federal judge issued a temporary restraining order on the U.S. Department of Justice, prohibiting the prosecution of California physicians who prescribed or recommended marijuana to their patients.

In Arizona, opponents of the legalized medical use of illegal drugs vowed to place two referenda on the November 1998 ballot that would repeal the major provisions of Proposition 200. Supporters of the original referendum promised a vigorous fight to defend its provisions if the referenda are placed on the ballot.

Controversy over managed care.
In March 1997, President Clinton named a 34-member panel to draft a health-care "bill of rights" for patients. The Advisory Commission on Consumer Protection and Quality in the Health Care Industry was also expected to focus on the need for the federal government to regulate private health insurance plans.

Proponents of the advisory panel, headed by Secretary of Health and Human Services Donna Shalala and former Acting Secretary of Labor Cynthia Metzler, said that the members will investigate the practices of health-care organizations and other forms of *managed care* (enrollment in organized health plans). However, Representative Bill Thomas (R., Calif.) said that the advisory commission would likely "rubber-stamp the president's desired governmental intervention into health care."

Expanding health-care coverage.
In his State of the Union address in February 1997, President Clinton announced his pledge to continue to give more families access to affordable, high-quality health care. Despite the failure of his universal coverage plan in 1993, the president said that he supported subsidized coverage for up to 5 million children. In his speech, Clinton said that an estimated 10 million American children were uninsured.

In a related issue, a bill in April 1997 cosponsored by Senators Edward Kennedy (D., Mass.) and Orrin Hatch (R., Utah) proposed increasing the federal cigarette tax to 67 cents a pack from the 1997 rate of 24 cents a pack in order to provide $20 billion a year in grants to states. The money would be used to provide insurance for children whose low-income working parents do not qualify for Medicaid.

Although both Republicans and Democrats supported the concept of expanding coverage for children, the tobacco tax proved controversial because of opposition from legislators who represented states where tobacco is a major crop. After much debate, both the House and Senate approved $16 billion from other sources to fund expanded children's health coverage.

However, the House bill gave states much more flexibility in terms of how they could use the money. The Senate version, cosponsored by Senators John Chafee (R., R.I.) and Jay Rockefeller (D., W. Va.), would add $8 billion from a 20 cent per pack tax on cigarettes, for a total of $24 billion, put more limits on states' spending options, and require a more extensive benefit package.

There were also private-sector initiatives in 1997. In June, Kaiser Permanente, the largest managed-care plan in California, announced that it will provide $100 million over the next five years to subsidize health coverage for up to 50,000 uninsured low-income children in the state. According to company officials, the plan will reach the children by working with schools and organizing a statewide coalition.

UNOS changes organ policy. In June 1997 the United Network for Organ Sharing (UNOS), a nonprofit Richmond, Virginia, organization that coordinates donations of healthy organs taken from people who recently died and allocates them to people in need of transplants nationwide, announced a new system that changed the priority structure for liver recipients. Patients at the top of the liver-transplant list—those critically ill patients considered most likely to survive with a transplant—would not be affected by the change in the priority structure. These patients include those who are acutely ill but otherwise healthy, such as a person who has suffered sudden poisoning or an infection that harms the liver. However, those patients who are chronically ill—with diseases such as hepatitis or cirrhosis, for example—will be given a lower priority.

Under UNOS' revised liver allocation policy, these chronically ill patients will be divided into two groups. The higher priority will go to those patients who have chronic disease, but whose condition has suddenly worsened; the lower priority will go to patients who also have chronic disease, but whose conditions are stable.

Andrew Klein, who chaired the UNOS liver and intestinal organ transplantation committee, said that the group hoped to make additional policy changes in the future that will make the waiting list even more fair.

Organ transplants in Japan. Japan's parliament approved a measure in June 1997 that will permit heart transplants in that country. Heart transplants have never been performed in Japan, and only a small number of kidney transplants are performed annually, because of a strong belief that death occurs only when the heart stops naturally beating. However, obtaining usable donor organs is almost impossible if most of the donor's bodily functions have ceased for a long period of time.

The new statute allows physicians to surgically remove organs for transplant when the heart is still beating, but the brain has ceased to function. However, the procedure can occur only when doctors have written consent from potential donors, and donors' families can stop the procedure if they object.

Supporters of the law said that heart, kidney, and other organ transplants would be more available to Japanese patients, who historically had little hope of receiving organs because of the stringent limitations imposed by law. However, some organ transplant advocates argued that the law was still too strict and predicted that it would result in few, if any, heart transplants.

Apology for Tuskegee. In May 1997, President Clinton apologized to five of the eight survivors of a 40-year government study in which low-income black men with *syphilis*, a se-

Young survivor
Alberta Pyle kisses the hand of her daughter, Cheyenne, as her husband, Stephen, looks on in the neonatal care unit at Jackson Children's Hospital in Miami, Florida. In November 1996, Cheyenne Pyle underwent surgery to replace an underdeveloped heart 90 minutes after being born. Physicians believe that she is the youngest patient ever to undergo a heart transplant.

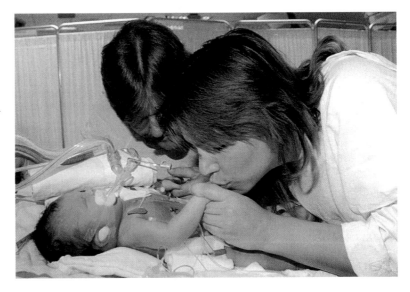

rious and potentially fatal sexually transmitted disease, were left untreated. The apology was made during a White House ceremony more than 25 years after public attention was drawn to the Tuskegee Syphilis Study. It also came more than 65 years after the study was begun by the United States Public Health Service.

The Tuskegee Syphilis Study began in 1932 to examine the effects of syphilis on the human body. About 400 men in Tuskegee, Alabama, were told that they had "bad blood" rather than syphilis. The men were led to believe that they were receiving free medical treatment for the imaginary ailment when the procedures doctors

were performing—including spinal taps and blood tests—were only for research purposes. Government physicians also failed to give the patients penicillin, which cures syphilis, when the drug became available in the late 1940's.

President Clinton said that the men participating in the study "were betrayed" and lied to by the Public Health Service and that "their rights were trampled upon." One survivor said he forgave the government, saying that "it is never too late to restore faith and trust."   • Emily Friedman

See also MEDICAL ETHICS. In the section Spotlight on Managed Care, see THE DEBATE ON MANAGED CARE.

In September 1996, the United States Food and Drug Administration (FDA) approved the marketing of an automatic external defibrillator, a device that can be used even by non-professionals to save the life of a person whose heart suddenly stops beating. Sudden cardiac arrest is a leading cause of death in the United States. It occurs when a normal heartbeat is abruptly replaced by *fibrillation* (rapid, irregular twitching of the heart muscle). This disorder of heart rhythm is fatal unless a normal heartbeat is restored within a few minutes. Cardiopulmonary resuscitation (CPR) can extend survival, but *defibrillation* (the reestablishment of normal rhythm) must be accomplished as quickly as possible.

Until recently, however, defibrillators were large devices that were kept in hospitals or on specially equipped ambulances, and only highly trained personnel, such as physicians or paramedics, were permitted to operate them. In an emergency, however, such highly trained people rarely arrive on the scene soon enough to use the devices effectively. For this reason, the survival rate in the United States from sudden cardiac arrest is only 5 percent.

The FDA approved a portable defibrillator, called the ForeRunner, marketed by HeartStream, Inc., of Seattle. The device uses an advanced computer to diagnose heart fibrillation, eliminating the need for a trained op-

erator. If fibrillation is detected, the device automatically delivers a measured electrical shock to defibrillate the patient. The ForeRunner is about the size of a hardcover book and weighs only 4 pounds (1.8 kilograms). It is practical for use by police officers, firefighters, and flight attendants. Doctors expected nationwide availability of the device to dramatically improve the survival rate of cardiac arrest patients.

Pacemakers and cell phones. Reports of electromagnetic interference with pacemaker function caused by digital cellular phones first appeared in Europe in 1994. But in May 1997, researchers from the Mayo Clinic and Foundation in Rochester, Minnesota, and two other U.S. medical centers reported that they found no risk that a digital cell phone would disrupt heartbeats in people with pacemakers unless it was placed close to the site of the pacemaker while turned on.

A pacemaker is a small, electronic device surgically implanted under the skin of patients with an abnormal heartbeat. The device is connected to electrodes placed on the heart. To preserve battery life, pacemakers are usually set so that they turn on only if unusual electrical heart activity is detected. Early models were sensitive to microwave ovens and other electronic devices, that emitted electromagnetic signals that the pacemakers misread as normal heart activity. Therefore,

Heart and Blood Vessels

- Life-saving device goes portable
- Pacemakers and cell phones
- Drugs as effective as surgery
- New drug prevents blood clots
- Cholesterol: lower is better
- Post-bypass brain injury

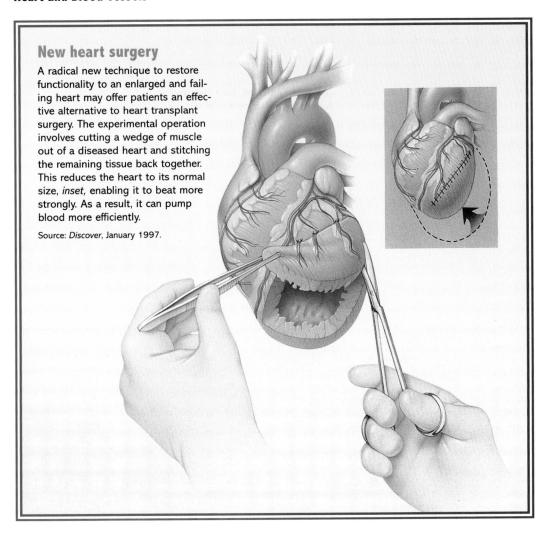

New heart surgery

A radical new technique to restore functionality to an enlarged and failing heart may offer patients an effective alternative to heart transplant surgery. The experimental operation involves cutting a wedge of muscle out of a diseased heart and stitching the remaining tissue back together. This reduces the heart to its normal size, *inset,* enabling it to beat more strongly. As a result, it can pump blood more efficiently.

Source: *Discover,* January 1997.

the pacemaker would fail to turn on even when needed. Advances in shielding and circuit design have made newer pacemakers resistant to this type of interference.

The researchers studied 980 patients with various brands of pacemakers and five types of cellular phones. They found that interference was significant only when a digital phone was held close to the chest, near the pacemaker. Interference did not occur when the phone was held up to the ear, away from the pacemaker. An analog cellular phone caused no significant interference. Analog telephones transmit continuous signals, while digital phones use pulsed signals. Digital phone sales were increasing in the United States

in 1997, but most cell phones were still of the older, analog type.

Pacemaker manufacturers were working to eliminate interference, but until then, many older pacemaker models would be vulnerable. The researchers said that people with a pacemaker should avoid carrying a digital cell phone in a breast pocket, or close to the pacemaker.

Drugs as effective as surgery. In October 1996, researchers from Seattle, Washington, and Stanford, California, published a study that compared angioplasty and drug therapy for heart attack. They announced that drug therapy was as effective as angioplasty and less costly in treating heart attack patients.

A heart attack can result when a blood clot blocks a *coronary artery,* an artery that supplies blood to the tissues of the heart. Blood clots form when fatty deposits on the arterial wall break down, causing small cell fragments in the blood called platelets to clump together and bind to the wall. These platelet clumps attract red blood cells and a protein called fibrin, which all bind together to form a blood clot that partially or completely blocks the artery.

The standard approach to treating heart attack has been to administer drugs that dissolve blood clots. Unfortunately, these drugs do not work in all cases, and so doctors must often perform angioplasty to clear a blockage. In angioplasty, a cardiologist inserts a small flexible tube, called a catheter, into the blocked artery. A tiny balloon on the end of the catheter is then inflated to break apart the clot and open the artery. This approach is more reliable than clot dissolving drugs, but it costs more in the short term. Therefore, there was concern among physicians about whether the higher success rate of angioplasty was worth the extra cost with regard to patient survival.

The researchers studied 3,145 patients who underwent either angioplasty or drug therapy and followed them for three years. The results showed that the survival rate in the hospital and during the follow-up period was not significantly different between the two treatment groups. Furthermore, treatment costs during the study period were 13 percent lower in the drug treatment group. Therefore, the researchers concluded that drug therapy was just as effective as angioplasty in terms of survival rate over three years after a heart attack and cost less in the short term. They suggested that angioplasty be used only in patients who cannot be given clot-dissolving drugs, such as patients who have a risk of serious bleeding in another organ because of recent surgery, stroke, or major injury.

New drug prevents blood clots.
Many researchers in 1996 and 1997 worked to develop new drugs to inhibit the role that platelets play in forming blood clots. The standard drugs used to prevent clots are aspirin and ticlopidine. Both are effective in preventing clots, but they have significant side effects: aspirin causes upset stomach in some people and can cause intestinal bleeding, and ticlopidine can suppress blood cell production, produce a skin rash, and cause diarrhea.

In November 1996 a report was published on a large multinational study in Europe that compared the effectiveness of aspirin and a new drug, clopidogrel, in preventing blood clots. A promising new strategy to prevent clots from forming is to block the sites on platelets to which fibrin proteins attach. Clopidogrel achieves

A new job for arterial stents?

Tiny devices called stents have been used for years to help prevent heart attacks by keeping arteries in the heart from becoming blocked. Some experts in 1997 said that stents could also be used to keep neck arteries open, thereby preventing strokes. Traditional surgery to clear *plaque* (hardened debris) from *carotid arteries* (arteries in the neck that keep the brain supplied with blood) involves a rather large incision to be made in the neck. Inserting a stent is much less invasive. In tests, using stents led to shorter hospital stays, but their long-term effectiveness remained unknown.

After making a small incision near the patient's groin, a surgeon runs a thin tube through a major artery into one of the carotid arteries.

A tiny balloon is inflated inside the artery to widen it. Then, a collapsed stent is run through the tube and placed at the proper point within the artery.

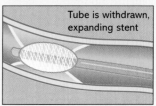

As the tube is withdrawn, the stent expands, propping open the walls of the artery. Some experts believe this will prevent accumulations of plaque from blocking the artery.

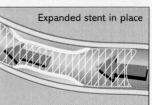

Source: Duke University Medical Center.

Fish linked to better heart health

The longest study yet on the possible benefit of eating fish to reduce the risk of heart attack in men was reported in April 1997 by researchers at Northwestern University Medical School in Chicago. The study followed 1,822 men for 30 years, taking routine surveys of their eating habits. The data showed that men who ate 8 ounces (224 grams) of fish each week had a 44 percent lower risk of heart attack compared with men whose diet typically included no fish. Previous studies have yielded similar results, but researchers have not yet identified exactly how fish protein protects against heart disease. Certain fatty acids in fish are thought to play a key role in preventing heart disease.

this by blocking the formation of these attachment sites on platelets, thereby reducing platelet clumping.

The study involved 19,185 patients with fatty deposits in their arteries, who were treated either with clopidogrel or aspirin and followed for two years. The rate of stroke, heart attack, or death was 9 percent lower in people taking clopidogrel. In addition, the two drugs produced similar side effects, but cases of serious bleeding occurred less often in the clopidogrel group. The investigators concluded that clopidogrel therapy was more effective than aspirin in the prevention of blood clots and just as safe. The effectiveness of clopidogrel compared to ticlopidine has not been studied. Clopidogrel was awaiting FDA approval in mid-1997 for sale in the United States.

Cholesterol: lower is better. Below-normal cholesterol levels may prevent heart attack deaths, according to a study reported in October 1996. High blood cholesterol is a risk factor for the development of fatty deposits in heart arteries, and studies have shown that reducing cholesterol lowers the risk of heart attack in patients with high cholesterol. However, studies have also shown that most heart attacks occur in people who do not have high cholesterol. Researchers theorized, therefore, that reducing cholesterol in patients with average cholesterol levels who suffered a heart attack might prevent a second

heart attack. A group of physicians and scientists at 80 medical centers in the United States and Canada tested this theory.

The researchers studied 4,159 heart-attack patients whose cholesterol levels were in the normal range (less than 240 milligrams per deciliter). The patients were divided into two groups that were given either the cholesterol-lowering drug pravastatin or a *placebo* (inactive substance) and followed for five years. Subjects in the pravastatin group experienced a 24 percent lower risk of death or another heart attack. Furthermore, the need for subsequent coronary artery bypass surgery or angioplasty was 10 percent in the placebo group but only 8 percent in the pravastatin group. The reduction in heart disease was greater in women and in subjects with the highest cholesterol levels. The researchers concluded that lowering cholesterol is beneficial even to heart attack victims who have low to average cholesterol levels. The National Institutes of Health recommended that all adults keep their cholesterol levels below 200 milligrams per deciliter.

Post-bypass brain injury. In December 1996, researchers from several American universities and medical centers reported the results of their study of brain injury following coronary artery bypass surgery. Stroke is the third most frequent cause of death in the United States. It occurs when the blood supply to a part of the brain is cut off. This is usually caused by a blood clot blocking a brain artery. Starved of blood, brain cells in the affected area begin to die. Several aspects of bypass surgery increase the risk of stroke and brain injury, but the link between the two is not well understood.

In 2,108 patients who had coronary artery bypass surgery, the researchers documented two types of brain injury: stroke and intellectual impairment, such as confusion, disorientation, or memory loss. Brain injury was detected in 6 percent of patients and was equally distributed between stroke and intellectual impairment.

Patients with brain injury had a higher death rate during surgery: 21 percent in those with stroke, 10 percent in those with intellectual impairment, and 2 percent in those who experienced no brain injury. Also, patients who had brain injury required significantly longer hospital stays.

Thus, the study showed that coronary bypass surgery was linked to a significant risk of brain injury, which slowed patient recovery and increased costs. The investigators said that further research was needed to reduce the risk to patients and develop better diagnostic and treatment strategies.   • Michael H. Crawford

In WORLD BOOK, see HEART.

A tuberculosis (TB) treatment method begun in the early 1990's proved to be effective and has the potential to curb the global epidemic. The World Health Organization (WHO), an agency of the United Nations based in Geneva, Switzerland, reported the results of the first widespread testing of the new treatment in March 1997.

Tuberculosis, an infectious disease that destroys the lungs, claims the lives of 2 million to 3 million people annually. The new TB treatment, called Directly Observed Treatment, Short-course (DOTS), combines powerful anti-TB drugs with new health management methods.

In the past, patients often took antibiotic treatments only until they felt better, but failed to finish the complete course of medication necessary for a cure. WHO reported that this incomplete use of TB medications led to the emergence of new strains of TB bacteria. The new strains are resistant to traditional drugs, more expensive to treat, and very difficult, and sometimes impossible, to cure.

DOTS overcomes those problems by using health workers called patient observers to watch TB patients swallow each dose of four medicines over the full six- to eight-month treatment. Hiroshi Nakajima, director-general of

Infectious Diseases

- Effective treatment for tuberculosis
- Decline of new tuberculosis cases in the United States
- Guinea worm disease
- Treatment for ear infections
- Decline in AIDS deaths
- Disease contracted from rats

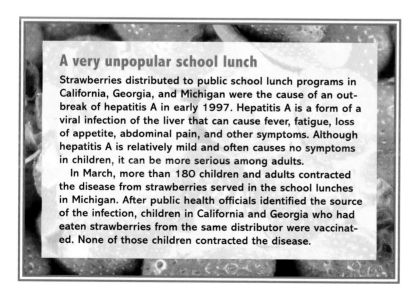

A very unpopular school lunch

Strawberries distributed to public school lunch programs in California, Georgia, and Michigan were the cause of an outbreak of hepatitis A in early 1997. Hepatitis A is a form of a viral infection of the liver that can cause fever, fatigue, loss of appetite, abdominal pain, and other symptoms. Although hepatitis A is relatively mild and often causes no symptoms in children, it can be more serious among adults.

In March, more than 180 children and adults contracted the disease from strawberries served in the school lunches in Michigan. After public health officials identified the source of the infection, children in California and Georgia who had eaten strawberries from the same distributor were vaccinated. None of those children contracted the disease.

WHO, predicted that DOTS would prevent at least 10 million TB deaths during the next 10 years.

Despite the optimism of the 1997 report, WHO noted that in Russia and many Eastern European countries cases of TB had surged. Since 1991, the TB cases in Russia, where DOTS is not used, rose 70 percent, and deaths rose 90 percent.

Decline in new tuberculosis cases. The number of new TB cases in the United States, which began to rise in the mid-1980's, decreased for the fourth straight year in 1996. The Centers for Disease Control and Prevention (CDC) in Atlanta, Georgia, re-

ported those findings in March 1997.

The CDC said that 21,327 new TB cases were reported in 1996, a decline of 7 percent from the 22,860 cases in 1995. Officials credited use of DOTS and greater emphasis on TB control programs for the decline. They cautioned, however, that continued emphasis on TB control was necessary to prevent another resurgence of the disease. TB cases had declined earlier in the 1900's and by the 1960's reached such a low level that officials regarded the disease as conquered.

Guinea worm disease. WHO announced in January 1997 that 21 countries, including Pakistan and Iran, had stopped the transmission of guinea worm disease, or dracunculiasis. The report marked the first time that any country had been declared free from transmission of the disease.

Dracunculiasis is caused by drinking water contaminated with a parasite that grows inside the human body, causing severe pain, fever, nausea, and vomiting, until the parasite emerges from the body. It is the largest tissue parasite affecting humans, with the worm growing to as long as 3.3 feet (1 meter). There are no medications or vaccines to prevent infection by the parasite.

WHO credited the eradication of the disease to a global campaign, begun in 1980, to eliminate guinea worms from drinking water. By 1997, further transmission of the disease had been eliminated from all except 9,900 villages throughout the world. Officials predicted that in "the near future," dracunculiasis would become the first parasitic disease to be completely eliminated from the world.

Treatment for ear infections. A single injection of the antibiotic ceftriaxone is as effective in treating ear infections in children as the traditional 10 days of oral medication, scientists reported in January 1997. Researchers from the Boston University Schools of Medicine and Public Health and the Boston Medical Center reported that the antibiotic, if approved by the U.S. Food and Drug Administration, may offer an alternative treatment to the oral medication.

Rabies prevention

Rabies is a viral infection that attacks the central nervous system and is transferred to humans through the saliva of infected animals. Vaccines are effective in preventing illness if a person receives treatment immediately after being bitten. However, once symptoms appear, the life-threatening disease is too advanced to treat. According to the U.S. Food and Drug Administration, taking preventive measures is a good defense against rabies.

- Keep pets' rabies vaccinations up to date.
- Don't leave chained-up dogs unattended, making them vulnerable to wild animals.
- Don't make the yard inviting to wild animals. Feed pets inside and keep garbage cans tightly sealed.
- Seal openings to basements and attics and cover chimneys with screens.
- Avoid wild or unfamiliar animals. Never touch a wild animal, even if it is dead.

According to the Boston researchers, parents do not often follow the traditional treatment of two doses a day for 10 days, and children sometimes vomit the medication or refuse to swallow it. The one-dose treatment, they claimed, could be used in such circumstances and could also combat bacteria resistant to current treatments. The new medication was not without risks, however. In the study, children receiving the one dose were more likely to develop diarrhea, and a large single dose of an antibiotic can make bacteria more likely to build resistance to the drug.

Decline in AIDS deaths. The number of Americans who died from acquired immune deficiency syndrome (AIDS) declined in 1996 for the first time since the epidemic began in 1981, the CDC announced in February 1997. The CDC reported that the estimated 22,000 AIDS deaths in the United States from January to June of 1996 was 13 percent fewer than the number of deaths during the same period in 1995.

The biggest decline, about 32 percent, occurred among American Indians and Alaskan Natives, with declines of 21 percent among whites, 10 percent among Hispanics, 6 percent among Asians and Pacific Islanders, and 2 percent among blacks. Officials said the decline resulted from better treatment with new combinations of drugs that are more effective against the AIDS virus.

Disease contracted from rats. Leptospirosis, the most common disease that rats transmit to humans, may be emerging as a threat to residents of deteriorating inner cities. Researchers from the National Institute of Allergy and Infectious Diseases (NIAID) in Bethesda, Maryland, issued the warning in November 1996.

People contract leptospirosis from contact with the bacterium *Leptospira interrogans* in rat urine or pools of infected water. Most people experience only mild, flulike symptoms that can be treated with antibiotics. But serious complications, occurring in 10 percent of cases, include high fever, kidney failure, internal bleeding, and sometimes death.

Bacterial meningitis outbreak in Africa

An outbreak of bacterial meningitis claimed the lives of more than 1,500 people in West Africa early in 1997. The World Health Organization (WHO), an agency of the United Nations based in Geneva, Switzerland, reported in April that as many as 11,000 people may have been infected. Burkina Faso, where more than 700 people died, was the worst hit country.

Bacterial meningitis is an inflammation of the membrane surrounding the spinal cord and brain. It is caused by a bacterial infection. In Africa, the fatality rate from bacterial meningitis is between 5 and 15 percent if the infection is diagnosed and treated early, but if not, the fatality rate is about 50 percent.

According to the Centers for Disease Control and Prevention (CDC) in Atlanta, Georgia, the region of Africa south of the Sahara Desert is known as the "meningitis belt" because of the large number of recurring outbreaks in the region. Since the 1980's, the frequency of these epidemics continued to increase. In May 1996, the CDC and WHO began working together to combat this trend. Beginning in the winter of 1997, the joint effort initiated a training program for epidemic surveillance in 15 different African countries. The program was also expected to help the governments of those countries improve the production and distribution of vaccinations.

Joseph M. Vinetz, an infectious disease specialist at NIAID who led the research, noted that a Baltimore, Maryland, hospital had reported three cases within one year, though no cases had been reported there in the previous decade. The researchers tested 21 rats at sites in the inner city where the three individuals were likely to have contracted the disease. They found that 19 of the rats carried the bacteria. Previous studies, noted by the authors of the report, had shown that city dwellers were at risk for contracting leptospirosis.

• Michael Woods

See also AIDS. In the section Medical and Safety Alerts, see How Safe Is Our Food Supply? In World Book, see Bacteria; Virus.

Kidney

Progress in *xenotransplantation,* the transplantation of an organ from one species into another species, was reported in January 1997 by researchers at Nextran, a private genetic research firm, and Duke University Medical Center in Durham, North Carolina. Increasing success in kidney transplantation has led to a shortage in the United States of donated kidneys. The shortage spurred scientists to find ways to make xenotransplants feasible.

Because of their size, physiology, and availability, pigs are the likeliest organ donors for human patients, but many barriers to success exist. When pig organs are transplanted into primates, an intense reaction, called *hyperacute rejection*, occurs, destroying the transplanted organ within minutes or hours. Rejection is caused by *antibodies,* proteins that are a normal part of the immune system, which ordinarily latch onto and destroy bacteria or viruses in the body. In a pig-primate transplant, the primate's antibodies attach to cells that line the blood vessels of the pig organ. This in turn activates *complement,* another protein, leading to cell damage. Ultimately, the blood vessels become blocked and begin to bleed, and the organ dies.

The Duke and Nextran team successfully blocked hyperacute rejection by using complement regulatory proteins, which normally line the walls of blood vessels and protect them from injury by complement. Pig complement regulatory proteins are not effective against primate complement, so the investigators infected several pigs with a virus that contained human complement regulatory protein-genes, thereby altering the pigs' genetic code. Over time, the organs of these pigs began to produce human complement regulatory protein instead of pig complement regulatory protein. When organs from these pigs were transplanted into baboons, they survived much longer than organs from normal pigs. This novel approach of modifying the donor rather than the recipient offered hope that further donor modifications may eventually make pig-to-human xenotransplants possible.

Implantable artificial kidneys. At the annual Scientific Meeting of the American Society of Nephrology held in November 1996, investigators from the University of Michigan and Nephros Therapeutics, Inc., a private medical research firm, reported on progress toward developing an implantable artificial kidney. The kidney is the only solid organ whose function can be adequately replaced in the long term by an artificial filtering mechanism. More than 200,000 Americans currently receive this treatment, known as dialysis. Dialysis, however, is far from an ideal substitute, and kidney transplantation is not always available or successful.

The proposed artificial kidney consists of two main components. The first, a hemofilter, is created by growing cells along the inside of a thin-walled tube. The cells are genetically modified to produce a blood thinner, so the blood won't clot within the filter. As blood flows through the tube, a filtered plasma is produced. This plasma is then passed to the second component, a renal tubule. The tubule is constructed like the filter, except it contains cells that reabsorb the healthy parts of the plasma and return them to the body. The investigators noted that full development of this device was still years away. In the meantime, elements of the system could be used to complement existing treatments.

Diabetes and kidney disease. In November 1996, researchers from various U.S. medical centers reported the results of a study among the Pima Indians, who have the world's highest rate of noninsulin dependent diabetes mellitus (NIDDM). NIDDM, also called Type II diabetes, is the leading cause of kidney failure in the United States, but the link between them is not well understood.

The researchers studied 194 Pima who had varying stages of diabetic kidney disease. They carefully measured the subjects' kidney filtering function and tested urine samples for *albuminuria*—the presence of a protein called albumin. Albuminuria indicates kidney damage and is the first sign of diabetic kidney disease.

The data showed that in people with newly diagnosed NIDDM, kidney filtering function was 16 percent higher than normal. Subjects who had microscopic traces of albumin in the urine had kidney filtering function 26 percent higher than normal. People with high urine albumin levels (a sign of advanced kidney disease) initially had a normal kidney function rate, but they were losing kidney function at a rate that would lead to kidney failure within about 10 years. This indicated that kidney filtering function increases at the onset of NIDDM and remains elevated until the kidneys are significantly damaged.

Albuminuria develops without symptoms and conventional blood and urine tests may fail to detect problems early. In subjects who had a high level of albumin in the urine at the start of the study, for example, blood tests for kidney function were normal, but they were already rapidly losing kidney function. Unfortunately, once kidney disease is established, only careful blood pressure control can slow the loss of kidney function. Doctors advise people with diabetes to modify risk factors for high blood pressure and begin taking medications at the first sign of albuminuria.

• Jeffrey R. Thompson

In WORLD BOOK, see KIDNEY.

A February 1997 announcement that researchers at the Roslin Institute in Edinburgh, Scotland, had *cloned* (made an exact genetic copy of) an adult sheep set off a storm of debate over the ethics of cloning. The procedure was heralded in the scientific community as a major accomplishment in the field of genetics, but news of the experiment stirred public concern—especially over the issue of cloning humans.

Although scientists had already cloned animal cells taken from *embryos* (a prebirth stage of an organism), this was the first time that a mammal had been cloned from an adult cell. Scientists cloned a 6-year-old *ewe* (female sheep) by fusing one of its cells with an empty egg cell from another ewe. The nucleus of the egg cell was removed so that only the genetic material from the first animal existed in the egg. The researchers placed the resulting embryo into the uterus of a surrogate mother ewe. On July 5, 1996, the ewe gave birth to a lamb named Dolly.

Some ethicists expressed fears that cloning could give rise to the practice of *eugenics*, a process that aims at improving the human race by selecting parents based on their inherited characteristics. Some critics of cloning feared this process could make possible the creation of a race of people with identical characteristics. Others raised concern that parents could clone a sick child in order to obtain organs or bone marrow for transplantation.

In March 1997, President Bill Clinton banned the use of federal funds for research on human cloning and asked that researchers voluntarily forego such research until its implications were explored. The president also asked the 18-member National Bioethics Advisory Commission, which was established in July 1996, to examine a variety of current bioethical issues, to investigate the ethical and legal implications of human cloning, and to recommend government actions to prevent abuse.

The commission announced in June 1997 that duplicating humans was "morally unacceptable" and recommended legislation to ban cloning experiments aimed at making a human. However, commission members also recommended that any law have a "sunset clause" that would expire in three to five years. Inclusion of such a clause would force the nation to reexamine the question of human cloning at that time, when the science of cloning may have improved.

Age limits for pregnancy. News of the successful pregnancy and birth of a baby to a 63-year-old mother in 1996 was announced in April 1997. The event raised questions about whether there should be an age limit for pregnancy and who should decide if a woman is too old to bear a child.

The woman, who had already gone

Medical Ethics

• Cloning and human reproduction
• Age limits for pregnancy
• Allocating transplantable livers

Medical Ethics

through menopause, was admitted to the fertility clinic at the University of Southern California after lying about her age. The clinic bars women over the age of 55. Doctors fertilized an egg from a much younger woman with sperm from the 63-year-old woman's husband. The doctors then implanted the donor egg into the woman's uterus. Doctors also gave the woman fertility drugs to assist implantation.

Following the news of the birth, some doctors said that it is unnatural and medically unsound for a woman to have a baby late in life. Others said that it is wrong for a child to grow up with a much older mother, who is more likely to become ill or to die when the child is still young.

Some medical professionals, however, supported birth by older women. Ronald Munson, an ethicist at the University of Missouri, said that denying birth to older women is a form of age discrimination. Others said that the procedure offers an option to older couples who want to have a child, but are turned down by adoption agencies because of their age.

Allocating transplantable livers. In June 1997, the United Network for Organ Sharing (UNOS), a nonprofit agency located in Richmond, Virginia, that coordinates donations of healthy organs taken from people who recently died and allocates them nationwide, announced plans for a new system for priority allocations. Under the new system, patients who are considered to be most likely to survive with a transplant will remain at the top of the list. This revision, announced in November 1996, includes patients whose livers suddenly failed because of an infection and patients who had had a transplant that failed. The change occurs in patients on the second tier of priorities, consisting of chronically ill people with diseases like hepatitis or alcoholic cirrhosis who are hospitalized. Patients whose disease suddenly worsened will now have priority over people whose condition is stable.

About 7,000 people in the United States in 1997 were waiting for transplantable livers. Only about 4,300 livers become available each year, the majority from young people who die in accidents. About 8 percent of people on waiting lists die before a usable liver becomes available.

Andrew Klein, chairman of the UNOS liver and intestinal organ transplantation committee that developed the new policy, said that the group hoped to make additional changes in the future to make the process fairer. Critics of the plan, including John Fung of the University of Pittsburgh, claimed that patients who are chronically ill are just as likely to do well with new livers as patients with a viral infection, for example, and argued that it is unfair to put them lower on the waiting list.   • Carol Levine

See also HEALTH CARE ISSUES.

A lamb named Dolly, *below*, the first clone of an adult mammal, was born on July 5, 1996. The birth set off a storm of controversy about the ethics of cloning and raised concerns about the possibility of cloning humans.

On Sept. 26, 1996, President Bill Clinton signed into law the Mental Health Parity Act of 1996, which mandates that certain features of health insurance can be no different for mental illnesses than they are for physical illnesses. That requirement for *parity,* or equality, in insurance coverage was scheduled to take effect Jan. 1, 1998.

Insurance plans generally provide less coverage for mental illness than for physical illness. Most policies that cover mental health services require higher than normal *copayments* (fees paid by patients at the time of treatment) or higher *deductibles* (payments made by patients before an insurance company contributes). Also, most policies impose lower annual and lifetime limits for mental health benefits. For example, although many insurance plans offer lifetime limits of $1 million for cancer treatment, most plans place lifetime limits for mental health benefits at $50,000 or less.

The new law prohibits insurance companies from imposing those lower annual and lifetime benefit limits for treatment of mental illness. The measure applies to group health plans provided by insurance companies and to self-insured businesses, companies that own their own group policies. The law does not require plans to offer mental health benefits, and the parity requirements do not apply to substance abuse treatment. The law also does not require parity in areas such as deductibles, copayments, and the maximum number of visits to a practitioner.

Self-insured businesses with fewer than 51 employees and individual insurance plans are exempt from the law. In addition, if an insurance provider can demonstrate that compliance with the new measure would increase costs by 1 percent or more, the provider could claim exemption.

Workers with mental illnesses. In April 1997, the Equal Employment Opportunity Commission (EEOC) issued guidelines for employers regarding the rights of employees with psychiatric or emotional disorders, including depression, schizophrenia, and obsessive-compulsive disorder. According to the EEOC, the guidelines were created to dispel "myths, fears, and stereotypes" about mental illness and to clarify how the Americans with Disabilities Act of 1990, which provides protection against discrimination, applies to employees with psychiatric disabilities.

The guidelines require employers to make "reasonable accommodation" for those employees. Accommodations may include adjusting work schedules or making physical changes in the work space. In addition, the guidelines prohibit companies from requiring job applicants to answer questions about their mental health

Depression often goes untreated

More than 17 million adults in the United States suffer from some *depressive disorder*, a condition that affects a person's body, feelings, behaviors, and thoughts. About 80 percent of people diagnosed with severe depression, however, can improve with current treatments, according to the National Institute of Mental Health. Unfortunately, only one in three depressed people seeks help for the condition. People may avoid treatment because they do not perceive feeling exhausted, worthless, helpless, or hopeless as treatable conditions. Also, some of the symptoms can themselves discourage taking the initiative to seek assistance unless another individual provides the necessary encouragement.

Mental health care providers

Selecting appropriate practitioners for mental health care can be daunting because of the varied professional services available. Understanding the expertise of each profession can help consumers make informed decisions.

Psychiatrists are medical doctors who specialize in the treatment of mental disorders. Because of their training, they can evaluate the biochemical connections to mental illnesses and coordinate medical treatment and counseling.

Clinical psychologists hold doctorate degrees and have completed extensive clinical training. They must pass a state licensing examination in order to practice. Psychologists focus on an individual's personality, behavior, and experiences to address emotional problems. They often coordinate treatment with psychiatrists.

Social workers hold at least a master's degree in social work and specialize in treating patients with emotional or psychiatric problems. They must also apply for a license to practice and often coordinate work with psychiatrists.

Mental health counselors provide a variety of counseling services, including concerns with career choices and spiritual matters. While some states have licensing requirements and guidelines for counselors, others have none.

Source: *The Columbia University College of Physicians and Surgeons Complete Guide to Mental Health.*

ment in response to what they perceived as an emphasis of insurance providers on profits rather than quality care. The groups planned to distribute the bill of rights to members of Congress and to managed care organizations (MCO's) as part of a campaign to promote mental health legislation and changes in the way MCO's cover mental health care.

The document stipulates that patients should have access to detailed information about their mental health benefits, including what their benefits are, how the insurance company decides which treatments to cover, and what treatment options are available. It also calls for MCO's to provide consumers with full access to information on practitioners' experience and credentials. The bill of rights also calls on MCO's to guarantee confidentiality about a patient's treatment. And it calls for guarantees of free choice in selecting mental health care professionals, parity in mental health coverage, and accountability from insurance companies to provide coverage for necessary treatment.

Impact of mental illness. Five of the 10 leading causes of disability worldwide are mental illnesses, according to a five-year study of worldwide public health trends. Those findings were announced in 1996 and 1997 in a 10-volume report, "The Global Burden of Disease," prepared by the Harvard School of Public Health in Boston; the World Health Organization, an agency of the United Nations (UN) in Geneva, Switzerland; and the UN's World Bank in Washington, D.C. The illnesses highlighted in the study were depression, alcoholism, manic-depression, schizophrenia, and obsessive-compulsive disorder.

The authors concluded that the global burden of mental illness had been significantly underestimated. They estimated that in 1990 mental illnesses made up about 10.5 percent of total disability cases—measured according to "disability adjusted life years," or years of healthy life lost—and projected that figure would rise to 15 percent by 2020.

Mental health care providers had long argued that mental illness takes a great toll on society, that it is not

history or from discriminating against qualified applicants who may be mentally ill. However, the guidelines do not require employers to lower their performance standards for employees with mental illness or to tolerate threats to coworkers from an employee with a mental illness.

Managed care and mental health. Nine organizations representing mental health professionals released a Mental Health Bill of Rights in February 1997 to educate people about their rights as consumers of mental health care. The groups—including the American Psychological Association, the American Psychiatric Association, and the National Association of Social Workers—prepared the docu-

treated as seriously as physical illness, and that treatment and research on mental illness receive inadequate funding. The authors of the study hoped that the report's findings would help policymakers allocate health care funds more effectively.

Alzheimer's and intelligence. High intelligence may compensate for the decline in brain function caused by Alzheimer's disease and may provide some protection against symptoms of the disease. Those findings were reported in February 1997 by the National Institute of Aging (NIA) in Bethesda, Maryland.

Alzheimer's disease, the most common form of *dementia* (deterioration of the mind) is caused by the *degeneration,* or gradual destruction, of brain cells. According to the American Psychiatric Association, Alzheimer's affects more than 50 percent of people over the age of 85.

The NIA researchers used positron emission tomography (PET) to measure the degeneration of the brains of 46 patients with dementia probably caused by Alzheimer's disease. (A diagnosis of Alzheimer's disease can only be confirmed after a patient's death.) PET scans produce images of the brain's chemical activity. The device uses sensors to pick up gamma ray signals from the brain. A computer then translates these signals into color images that show the rate of chemical activity in specific brain regions. The NIA researchers could make judgments about the degree of degeneration by comparing the PET scans of the people with dementia to those of healthy individuals.

The people with Alzheimer's symptoms all showed a similar degree of dementia, but they differed in level of intelligence. Intelligence scores were based on reading tests and education levels achieved. The researchers found that the brains of the more intelligent patients had more severe brain degeneration than the brains of the less intelligent subjects. The results suggested that the brains of the more intelligent people had to degenerate further before they showed symptoms of dementia.

Treatment for Alzheimer's disease. The U.S. Food and Drug Administration (FDA) approved the use of donepezil hydrochloride in November 1996 to treat the symptoms of Alzheimer's disease. The drug, marketed in the United States by Pfizer Inc., under the name Aricept, became only the second medication for treating Alzheimer's patients. The other drug is tacrine hydrochloride, or Cognex.

Neither drug slows degeneration, but both relieve symptoms of dementia by helping the brain use the neurotransmitter acetylcholine more effectively. Neurotransmitters are chemicals that convey nerve signals

Creativity and mental illness

In the last 19 months of his life, Vincent Van Gogh, the Dutch artist of the 1800's, painted numerous works between bouts of depression. Van Gogh's illness and the lives of other creative geniuses—visual artists, writers, and musicians—have inspired much research about creativity and mental illness. Many studies have shown an unusually high number of mental disorders among renowned artists. According to psychologist Sybil Barten of Purchase College, State University of New York, explanations for the link between mental illness and creativity are based on the assumption that both characteristics deal with the unconscious. At a conference at Purchase in April 1997, art historian Jane Kromm noted, however, that Van Gogh himself saw his depression as a hindrance, not a help to his work.

between *neurons* (nerve cells). Aricept appears to cause fewer and less dangerous side effects than Cognex.

The American Psychiatric Association published its first set of guidelines in May 1997 for the treatment of Alzheimer's and other dementias associated with aging. The guidelines, based on a review of existing research and clinical studies, recommended that physicians specifically prohibit patients with moderate to severe Alzheimer's from driving. In addition, they promoted the use of vitamin E as well as prescription medications that enhance the activity of the brain and, therefore, slow the progression of the disease's symptoms.

Obsessive-compulsive disorder in children may be linked to streptococcal infection, one of the most common bacterial infections. Researchers led by pediatrician Susan Swedo at the National Institute of Mental Health (NIMH) in Bethesda, Maryland, announced that finding in January 1997. Symptoms of OCD include repetitive, ritualized behaviors, such as counting, hoarding objects, or hand washing; obsessive fear of threats, such as germs; or a fear of committing violent acts.

The researchers theorized that an *antibody* (immune system cell) may actually cause OCD. The antibody, called D8/17, is produced to fight the streptococcus bacterium that causes rheumatic fever. In some children, however, D8/17 may attack healthy cells in the brain's basal ganglia region, which helps control basic movement sequences, such as walking or eating.

In the NIMH study, the researchers compared the blood of 27 children diagnosed with OCD symptoms with the blood of 24 healthy children. They found that the blood of 23 of the children with OCD contained D8/17. In contrast, only four of the healthy children had the antibody.

In clinical trials conducted since 1986, the NIMH team also found that treatments that removed the antibodies from the bloodstream relieved symptoms of OCD in children. The researchers hoped that their findings would provide a way to identify children susceptible to OCD and lead to better understanding of other physiological causes of OCD in adults as well as children.

In March 1997, the FDA approved the use of the drug fluvoxamine maleate, or Luvox, to treat OCD in children. Luvox, previously approved to treat adults, prevents the neurotransmitter serotonin from being reabsorbed into neurons. An inadequate level of serotonin in the *synapses* (spaces) between neurons has been linked to several mental illnesses, including OCD.   • Lisa Klobuchar

See also BRAIN AND NERVOUS SYSTEM. In WORLD BOOK, see MENTAL ILLNESS.

Nutrition and Food

- Selenium and cancer
- Alzheimer's disease and vitamin E
- Zinc and common colds

The mineral selenium may reduce the risk of some cancers when taken as a dietary supplement, according to the results of a study published in December 1996. But some health professionals who claimed that the study was flawed questioned the benefits of selenium.

Selenium, a mineral found in seafood, egg yolk, liver, kidney, and whole grain products, is an *antioxidant*, a chemical compound that prevents cell damage by blocking the effects of unstable molecules called free radicals. Scientists have linked free radicals to a number of diseases, including cancer.

Researchers from the Arizona Cancer Center in Tucson in 1983 began to study the effects of selenium in 1,321 patients with skin cancer. One group of patients participating in the National Prevention of Cancer Study was given a supplement containing 200 micrograms of selenium and another group was given a *placebo* (an inactive substance).

The researchers concluded that though selenium had no effect on skin cancer, the risk of developing other forms of cancer was dramatically reduced in the patients taking selenium compared with patients taking the placebo. The group taking selenium experienced a 63 percent lower rate of prostate cancer, a 58 percent lower rate of colon/rectal cancer, and a 45 percent lower rate of lung can-

Reducing iron overload

Some health experts expressed concern in 1997 that overconsumption or overabsorption of iron might be a cause of or a contributor to ailments such as heart disease and cancer. Iron overload can result when the diet is overly rich in iron from the excessive consumption of red meat or from iron supplements taken when the body is not iron-deficient. Some researchers suggest that excessive iron in the tissues can promote coronary artery disease or the growth of some cancers. Adults require between 10 and 15 milligrams of iron daily, depending on their age and gender. Blood tests can detect the amount of iron in the body. People with excessive amounts of iron in their blood may be able to reduce iron overload in the following ways:

- Stop smoking.
- Drink more tea, which has acids called tannins that trap iron and reduce its absorption.
- Avoid taking vitamin C or foods rich in vitamin C with iron-containing supplements or iron-rich foods.
- Reduce the amount of red meat in the diet.
- Increase the amount of exercise.
- Eat bran and other whole grains that contain phytic acid, which combines with iron and keeps it out of the circulatory system.
- Drink less alcohol, which increases the solubility of iron, making it easier to store.
- Avoid iron-enriched cereals and bread and supplements with iron.
- Donate blood several times each year.

Source: U.S. Food and Drug Administration.

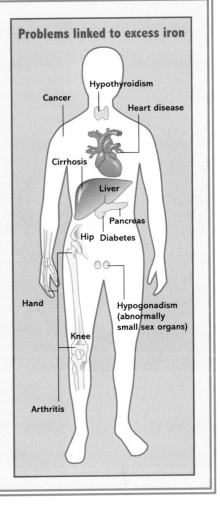

Problems linked to excess iron

Cancer
Hypothyroidism
Heart disease
Cirrhosis
Liver
Pancreas
Hip Diabetes
Hand
Hypogonadism (abnormally small sex organs)
Knee
Arthritis

cer than the group taking the placebo. The group taking selenium also experienced a 50 percent lower rate of death from all forms of cancer.

The researchers theorized that the mineral had no effect on skin cancer because patients did not take selenium supplements for a sufficient period of time. The researchers also suggested that selenium may be most effective in battling cancer in its later stages of development.

Although the results of the study looked promising, some scientists questioned the methods used to produce the results. For example, the study was originally designed to examine the effects of selenium on skin cancer. In 1990, the researchers decided to study selenium's effect on other cancers, including lung, colon, rectal, and prostate cancers.

Critics pointed out that the number of people used in the study was relatively small compared with other cancer studies, and that patients were recruited from the East Coast of the United States—a region with relatively low selenium levels in soil and crops and high rates of skin cancer. The patients, in fact, had blood selenium concentrations lower than most other Americans. Some scientists, including Larry Clark, a researcher at the Arizona Cancer Center who worked on the selenium study, stressed that long-term research must be performed on selenium before its true effects are known.

Alzheimer's disease and vitamin E.

The results of two studies released in 1997 stressing the benefits of vitamin E caused health professionals to look at the vitamin in a new light. Researchers announced that vitamin E may help treat Alzheimer's disease patients and may increase the strength of the immune system in elderly people.

Alzheimer's disease is a disorder in which brain cells degenerate and die, causing memory problems and, eventually, a complete loss of mental function. A study published in April 1997 found that people with moderately advanced cases of Alzheimer's disease who take 2,000 International Units (IU) of vitamin E daily can delay the loss of ability to groom and feed themselves by seven months and the need for 24-hour care by seven months. The treatment may also prolong life.

The research team, headed by neuropsychologist Mary Sano of Columbia University in New York City, studied 341 Alzheimer's patients for two years. The patients were given either 2,000 IU of vitamin E, 10 milligrams of *selegiline* (a prescription drug used to treat Parkinson disease), a combination of vitamin E and selegiline, or a placebo.

The rate of mental decline slowed by 25 percent in patients who took vitamin E and in those who took selegiline, compared with those who took the placebo. Researchers found, however, that the combination of the treatments was not as effective in slowing the rate of decline. No treatment completely halted or reversed the progression of the disease.

The research team theorized that because vitamin E and selegiline are both antioxidants they reduce oxidative stress, a process by which a highly reactive form of oxygen breaks down brain cell structure, making cells unable to function normally. According to the researchers, an increased rate of oxidative stress speeds cell destruction, which in turn quickens the progression of Alzheimer's disease.

Researchers in mid-1997 planned to give vitamin E and selegiline to patients in the earliest stages of Alzheimer's. Their hope was that these or other drugs in development might postpone the disease indefinitely.

In an unrelated study also published in May 1997, researchers at Tufts University in New York City found that daily doses of 200 IU of vitamin E significantly improved the strength of the immune system and possibly prevented infectious diseases in people age 65 and older.

The strength of the immune system declines with age, which the researchers said may explain why the elderly are more likely to suffer from infections and from diseases, such as arthritis, that are caused by malfunctioning immune systems. The researchers believed that vitamin E

Wrapped in fat and calories

Many restaurants promote wraps—grilled vegetables, chicken, tuna, or other ingredients wrapped in flat breads—as a healthy alternative to other menu items. However, according to an analysis conducted by Tufts University in New York City, the wraps are high in fat and calories because of the large serving size—usually between 8 and 15 ounces.

Product	Calories	Fat grams	Saturated fat grams	Sodium grams
Au Bon Pain				
Chicken	630	31	8	1,140
Tuna	950	64	17	1,230
Turkey	550	12	1	1,610
Taco Bell				
Chicken	460	21	6	1,220
Supreme	500	25	8	1,230
Steak	460	21	6	1,130
Supreme	510	25	8	1,140
Veggie	420	19	5	920
Supreme	460	23	8	930
Wendy's				
Chicken	490	17	5	1,300
Greek	430	19	7	1,070
Ranch/chicken	480	17	4	1,170
Veggie	390	15	3	780

supplements might reduce the risks of infectious disease that often accompany aging.

In the study, 88 people age 65 and older were given daily doses of either 60 IU, 200 IU, or 800 IU of vitamin E, or a placebo for eight months. The patients were also given vaccinations and booster shots containing dead or weakened strains of the microorganisms responsible for causing hepatitis B, tetanus, diphtheria, and pneumonia. In addition, the patients were pricked in the arm with a small, multipronged device that contained triggers, such as diphtheria or tuberculosis. The vaccinations, booster shots, and triggers all alerted white blood cells called T cells to the presence of a disease in the body. T cells are among the immune system components that attack infectious microorganisms. The researchers used a skin sensitivity test, called the delayed type hypersensitivity test, to gauge the strength of the patient's immune system response to the different diseases.

After only four months of treatment, T cell response grew 65 percent stronger in patients who took 200 IU of vitamin E. In addition, the patients had more *antibodies* (disease-fighting proteins) to fight hepatitis B and tetanus than the patients who took the placebo.

The patients who took 800 IU of vitamin E also developed more antibodies against hepatitis B, but they were no more protected against tetanus than patients who took the placebo. Their T cell response also was no stronger than that found in the placebo group.

Patients who took 60 IU of vitamin E showed a slightly greater resistance to diphtheria and tuberculosis than the placebo group. However, their bodies were no more protected against hepatitis B or tetanus than those patients who took a placebo.

Zinc and common colds. A study published in July 1996 that suggested the mineral zinc may relieve symptoms of the common cold resulted in a huge increase in the sale of zinc lozenges. Researchers at the Cleveland Clinic in Cleveland, Ohio, studied the effects of zinc on 100 people who had experienced cold symptoms

within 24 hours of treatment. The patients were divided into two groups. One group received lozenges containing 13 milligrams of zinc, a mineral that helps the body use carbohydrates, proteins, and fats, and aids in cell growth and repair. The other group received placebo lozenges—lozenges containing no zinc. The patients took the lozenges every two hours while they were awake until they no longer had cold symptoms.

After the first day of treatment, 46 percent of the patients taking the placebo and 59 percent of those taking zinc said that the lozenges had helped alleviate cold symptoms. By the end of the 18-day study, all but eight of the patients reported that the cold symptoms had disappeared—

Cholesterol-free milk
A fat-free, cholesterol-free milk that, when combined with a balanced diet, can help reduce total blood cholesterol and thereby lessen the risk of heart disease, was expected to store shelves in mid-1997. The product, marketed under the name Replace—Beta-Glucan Factor, was developed by Golden Jersey Products, Incorporated, of Vero Beach, Florida. The product is made by combining skimmed milk with hydrolyzed oat flour, which is used as a replacement for fat.

Removing fat from ground beef

Half the fat from ground beef used in recipes that call for crumbled ground meat can be removed by first placing the meat in a microwave. Crumble the beef into a bowl and microwave it on high for a few minutes. Using a fork, break up the meat and pour off the grease. Microwave the beef again until the meat looks cooked. Place the cooked meat in a strainer and press out more of the fat, or place the meat on paper towels and blot it. To remove additional amounts of fat from the beef, place the cooked meat in a strainer or colander and rinse it with hot, but not boiling, water. Then dry the meat completely.

Source: University of California-Berkeley Wellness Letter, March 1997.

with 44 percent of the placebo group and 59 percent of the zinc group claiming that the lozenges had helped them. On average, patients in the zinc group experienced cold symptoms for 4.4 days compared with patients in the placebo group, who experienced symptoms for 7.6 days. However, the patients taking zinc reported side effects including nausea and a bad aftertaste.

The researchers admitted that the study had some flaws. The researchers did not check zinc levels in patients' bodies to gauge if there was a relation between blood zinc levels and cold symptoms. The patients were also instructed to take lozenges every two hours, which would have been seven to eight daily; instead, they took four to eight lozenges daily.

Previous studies have shown that zinc inhibits replication of the cold virus and that the mineral binds with a nerve in the nose—a process that may inhibit sneezing. Other studies have suggested that zinc may stabilize cell membranes, making them invulnerable to viral attack. Some studies have found that zinc does not relieve cold symptoms. The researchers agreed that further study was needed to identify the effects zinc has on combating symptoms of the common cold.   • Jeanine Barone

In WORLD BOOK, see NUTRITION.

Pregnancy and Childbirth

- Minimum hospital stay for childbirth
- Reducing risk of infection in newborns
- Medication linked to birth defects
- Testing for cystic fibrosis

President Bill Clinton signed into law the Newborns' and Mothers' Health Protection Act in September 1996, guaranteeing a minimum length of a hospital stay for childbirth. The law was strongly supported by consumers and professional organizations, such as the American Academy of Pediatrics in Elk Grove Village, Illinois, and the American College of Obstetricians and Gynecologists in Washington, D.C.

The law, scheduled to go into effect Jan. 1, 1998, mandates that health-care insurers provide for a minimum of 48 hours of hospital care following an uncomplicated vaginal delivery and 96 hours following a cesarean delivery. A shorter period is acceptable only if the mother and the health-care provider agree. Insurers cannot require a physician to seek advance approval for a 48- or 96-hour stay, nor can the insurer impose any penalty on the health-care provider for authorizing it.

With the advent of managed health care, hospital stays had been shortened in an effort to control costs. Fearing that cost-cutting measures could be harmful to patients, physicians and other groups led efforts to limit managed-care organizations' ability to restrict care. The new law stemmed from concerns that arose over mothers and babies having problems after being discharged from the hospital soon after birth.

Tests during pregnancy

Assessing the condition of a fetus or unborn baby has always been a challenge. Doctors use several standard tests as well as new sophisticated technology to detect problems that may occur during pregnancy.

Test	Purpose	Timing
Laboratory tests:	Determine what conditions are normal for a mother and detect possible problems. (Tests include blood type, pap test, urine culture, and hemoglobin/hematocrit.)	First prenatal exam
Tests for infections:	Detect infections—hepatitis B, rubella, syphilis, gonorrhea, and HIV—that could affect the fetus or complicate the pregnancy.	First prenatal exam
Chorionic villus sampling:	A sample of tissue from the placenta is removed and analyzed to detect genetic disorders.	10–12 weeks
Amniocentesis:	Amniotic fluid surrounding the fetus is removed and analyzed to detect genetic disorders or, later in pregnancy, to see if the baby's lungs are mature.	14–18 weeks
Maternal serum screening:	Substances in blood are tested to detect birth defects, such as Down syndrome and neural tube defects.	15–18 weeks
Ultrasound:	Sound waves create an image of the fetus to assess age, growth, position, movement, and possible problems.	As needed
Nonstress test:	Fetal heart rate is measured through a device attached to mother's stomach to assess whether the fetus is getting enough oxygen.	As needed, usually in last 10 weeks
Contraction stress test:	Fetal heart rate is measured in response to mother's contractions to see if the fetus is under stress.	As needed, usually in last 10 weeks
Biophysical profile:	Combination of tests to assess the fetus's breathing and movement and to verify the results of other tests.	As needed
Doppler velocimetry:	A form of ultrasound that measures blood flow in the umbilical cord and thus the oxygen supply to the fetus.	Used with growth-restricted fetuses

Source: American College of Obstetricians and Gynecologists.

In response, physician groups defined what they considered an adequate length of care and launched a campaign to have it enacted nationwide. Although some states had already joined the effort and passed regulations, those laws did not extend guarantees to women covered by self-insured plans. The new law ensures coverage for a minimum stay for all insured women giving birth.

Reducing risk of infection. In March 1997, the American Academy of Pediatrics announced its support of guidelines to prevent group B streptococcal (GBS) infection in newborns. The guidelines were developed by the U.S. Centers for Disease Control and Prevention (CDC) in Atlanta, Georgia, in collaboration with the American College of Obstetricians and Gynecologists.

Group B streptococci are bacteria that can be found in the digestive, urinary, respiratory, and reproductive tracts of men and women. GBS occurs in 10 to 30 percent of pregnant women, most often in the vagina and rectum. In many cases the bacteria do not cause any symptoms and treatment is not needed. During pregnancy, however, the bacteria can be passed to the baby. This can cause serious illness, usually within six hours of birth. GBS infection occurs in about 7,600 newborns annually, resulting in about 310 deaths of infants less than 90 days of age.

The new guidelines were designed

to identify those women at risk of passing the infection to their newborns during labor and delivery. Women who develop a fever in late pregnancy or who have preterm labor or ruptures of *membranes* (the sac that holds the baby in the woman's uterus) are at higher risk of passing the infection to their babies.

The new guidelines suggested two approaches that, according to the CDC, can significantly reduce the number of infants born with this potentially life-threatening infection. One approach is testing all women for the presence of GBS at 35 to 37 weeks of pregnancy. (An average pregnancy is 40 weeks.) Testing is done by taking cultures from the woman's rectum or vagina, which are then analyzed in a laboratory. The results are not accurate earlier in a pregnancy or if only a small amount of bacteria are present. Women whose test results show the presence of GBS at 35 to 37 weeks of pregnancy can receive an antibiotic treatment during labor that helps prevent transferring the infection. The other approach is giving antibiotic treatments during labor to a woman with risk factors even if she has not been tested.

Medication linked to birth defects. Birth defects linked to the use of certain high blood pressure medication can be prevented if drug use is discontinued during the first trimester of pregnancy. The CDC reported those conclusions in March 1997 based on a multiorganizational study of surveys on birth defects.

Angiotensin-converting enzyme inhibitors (ACEI's), drugs promoted as first-line therapy for long-term high blood pressure, became widely used in the 1980's. In 1992, however, the U.S. Food and Drug Administration warned that ACEI's taken during the second and third trimesters of pregnancy were a known link to birth defects. The new study was done to determine if the drug also produced harmful effects when taken in the early stages of pregnancy.

In a review of 79 pregnancies, the researchers found no evidence of birth defects with use of ACEI's in the first 14 weeks of pregnancy. The CDC recommended, however, that whenever possible, pregnant women or women who are planning pregnancy and who are using ACEI's switch to another medication to maintain normal blood pressure.

Testing for cystic fibrosis. All couples expecting or planning to have a child should be offered testing for cystic fibrosis. The National Institutes of Health (NIH) in Bethesda, Maryland, issued that statement in April 1997 because of the serious impact of the disease, its prevalence, and the availability of accurate tests to identify the risks.

Baby, baby, baby, etc.

The number of triplets, quadruplets, and quintuplets born annually in the United States increased by more than four times from 1971 to 1994. Some of that increase can be attributed to a greater number of mothers 30 years of age or older, who are more likely to have multiple births. The primary cause, however, was the rise in the use of fertility drugs, which tend to promote the production of multiple eggs.

In addition to increasing the size of a family significantly, multiple births are much riskier pregnancies. The babies tend to arrive earlier and are smaller than single-birth babies. For example, the average birth weight of a triplet is only half the average weight of a single infant. Babies born in multiples, consequently, have higher mortality rates and greater risks of lifelong health problems.

Source: U.S. Department of Health and Human Services.

Cystic fibrosis is a genetic disorder that causes mucus to build up in several parts of the body, particularly in the lungs and the pancreas. It affects more than 25,000 Americans and is one of the most common inherited disorders in people of Northern European descent. The disease is usually detected before the first year of age, and those affected live on average about 30 years. Ninety percent of those who have cystic fibrosis die from lung disorders. Although there have been advances in treatment of complications, there is no cure.

Cystic fibrosis is caused by a defective gene. A person who has one such gene will not have cystic fibrosis but is still a carrier who can pass on the gene to children. Cystic fibrosis occurs only when both parents pass the defective gene to their child. The tests recommended by the NIH can identify carriers of the gene with an accuracy of more than 90 percent.

The NIH panel recommended that individuals with a family history of cystic fibrosis and partners of people with cystic fibrosis should also be offered testing. The NIH stressed that testing should be voluntary and accompanied by education and counseling about the results so that parents could make informed decisions.

• Rebecca Rinehart

In WORLD BOOK, see PREGNANCY.

• Evaluating asthma treatment strategies
• New asthma drugs
• Treating severe lung injury

Both the number of new asthma cases and the rate of asthma-related deaths continued to rise at an alarming rate in the United States and in many other industrialized areas of the world in 1997. This increase occurred despite a growing understanding of the causes of asthma and greatly improved methods for treating the disease. In March 1997, researchers at the Harvard Medical School and the Harvard Pilgrim Health Care System in Boston published the results of a study in which they assessed the effectiveness of treatment with inhaled steroids in reducing or preventing asthma-related hospital admissions.

The major problem in asthma is *bronchoconstriction* (tightening and narrowing of lung airways). Drug treatment of the disease, therefore, has primarily involved the use of *bronchodilators,* drugs that relax muscle tissue surrounding the airway. But research into the nature of asthma indicated that the condition was actually a chronic inflammatory disease. This discovery led researchers to search for anti-inflammatory drugs that might be more effective and safer treatments for asthma. Anti-inflammatory drugs, such as oral or inhaled corticosteroids, became an important part of asthma therapy.

The Boston researchers reviewed the medical histories of 16,941 people with asthma who were enrolled in the Harvard Pilgrim Health Care System plan from October 1991 through September 1994. Analysis of medical records revealed, among other things, that people who were treated with inhaled steroids were hospitalized 50 percent less often than those who were not using inhaled steroids. In addition, the simultaneous use of inhaled corticosteroids and bronchodilators in this group was associated with a marked reduction in hospital admissions compared with patients who used bronchodilators alone. The researchers also found that the use of commonly prescribed bronchodilator medications quadrupled the risk of hospitalization when more than four prescriptions for these drugs were issued a year. However, this result may have been due to the severity of the asthma rather than the treatment.

The researchers concluded that the use of anti-inflammatory drugs in the management of asthma benefitted patients who had persistent symptoms. Inhaled corticosteroids were also found to be safe and reduced the need for hospitalization. Future trials may determine whether this improvement will result in a drop in the observed death rate from asthma.

New asthma drugs. In 1996, two new medications designed to reduce inflammation caused by asthma were approved for use in the United States. In February 1997, researchers from hospitals in Montreal, Canada, and Bogota, Colombia, reported on the therapeutic and cost benefits of one of these drugs, zafirlukast (sold as Accolate), in patients with mild to moderate asthma.

Anti-inflammatory asthma drugs target *leukotrienes,* inflammatory biochemicals that result from the breakdown of arachidonic acid, which is a common substance in the human body. Leukotrienes contribute to the inflammation of lung tissues, which causes swelling and constriction of the airways. Zafirlukast prevents inflammation by blocking the sites, called receptors, on lung cells to which leukotrienes attach.

The research group compared 103 patients treated with a bronchodilator and zafirlukast with 43 patients who were treated with a bronchodilator and a *placebo* (inactive substance) instead of zafirlukast. The zafirlukast-treated patients had significantly fewer symptoms, used the bronchodilator less, and had more days without episodes of asthma. In addition, the researchers found the use of zafirlukast to be a cost-effective treatment because patients needed less time with health care workers, had fewer absences from school or work, and required less bronchodilator medication. The authors concluded that the daily use of zafirlukast in mild to moderate asthma provided better and more cost-effective asthma care and might be an alternative to the use of inhaled steroids as anti-inflammatory therapy in asthma treatment.

Does zinc help fight colds?

Researchers at the Cleveland Clinic in Cleveland, Ohio, published a report in July 1996 indicating that zinc was effective in fighting a cold. Several small studies of zinc's effect on the common cold had been conducted in the past but had yielded conflicting results.

The Ohio researchers studied 100 people who reported having symptoms of a cold. The subjects were divided into two groups; one received lozenges containing zinc, while the other received a *placebo* (lozenges containing no zinc at all). At the conclusion of the study, the team found that the cold symptoms disappeared after an average of 7.6 days in the placebo group, but after only 4.4 days in the zinc-treated group. However, critics said that the study was of limited scientific value because, for example, the researchers collected no evidence to confirm the diagnosis of a cold and took no physical samples to confirm that the subjects had taken the lozenges as directed. Nevertheless, after widespread publicity of the study, zinc lozenges became a hot-selling cold remedy of the following winter.

Treating severe lung injury. In February 1997, researchers at the Service de Réanimation at the Hôpital de la Croix Rousse in Lyon, France, reported the results of a study examining whether turning patients from the *supine* position (lying flat on the back) to the *prone* position (lying face down) improved gas exchange in the lungs. The poor exchange of oxygen and carbon dioxide between the lungs and circulatory system even with the aid of a mechanical ventilator is a characteristic of acute respiratory distress syndrome (ARDS). Despite the introduction of new treatments, patients with ARDS have a high rate of complications and death. The difficulty in getting damaged lungs to absorb sufficient oxygen may be linked to both the high death rate and complications in other organs and systems in the body.

Some experts had suggested that changing the position of severely ill ARDS patients from supine to prone might improve chances for survival. The French researchers evaluated this technique on 32 patients with ARDS who required breathing assistance from a ventilator.

The study involved taking measurements of gas exchange in the lungs at specific intervals after the patients were turned from the supine to the prone position. Poor gas exchange is indicated by a severe drop in the oxygen level of arterial blood. In the study, 78 percent of the patients experienced an increase in the level of oxygen in the arterial blood after one hour in the prone position, indicating improvement in gas exchange after being turned. When these patients were later returned to the supine position, 57 percent maintained the improvement. In addition, repeated intervals in the prone position frequently resulted in further improvement.

While not all patients appeared to benefit from this therapy, the researchers said, the maneuver was safe and led to no major complications. In an accompanying editorial, Richard K. Albert of the Section of Pulmonary and Critical Care Medicine of the University of Washington Medical Center in Seattle, Washington, emphasized the safety of the technique and stated that the benefit of the prone position appeared to be that lying face down better suited the natural pumping motion of the lungs compared with the supine position. Albert stressed that care must always be taken when turning critically ill patients over to the prone position. But this simple change of position, taking advantage of a basic principle of body mechanics, may dramatically improve the outcome for people with severe lung injury.   • Robert A. Balk

In WORLD BOOK, see ASTHMA; LUNG; RESPIRATION.

The National Safety Council (NSC) reported in October 1996 that the number of accidental deaths in the United States increased for the third straight year in 1995. NSC, a non-profit organization based in Itasca, Illinois, is devoted to preventing unintentional injuries and deaths.

According to the NSC, 93,300 fatal injuries occurred in 1995, an increase of 2 percent from the 91,400 accidental deaths in 1994. In 1992, fatal injuries declined by 3 percent to 86,777, the lowest recorded number of deaths since 1924. Jerry Scannell, president of the NSC, attributed the increase in fatal accidents mainly to people driving after drinking alcohol and driving without seat belts.

Motor vehicle accidents caused 43,900 deaths in 1995, an increase of 3 percent from 1994. Such accidents were the leading cause of fatal injuries. Home accidents were the second highest cause of death, resulting in 26,400 deaths, followed by 20,100 deaths from fatal injuries in public places and 5,300 accidental deaths in the workplace.

NSC cited increased drinking and driving as a major factor in the rise in highway fatalities. Alcohol-related traffic deaths increased by 4 percent in 1995, the first increase since

• Increase in accidental deaths

• New food safety program

• Don't dial and drive

• Airbag precautions

• New rules for buckling up

• Computer keyboards

• Gas-powered engines and tools

Safer skating
Wrist guards and elbow pads can prevent more than one-third of the 100,000 injuries that children sustain each year while in-line skating. The Centers for Disease Control and Prevention (CDC) in Atlanta, Georgia, reported this finding in November 1996. According to the CDC study, a child wearing wrist guards and elbow pads may be 10 times less likely to break a wrist or injure an elbow than one not wearing guards or pads.

1985. Alcohol was a factor in 41 percent of the fatal crashes. The NSC said that there was insufficient data to determine whether higher speed limits, which began to go into effect in many states in late 1995, also contributed to the increase.

The number of fatal poisonings rose in 1995 as well, surpassing falls for the first time as the leading cause of accidental death in the home. Accidental poisonings claimed 10,000 lives. The number of accidental poisonings rose by 144 percent since 1985. Most of the increase was attributed to overdoses of cocaine and other illegal drugs.

The NSC noted that accidents cost society $434.8 billion in 1995. Accidents were the fifth leading cause of death, after heart disease, cancer, stroke, and chronic lung disease.

New food safety program. The safety of America's food supply was the focus of a new government program proposed by President Bill Clinton in January 1997 and announced by Vice President Al Gore in May. The program aimed to improve food safety by requiring stricter precautions in handling such products as seafood, eggs, and fruit and vegetable juices.

According to the vice president, the program would include consumer education on food handling practices, improved food inspection efforts, and research on better ways of detecting contaminated food products. It would also include new research efforts to determine why food-poisoning microorganisms become resistant to traditional food preservation methods such as boiling and freezing. The proposed $43-million program, part of the 1998 federal budget, was subject to approval by the U.S. Congress.

The vice president announced the program following outbreaks of several foodborne illnesses throughout the United States. One of the outbreaks involved the spread of hepatitis A in March 1997 among students and staff in Calhoun County, Michigan. Hepatitis A is a highly contagious—but rarely fatal—viral disease that affects the liver. The disease causes such symptoms as fever, stomach pain, and nausea and is often spread by consumption of food or water contaminated with sewage.

Health officials traced the Michigan outbreak to strawberries imported from Mexico that were processed in California and distributed to school lunch programs in five states. Michigan was the only state to report an outbreak of illness. Those exposed to the infection were given immunoglobulin shots, which can prevent hepatitis A if administered within 14 days of infection.

Don't dial and drive. People who talk on a cellular telephone while driving a car have a higher risk of crashing than drivers who do not carry on phone conversations. That was the

Is your home office safe for children?

A home office is filled with potential dangers—from thumbtacks to copy machine toner— particularly for children under the age of 6. When possible, experts advise, keep the door to a home office locked to prevent unsupervised children from getting in. When locking the door is not possible, the following precautions can help make a home office a safer place:

- Choose office furniture with no sharp edges, or cover such edges with plastic or rubber shields.
- Store dangerous supplies—such as office chemicals or small and sharp objects—on high shelves.
- Lock filing cabinet drawers or install safety latches.
- Use plastic covers on exposed electrical outlets and use safety plugs or locking devices to keep plugs in place.
- Enclose dangling electric cords in a cord-housing unit.
- Warn older children using an office computer to never reveal personal information, such as last name, address, or phone number, on the Internet.

Source: Parlapiano, Ellen H., and Cobe, Patricia. *Mompreneurs: A Mothers' Practical Step-by-Step Guide to Work-at-Home Success.* Berkley Publishing, 1996.

conclusion of a study reported in February 1997 by researchers at the University of Toronto in Canada.

Donald A. Redelmeier, a preventive medicine specialist, headed the study of 699 drivers who had cell phones and who had been involved in highway accidents that caused property damage but no personal injury. The drivers had made a total of 26,798 cell phone calls during the 14-month study period. Researchers compared the number of accidents that occurred during cell phone use with the number of accidents when a phone was not in use. The risk of an accident was more than four times higher during phone conversations.

According to the researchers, the study verified the widely held belief that cell phone conversations distract drivers and make them more accident prone. The researchers recommended that drivers eliminate unnecessary calls and keep important calls brief while driving.

Airbag precautions. The National Highway Traffic Safety Administration (NHTSA), an agency of the U.S. Department of Transportation, made several recommendations in November 1996 to improve automobile airbag safety. The recommendations were made in response to public concern about the dangers of airbags. From 1986 to early 1997, 38 children under age 12 and 24 adults died from injuries caused by deploying airbags. Airbags, however, saved the lives of at least 1,750 drivers and passengers during that same time, according to the NHTSA.

Airbags deploy at speeds up to 200 miles (320 kilometers) per hour. They were designed to protect an average adult male not wearing a seat belt. When children or short adults sit in seats with airbags, the bags can strike them in the head or neck, causing injuries they may not have otherwise sustained. Although most of the children who died were not properly buckled into safety seats, some who were properly restrained died because the force of the airbag was too great for a child.

The NHTSA recommended that infants in rear-facing child-safety seats always ride in the back seat. Children

under age 12 should also ride in the back seat, and all passengers should wear shoulder and lap belts, even in cars equipped with airbags.

In addition, the NHTSA urged manufacturers to develop "smart bags"— airbags that gauge a person's size and position on the seat and deploy with appropriate force. Until smart bags become available, the agency recommended that all new cars and light trucks—as well as all child safety seats—carry prominent warning stickers to caution drivers about airbag hazards.

The NHTSA said that it would continue to allow installation of manual cut-off switches to deactivate airbags in vehicles with no rear seat, such as pickup trucks. In addition, the agency

Car phone danger
A study by researchers at the University of Toronto in Canada provided the first direct evidence that speaking on a cellular phone while driving increases the chance of an accident. The study, published in February 1997, analyzed the activities of 699 drivers with cell phones who were involved in car accidents. The researchers found that drivers were four times more likely to have an accident while speaking on a cell phone than they were when they were not using the phone.

Handle with care

Fire officials warned in 1997 that people who fill gasoline cans in the bed of a pickup truck are at risk of starting a fire. Several such fires have occurred in pickup trucks with vinyl bed liners. Vinyl bed liners provide insulation that prevents the static electricity produced as gasoline flows through the hose from bleeding off through the truck body and the tires into the ground. A spark produced as the nozzle rubs the edge of the can may ignite the gas vapors. The solution? Place the gas can on the ground during fill-up. The static will dissipate as it is produced.

Source: Monmouth County (New Jersey) Fire Academy.

child safety seat attachment. The attachment would simplify installation of more than 100 models of child safety seats in 900 models of cars and light trucks. Safety officials noted that up to 80 percent of child safety seats are improperly attached.

In April 1997, the president announced a new effort to increase Americans' use of seat belts to 85 percent by the year 2002. Transportation Secretary Rodney E. Slater cited studies showing that only 68 percent of Americans use seat belts. Increasing seat belt use to 85 percent, according to Slater, would annually save more than 4,000 lives, prevent more than 100,000 injuries, and save more than $6.7 billion in medical and other costs. The program would include public education about the benefits of seat belts. The president also urged that states enact laws to enforce seat belt use and conduct highly visible enforcement of the laws.

Computer keyboards with a non-traditional design provide no significant increase in user comfort. That was the conclusion of a study reported in January 1997 by the National Institute for Occupational Safety and Health (NIOSH) in Washington, D.C., an agency of the Centers for Disease Control and Prevention in Atlanta, Georgia.

Public concern over fatigue and pain in the wrists, arms, and back thought to be caused by keyboard design had led to the marketing of a new generation of keyboards. But few studies had been conducted to determine whether alternative keyboards are more beneficial than standard designs. NIOSH researchers studied 50 female clerical workers who typed on either a conventional keyboard or one of three alternative-design keyboards for two days. The alternative units varied in some design elements, but each had a split-configuration, with keys for the left and right hands on separate units.

The workers reported only low levels of fatigue and discomfort with both the traditional and nontraditional designs. The researchers concluded that keyboard design is not a significant factor affecting user comfort.

allowed auto dealers to deactivate airbags at the request of an owner.

In March 1997, the NHTSA gave airbag manufacturers permission to reduce the deployment speed of airbags by up to 35 percent. Manufacturers planned to install such airbags on all new cars by the end of the 1998 model year. In June 1997, the agency asked that all 50 states make it illegal for a child under the age of 13 to ride in the front seat of a car.

New rules for buckling up. President Bill Clinton addressed the issue of auto safety with recommendations for child safety seats and seat belt use. In February 1997, the president proposed regulations that would require equipping cars with a universal

Gas-powered engines and tools are not safe to use indoors, even in well-ventilated areas. The National Institute of Occupational Health and Safety (NIOSH) and several other federal agencies issued that warning in January 1997.

According to NIOSH, a wide range of tools—including concrete cutting saws, high-pressure washers, floor buffers, welders, pumps, and compressors—produce carbon monoxide, a colorless, odorless poison gas. Carbon monoxide can accumulate quickly in enclosed or semienclosed spaces and cause serious illness or death without warning. Even opening doors or windows or running exhaust fans

may not eliminate the gas.

NIOSH recommended that people substitute engines or tools powered by electricity or compressed air for gasoline-powered equipment when working indoors whenever possible. The agency also recommended placing the engine unit of gasoline-powered tools outdoors, away from ventilation air intakes. Workers in professions such as plumbing, floor installation, farming, and drywall finishing should be provided with personal carbon monoxide monitors with audible alarms, so that they can be warned of dangerous levels of carbon monoxide.   • Michael Woods

In WORLD BOOK, SEE SAFETY.

The United States has the highest rate of sexually transmitted diseases (STD's) of any industrialized country in the world and no effective national system to combat the epidemic. This was the conclusion of a report released in November 1996 by a committee of the Institute of Medicine, a branch of the National Academy of Sciences.

The report said that international studies showed the rates of STD's in the United States exceeded those of every other industrialized country. Gonorrhea, for example, infects 150 of every 100,000 Americans, compared with 3 of every 100,000 people in Sweden and 18.6 per 100,000 people in Canada.

One-fourth of the estimated 12 million new cases of STD's that occur in the United States each year involve adolescents, who are at greater risk because they are more likely to engage in more unprotected sex and other high-risk sexual behavior than adults, according to the report. The most common STD's included chlamydia infection, syphilis, gonorrhea, herpes, and hepatitis B virus, according to the report. Sexually transmitted diseases can cause infertility, cancer, birth defects, miscarriages, and even death.

Herpes virus linked to cancer. A sexually transmitted herpes virus may cause a cancer in AIDS patients, according to researchers at Cornell Uni-

versity Medical College in New York. The researchers identified a gene in human herpesvirus 8 (HHV8) that may induce Kaposi's sarcoma, a cancer that affects more than 20 percent of patients with AIDS.

Since 1994, when fragments of viral DNA were found in the cancer's characteristic purplish skin lesions, scientists suspected that a sexually transmitted virus may cause the disease. Previous studies found HHV8 in the skin lesions, but researchers were unable to find a direct link between the virus and the cancer. The Cornell researchers, however, discovered an HHV8 gene whose protein can cause cells to multiply at an abnormally fast rate, which may accelerate the growth of cancer cells. In 1997, scientists were attempting to prove that the gene's protein induces growth of Kaposi's sarcoma tumors. The scientists planned to look for drugs that will interact with the protein and inhibit its ability to cause cell growth.

Benefits of chlamydia testing. Routine testing for chlamydia could prevent infertility and other complications in thousands of women every year, according to a report published in July 1996 in the *New England Journal of Medicine*. Chlamydia is a common sexually transmitted disease. More than 4 million women are diagnosed with the disease in the United States annually. Many more cases go unrecognized because the disease is

Sexually Transmitted Diseases

- United States has highest rate of STD's
- Herpes virus linked to Kaposi's sarcoma
- Benefits of chlamydia testing
- Husband's affairs put wife at risk of disease
- Syphilis originated in North and South America

STD's and the risk of infertility

The American Social Health Association (ASHA) is a national, nonprofit organization dedicated to stopping sexually transmitted diseases (STD's). As a part of National STD Awareness Month in April 1997, ASHA included the following facts, entitled "Protect Your Fertility and Your Future," on its World Wide Web home page:

- At least 15 percent of all infertility cases in American women are caused by pelvic inflammatory disease (PID), which is usually a complication of sexually transmitted diseases.

- The STD's most often associated with PID are chlamydia and gonorrhea.

- Chlamydia and gonorrhea rank first and second among the most commonly reported infections in the United States, according to the Centers for Disease Control and Prevention.

- Four million cases of chlamydia and 800,000 new cases of gonorrhea are reported each year in the United States. But because these infections often have no noticeable symptoms, experts estimate that the actual number is probably much higher.

- Chlamydia and gonorrhea can cause sterility in men as well as women.

Source: American Social Health Association home page
(http://sunsite.unc.edu/ASHA.html)

previously shown that exposure to certain types of human papillomavirus, a virus that is sexually transmitted, heightens a woman's risk of developing cervical cancer. The researchers interviewed the husbands of women who had cervical cancer and the husbands of women who were cancerfree. They asked the men about extramarital affairs and conducted a test that looked for viral DNA in a sample obtained from the outside of the penis.

The researchers discovered that the presence of viral DNA on a husband's penis increased the wife's risk of cervical cancer by five times the normal risk. The study also showed that the prevalence of the viral DNA and the wife's risk of cervical cancer increased with the number of the husband's extramarital affairs. The risk was especially great when a husband had sex with a prostitute. Wives of the men who reported having had sex with a prostitute at least 10 times during the marriage had 11 times the risk of developing cervical cancer as the wives of men who had no contact with prostitutes. The number of sexual partners a man had before marriage did not appear to influence the wife's risk of cervical cancer.

Syphilis originated in Americas. People living in North and South America were infected with syphilis long before the 1492 expedition of Christopher Columbus. This finding was reported in October 1996 by Bruce Rothschild, a paleopathologist at the Arthritis Center of Ohio.

Rothschild studied 687 skeletons from eight different populations in North and South America, ranging in age from 400 to 6,000 years old. Skeletons from Florida, Ecuador, and New Mexico all showed clear signs of syphilis, at least 800 and perhaps 1,600 years ago.

Rothschild did not find any evidence of syphilis in 1,000 skeletons from Europe, Africa, or Asia. He believes syphilis originated in the Americas, and that Columbus and his crew contracted syphilis and caused an outbreak in Europe upon their return.

• Victoria Peters

SEE ALSO AIDS. In WORLD BOOK, see SEXUALLY TRANSMITTED DISEASE.

often symptom free. If left untreated, it can lead to pelvic inflammatory disease, infertility, and chronic pelvic pain. A study of 2,607 single, sexually active women at the Group Health Cooperative of Puget Sound, a health plan in the Pacific Northwest, found that women who were not tested for chlamydia were almost twice as likely to develop pelvic inflammatory disease as women who were tested.

Husband's affairs put wife at risk. A husband's extramarital affairs may put his wife at risk of cervical cancer, according to a study released in August 1996 by researchers at Johns Hopkins Medical Institutions in Baltimore, Maryland. The researchers had

Pulsed carbon-dioxide lasers, which deliver short bursts of hot laser light, remove acne scars and wrinkles from skin more effectively than continuous-wave lasers. Dermatologists Jeffrey S. Dover and Kenneth A. Arndt of Harvard Medical School in Boston reported this finding in June 1996.

The doctors reviewed studies of patients who had had skin surgery since the late 1980's. They found that continuous-wave lasers were significantly better than older techniques—such as facelifting, dermabrasion, and chemical peeling—at repairing the effects on the skin of aging, excessive sun exposure, and acne. However, continuous-wave lasers also damaged skin and caused scarring if the laser was held too long over an area.

Pulsed lasers, which use short bursts of laser light, destroy only thin layers of skin, according to the dermatologists. Doctors can better control the amount of heat applied to the skin with pulsed lasers, which results in a decreased risk of skin damage.

The dermatologists noted that, because pulsed lasers are a relatively new development, little is known about their long-term effects. Some patients experienced *pigmentation* (discoloration) in new skin after treatment with the pulsed laser. In addition, doctors do not know how long improvements in skin appearance will last. However, patients treated with pulsed lasers showed continuous improvement in skin appearance at 3-month and 6-month follow-ups, leading the dermatologists to theorize that the improvements may be sustained over time.

Moles and skin cancer risk. A study led by Margaret Tucker of the National Cancer Institute in Bethesda, Maryland, showed that the number, size, and appearance of moles on the skin are related to a patient's risk for developing melanoma, the most lethal form of skin cancer. The study, published in May 1997, involved patients at the Pigmented Lesion Clinic of the Hospital of the University of Pennsylvania in Philadelphia and at the Melanoma Clinic of the University of California in San Francisco.

Researchers examined 716 people with recently diagnosed melanoma and 1,014 people treated at outpatient clinics for conditions other than melanoma. The researchers counted all moles larger than 2 millimeters (about ½ inch) on each person's body. They then classified the moles according to size and according to whether the mole was normal or abnormal. Abnormal moles vary in color, have irregular shapes, and are either totally or partially flat.

The researchers found that patients with 50 or more small, but normal, moles had twice the risk of develop-

- Better laser to treat scars and wrinkles
- Moles and skin cancer risk
- Glue instead of stitches
- New cream helps heal cold sores

Artificial skin
A technician at Integra Life-Sciences Corporation in Plainsboro, New Jersey, moves trays of *collagen* (a type of protein) into a freeze-drier in the process of making artificial skin. The artificial skin, approved by the U.S. Food and Drug Administration in 1996 to treat burn victims, is made of collagen drawn from calf tendons and from a chemical derived from shark cartilage. These ingredients form a layer that protects the body from infection and dehydration, and helps injured skin to regrow.

Bee sting? Act quickly...

The best way to treat a honey bee sting is to remove the stinger quickly, in any way possible. That was the conclusion reported in August 1996 by a research team led by P. Kirk Visscher, an *entomologist* (insect expert) at the University of California in Riverside. Conventional wisdom has always stressed that stingers should be scraped off with a flat-edged object, such as a knife or credit card, because pinching the stinger by using tweezers or fingers will release more venom, making the sting more painful and more dangerous for people allergic to bee venom. But Dr. Visscher and his colleagues—who allowed themselves to be repeatedly stung by honey bees—found that less venom was released when the stinger was removed quickly, even if the stinger was pinched during removal.

ing melanoma as patients with 25 or fewer small, normal moles. Patients with one abnormal mole had twice the risk of developing melanoma as those with no abnormal moles. And patients with 10 or more abnormal moles had 12 times the risk of developing melanoma as patients with no abnormal moles. The researchers also found that, among patients with no abnormal moles, those with the most freckles had 3 times the risk of developing melanoma as those with few or no freckles. Moles present at birth, the researchers found, did not pose a greater risk for developing melanoma.

The researchers suggested that doctors screen patients for moles and regularly examine the skin of people with many moles or unusual moles. Melanoma is curable with early detection, the researchers noted.

Glue instead of stitches. Doctors at the University of Michigan in Ann Arbor and at the University of Ottawa in Ontario reported in May 1997 that sterilized glue closed some wounds more effectively than stitches. The glue made wound-closure less painful and took less time than stitches.

The doctors treated 130 patients by either gluing or stitching their wounds closed. After three months, the wounds of those treated with glue had healed as well as the

New lotion protects against poison ivy

IvyBlock, the first drug to protect against poison ivy, poison oak, and poison sumac, was approved by the U.S. Food and Drug Administration in August 1996. The claylike lotion contains quaternium-18 bentonite, a substance that prevents *urushiol* from coming into contact with the skin. Urushiol is the oil in poison ivy, oak, and sumac that causes the rash. IvyBlock is sold without a prescription and washes off with soap and water. It must be applied to the skin at least 15 minutes before possible contact with the poisonous plants and reapplied every 4 hours. Dermatologists at four clinics throughout the United States who tested IvyBlock emphasized that the lotion is ineffective when applied after contact with the poisonous plants. The doctors also noted that, in rare instances, IvyBlock has caused allergic reactions in people. The best protection against poison ivy, oak, and sumac, according to the doctors, is wearing protective clothing in areas that may harbor the "leaves of three."

wounds of those treated with stitches. The doctors noted, however, that wounds on the feet, hands, or joints should not be glued, because frequent movement of those areas could cause the wound to open and become infected.

New cream helps heal cold sores.

Researchers reported in May 1997 that a cream called penciclovir helps cold sores to heal more quickly and shortens the time that they are painful and contagious. Cold sores are caused by the herpes simplex virus.

The researchers, led by S. L. Spruance of the University of Utah in Salt Lake City, studied 1,573 patients with cold sores in 31 clinics throughout the United States. Some patients applied penciclovir at the first sign that a cold sore was developing while others applied an inactive cream.

The researchers found that the cold sores of patients treated with penciclovir healed more quickly than those of the patients using the inactive cream. The researchers were especially pleased with the study results because the common treatment for recurrent cold sores has been an oral antiviral medication that must be taken continuously, a treatment that is not appropriate for most people who develop cold sores.   • Cindy Jones

In WORLD BOOK, see SKIN.

The smallest of the major United States tobacco companies acknowledged in March 1997 that cigarettes are addictive and cause cancer. The acknowledgment by Liggett Group Incorporated of Durham, North Carolina, was part of a settlement with the attorneys general from 22 states who, in March 1997, filed lawsuits against every major tobacco company to seek compensation for the estimated $6 billion in annual state health-care costs tied to smoking.

Liggett also acknowledged that some tobacco marketing has been directed toward minors. The settlement required Liggett to pay 25 percent of its pretax profits, plus up to $25 million, to the suing 22 states over the next 25 years.

Cigarette makers reach accord.

Negotiations between 37 state attorneys general, health groups, and tobacco companies ended in June 1997 with a settlement proposal to provide billions of dollars in compensation to states and to change the way cigarettes are marketed. In mid-1997, the agreement was still awaiting final approval by Congress and President Bill Clinton.

Under the terms of the settlement, tobacco manufacturers—Philip Morris Companies; RJR Nabisco Holdings Corporation; B.A.T. Industries P.L.C., the British parent of the Brown & Williamson Tobacco Corporation; and the Loews Corporation, which owns the Lorillard Tobacco Company—would be required to pay $368.5 billion in the first 25 years following approval of the agreement to cover health-care costs. After 25 years, the annual fee would be $15 billion. The settlement ended 40 state lawsuits, and 17 class-action lawsuits filed against the tobacco industry, by requiring the immediate payment of $50 billion.

A requirement of the agreement included the need for cigarette packaging to carry larger, stronger warnings, covering 25 percent of the front cover and explicitly stating that cigarettes are addictive and that tobacco smoke causes fatal diseases in nonsmokers. Under the settlement, the tobacco industry also agreed to pay a $2 billion fine per year if there is not a 67 percent drop in youth smoking within 10 years following federal approval of the agreement.

The pact had cleared the way for the U.S. Food and Drug Administration (FDA) to regulate nicotine as a drug. However, in July 1997, the White House rejected that element of the tobacco deal, claiming it would impose broad new restrictions on federal authority to regulate nicotine in cigarettes. Presidential advisers in mid-1997 planned to rewrite that portion of the settlement.

Quitting the smoking habit. Smokers who are able to go without a cigarette for at least three months

Smoking

- Liggett settles lawsuit
- Cigarette makers reach accord
- Quitting the smoking habit
- Dangerous secondhand smoke
- Cigars popular with teens

Smoking

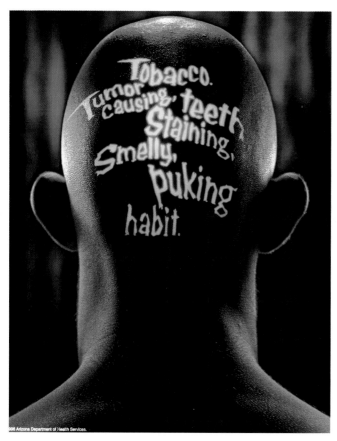

'96 Arizona Department of Health Services.

Appealing to kids

An antismoking advertising campaign that originated in Arizona was made available to other states and antitobacco groups in 1997 by the Centers for Disease Control and Prevention (CDC) in Atlanta, Georgia. The campaign uses the slogan "Tobacco: tumor-causing, teeth-staining, smelly, puking habit," and is designed to "speak to teens in their own language," according to the CDC's Office on Smoking and Health.

have a greater chance of being able to stop smoking entirely than other smokers. That was the conclusion of a National Cancer Institute study released in April 1997.

The two-year study of 24,296 smokers and former smokers revealed that 90 percent of participants who had quit smoking for more than three months and 95 percent who had quit for more than one year had not returned to smoking by the end of the study period.

Although the study provided encouraging news to people who want to stop smoking, the researchers reported that many smokers try to quit repeatedly before succeeding. Other studies have revealed that about one-third of all smokers make at least one attempt to quit during the year.

Dangerous secondhand smoke.
The results of a study published in May 1997 found that secondhand cigarette smoke is more dangerous

than health experts originally believed. As part of a 10-year study on the effects of secondhand smoke, researchers from Harvard School of Public Health in Boston, Massachusetts, tracked 32,046 healthy women who had never smoked. The women were between the ages of 30 and 55 when the study began in 1976. The study was originally designed to examine the health habits of nurses.

The participants filled out questionnaires every two years about their health habits. Beginning in 1982, the women were asked about their exposure to secondhand smoke. The researchers then began monitoring the participants for heart disease.

The researchers reported that regular exposure to secondhand smoke almost doubled the risk of heart disease among the women. The women who reported regular exposure to cigarette smoke had a 91 percent higher risk of heart attack than those with no exposure.

Other researchers previously identified several ways in which chemicals in secondhand smoke can contribute to heart disease. Besides reducing a person's oxygen supply, the chemicals can damage arteries, lower the levels of a beneficial form of cholesterol called high-density lipoprotein, and increase the risk of blood clots that can trigger a heart attack.

The study supported several U.S. Occupational Safety and Health Administration proposals to regulate smoking in the workplace. State and local legislative bodies planned to use the study as a basis to limit smoking in areas such as restaurants and bars.

Cigars popular with teens. An estimated 6 million teen-agers—more than 25 percent of all boys and girls between the ages of 14 and 19—smoked at least one cigar in 1996, according to a report issued in May 1997 by the Centers for Disease Control and Prevention (CDC) in Atlanta, Georgia.

The report was based on three studies that surveyed the cigar smoking habits of teen-agers. A nationwide survey of 16,117 young people in grades 9 through 12 conducted by the Robert Wood Johnson Foundation

Liggett Group Inc. acknowledges effects of smoking

Liggett Group Incorporated, a Durham, North Carolina-based tobacco company, admitted in March 1997 that cigarettes are addictive and cause cancer. The acknowledgement by Liggett—which is the smallest of the country's five leading cigarette makers— was made as part of a legal settlement with 22 states. The states had accused the tobacco industry of hiding knowledge of the adverse health effects of tobacco. In exchange for a release from liability of treating smokers' health problems in the 22 states, Liggett agreed to:

- Acknowledge that smoking is addictive and say so in warning labels on cigarettes.
- Acknowledge that smoking causes cancer.
- Acknowledge that some tobacco marketing has been directed toward minors, and avoid doing so in the future.
- Cooperate in lawsuits against other companies, turn over documents, and allow its employees to testify in court.
- Pay a quarter of its pretax profits, plus up to $25 million, to the states annually for the next 25 years.

found that 3.9 percent of the boys and 1.2 percent of the girls surveyed were frequent cigar smokers, each having consumed more than 50 cigars in 1996. A Massachusetts Department of Public Health survey of 6,844 teen-agers in grades 6 through 12 revealed that 28.1 percent of high school students reported having smoked at least one cigar. A survey of tobacco use among 9,916 ninth-graders in two New York counties conducted by the Roswell Park Cancer Institute showed that between 12.7 percent and 14.8 percent of

students questioned reported having smoked a cigar in the 30 days prior to the survey.

In response to the CDC survey, health advocates asked the FDA to place warning labels—similar to those found on cigarette packages—on cigars and to extend antismoking campaigns to include cigars. The FDA reacted cautiously to the survey, saying that reducing the use of cigarettes and smokeless tobacco by teen-agers was considered its main priority.   • David C. Lewis

In WORLD BOOK, see SMOKING.

The blood thinner warfarin could cut the risk of stroke caused by atrial fibrillation by 67 percent, according to a study published in December 1996 by *The Archives of Internal Medicine.* The drug, however, has been drastically underused, according to the study.

About 2 million Americans suffer from *atrial fibrillation*, a heart rhythm disturbance that increases the risk of a blood clot's breaking free. Without a blood thinner, a clot can move to the brain, causing stroke.

Warfarin was prescribed in only about 32 percent of atrial fibrillation patients between 1980 and 1993, said the researchers. Based on the study of 1,062 random patient visits

drawn from the National Ambulatory Care Surveys performed in eight of those years, the researchers concluded that warfarin treatment could eliminate 50,000 of the 75,000 strokes Americans suffer each year. The researchers noted that warfarin use increased quickly from 1990 to 1993. The report did not include any information on warfarin use since 1993.

Doctors may be reluctant to prescribe warfarin because patients taking the drug require extremely close monitoring. The drug might also cause bleeding in some patients— from nosebleeds to serious internal bleeding, though other research indicates the drug is safer than previously believed.

Stroke

- Warfarin cuts risk of stroke
- Test predicts stroke damage
- Therapy as effective as drugs

Stroke

The annual incidence of new and recurrent strokes increases significantly among Americans who are 65 years of age or older. On average, the number of men suffering from strokes is about 19 percent greater than the number of women.

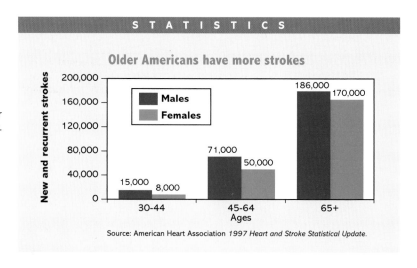

STATISTICS

Older Americans have more strokes

Source: American Heart Association *1997 Heart and Stroke Statistical Update*.

Test predicts stroke damage. A simple blood test can predict which patients are most likely to deteriorate in the first day or two after a stroke. This finding was reported in January 1997 by researchers at the Hospital Doctor Josep Trueta in Girona, Spain. The blood test, which detects abnormally high levels of a potentially harmful substance called glutamate, may allow doctors to determine which patients are most in need of aggressive treatment aimed at minimizing brain damage.

Glutamate came under intense study in the 1990's because it is thought to contribute to brain damage in people with head injuries and various neurological disorders, including stroke. Glutamate is an *amino acid*, one of the building blocks of proteins in the body. It is also a normal component of nerve cells, where it acts as a neurotransmitter, or a chemical messenger, secreted in minute amounts by cells to signal each other. But excessively high levels of glutamate, released from brain cells that are damaged or oxygen-starved, can actually kill neighboring nerve cells.

The researchers measured glutamate levels in the blood and spinal fluid of 128 patients within 24 hours of onset of stroke. The researchers found that one-third of the patients showed progressive deterioration, and that they were also the ones with the highest blood levels of glutamate.

According to the researchers, the glutamate test will allow doctors to predict stroke progression in 97 percent of patients. They noted that the findings supported the idea that drugs to lower glutamate levels might limit brain damage in some stroke patients.

Therapy as effective as drugs. Physical therapy is just as effective as drug therapy in treating the effects of stroke. This finding was reported in July 1996 by researchers at the University of Texas Health Science Center.

The researchers mimicked strokes in the brains of nine monkeys by creating small lesions in a region of the brain that partially controls the hand. In the month that followed, four of the nine monkeys were retrained in fine motor skills with a repetitive exercise. The remaining five monkeys received no rehabilitation.

The researchers found that rehabilitation seemed to encourage healthy brain tissue to take over the damaged area's function. Although the monkeys that did not receive rehabilitation eventually recovered basic motor abilities, they did it more slowly than the monkeys who underwent rehabilitation.

The researchers concluded that stroke patients who undergo rehabilitation will regain motor function more quickly and effectively if they are forced to perform repetitive, rehabilitative exercises.   • **Victoria Peters**

In the section On the Medical Frontier, see COMBATING THE EFFECTS OF STROKE. In WORLD BOOK, see STROKE.

A study published in April 1997 found that rectal cancer patients who receive radiation treatment prior to surgery live longer and have less risk of a recurrence of cancer than those patients who undergo surgery without radiation. This was the first study to indicate that *preoperative radiation* (radiation before surgical removal of cancerous tissue) increases the survival rate of rectal cancer patients. According to the study's researchers at the University of Uppsala in Sweden, another benefit of preoperative radiation is that it may shrink the cancerous tissue enough to allow surgeons to remove all of it without destroying the *anal sphincter* (the ring of muscles that enable a person to control bowel movements). When the anal sphincter is destroyed, as often happens in rectal surgery, the patient must permanently wear a *colostomy bag* (a bag into which the large intestine deposits feces).

Preoperative radiation is commonly used by physicians in Europe to treat rectal cancer patients. In the United States, however, physicians generally do not use it, because they are concerned that it might increase the risk of complications during surgery and that it may necessitate a delay of up to three months in performing surgery (to allow time for the radiation to have an effect). American physicians also noted a lack of evidence that preoperative radiation increases survival rate. Because of these concerns and because of the tendency of rectal cancer to recur after surgery, American physicians typically use radiation treatment and *chemotherapy* (drug treatment) following surgery.

The Swedish researchers studied more than 1,000 patients younger than 80 years of age who were treated for rectal cancer between March 1987 and February 1990. There were 553 patients who received radiation prior to surgical removal of rectal cancer, and 557 who had rectal cancer surgery without receiving radiation. The radiation was administered to each patient in five high doses over a period of one week. Surgical removal of cancerous tissue was performed within one week of the completion of radiation therapy.

Five years after treatment, rectal cancer had recurred in 11 percent of the patients who had received preoperative radiation therapy. In contrast, the cancer had recurred in 27 percent of the patients who had undergone only surgery. Nine years after treatment, 74 percent of the patients who had received preoperative radiation therapy were still alive, as opposed to 65 percent of the patients treated only with surgery. The researchers said that additional studies were needed to confirm the advantages of preoperative radiation.

Surgery

- Radiation before surgery helps rectal cancer patients
- Tissue glue better than sutures
- Laparoscopic surgery decreases hernia recurrence

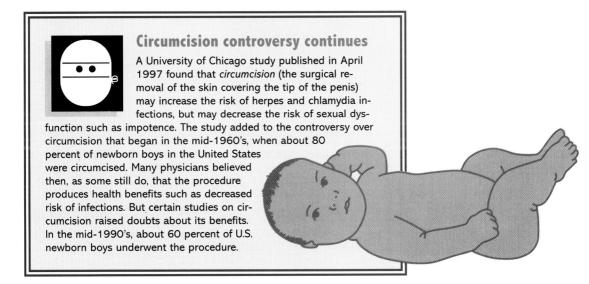

Circumcision controversy continues

A University of Chicago study published in April 1997 found that *circumcision* (the surgical removal of the skin covering the tip of the penis) may increase the risk of herpes and chlamydia infections, but may decrease the risk of sexual dysfunction such as impotence. The study added to the controversy over circumcision that began in the mid-1960's, when about 80 percent of newborn boys in the United States were circumcised. Many physicians believed then, as some still do, that the procedure produces health benefits such as decreased risk of infections. But certain studies on circumcision raised doubts about its benefits. In the mid-1990's, about 60 percent of U.S. newborn boys underwent the procedure.

Surgery

Surgery with MRI

In 1997, a new type of MRI (magnetic resonance imaging) device was being used by surgeons at Brigham and Women's Hospital in Boston. The machine produces detailed images of internal tissues during surgery. The images, which are displayed on a monitor, help the surgeon perform precise procedures, such as tumor removal, through a small incision in the patient's body.

Tissue glue better than sutures.

Medical researchers at the University of Michigan in Ann Arbor and the University of Ottawa in Canada said in May 1997 that a new type of chemical adhesive called octylcyanoacrylate has several advantages over conventional nylon sutures in closing *lacerations* (torn, jagged wounds). Octylcyanoacrylate belongs to a family of chemical compounds called cyanoacrylates, which were first described by scientists in 1949. These compounds have been used as tissue adhesives in Europe, Canada, and Japan since the 1970's, in such procedures as skin and cartilage grafting and head and neck surgery. However, the

U.S. Food and Drug Administration (FDA) withheld approval of these substances because certain studies raised questions about their effectiveness and safety.

Octylcyanoacrylate, which was tested on 130 patients, was found to cause less pain and provide a faster, as well as a less expensive, method of wound repair than sutures. The researchers said the adhesive may also reduce the risk of infection that occurs with sutures. In addition, the adhesive was as effective as suturing in reducing the risk of scars resulting from wounds and surgical incisions. The adhesive, however, did not work well on skin that underwent a great

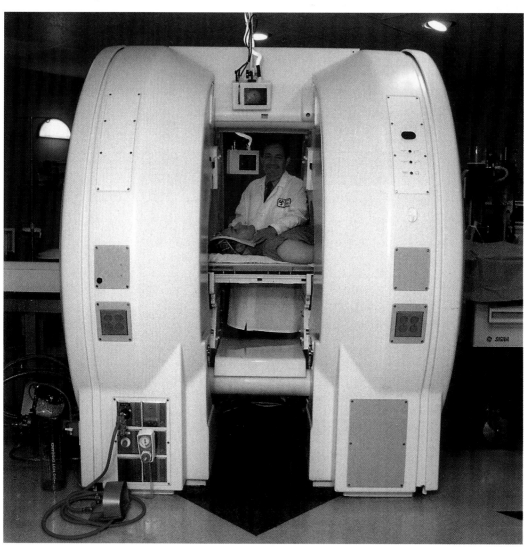

deal of movement, such as the skin of the hands. The researchers said that if additional studies prove that octylcyanoacrylate is safe with long-term use, it could eliminate the need for suturing many lacerations and surgical incisions. According to the researchers, the study indicated that octylcyanoacrylate is more effective than other cyanoacrylates—an important factor that works in favor of FDA approval of the substance.

Laparoscopic hernia repair. A group of researchers from several medical institutions in the Netherlands reported in May 1997 that people with *inguinal hernias* (a protrusion of an abdominal organ through a weak area in the abdominal wall) recover quicker and are less likely to have hernia recurrences if they undergo laparoscopic surgery rather than conventional open surgery. In laparoscopic surgery—which has been used to repair hernias since the late 1980's—the surgeon operates through an incision the width of a pencil. A thin instrument called a laparoscope, equipped with surgical tools and viewing lenses, is inserted through the incision. The ruptured abdominal wall is then closed with a mesh patch. In contrast, in open surgery the incision is about 3 inches (7½ centimeters) long, and the abdominal wall is closed with either a mesh patch or sutures. Though

previous studies found that laparoscopic surgery reduces recovery time compared with conventional surgery, the Netherlands study was the first one to effectively demonstrate a decreased risk of hernia recurrence.

In the Netherlands study, the hernias in 487 patients were repaired with laparoscopic surgery. The hernias of 507 patients were repaired with open surgery, usually by suturing. The patients who had laparoscopic surgery were able to resume normal daily activities in about six days, whereas the patients who had open surgery needed about 10 days to do so. The laparoscopic patients returned to work in about 14 days, compared with about 21 days for the open surgery patients. Physical examinations two years after surgery found that hernias had recurred in 3 percent of the patients who had laparoscopic surgery and 6 percent of the patients who had open surgery.

The researchers noted, however, that laparoscopic surgery requires the use of a *general* anesthetic, which renders the patient unconscious and has more risk than the *local* (spinal) anesthetic typically used in open surgery. Other studies indicated that open surgery using mesh patches instead of sutures can produce hernia recurrence rates at least as good as those produced with laparoscopic surgery.   • Richard A. Prinz

In WORLD BOOK, see SURGERY.

A new method for treating benign prostatic hyperplasia (BPH), called transurethral needle ablation (TUNA), was approved by the U.S. Food and Drug Administration (FDA) in November 1996. BPH is a noncancerous growth of the prostate gland that commonly occurs as men age. An enlarged prostate can block the flow of urine through the *urethra* (the passage that carries urine from the bladder out of the body), leading to a variety of urinary symptoms. These include difficulty starting urine flow, increased frequency of urination during the day and night, and a decrease in the force of the urinary stream.

Since the 1930's, the most common treatment for men with an en-

larged prostate was surgery to reduce the size of the gland. This procedure, known as a transurethral resection of the prostate (TURP), involved the use of a wire loop that carried electric current to shave away excess prostate tissue. In the 1980's, a variety of drugs instead of surgery became available to treat urinary symptoms caused by BPH. However, these medications did not help all patients and many men still required surgery.

The TUNA procedure employs a fiberoptic instrument that, like TURP, is inserted into the urethra. But instead of electric current, the TUNA device transmits low-level radio frequency waves into the prostate. The

• **New device for prostate surgery**
• **Improved impotence treatment**

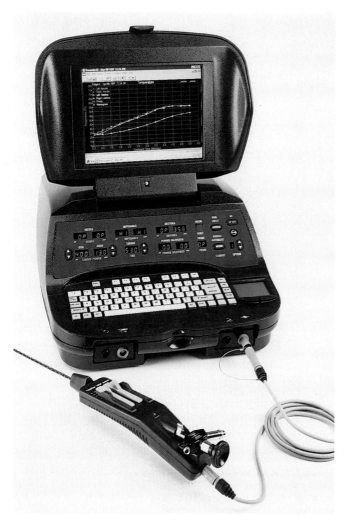

Tuning in on the prostate

A new method to treat men with a noncancerous enlarged prostate gland was cleared for use in the United States in November 1996. In the procedure, known as transurethral needle ablation (TUNA), a small probe is inserted into the urethra toward the prostate. The probe emits radio waves that burn away excess prostate tissue without damaging the surrounding tissue.

radio energy heats the prostate tissue to greater than 212 °F (100 °C), destroying prostate cells. This reduces the size of the prostate and relieves the blockage. Two of the main advantages of TUNA are that it can be performed with little or no anesthesia and does not require hospitalization.

Although TURP was still widely used in 1997, TUNA was one of many new methods developed in an attempt to minimize the discomfort, recovery period, and need for hospitalization associated with prostate surgery. Early trials indicated that TUNA significantly improved urinary symptoms and the degree of obstruction, but the results were less impressive than those seen with TURP. However, the risk of side effects, such as

incontinence (involuntary loss of urine) and sexual dysfunction were minimal with TUNA. Although the results with TUNA were promising, most urologists said that a larger study with a longer follow-up period was necessary before its effectiveness in treating BPH could be fully assessed.

Improved impotence treatment. In December 1996, a new form of alprostadil, a drug treatment for impotence (the inability of a man to achieve an erection) was approved by the FDA. In 1995, the FDA approved a form of the drug that was delivered by a hypodermic injection into the base of the penis. The new system delivered alprostadil in the form of a pellet placed into the urethra using a small plastic applicator. The drug is absorbed into penile tissues through the urethra.

Impotence affects between 10 million and 20 million men in the United States. Although there are a number of potential causes for impotence, the most common cause is inadequate blood flow to the penis due to a buildup of fatty deposits and plaques in blood vessels. Since diminished blood flow occurs more frequently as men age, impotence is increasingly common in older patients.

In clinical trials of the new delivery system, involving more than 1,500 men at several centers in the United States, 66 percent of men achieved erections that were sufficient for sexual intercourse. The most common side effect was the mild penile pain experienced by 10 percent of the patients. However, this rarely caused patients to stop using the medication. The most severe side effect was low blood pressure, which occurred in slightly more than 3 percent of men. This side effect was one of the most important reasons why transurethral alprostadil must initially be administered under a doctor's supervision.

Overall, doctors said, alprostadil given in pellet form appeared to be an effective alternative for men with impotence. Although the medication was not effective in all cases, it was easier to use and less traumatic than a penile injection and caused few side effects.   • Glenn S. Gerber

In WORLD BOOK, see PROSTATE GLAND.

• New rules to fight food poisoning
• Bison killed to protect cattle
• Why pets are given to shelters

In November 1996, the Food Safety and Inspection Service, an agency of the United States Department of Agriculture, and the U.S. Food and Drug Administration announced that they would strengthen regulations regarding the handling, storage, and transportation of foods susceptible to bacterial contamination. Such foods include eggs, egg products, milk, poultry, red meat, and seafood. The two agencies hoped that the new rules, which were expected to be made public before the end of 1997, would help combat a growing number of food poisoning cases in the United States—a major concern of livestock veterinarians working in the area of public health.

One of the main causes of food poisoning is eating foods contaminated with bacteria called *Salmonella,* which cause a potentially fatal disease called salmonellosis. This disease produces symptoms such as diarrhea, abdominal pain, and fever. It is best prevented by the proper refrigeration and cooking of foods that may carry the bacteria. For example, public health experts warn that eggs, which are among the foods most commonly contaminated with *Salmonella,* should be refrigerated at temperatures of at least 40 °F (4 °C) and cooked until the yolks are firm. It was expected that the new regulations would help decrease the chance that eggs bought by consumers would carry *Salmonella.*

Bison killed to protect cattle. In August 1996, the National Park Service announced a plan to ease the fears of Montana ranchers who were concerned that bison wandering out of Yellowstone National Park would transmit a disease called brucellosis to cattle. Brucellosis, a bacterial infection carried by many of the bison in Yellowstone, can cause abortions and reduce fertility and milk production in cattle. People who consume milk or meat from infected cattle can become ill and die from complications caused by the disease.

The plan called for bison wandering beyond the northern and western boundaries of the park in Montana to be captured and either killed or relocated inside the park. Bison often wander outside the park during winter to forage for food. During the winter of 1996-1997, in compliance with the plan, more than 1,000 bison were either sent to slaughter or shot by the National Park Service or the Montana Department of Livestock. About 150 bison that tested negative for brucellosis were relocated.

Ranchers were afraid that if any cattle were infected by brucellosis, all Montana cattle would lose the "brucellosis-free" certification—resulting in serious economic consequences.

Dangerous dogs
The number of dog bites serious enough to require medical care increased 37 percent between 1986 and 1994, according to the Centers for Disease Control and Prevention (CDC) in Atlanta, Georgia. The CDC reported that 26 percent of bites in children needed medical attention, and children 10 years old or younger were the victims of 60 percent of fatal dog attacks. The CDC advised dog owners to train their pets properly and to make sure that dogs are not left alone with young children.

Critics of the plan argued that there were no confirmed cases of bison transmitting brucellosis to cattle. The National Park Service hoped that a vaccine tested in 1997 would eliminate brucellosis in Yellowstone bison by the year 2010.

Why pets are given to shelters.
According to data published in May 1997 from a year-long study by the National Council on Pet Population Study and Policy (NCPPSP), the main reasons pet owners turn their pets over to animal shelters are the following: the pet is sick or old; the owner is moving; the owner found the animal but doesn't want it; the landlord doesn't allow pets; the owner has too many pets; the pet is too expensive to own; there are allergies in the family; and the pet is soiling the house.

The study, which was based on interviews of more than 3,000 pet owners, was part of an effort by the NCPPSP to prevent the yearly *euthanasia* (painless killing) of millions of unwanted pets. The NCPPSP is a coalition of 10 major animal organizations, including the American Kennel Club and the American Veterinary Medical Association.   • Philip H. Kass

In the section Medical and Safety Alerts, see HOW SAFE IS OUR FOOD SUPPLY? In WORLD BOOK, see VETERINARY MEDICINE.

Weight Control

- Virus linked to obesity
- Obesity genes found
- Drug prevents fat absorption
- Diet pills linked to heart ailment

A virus that causes some animals to gain weight may be linked to obesity in humans, researchers at the University of Wisconsin announced in April 1997. The virus, called Ad-36, is a member of a fairly common family of viruses that causes mild respiratory infections.

The researchers found *antibodies* (substances produced by the immune system to fight off infection) against the Ad-36 virus in 18 percent of the 105 obese patients involved in the study. The antibodies represented the presence of infection by the Ad-36 virus. Antibodies were not present in any of the 23 lean patients involved in the study.

The researchers began the study after completing another study showing that injections of the Ad-36 virus fattened chickens. The researchers learned that as the chickens gained fat, they did not experience increases in levels of cholesterol and a related blood-fat called triglyceride. High levels of these substances increase the risk of heart disease, stroke, and high blood pressure. Patients with Ad-36 antibodies also had normal cholesterol and triglyceride levels. Obese patients who did not have Ad-36 antibodies had significantly higher cholesterol and triglyceride levels.

The researchers described the evidence as circumstantial but "tantalizing." According to the researchers, the only way to prove that the virus causes obesity is to inject the virus into thin people and then examine them for weight gain. Because of possible danger, scientists in 1997 did not plan to try the procedure.

The researchers did not speculate on how the virus could cause obesity. Although the results were preliminary, the scientists claimed they were sufficient to prompt additional research.

Obesity genes found. The results of two studies released in June 1997 by researchers in Cambridge, England, linked two defective genes to human obesity. Previous studies suggested that genes could be responsible for obesity in animals, but scientists did not know whether genes in humans could contribute to obesity.

In one study, the researchers examined two obese cousins—an 8-year-old girl who weighed 190 pounds (86 kilograms) and a 2-year-old boy who weighed 64 pounds (29 kilograms). In both cousins, the researchers discovered a defect in the gene for leptin, a hormone that scientists believe helps control weight by telling the body that it is full.

In a separate study, researchers discovered mutations in a gene for an enzyme that helps process hormones called prohormone convertase (PC1) in a woman who was severely obese as a child. The PC1 gene helps the body process insulin and aids other hormones that scientists believe are connected to weight control.

The researchers admitted that the

discoveries are unlikely to produce benefits for most overweight people because the genetic defects are considered rare. However, the scientists said that the discoveries may provide clues to other genetic defects connected with obesity.

Drug prevents fat absorption. In May 1997, the U.S. Food and Drug Administration's (FDA) Endocrinology and Metabolic Drugs Advisory Committee unanimously recommended approval of orlistat, an antiobesity drug that prevents fat absorption. The FDA usually, but not always, follows the advice of such panels. The drug, to be sold under the name Xenical, is taken with each meal and binds to pancreatic enzymes, blocking digestion of 30 percent of the fat consumed in a diet. It is the first weight-loss drug slated for FDA approval that works in the gastrointestinal tract and not by altering brain chemistry.

Researchers at the drug's manufacturer, Hoffman-LaRoche Incorporated in Nutley, New Jersey, tested orlistat on more than 4,000 patients in the United States and Europe over a two-year period. Patients took capsules containing 120 milligrams of Xenical three times a day. Another group received a *placebo* (an inactive substance). Participants were placed on a moderate diet, reducing their daily

Working up a sweat

Researchers at the Medical College of Wisconsin and the Veterans Affairs Medical Center in Milwaukee compared the number of calories people burn on various exercise machines. Participants used the machines for five minutes at three exertion levels. The chart, *right,* lists the average number of calories burned per hour for each exercise.

Machine	Exertion levels and calories burned		
	Fairly light	Somewhat hard	Hard
Treadmill	552	705	865
Stair-climber	505	627	746
Rowing machine	511	606	739
Ski machine	507	595	678
Stationary bike	405	498	604
Stationary bike with arm levers	344	509	709

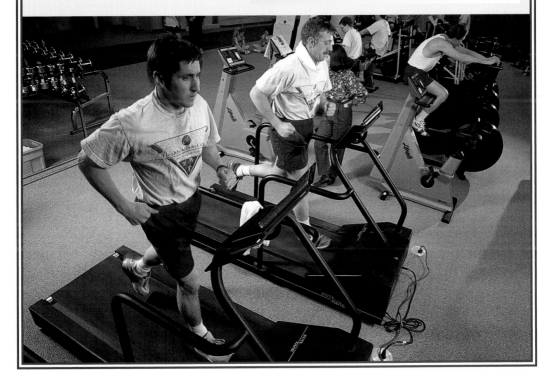

How Americans say they try to lose weight

According to a 1997 report by researchers from Medical University of South Carolina in Charleston, Americans use a wide variety of techniques and products—not all of which are medically acceptable—in efforts to control weight.

Activity	Percentage of females surveyed	Percentage of males surveyed
Adults		
Weighing oneself	71	70
Walking	58	44
Drinking diet soda	52	45
Vitamins & minerals	33	26
Counting calories	25	17
Skipping meals	21	20
Taking diet pills	14	7
Using commercial meal replacements	15	13
Organized weight loss program	13	5
Adolescents		
Exercising	51	30
Skipping meals	49	18
Taking diet pills	4	2
Vomiting	3	1

food consumption by about 600 calories. Patients' fat intake was limited to 30 percent of their total calories, compared with the average American's intake of up to 40 percent of total daily calories from fat.

On the average, patients who took Xenical lost 10 percent of their total body weight in a year, according to the researchers. Between 40 percent and 57 percent of the patients lost at least 5 percent of their body weight, compared with 24 percent to 31 percent of those patients who took a placebo. Patients taking Xenical also slightly reduced their levels of cholesterol, blood sugar, and blood pressure, which suggested that the drug might also lower the risk of heart disease in obese patients.

In the second year of the study, patients who stopped dieting but continued to take Xenical regained 26 percent of the weight they had lost the first year. Participants who took a placebo during the first year of the study and went off their diets in the second year regained half of the weight they had lost.

The drug has some side effects. The researchers said that 26 percent of the patients experienced gas and diarrhea. Another 20 percent had trouble absorbing vitamin D, vitamin E, and beta-carotene. Eleven women in the study were also diagnosed with breast cancer shortly after the study began, compared with only one woman diagnosed with breast cancer in the placebo group. Although the researchers discovered no link between Xenical and breast cancer, the FDA panel recommended that the label on the product warn users about possible side effects.

Diet pills linked to heart ailment. The FDA warned in July 1997 that a diet-drug combination may cause rare but potentially life-threatening health problems. Physicians at the Mayo Clinic in Rochester, Minnesota, reported that 24 otherwise healthy women who were taking a combination of fenfluramine and phentermine, called fen-phen, to lose weight had developed a rare heart valve deformity. Eight of the 24 women also had developed a potentially fatal condition called *pulmonary hypertension*, in which the arteries that supply blood to the lungs constrict, or tighten.

The women sought medical attention after experiencing symptoms of heart problems such as fatigue, shortness of breath, and an accumulation of fluid in the ankles or abdomen. Doctors then made the connection to the diet pill combination.

Because the conclusions were reached through normal medical examinations and not as part of a clinical study, the physicians did not conclude how the diet pills may cause heart or lung ailments. However, FDA officials said that they were concerned and warned doctors to check patients taking the drugs for possible health problems.   • Lauren Love

In WORLD BOOK, see WEIGHT CONTROL.

1997-1998 DIRECTORY OF HEALTH INFORMATION

ADDICTIONS

Alcohol and Drug Help Line provides referrals to local treatment centers nationwide 24 hours a day, 7 days a week.
Phone: 800-821-4357

Alcoholics Anonymous provides support and counseling to alcoholics, their families, and their friends.
Phone: 212-870-3312
Mailing address: A.A. World Services, P.O. Box 459, Grand Central Station, New York, NY 10163
Web site: http://www.moscow.com/Resources/SelfHelp/AA/

American Council on Alcoholism answers questions and provides written information and educational materials.
Phone: 800-527-5344
Mailing address: 2522 St. Paul Street, Baltimore, MD 21218

Center for Substance Abuse Treatment sends written information, provides counseling, and refers callers to treatment centers and support groups.
Phone: 800-662-HELP

HabitSmart web site offers an electronic magazine on addictive behaviors that features articles, practical guides, interactive self-help tests, and links to other sites dealing with addiction.
Web site: http://www.cts.com:80/~habtsmrt

National Clearinghouse for Alcohol and Drug Information offers statistics, brochures, educational programs, and the most recent information on drugs and drug abuse.
Phone: 410-225-6910
Mailing address: Office of the Director, Center for Substance Abuse Prevention, Substance Abuse and Mental Health Services Administration,
5600 Fishers Lane, Rockwall II Building, Rockville, MD 20857
Web site: http://www.health.org

National Cocaine Hotline provides referrals to local treatment centers.
Phone: 800-262-2463

National Council on Alcoholism and Drug Dependence, Inc., provides referrals through voice mail to affiliates that offer counseling and answer questions.
Phone: 800-622-2255

Recovery Homepage offers a comprehensive listing of 12-step recovery programs and provides information and support for people suffering from a variety of addictions.
Web site: http://www.shore.net/~tcfraser/recovery.htm
E-mail: tcfraser@shore.net

Web of Addictions web site provides information on addiction and treatment.
Web site: http://www.well.com/user/woa/
E-mail: Razer@ix.netcom.com

ADDISON'S DISEASE

National Adrenal Diseases Foundation provides information and support to individuals suffering from adrenal diseases, especially Addison's disease, which results from insufficient production of several vital hormones by the adrenal gland.
Phone: 516-487-4992
Mailing address: 505 Northern Boulevard, Suite 200, Great Neck, NY 11021

AGING

American Association of Homes and Services for the Aging provides information on not-for-profit nursing homes, housing, retirement communities, and health-related facilities and services.
Phone: 202-783-2242
Mailing address: 901 East Street, Suite 500, Washington, DC 20004-2037

Association of Caregivers develops resources, leadership, and programs for caregivers of the elderly.
Phone: 800-323-8039
Mailing address: 1451 Dundee Avenue, Elgin, IL 60120

Children of Aging Parents offers education, support, guidance, and development of coping skills to caregivers of the elderly and provides a referral service.
Phone: 800-227-7294
Mailing address: Woodbouro Office Campus, Suite 302A, 1609 Woodbourne Road, Levittown, PA 19057-1511

Eldercare Locator answers questions, provides written information, and makes referrals to local support groups and sources of assistance for the elderly.
Phone: 800-677-1116

Elder Watch web site offers articles, summaries of articles, and links to other healthcare sites.
Web site: http://www.wellweb.com/seniors/eldership.htm
E-mail: seniors@wellweb.com

Eldercare web site offers Internet resources for seniors and caregivers.
Web site: http://www.ice.net/~kstevens/elderweb.html
E-mail: Kstevens@ice.net

Little Brothers of the Poor—Friends of the Elderly provides friendship and assistance to the elderly who do not receive emotional and physical support from relatives. Offers information, referrals, and contacts with other private and public agencies.
Phone: 312-477-7702
Mailing address: 1658 West Belmont Avenue, Chicago, IL 60657

National Association of Nutrition and Aging provides information on home-delivered nutrition services for the elderly.
Phone: 800-999-6262
Mailing address: 2675 44th Street Southwest, Suite 305, Grand Rapids, MI 49509

National Council on Aging provides national information and consultation centers, recruits and trains older volunteers to work with chronically ill children.
Phone: 202-479-1200
Mailing address: 409 3rd Street Southwest, Suite 200, Washington, DC 20024

National Institute on Aging Information Center provides written information and referrals on various issues affecting aging.
Phone: 800-222-2225; hearing-impaired people can reach the institute by TDD at 800-222-4225.
Mailing address: P.O. Box 8057, Gaithersburg, MD 20898
Web site: http://www.aoa.dhhs.gov/aoa/resource.html

National Voluntary Organizations for Independent Living for the Aging provides information on voluntary organizations that offer in-home and community-based health and social services.
Phone: 202-479-6682
Mailing address: 409 3rd Street Southwest, Suite 200, Washington, DC 20024

Older Women's League provides written information, answers questions, and makes referrals to support groups and local chapters.
Phone: 800-825-3695
Mailing address: 666 11th Street Northwest, Suite 3700, Washington, DC 20001
E-mail: seidokid@aol

AIDS

American Foundation for AIDS Research offers educational programs about AIDS prevention.
Phone: 800-39-AMFAR
Mailing address: 733 3rd Avenue, 12th Floor, New York, NY 10017

The Body: A Multimedia AIDS and HIV Information Resource web site offers educational articles and information on political action, legal, and financial issues, hotlines, community service organizations, and newsgroups.
Web site: http://www.thebody.com
E-mail: info@the body.com

Body Positive Hotline provides support services for people who are HIV-infected and their family and friends.
Phone: 800-566-6599

The Centers for Disease Control AIDS Clearinghouse, a service of the Centers for Disease Control and Prevention, offers information on HIV/AIDS and provides a referral service.
Phone: 800-458-5231
Web site: http://cdcnac.aspensys.com:86

HIV/AIDS Clinical Trials Information Service answers questions and sends written materials on trials for drugs and experimental therapies.
Phone: 800-874-2572
Mailing address: P.O. Box 6421, Rockville, MD, 20849-6421
Web site: http://www.actis.org
E-mail: actis@cdcnac.org

HIV/AIDS Treatment Information Service web site, operated by the National Library of Medicine, features discussions on scientific issues and research.
Web site: http://test.nim.nih.gov/atis/list.html

HIV/AIDS Treatment Service provides information on treatment options and treatment guidelines and refers callers to sources of additional information on these topics.
Phone: 800-448-0440
Mailing address: P.O. Box 6303, Rockville, IL 20847-6303
Web site: http://www.hivatis.org
E-mail: atis@cdcnac.org

National AIDS Hotline, operated by the Centers for Disease Control and Prevention, provides information and referrals 24 hours a day, 7 days a week.
Phone: 800-342-AIDS; Spanish-language information is available at 800-344-7432; people who are hearing impaired can call 800-243-7889
Mailing address: P.O. Box 13827, RTP, NC 27709
Web site: http://sunsite.unc.edu/ASHA/

National Directory of AIDS Care Hotline provides information on care, education, and support services for AIDS patients.
Phone: 800-584-7972

National Minority AIDS Council Hotline offers information on how AIDS affects the minority community and provides education and research information.
Phone: 800-544-0586

Pediatric AIDS Foundation offers support networks and programs for children with AIDS.
Phone: 800-828-3280
Mailing address: 50 West 17th Street, 8th Floor, New York, NY 10011

Project Inform National HIV/AIDS Treatment Hot Line answers questions about treatment of HIV and AIDS and provides referrals to local sources of assistance for HIV- and AIDS-related problems.
Phone: 800-822-7422
Web site: http://www.projinf.org/

The TB/HIV Laboratory web site, operated by the TB/HIV Laboratory at Brown University, provides summaries of the lab's current projects, information on TB/HIV (including a history of tuberculosis), a list of related TB/HIV resources on the Internet, and articles published by lab staff.
Web site: http://www.brown.edu/Research/TB-HIV_Lab/
E-mail: William_Jesdale@brown.edu

Teens Teaching AIDS Prevention Hotline provides teens with information about AIDS.
Phone: 800-234-8336

 ## ALZHEIMER'S DISEASE

Alzheimer's Association provides written information and referrals to local chapters. The web site provides an electronic version of the Alzheimer's Association's quarterly journal, on-line versions of association publications, medical information on Alzheimer's, and public policy statements.
Phone: 800-272-3900
Mailing address: 919 North Michigan Avenue, Suite 1000, Chicago, IL 60611
Web site: http://www.alz.org/
E-mail: greenfld@alz.org

Alzheimer's Disease Education and Referral Center answers questions, provides written materials, makes referrals to research centers for diagnosis and treatment, provides information on state services for patients, publishes information on research, and provides an on-line database of information.
Phone: 800-438-4380
Mailing address: P.O. Box 8250, Silver Springs, MD 20907-8250
Web site: http://www.alzheimers.org/adear

Alzheimer's Disease International offers information and support to families affected by the disease.
Phone: 312-335-5777
Mailing address: 12 South Michigan Avenue, Chicago, IL 60603

Alzheimer Web Home Page provides information on the basics of Alzheimer's disease, a bulletin on recent research developments, a list of research labs on the Internet, a bibliography of articles, books, and journals on Alzheimer's disease, and a list of upcoming conferences.
Web site: http://werple.mira.net.au/~dhs/ad.html
E-mail: david_small@muwayf.unimelb.edu.au

AMYOTROPHIC LATERAL SCLEROSIS
(Lou Gehrig's disease)
Amyotrophic Lateral Sclerosis (ALS) Association National Office answers questions, supplies written information, and provides referrals to support groups and local chapters.
Phone: 800-782-4747
Web site: http://www.alsa.org

ALS web site provides information on cause and treatment of the disease.
Web site: http://www.pslgroup.com/als.htm

ANIMAL WELFARE
American Dog Owners Association provides written information on the care and feeding of dogs.
Phone: 518-477-8469
Mailing address: 1654 Columbia Turnpike, Castleton, NY 12033

American Feline Society provides written information on alleviating cat suffering and abuse, cat history, care, and feeding.
Mailing address: 220 West 19th Street, Suite 2A, New York, NY 10011

American Humane Education Society provides information on the treatment of animals.
Phone: 617-541-5095
Mailing address: 350 South Huntington Avenue, Boston, MA 02130
Web site: http://www.mspcu.org

American Society for the Prevention of Cruelty to Animals provides educational information on the treatment and care of animals.
Phone: 212-876-7700
Mailing address: 424 East 92nd Street, New York, NY 10128
Web site: http://www.aspca.org

Electronic Zoo web site provides a listing of animal-health sites on the Internet.
Web site: http://netvet.wustl.edu/e-zoo.htm

Project Breed Rescue Efforts and Education, a national clearinghouse and reference source, provides written information on animal protection efforts, animal rescue, rehab, adoption, and education.
Mailing address: P.O. Box 15888, Chevy Chase, MD 20825-5888

Veterinary Medicine web site, operated by Washington University, provides information on animal-health issues.
Web site:
http://netvet.wustl.edu/vetmed.htm

ANXIETY DISORDERS
Council on Anxiety Disorders provides information, referrals, assistance, and consultation for people with anxiety disorders.
Phone: 910-722-7760
Mailing address: P.O. Box 17011, Winston-Salem, NC 27116

APHASIA
Academy of Aphasia provides research and educational information about aphasia, a speech disorder that often affects victims of stroke.
Phone: 310-206-3206
Mailing address: UCLA, Department of Linguistics, Los Angeles, CA 90024

APLASTIC ANEMIA
Aplastic Anemia Foundation of America serves as an information source for individuals with aplastic anemia, an often fatal disease in which bone marrow fails to produce new blood cells.
Phone: 800-747-2820
Mailing address: P.O. Box 22689, Baltimore, MD 21203

ARTHRITIS
American Juvenile Arthritis Organization provides information to parents of children with juvenile arthritis.
Phone: 404-872-7100
Mailing address: 1314 Spring Street, Atlanta, GA 30309

Arthritis Foundation sends written information on treatment and local chapters to callers who leave their names and addresses on its answering machine. Callers also may listen to taped information. The web site offers practical tips on living with arthritis, sample articles from *Arthritis Today*, on-line order forms for free brochures, and information on local chapters.
Phone: 800-283-7800
Mailing address: 1314 Spring Street NW, Atlanta, GA 30309
Web site: http://www.arthritis.org
E-mail: help@arthritis.org

The American Lupus Society sends written information to those who leave their names and addresses on its answering machine.
Phone: 800-331-1802

Lupus Foundation of America provides written information on the cause and treatment of lupus.
Phone: 800-558-0121
Mailing address: 4 Research Place, Suite 180, Rockville, MD 20850-3226

Lupus Network provides information on the cause and treatment of lupus.
Phone: 203-372-5795
Mailing address: 230 Ranch Drive, Bridgeport, CT 06606

National Arthritis and Musculoskeletal and Skin Diseases Information Clearinghouse provides information about arthritis and musculoskeletal and skin diseases.
Phone: 301-495-4484
Mailing address: 9000 Rockville Pike, P.O. Box AMS, Bethesda, MD 20892-2903

ASTHMA AND LUNG DISORDERS

Allergy and Asthma Network/Mothers of Asthmatics Inc. provides information and referrals and publishes a monthly newsletter.
Phone: 703-385-4403
Mailing address: 3554 Chain Bridge Road, Suite 200, Fairfax, VA 22030
Web site: http://www.podi.com/health/aanma

Allergy, Asthma, and Immunology Online web site, operated by the American College of Allergy, Asthma and Immunology, provides information on these disorders.
Web site: http://allergy.mcg.edu/

American Academy of Allergy, Asthma, and Immunology web site provides information and links to other web sites.
Web site: http://allergy.mcg.edu/

American Academy of Allergy, Asthma, and Immunology provides research and educational information on allergies and asthma.
Phone: 414-272-6071
Mailing address: 611 East Wells Street, Milwaukee, WI 53202

American Allergy Association provides information on diet, environmental concerns, and other facets of allergies.
Phone: 415-322-1663
Mailing address: P.O. Box 7273, Menlo Park, CA 94026

American Lung Association provides information and educational material on asthma.
Phone: 212-315-8700
Mailing address: 1740 Broadway, New York, NY 10019-4374
Web site: http//www.lungusa.org

Asthma and Allergy Foundation of America provides written information on asthma and allergies.
Phone: 800-7-ASTHMA
Mailing address: 1125 15th Street Northwest, Suite 502, Washington, DC 20005

Lungline provides written information on respiratory and immunological problems and an opportunity to speak with a registered nurse.
Phone: 800-222-LUNG
Web site: http://www.hjc.org

National Asthma Education and Prevention Program Information Center provides pamphlets, fact sheets, and articles.
Phone: 301-251-1222
Mailing address: P.O. Box 30105, Bethesda, MD 20824-0105
Web site: http://www.nhlbi.nih.gov/nhibi/nhibi.htm

National Institute of Allergy and Infectious Diseases web site contains information about these disorders.
Web site: http://web.fie.com/web/fed/nih/

Practical Allergy Research Foundation provides information on allergies, their symptoms, and remedies.
Phone: 800-787-8780
Mailing address: P.O. Box 60, Buffalo, NY 14223

ATTENTION-DEFICIT DISORDER
Attention Deficit Disorder Advocacy Group provides educational information and legislative news about the disorder.
Phone: 303-690-7548
Mailing address: 8091 South Ireland Way, Aurora, CO 80016

Attention Deficit Disorder Archive web site provides resources on attention deficit disorder to people with this disability.
Web site: http://www.seas.upenn.edu/~mengwong/add/
E-mail: mengwong@poxbox.com

Attention Deficit Disorder Association provides information on the disorder.
Phone: 800-487-2282
Mailing address: 4300 West Park Boulevard, Plano, TX 75093

Children and Adults with Attention Deficit Disorder (CHADD) Online delivers information about attention deficit disorder and about CHADD, a nonprofit, parent-based organization.
Web site: http://www.chadd.org

National Attention-Deficit Disorder Association Hotline provides written information, including referrals to local support groups, to people who leave their names and addresses on its answering machine.
Phone: 800-487-2282

AUTISM
Autism Network International offers information and tips on coping with autism.
Mailing address: P.O. Box 448, Syracuse, NY 13210-0448
E-mail: jisincla@mailbox.syr.edu

Autism Resources web site, operated by Syracuse University, provides information on the causes and treatment of autism.
Web site: http://web.syr.edu/~jmwobus/autism/

Autism Services Center assists families affected by autism.
Phone: 304-525-8014
Mailing address: Prichard Building, 605 9th Street, P.O. Box 507, Huntington, WV 25710

Autism Society of America offers information on the symptoms and problems of children and adults with autism.
Phone: 800-3-AUTISM
Mailing address: 7910 Woodmont Avenue, Suite 650, Bethesda, MD 20814

BEHCET'S SYNDROME
American Behcet's Disease Association offers educational and research information on Behcet's syndrome, a disease characterized by painful oral ulcers.
Phone: 800-723-4238
Mailing address: P.O. Box 27494, Tempe, AZ 85285-7494

BIRTH DEFECTS
Association of Birth Defect Children Hotline provides information on birth defects and offers help in adjusting to the problems faced by people with physical malformations.
Phone: 800-313-ABDC

Cornelia De Lange Syndrome Foundation seeks to ensure early and accurate diagnosis of the syndrome (a birth defect of unknown cause resulting in babies who continue to develop—mentally and physically—at a slower rate).
Phone: 800-223-8355
Mailing address: 60 Dyer Avenue, Collinsville, CT 06022-1273

International Federation of Teratology Societies provides an information exchange on the prevention and treatment of birth defects. (Teratology is the study of birth defects.)
Mailing address: University of Sydney, Department of Anatomy, Sydney, NSW 2006, Australia

IVH Parents provides information to parents of children with intraventricular hemorrhage, which can occur in an infant after premature or traumatic birth.
Phone: 305-232-0381
Mailing address: P.O. Box 56 1111, Miami, FL 33256-1111

Klippel-Trenaunay Support Group offers information to people affected by the syndrome—a congenital malformation characterized by birthmarks the color of port wine, excessive growth of soft tissue and bone, and varicose veins.
Phone: 612-925-2596
Mailing address: 4610 Wooddale Avenue, Minneapolis, MN 55424

March of Dimes Birth Defects Foundation promotes the prevention of birth defects by focusing on maternal and child health issues.
Phone: 914-428-7100
Mailing address: 1275 Mamaroneck Avenue, White Plains, NY 10605
Web site: http://www.modimes.org

National Congenital Port Wine Stain Foundation collects and disseminates information on the symptoms, diagnosis, treatment, and prevention of congenital port wine stains and related disorders.
Phone: 516-867-5137
Mailing address: 125 East 63rd Street, New York, NY 10021

Organization of Teratology Information Services provides information on birth defects.
Phone: 617-466-8474
Mailing address: 40 Second Avenue, Suite 460, Waltham, MA 02154

Rubinstein-Taybi Parent Group provides information and support to families with children diagnosed with the syndrome.
Phone: 913-697-2984
Mailing address: P.O. Box 146, Smith Center, KS 66967

BLADDER DISORDERS

Bladder Health Council, operated by the American Foundation for Urologic Disease, provides written materials on bladder cancer and urinary tract infections. Callers can also obtain information on other urologic disorders, such as prostate disease, kidney disease, and sexual function.
Phone: 800-242-2383
Web site:http://www.access.digex.net~afud

BLOOD

National Rare Blood Club offers information to people with rare blood types.
Phone: 212-889-8245
Mailing address: Associated Health Foundation, 99 Madison Avenue, New York, NY 10016

BRAIN INJURY

Brain Injury Association Family Help Line (formerly National Head Injury Foundation) answers questions, provides written information, and makes referrals to local resources.
Phone: 800-444-6443

Traumatic Brain Injury web site provides information and links to other web sites.
Web site: http://canddwilson.com/tbi/tbiepil.htm

BREAST DISEASE

American Society of Breast Disease
provides information on diseases of the breast.
Phone: 214-368-6836
Mailing address: P.O. Box 140186, Dallas, TX 75214

Breast Cancer Advisory Group provides information to patients concerning ongoing research.
Mailing address: P.O. Box 224, Kensington, MD 20895

Breast Cancer Information Clearinghouse provides information and free publications and brochures on breast cancer detection and treatment. The web site, operated by New York State Education and Research Network, offers patient education materials from the American Cancer Society and the National Cancer Institute, listings of support groups from around the country, listings of toll-free telephone numbers and hotlines, and state and federal legislation related to breast cancer.
Phone: 800-4-CANCER
Web site: http://nysernet.org/bcic/
E-mail: kennett@nysernet.org

A Patient's Guide to Breast Cancer Treatment web site provides information on breast cancer and its treatment.
Web site: gopher://nysernet.org:70/00/bcic/sources/strang-

BURNS

American Burn Association offers information on the treatment and care of burns.
Phone: 800-548-2876
Mailing address: New York Hospital-Cornell Medical Center, 525 East 68th Street, Room L-706, New York, NY 10021
Web site: http://www.ameriburn.org

Burns United Support Group provides support services and information on burn care and prevention.
Phone: 313-881-5577
Mailing address: 441 Colonial Court, Grosse Pointe Farms, MI 48236

National Burn Victim Foundation provides information on burn treatment and care. Maintains 24-hour emergency burn referral.
Phone: 800-803-5879
Mailing address: 32 34 Scotland Road, Orange, NJ 07050

National Institute for Burn Medicine offers information on preventing burn injuries, improving the survival rate, and improving the quality of life for burn victims.
Phone: 313-769-9000
Mailing address: P.O. Box 15138, Ann Arbor, MI 48106-5138

Phoenix Society for Burn Survivors offers a self-help service for burn survivors and their families.
Phone: 800-888-BURN
Mailing address: 11 Rust Hill Road, Levittown, PA 19056

CANCER

American Association for Cancer Education provides information on prevention, early detection, treatment, and rehabilitation.
Phone: 713-792-3020
Mailing address: Anderson Cancer Center, Department of Epidemiology, 189, 1515 Holcombe Boulevard, Houston, TX 77030

American Brain Tumor Association provides information on brain tumors and brain tumor research.
Phone: 800-886-2282
Mailing address: 2720 River Road, Suite 146, Des Plaines, IL 60018

American Cancer Society provides special services to cancer patients.
Phone: 800-ACS-2345
Mailing address: 1599 Clifton Road NE, Atlanta, GA 30329
Web site: http://www.cancer.org

Association for Research of Childhood Cancer offers information on various pediatric cancers.
Phone: 716-681-4433
Mailing address: P.O. Box 251, Buffalo, NY 14225-0251

Cancer Care offers services to cancer patients and their families.
Phone: 212-221-3300
Mailing address: 1180 Avenue of the Americas, New York, NY 10036

Cancer Information Service of the National Cancer Institute answers questions and provides written information and referrals to treatment centers, mammography facilities, and support groups. The web site offers educational materials and a medicine online library.
Phone: 800-4-CANCER; hearing-impaired people can reach the service by TDD at 800-332-8615
Web site: http://www.icic.nci.nih.gov
E-mail: comcowic@meds.com

Cancer Pain Education for Patients and Families web site, operated by the University of Iowa, provides information about pain control.
Web site: http://coninfo.nursing.uiowa.edu/www/nursing/apn/cncrpain/toc.htm

Cancer Response System of the American Cancer Society provides written information and referrals to local ACS programs and resources.
Phone: 800-ACS-2345
Web site: http://www.cancer.org

Candlelighters Childhood Cancer Foundation educates, supports, serves, and advocates for families and individuals touched by childhood cancer.
Phone: 800-366-2223
Mailing address: 7910 Woodmont Avenue, Suite 460, Bethesda, MD 20814-3015

Cansearch: A Guide to Cancer Resources web site, operated by the National Coalition for Cancer Survivorship, features step-by-step instructions on how to access resources, including how to look for specific information. The site provides a guide to medical terms and descriptions of resources on specific types of cancer.
Web site: http://access.dignex.net/~mkragen/cansearch.html

Children's Leukemia Research Association provides financial aid to leukemia patients and their families. Offers children's services and conducts a referral service.
Phone: 516-222-1944
Mailing address: 585 Stewart Avenue, Suite 536, Garden City, NY 11530

International Myeloma Foundation provides research information on myeloma, a blood cancer.
Phone: 800-452-CURE
Mailing address: 2120 Stanley Hills Drive, Los Angeles, CA 90046
Web site: http://www.comed.com/Aboutccihf.spml

Leukemia Society of America provides information and financial aid for patients and sponsors support groups.
Phone: 800-955-4LSA
Mailing address: 600 3rd Avenue, New York, NY 10016

National Coalition for Cancer Survivorship provides information and support groups for cancer survivors.
Phone: 301-650-8868
Mailing address: 1010 Wayne Avenue, 5th Floor, Silver Spring, MD 20910

OncoLink web site, operated by the University of Pennsylvania, offers patient-oriented information guides on the nature of cancer, its causes, and screening and prevention, information on clinical trials, financial guides on topics such as how to obtain financial assistance, articles, and a feature for children complete with articles and statistics about childhood cancer, support groups, and artwork by young cancer patients.
Web site: http://cancer.med.upenn.edu/
E-mail: editors@oncolink.upenn.edu

Ovarian Cancer Prevention and Early Detection Foundation offers information on research and education.
Mailing address: 841 Bishop Street, Suite 1615, Honolulu, HI 96813-3821

Patient Advocates for Advanced Cancer Treatment provides educational materials to individuals with prostate cancer.
Phone: 616-453-1477
Mailing address: 1143 Parmelee NW, Grand Rapids, MI 49504-3844

People Against Cancer provides information on cancer therapy and prevention.
Phone: 800-NO-CANCER
Mailing address: 604 East Street, P.O. Box 10, Otho, IA 50569-0010

Prostate Cancer Infolink web site provides information and resources for patients with prostate cancer.
Web site: http://www.comed.com/prostate/

Prostate Cancer Support Network sends written information and provides referrals to local support groups.
Phone: 800-828-7866
Web site: http://www.access.digex.net~afud

Quick Information about Cancer for Patients and Their Families web site, operated by the University of Michigan School of Medicine, provides information on causes of cancer, treatment, support, and a list of databases.
Web site: http://asa.ugl.lib.umich.edu/chdocs/cancer/

Skin Cancer Foundation offers information on the prevention and early recognition of skin cancer.
Phone: 800-SKIN-490
Mailing address: 245 5th Avenue, Suite 2402, New York, NY 10016

Y-ME National Breast Cancer Organization allows callers to speak to counselors who have survived breast cancer; offers a men's hotline staffed by male counselors; provides written information; and supplies wigs and prostheses to women who cannot afford them. The line operates 7 days a week, 24 hours a day.
Phone: 800-221-2141; Spanish speakers may call 800-986-9505
Web site: http://www.y-me.org

CELIAC DISEASE

Celiac Disease Foundation provides services, information, and support to individuals with celiac disease (the small intestine is damaged by ingestion of certain foods) and its related skin disorder.
Phone: 818-990-2354
Mailing address: 13251 Ventura Boulevard, Suite 3, Studio City, CA 91604-1838

CEREBRAL PALSY

United Cerebral Palsy Associations provides information and referral services.
Phone: 800-USA-5UCP
Mailing address: 1522 K Street NW, Suite 1112, Washington, DC 20005
Web site: http://www.ucpa.org
E-mail: uspnatl@ucpa.org

CHILD ABUSE AND NEGLECT

American Humane Association Children's Division offers evaluation and technical assistance to communities and conducts ongoing research into the nature of child maltreatment.
Phone: 800-227-4645
Mailing address: 63 Inverness Drive, East Englewood, CO 80112-5117

Boys Town National Hotline provides counseling to young people and adults and makes referrals to local counselors, shelters, and social services.
Phone: 800-448-3000

Childhelp/IOF Foresters National Child Abuse Hotline provides trained professional counselors for crisis intervention 24 hours a day, 7 days a week. Written information and referrals to local resources and agencies for assistance with issues related to child abuse, adult survivors of abuse, domestic violence, and parenting are also available.
Phone: 800-4ACHILD; hearing-impaired people can reach the hotline at 800-2ACHILD

Child Quest International offers referrals for abused and exploited children.
Phone: 800-248-8020
Mailing address: 1625 The Alameda, Suite 400, San Jose, CA 95126

Committee for the Children provides information on preventing sexual abuse, physical abuse, and youth violence.
Mailing address: 2203 Airport Way South, Suite 500, Seattle, WA 98134-2027

Missing Children Help Center provides a hotline for reporting missing children or sighting missing children.
Phone: 800-USA-KIDS
Mailing address: 410 Ware Boulevard, Suite 400, Tampa, FL 33619

National Center for Missing and Exploited Children provides a national clearinghouse of information on the protection of children.
Phone: 800-843-5678
Mailing address: 2101 Wilson Boulevard, Suite 550, Arlington, VA 22201

National Clearinghouse on Child Abuse and Neglect Information is a government sponsored clearinghouse that provides information on child abuse and neglect.
Phone: 800-394-3366
Mailing address: P.O. Box 1182, Washington, DC 20013-1182

National Committee to Prevent Child Abuse provides resources on child maltreatment and prevention.
Phone: 800-CHILDREN
Mailing address: 332 South Michigan Avenue, Suite 1600, Chicago, IL 60609

National Exchange Club Foundation for the Prevention of Child Abuse works with abusive parents and children to rehabilitate and train parents to cope in nonviolent child-rearing techniques.
Phone: 800-760-3413

National Resource Center for Youth Services offers education on preparing adolescents for the challenges of life.
Phone: 918-585-2986
Mailing address: 202 West 8th Street, Tulsa, OK 74119-1419

National Safe Kids Campaign provides information on creating safer homes and communities for children.
Phone: 202-884-4993
Mailing address: 111 Michigan Avenue Northwest, Washington, DC 20010

Orphan Foundation of America provides information and emergency help to children raised outside of the traditional family setting.
Phone: 800-950-4673
Mailing address: 1500 Massachusetts Avenue North, Suite 448, Washington, DC 20005

Society for Young Victims provides advice and assistance to parents whose children have been abducted or retained in connection with child custody disputes and offers information on how to prevent abductions and facilitate recovery.
Phone: 800-999-9024
Mailing address: 1920 Mineral Spring Avenue, No. 10, North Providence, RI 02904-3742

CHILDHOOD DISEASES

American Pediatric Gastroesophageal Reflux Association provides information and support to parents of children who suffer from gastroesophageal reflux, a disease that produces symptoms including regurgitation, crankiness, respiratory problems, and poor weight gain.
Phone: 617-926-3586
Mailing address: 23 Acton Street, Watertown, MA 02172

Children's Blood Foundation provides information on diseases of the blood in children, such as leukemia, hemophilia, and diseases of the immune system.
Phone: 212-297-4336
Mailing address: 333 East 38th, 8th Floor, New York, NY 10016

Children's Medical Center web site, sponsored by the University of Virginia Health Sciences Center, provides information on research, childhood diseases, and education.
Web site: http://galen.med.virginia.edu/~smb4v/cmchome.html

Cyclic Vomiting Syndrome Association provides support and information to individuals suffering from cyclic vomiting syndrome, a disorder that usually affects children aged 3 to 7 and is characterized by recurrent attacks of nausea and vomiting.
Phone: 414-784-6842
Mailing address: 13180 Caroline Court, Elm Grove, WI 53122

National Vaccine Information Center provides information about childhood vaccines.
Phone: 800-909-SHOT
Mailing address: 512 Maple Avenue West, Suite 206, Vienna, VA 22180

Pedinfo web site, sponsored by University of Alabama School of Medicine—Department of Pediatrics, provides information on childhood diseases, on-line publications, support groups, and links to dozens of other sites.
Web site:
http://www.lhl.uab.edu:80/pedinfo/
E-mail: spooner@aol.com

CHRONIC FATIGUE SYNDROME

Chronic Fatigue and Immune Dysfunction Syndrome Association of America provides free information, including lists of local support groups, to callers who leave a message on its answering machine.
Phone: 800-442-3437

Chronic Fatigue Syndrome web site offers information and resources.
Web site: http://www.cais.com/cfs-news/

National Chronic Fatigue Syndrome and Fibromyalgia Association provides educational material about the illnesses.
Phone: 816-931-4777
Mailing address: 3521 Broadway, Suite 222, Kansas City, MO 64111

CHRONIC PAIN

American Academy of Head, Neck, and Facial Pain serves as a referral service for patients suffering from head, facial, and neck pain.
Phone: 800-322-8651
Mailing address: 520 West Pipeline Road, Hurst, TX 76053-4924

American Chronic Pain Association offers support and information to individuals suffering from chronic pain.
Phone: 916-632-0922
Mailing address: P.O. Box 850, Rocklin, CA 95677

The National Chronic Pain Outreach Association Hotline provides information and referrals.
Phone: 540-997-5004

The Worldwide Congress on Pain web site offers information and educational material on chronic pain.
Web site: http://www.pain.com

CLEFT PALATE

Children's Craniofacial Association provides financial assistance and a referral service to craniofacially deformed individuals.
Phone: 800-535-3643
Mailing address: 10210 North Central Expressway, Suite 230, Lockbox 37, Dallas, TX

Cleft Lip and Palate web page provides a collection of Internet resources on the disorders.
Web site:
http://www.samizdat.com/pp3.html

Cleft Palate Foundation offers information about cleft lip and palate and provides research programs and children's services.
Phone: 800-24-CLEFT
Mailing address: 1218 Grandview Avenue, Pittsburgh, PA 15211

Forward Face provides medical, psychological, and financial support services.
Phone: 800-FWD-FACE
Mailing address: 317 East 34th Street, New York, NY 10016

COMA

Coma Recovery Association provides support to coma and head injury survivors and their families.
Phone: 516-355-0951
Mailing address: 570 Elmont Road, Suite 104, Elmont, NY 11003

COSMETIC SURGERY

National Foundation for Facial Reconstruction sponsors surgical and rehabilitation service programs for patients suffering facial disfigurements.
Phone: 800-422-FACE
Mailing address: 317 East 34th Street, Suite 901, New York, NY 10016

Plastic Surgery Educational Foundation provides educational and research ma-terials.
Phone: 708-228-9900
Mailing address: 444 East Algonquin Road, Arlington Heights, IL 60005

CROHN'S DISEASE AND COLITIS

Crohn's and Colitis Foundation of America, Inc. provides written information and referrals to physicians and support groups.
Phone: 800-932-2423
Mailing address: 386 Park Avenue, New York, NY 10016-7374
E-mail: mhda37b@prodigy.com

Crohn's Disease, Ulcerative Colitis, and Inflammatory Bowel Disease web site provides information on the causes and treatments of these disorders.
Web site: http://qurlyjoe.bu.edu/

CYSTIC FIBROSIS

Cystic Fibrosis Foundation provides written information and referrals to accredited cystic fibrosis care centers.
Phone: 800-FIGHT CF
Mailing address: 6931 Arlington Road, Bethesda, MD 20814
Web site: http://www.cff.org

The Cystic Fibrosis web site provides a collection of online information about the disease.
Web site:
hppt:www.ai.mit.edu/people/mernst/cf/
E-mail: rcalhoun@mit.edu

A Family Guide to Cystic Fibrosis Testing web site provides information about the disease and testing procedures.
Web site:
http://www.phd.msu.edu/cf/fam.html

DEATH AND DYING

Bereavement: A Guide to Internet Resources web site, operated by the University of Michigan, provides a list of support resources on the Internet, including electronic discussion groups.
Web site: gopher://una.hh.lib.umich.edu/00/netdirsstacks/emotsupport/3ajunpow

Crisis, Grief, and Healing web site provides information on coping with grief and loss.
Web site: http://www2.dgsys.com/~tgolden/1grief.html
E-mail: tgolden@dgsys.com

DeathNet web site, operated by the Right-to-Die Society, offers a wide range of material on the legal, moral, medical, historical, and cultural issues related to dying. Includes information on living wills, insurance, funeral arrangements, and media coverage of death and dying.
Web site: http:www.rights.org/~deathnet/homepage.html
E-mail: rights@rights.com

GriefNet web site provides resources to help people cope with and overcome loss and grief.
Web site: http://rivendell.org/
E-mail: griefnet@falcon.ic.net

Sociology of Death and Dying web site, operated by Trinity University, provides a list of Internet resources related to death and dying.
Web site:
http://www.trinity.edu/~mkearl/death.html

DEGENERATIVE DISEASES

Independent Citizens Research Foundation for the Study of Degenerative Diseases provides information on the causes of degenerative diseases, testing procedures for early detection, and approaches to therapy and prevention.
Phone: 914-478-1862
Mailing address: P.O. Box 91, Ardsley, NY 10502

DENTISTRY

Academy of Dentistry for Persons with Disabilities
promotes the importance of oral health for people with special needs.
Phone: 312-440-2661
Mailing address: 211 East Chicago Avenue, Suite 948, Chicago, IL 60611

American Academy of the History of Dentistry
provides information on the study, research, and history of dentistry.
Phone: 708-670-7561
Mailing address: 100 South Vail Avenue, Arlington Heights, IL 60005-1866

American Academy of Oral Medicine
provides information on the cause, prevention, and the control of diseases of the teeth.
Phone: 703-684-6649
Mailing address: 631 29th Street South, Arlington, VA 22202-2312

American Dental Association
provides news and information on dental health.
Phone: 312-440-2500
Mailing address: 211 East Chicago Avenue, Chicago, IL 60611
Web site: http://www.ada.org
E-mail: wwwedit@www.ada.org

Dental-Related Internet Resources
web site, operated by New York University College of Dentistry, provides a comprehensive listing of dental information on the Internet.
Web site: http://www.nyu.edu/dental/

National Oral Health Information Clearinghouse
collects and maintains a catalog on oral health and diseases of the teeth.
Phone: 301-402-7364
Mailing address: 1 NOHIC Way, Bethesda, MD 20892-3500

DERMATOLOGY

American Dermatological Association
provides educational and research information.
Phone: 706-721-6496
Mailing address: Medical College of Georgia, Department of Dermatology, Augusta, GA 30912-2900

American Hair Loss Council
provides information regarding treatments for hair loss in both men and women.
Phone: 800-274-8717
Mailing address: 401 North Michigan Avenue, 22nd Floor, Chicago, IL 60611-4212

American Society of Dermatopathology
provides information on treatment of dermatopathology (abnormal skin conditions).
Phone: 806-743-1106
Mailing address: 3601 4th Street, Suite 4A-118, Lubbock, TX 79430

Dystrophic Epidermolysis Bullosa Research Association of America
offers information on the cause and treatment of dystrophic epidermolysis bullosa, a group of inherited disorders of the skin characterized by formation of blisters.
Phone: 212-693-6610
Mailing address: 40 Rector Street, New York, NY 10006

Eczema Association for Science and Education
provides research and educational information on eczema.
Phone: 503-228-4430
Mailing address: 1221 Southwest Yamhill, No. 303, Portland, OR 97205

Foundation for Ichthyosis and Related Skin Types
provides information and support to people suffering from ichthyosis, a hereditary disease that causes the skin to be thick, dry, taut, and scaly.
Phone: 800-545-3286
Mailing address: P.O. Box 20921, Raleigh, NC 27619

International Livedo Reticularis Network
provides information to people suffering from livedo reticularis, a condition characterized by a reddish-blue mottling of the skin.
Phone: 512-353-7451
Mailing address: 215 Lazy Lane, San Marcos, TX 78666

National Association for Pseudoxanthoma Elasticum provides support and information to people suffering from pseudoxanthoma elasticum, a skin disease marked by an exaggeration of the normal creases and folds of the skin.
Phone: 303-832-5055
Mailing address: 1420 Ogden Street, Denver, CO 80218

National Psoriasis Foundation provides information and support to people suffering from psoriasis (a chronic skin disease characterized by red patches covered with white scales) or psoriatic arthritis.
Phone: 800-723-9166
Mailing address: 6600 Southwest 92nd, Suite 300, Portland, OR 97223-7195
Web site: http://www.psoriasis.org/

National Vitiligo Foundation provides counseling and information to people suffering from vitiligo, a skin disease that destroys pigment cells causing smooth, white patches of skin.
Phone: 903-534-2925
Mailing address: P.O. Box 6337, Tyler, TX 75711

Psoriasis Research Association provides information on the cause and cure of psoriasis.
Phone: 415-593-1394
Mailing address: 107 Vista del Grande, San Carlos, CA 94070

Psoriasis Research Institute provides information on the study, diagnosis, treatment, and cure of psoriasis.
Phone: 415-326-1848
Mailing address: 600 Town and Country Village, Palo Alta, CA 94301

 ## DIABETES

American Diabetes Association answers questions and provides written information. The web site offers information on the nature of diabetes and how to cope with it, legislative and advocacy issues, events and programs, and opportunities to volunteer.
Phone: 800-ADA-DISC
Web site: http://www.diabetes.org

The Diabetic Foot web site, operated by the Foot and Ankle Institute of St. George, Utah, provides information on foot problems associated with diabetes.
Web site: http://www.infowest.com/doctor/index.html

Diabetes Home Page offers information on support groups and organizations, medical research, and sources of insulin pumps, sugar-free chocolates, and diet plans.
Web site: http://www.nd.edu/~hhowisen/diabetes.html
E-mail: hhowisen@argon.helios.nd.edu

Diabetes Research Institute Foundation serves as an information clearinghouse and offers a referral service.
Phone: 800-321-3437
Mailing address: 3440 Hollywood Boulevard, Suite 100, Hollywood, FL 33021

International Diabetic Athletes Association provides a network and support group for athletes with diabetes.
Phone: 800-898-IDAA
Mailing address: 1647 West Bethany Home Road, No. B, Phoenix, AZ 85015

Juvenile Diabetes Foundation International Hotline answers general questions and supplies written information.
Phone: 800-223-1138
Web site: http://www.jdfcure.com
E-mail: info@jdfcure.com

Managing Your Diabetes web site features a diabetes reference manual and provides information on the disease.
Web site: http://www.Lilly.com/diabetes

The National Institute of Diabetes and Digestive and Kidney Disease of the National Institutes of Health web site offers educational materials and information on several disorders.
Web site: http://www.niddk.nih.gov/
E-mail: kranzfeldk@hq.niddk.nih.gov

DIGESTIVE DISEASE

Digestive Disease National Coalition
offers information on digestive diseases
and related nutrition.
Phone: 202-544-7497
Mailing address: 711 2nd Street
Northeast, Suite 200,
Washington, DC 20002

**Intestinal Digestive Diseases Informa-
tion Clearinghouse** serves as a central information resource on the prevention and
management of digestive diseases.
Phone: 301-654-3810
Mailing address: 2 Information Way,
Bethesda, MD 20892-3570

**North American Society for Pediatric
Gastroenterology and Nutrition** provides
information on gastrointestinal disorders.
Phone: 216-844-1767
Mailing address: Rainbow Babies and
Children's Hospital, 2074 Abington Road,
Cleveland, OH 44106

DISABILITY AND REHABILITATION

Accent on Information provides a computerized retrieval system that offers access to information on products and services available to the disabled.
Phone: 309-378-2961
Mailing address: P.O. Box 700,
Bloomington, IL 61702

American Amputee Foundation offers
peer counseling to new amputees and
their families, legal assistance, and referral
concerning prosthetics.
Phone: 501-666-2523
Mailing address: P.O. Box 250218,
Hillcrest Station, Little Rock, AR 72225

American Disability Association provides information on disability issues, children's services, and educational and support services.
Phone: 205-323-3030
Mailing address: 2121 8th Avenue North,
Suite 1623, Birmingham, AL 35203

**Americans with Disabilities Act (ADA)
Document Center** web site contains information on ADA implementation, the rights
of the disabled, the definition of disability, regulations, instructions on how to file
a complaint, and disability-related tax
provisions.
Web site: http://janweb.icdi.wvu.edu/
kinder/
E-mail: dckinder@ovnet.com

Amputee Shoe and Glove Exchange
facilitates swaps of unneeded shoes and
gloves by amputees.
Mailing address: P.O. Box 27067,
Houston, TX 77227

The Association of Retarded Citizens
answers questions on problems such as
Down's syndrome, fetal alcohol syndrome,
or neural tube defects, and provides infor-
mation on legislation, support services,
and publications.
Phone: 202-467-4179
Mailing address: Department of
Government Affairs, 1522 K Street
Northwest, S-516,
Washington, DC 20005-1247
Web site: http://TheArc.org/welcome.html
E-mail: arcga@radix.net

Canine Companions for Independence
offers information on obtaining specially
trained dogs for the disabled.
Phone: 800-767-2275
Mailing address: P.O. Box 446,
Santa Rosa, CA 95402

**Center for Information Technology
Accommodation** web site provides a list
of accessibility resources, a handbook on
information technology issues, a section
on legislative issues, and links to other
web sites.
Web site: http://www.gsa.gov/coca/
E-mail: Susan.Brummel@gsa.gov

Clearinghouse of Disability Information
provides information on federally funded
programs serving the disabled.
Phone: 202-205-8241
Mailing address: U.S. Department of
Education, Office of Special Education
and Rehabilitative Services,
Switzer Building, Room 3132,
Washington, DC 20202-2524

Direct Link for the Disabled serves as an information resource and referral service linking local, state, and national resources for all disabilities, health conditions, and rare disorders.
Phone: 805-688-1603
Mailing address: P.O. Box 1036, Solvang, CA 93464

Federation for Children with Special Needs is a coalition of parents' organizations acting on behalf of children and adults with disabilities that offers educational material and referrals.
Phone: 800-331-0688
Mailing address: 95 Berkley Street, Suite 104, Boston, MA 02116

Job Accommodation Network provides international information and referral services for people with disabilities.
Electronic bulletin board: 800-DIALJAN
Phone: 800-526-7234; hearing-impaired people can call the TD line at 800-526-7234
Mailing address: HRE/WVRRTC, West Virginia University, P.O. Box 6080, Morgantown, WV 26506

National Information Center for Children and Youth with Disabilities provides information and referrals to other organizations, prepares information packets, and assists parents.
Phone: 800-695-0285
Mailing address: P.O. Box 1492, Washington, DC 20013

National Information Clearinghouse for Infants with Disabilities and Life-Threatening Conditions provides information, assistance, and referrals to caregivers.
Phone: 800-922-9234
Mailing address: University of South Carolina, Center for Developmental Disabilities, Benson Building, First Floor, Columbia, SC 29208

National Institute for Rehabilitation Engineering is a service organization of electronic engineers, physicists, psychologists, and optometrists who offer advice to disabled people regarding custom-designed and custom-made tools and devices and training.
Phone: 800-736-2216
Mailing address: P.O. Box T, Hewitt, NJ 07421

National Rehabilitation Information Center acts as a library on topics relating to disability and rehabilitation by searching databases and providing written information. The center also answers questions and provides referrals.
Phone: 800-346-2742
Web site: http://www.naric.com/naric

Rehabilitation Learning Center web site, operated by Harborview Medical Hospital, Seattle, Washington, features a demonstration slide show that explains how spinal-cord-injury patients can master tasks such as getting in and out of a car, bed, shower, or wheelchair. Anatomic drawings allow patients to access detailed diagrams of the spinal cord and spot the location of an injury.
Web site:
http://weber.u.washington.edu/~rlc/
E-mail: rlc@washington.edu/~rlc

DOWN SYNDROME

Association for Children with Down Syndrome provides resources and information about Down syndrome.
Phone: 516-221-4700
Mailing address: 2616 Martain Avenue, Bellmore, NY 11710

Down Syndrome Web Page includes Internet resources on Down syndrome and basic scientific information.
Web site: http://www.nas.com/downsyn/
E-mail: trace@nas.com

Mental Retardation Association of America provides information, referrals, and educational material.
Phone: 801-328-1575
Mailing address: 211 East 300 South, Suite 212, Salt Lake City, UT 84111

National Down Syndrome Society

Hotline answers questions, supplies written information, and provides referrals to local parent-support groups.
Phone: 800-221-4602
Web site: http://www.pcsltd.com/ndss/

DRINKING WATER

Safe Drinking Water Hotline, operated under contract for the Environmental Protection Agency, answers questions and provides written information about federal regulation of public water.
Phone: 800-426-4791

DYSLEXIA

Dyslexia Archive web site, operated by the University of Kent, provides a collection of material covering all aspects of dyslexia.
Web site: http://www.hensa.ac.uk/dyslexia/www/homepage.html

The Orton Dyslexia Society sends written information to callers who leave their names and addresses on its answering machine.
Phone: 800-222-3123—answering machine; staff members answer questions at 410-296-0232.

EATING DISORDERS

American Anorexia/Bulimia Association serves as an information and referral service.
Phone: 800-924-2643
Mailing address: 293 Central Park West, Suite 1R, New York, NY 10024

Anorexia Nervosa and Related Disorders provides support groups, medical referrals, and counseling for anorectics, bulimics, and their families.
Phone: 541-344-1144
Mailing address: P.O. Box 5102, Eugene, OR 97405

International Association of Eating Disorders provides information and referrals.
Phone: 918-481-4044
Mailing address: 6655 South Yale Avenue, Tulsa, OK 74136

National Association of Anorexia Nervosa and Associated Disorders

provides information on illnesses related to the cause of eating disorders, methods of prevention, types of treatment and their effectiveness, and facts about victims.
Phone: 847-831-3438
Mailing address: Box 7, Highland Park, IL 60035

EPILEPSY

American Epilepsy Society provides information on treatment and care of epilepsy.
Phone: 203-586-7565
Mailing address: 638 Prospect Avenue, Hartford, CT 06105-4298

Epilepsy Concern Service Group provides information and support to people trying to deal with epilepsy.
Phone: 407-683-0044
Mailing address: 1282 Wynnewood Drive, West Palm Beach, FL 33417

Epilepsy Foundation of America answers questions; provides information; and makes referrals to physicians, local support groups, and organizations that supply assistance on issues such as employment and legal matters.
Phone: 800-EFA-1000
Mailing address: 4351 Garden City Drive, Landover, MD 20785
Web site: http://www.efa.org
E-mail: postmaster@efa.org

Epilepsy Support Organizations Guide web site, operated by Massachusetts General Hospital, provides addresses and phone numbers of worldwide organizations providing support and education for people with epilepsy and their families.
Web site: http://neurosurgery.mgn.harvard.edu/ep-resrc.htm

Washington University Epilepsy Links web site provides a comprehensive list of epilepsy-related resources.
Web site: http://www.neuro.wustl.edu/epilepsy/

EYES AND VISION

American Council of the Blind answers questions, makes referrals, and provides information on consumer items for blind people. An answering service provides updates on legislation affecting the blind.
Phone: 800-424-8666
Mailing address: 1155 15th Street Northwest, Suite 720, Washington, DC 20005
Web site: http://www.acb.org

American Foundation for the Blind provides information to individuals who are blind or visually impaired.
Phone: 800-AFB-LINE
Mailing address: 11 Penn Plaza, Suite 300, New York, NY 10001

Association for Macular Diseases provides information on the causes, treatment, and possible prevention of macular diseases, which include inflammations, tumors, retinal growths, and degenerative problems.
Phone: 212-605-3719
Mailing address: 210 East 64th Street, New York, NY 10021

Council of Citizens With Low Vision provides information and referral to people who are partially sighted and to people with low vision.
Phone: 800-733-2258
Mailing address: 1400 North Drake Road, No. 218, Kalamazoo, MI 49006

Eyenet web site, operated by the American Academy of Ophthalmology, features a forum where ophthalmologists answer frequently asked questions about eye disorders, an eye care quiz, eye care news, and a detailed illustration of the human eye.
Web site: http://www.eyenet.org

Glaucoma Research Foundation provides information about glaucoma and offers referrals and support services.
Phone: 800-826-6693
Mailing address: 490 Post Street, Suite 830, San Francisco, California 94102

Glaucoma 2001 provides information for people suffering from glaucoma.
Phone: 800-391-EYES
Mailing address: Foundation of the American Academy of Ophthalmology, 655 Beach Street, P.O. Box 7424, San Francisco, California 94120-7424

Guide Dog Foundation for the Blind, Inc. provides guide dogs free of charge to qualified people who are legally blind. The toll-free line has information specialists who answer questions.
Phone: 800-548-4337
Web site: http://www.guidedog.org
E-mail: ebiegel@guidedog.org

National Association for Parents of the Visually Impaired answers questions and provides referrals to support groups.
Phone: 800-562-6265

National Eye Care Project provides referrals to physicians who treat on a volunteer basis people 65 years and older who are unable to afford eye care. Callers also can request written materials on various subjects related to the eyes.
Phone: 800-222-EYES

National Eye Research Foundation answers questions, sends out written information, and provides referrals.
Phone: 800-621-2258
E-mail: nerf1955@aol.com

Prevent Blindness America answers general questions and provides written information on vision, eye health, care, and safety.
Phone: 800-331-2020
Web site: http://www.prevent-blindness.org
E-mail: 74777.100@compuserve.com

FEET

American Academy of Orthopedic Surgeons provides written information about problems that affect the feet.
Phone: 800-346-AAOS
Mailing address: 6300 North River Road, Rosemont, IL 60018-4226

**American Orthopedic Foot and Ankle
Society** provides information about problems that affect the feet and offers professional referrals.
Phone: 800-235-4855
Mailing address: 701 16th Avenue,
Seattle, WA 98122

Foot Care Information Center Hotline,
operated by the American Podiatric
Medical Association, provides written
materials and referrals to callers who
leave their names and addresses on its
voice mail.
Phone: 800-FOOT CARE

Podiatric Footwear Association provides
informational material about foot care.
Phone: 800-673-8447
Mailing address: 9861 Broken Land
Parkway, Columbia, MD 21046-1151

FERTILITY

**American Society for Reproductive
Medicine** offers resource information on
all aspects of fertility and problems of infertility and reproduction.
Phone: 205-978-5000
Mailing address: 1209 Montgomery
Highway, Birmingham, AL 35216-2809

Fertility Research Foundation provides
consultation for childless couples.
Phone: 212-744-5500
Mailing address: 877 Park Avenue,
New York, NY 10021

National Infertility Network Exchange
provides referrals and support for individuals and couples suffering from infertility.
Phone: 516-794-5772
Mailing address: P.O. Box 204, East
Meadow, NY 11554

Reproductive Toxicology Center provides
information on the effects of the chemical
and physical environment on fertility,
pregnancy, and fetal development.
Phone: 202-293-5137
Mailing address: 2440 M Street
Northwest, Suite 217,
Washington, DC 20037-1404

Resolve, Inc. offers information, referral,
and support to people with problems of
infertility.
Phone: 617-623-0744
Mailing address: 1310 Broadway,
Somerville, MA 12144-1731
Web site: http://www.resolve.org/

FOOD AND NUTRITION

Ask the Dietitian web site provides an
interactive forum on nutrition.
Web site:
http://www.hoptechno.com/rdindex.htm
E-mail: jlarsen@skypoint.com

Center for Food Safety and Nutrition
web site, operated by the Food and Drug
Administration, contains information
about food safety, cosmetics, product
labeling, and proper nutrition.
Web site: http://vm.cfsan.fda.gov/list.html
E-mail: lrd@vm.cfsan.fda.gov

**Consumer Nutrition Hotline of the
American Dietetic Association's
National Center for Nutrition and
Dietetics** provides registered dietitians
who answer questions on food and nutrition and offer referrals to local dietitians
weekdays from 9 a.m. to 4 p.m. Central
time. Callers can listen to taped messages
on food and nutrition from 8 a.m. to 8
p.m. Central time.
Phone: 800-366-1655
Web site: http://www.eatright.org

Food and Nutrition Information Center
provides publications on food and nutrition. The web site, operated by the U.S.
Department of Agriculture, offers a
healthy eating index, food and nutrition
software, educational materials, and information on the USDA research service and
library.
Phone: 301-504-5719
Mailing address: National Agriculture
Library—USDA, 10301 Baltimore
Boulevard, Room 304,
Beltsville, MD 20705-2351
Web site: //www.nalusda.gov/fnic/
E-mail: fnic@nalusda.gov

International Food Information Council provides information about food and nutrition. The web site provides information on scientific research and tips for healthy eating.
Mailing address: 1100 Connecticut Avenue Northwest, Suite 430, Washington, DC 20036
Web site: http://ificinfo.health.org/
E-mail: carbog@ific.health.org

Meat and Poultry Hotline, operated by the United States Department of Agriculture, provides an opportunity to speak to a food safety specialist weekdays from 10 a.m. to 4 p.m. Eastern time. Callers can listen to recorded messages 24 hours a day.
Phone: 800-535-4555
Web site: http://www.usda.gov/agency/fsis/homepage.htm

North American Vegetarian Society web site provides information on vegetarian events, conferences, and nutrition.
Web site: http://mars.superlink.com/user/dupre/navs/index.html
E-mail: dupre@mars:superlink.com

Seafood Hotline, operated by the United States Food and Drug Administration, provides written information and answers questions weekdays from noon to 4 p.m. Eastern time. Taped messages are provided 24 hours a day.
Phone: 800-FDA-4010
Web site: http://www.fda.gov/

GENERAL HEALTH INFORMATION

Agency for Health Care Policy and Research provides information on clinical practice guidelines and written information on a variety of health-related topics. The web site, sponsored by The National Library of Medicine of the National Institutes of Health, offers information on pain management, urinary incontinence, prevention and treatment of pressure ulcers, cataracts, and heart failure.
Phone: 800-358-9295
Mailing address: Center for Health Information Dissemination, Executive Office Center, Suite 501, Rockville, MD 20852
Web site: http://text.nlm.nih.gov/

American Medical Association offers information about studies and research materials to consumers and medical professionals. The web site provides information about the activities and policies of the AMA, access to abstracts of its journals and publications, and other healthcare resources.
Phone: 312-464-5000
Mailing address: 515 North State Street, Chicago, IL 60610
Web site: http://www.ama-assn.org
E-mail: webAdmin@web.ama-assn.org

The American Red Cross web site provides information on current relief efforts, Red Cross services, locating the Red Cross chapter near you, and volunteering.
Web site: http://www.crossnet.org/

CenterWatch web site provides information about clinical trials and new drug therapies recently approved by the Food and Drug Administration.
Web site: http://www.CenterWatch.com

Department of Health and Human Services provides consumer-oriented healthcare information. The web site provides information on health concerns and issues, financial assistance, legal documents, and educational materials.
Mailing address: Hubert H. Humphrey Building, 200 Independence Avenue, SW, Washington, DC 20201
Web site: http://www.os.dhhs.gov/
E-mail: tthomso@os.dhhs.gov

FedWorld web site, operated by the U.S. Department of Commerce, provides an online resource for locating, ordering and receiving U.S. government information, such as information on federal healthcare agencies, background on more than 2 million U.S. government information products, and updates on federal research projects.
Web site: http://www.fedworld.gov
E-mail: helpdesk@fedworld.gov

Health Care Financing Administration
provides information about Medicare and Medicaid programs. The web site, operated by the U.S. Department of Health and Human Services, offers an overview of these programs complete with names, phone numbers, and fax numbers of both federal and state agencies.
Phone: 410-786-3000
Mailing address: 7500 Security Boulevard, Baltimore, MD 21244
Web site: http://www.hcfa.gov/
E-mail: medicarestats@hcfa.gov

Global Health Network web site, sponsored by the University of Pittsburgh, offers thousands of Internet links to schools, organizations, associations, publications, and people dedicated to the goal of improving global health.
Web site:
http:www.pitt.edu/home/ghnet/ghnet.html
E-mail: rlaporte@vms.cis.pitt.edu

The Good Health web site offers a database of more than 1,000 health organizations, an interactive forum, health-related newsgroups, and an electronic journal.
Web site: http://www.social.com/health/index.html
E-mail: webmaster@social.com

Health Information Resources web site, operated by the National Information Center, lists toll-free numbers of medical organizations that provide health-related information.
Web site: http://nhic-nt.health.org/

HealthNet web site offers information on hospitals, government, and private medical practices, and provides links to hundreds of other web sites.
Web site:
http://debra.dgbt.doc.ca/~mike/healthnet/
E-mail: x-man@mgcheo.med.uottawa.ca

MedAccess web site offers a consumer's guide to health insurance, healthcare professionals, and facilities.
Web site: http://www.medaccess.com

Med Help International web site offers up-to-date information on most known illnesses and diseases.
Web site:
http://medhlp.netusa.net/index.html
E-mail: staff@medhlp.netusa.net

Medic Alert Foundation operates a worldwide medical information service. Members receive a pendant that alerts medical personnel to wearer's medical conditions, allergies, or medications. Members also are registered with a 24-hour emergency response center that transmits vital medical facts worldwide.
Phone: 800-825-3785
E-mail: info@medicalert.org

Medical Education Information Center web site, operated by University of Texas—Department of Pathology and Lab Medicine, provides a variety of healthcare tutorials and information on dozens of healthcare topics.
Web site: http://hyrax.med.uth.tmc.edu/
E-mail: lemaist@casper.med.uth.tmc.edu

Medical Source web site offers articles, tips, guides on healthcare, and more than 1,000 links to other health-related sites.
Web site: http://www.medsource.com

Med Net USA web site offers a medical resource center containing information for both medical professionals and consumers. The site provides links to every U.S. hospital that maintains a web site; first aid resources; nutrition information; reference library; and referral data base.
Web site: http://www.mednetna.com/
E-mail: Tim@Marpleinfo.com

MedWeb—BioMedical Internet Resources web site, sponsored by Emory University Health Sciences Center Library, offers an Internet resource guide to electronic journals, information sites, libraries, and bulletin boards.
Web site: http://www.emory.edu/WHSCL/medweb.hml
E-mail: libsf@web.cc.emory.edu

Morbidity and Mortality Weekly Report
web site provides the latest health-related information and documents the research activities of the Centers for Disease Control and Prevention.
Web site: http://www.crawford.com/cdc/mmwr/mmwr.html

National Committee for Quality Assurance, a nonprofit group that rates and accredits health plans, HMOs, and other health-care providers, offers information on the accreditation process. The web site provides a list of accredited health plans and offers tips on how to choose a health plan.
Phone: 202-955-3500
Mailing address: 2000 L Street, NW, Suite 500, Washington, DC 20036
Web site: http://www.ncqa.org/
E-mail: webmaster@ncqa.org

National Council Against Health Fraud Inc. provides information about health fraud and quackery. The web site offers a library of articles that provide a contrary view of alternative medicine and a hotline for people who believe they have been victimized by an unscientific health practice.
Phone: 909-824-4690
Mailing address: P.O. Box 1276, Loma Linda, CA 92354
Web site: http://www.primenet.com/~ncahf
E-mail: arlong@netcom.com

National Health Information Center provides referrals to national health organizations and support groups. Recorded messages about some organizations can be heard 24 hours a day.
Phone: 800-336-4797
Web site: http://nhic-nt.health.org
E-mail: nhicinfo@health.org

The Patient's Network web site, created by caregivers and patients, offers patient education materials, interactive areas, and links to resources.
Web site: http://www.pond.com/wellness/
E-mail: feedback@wellweb.com

Physicians Who Care provides information on health-care issues, managed care, and the role of the doctor-patient relationship. The web page features a newsletter and information on healthcare reform.
Mailing address: 10715 Gulfdale, Suite 275, San Antonio, TX 78216
Web site: http://www.pwc.org/
E-mail: comment@pwc.org

Public Health Services web site, operated by the Department of Health and Human Services, provides Internet access to all government resources related to healthcare—from large agencies like the Centers for Disease Control to small departments like the Office of Research Integrity.
Web site:
http://phs.os.dhhs.gov/phs/phs.html
E-mail: asmith2@oash.ssw.dhhs.gov

The Virtual Medical Center web site showcases thousands of medical research reports covering a wide range of topics.
Web site: http://www-sci.lib.uci.edu/~martindale/Medical.html
E-mail: jmartindale@vmsa.oac.uci.edu

GENETIC DISEASES

Alliance of Genetic Support Groups provides callers with information on how to contact genetic services and national support groups for various genetic disorders.
Phone: 800-336-GENE
Web site:
http://medhelp.org/www/agsg.htm
E-mail: alliance@capaccess.org

HEADACHE

National Headache Foundation answers questions, supplies written information, provides referrals to support groups, and offers audiotapes, books and a videotape for sale.
Phone: 800-843-2256
Web site: http://www.headaches.org

HEARING

American Association of the Deaf-Blind
provides services to deaf-blind individuals.
Mailing address: 814 Thayer Avenue, Suite
302, Silver Spring, MD 20910

American Auditory Society provides information on disorders of the ear, hearing,
and balance.
Phone: 602-789-0755
Mailing address: 512 East Canterbury
Lane, Phoenix, AZ 85022

American Hearing Research Foundation
provides medical information on deafness
and other hearing disorders.
Phone: 312-726-9670
Mailing address: 55 East Washington
Street, Suite 2022, Chicago, IL 60602

**American Speech-Language-Hearing
Information Resource Center** provides
information on speech, language, and
hearing disorders as well as referrals.
Phone: 800-638-8255
Web site: http://www.asha.org

Association of Late-Deafened Adults
provides information, support, and social
opportunities to individuals who have
become deaf as adults.
Phone: 708-445-0860
Mailing address: 10310 Main Street, No.
274, Fairfax, VA 22030-2410

Deaf World web site provides deaf resources organized by country, pen pals for
deaf children, and a discussion forum.
Web site: http://deafworldweb.org/
deafworld/
E-mail: dww@deafworldweb.org

Dial a Hearing Screening Test answers
questions, sends written information, and
makes referrals to local physicians, audiologists, and hearing-aid specialists. The organization also puts callers in touch with
regional centers that give free hearing
screening tests over the phone.
Phone: 800-222-EARS
E-mail: dabiddle@aol.com

Hearing Aid Helpline, operated by the
International Hearing Society, answers
questions, sends written information on
hearing aids and hearing loss, and makes
referrals to local hearing-aid specialists.
Phone: 800-521-5247

Hearing Helpline provides written information to the hearing impaired.
Phone: 800-EAR-WELL

**John Hopkins Center for Hearing and
Balance** web site provides information on
research projects and disorders related to
hearing and balance.
Web site:
http://www.bme.jhu.edu/labs/chb/
E-mail: jhuchb@bme.jhu.edu

HEART DISEASE

American Heart Association provides
written information on cholesterol and all
aspects of heart disease as well as referrals to local chapters weekdays during local business hours. The web site provides
resources related to heart disease and
stroke.
Phone: 800-AHA-USA-1
Web site: http://www.amhrt.org
E-mail: inquire@amhrt.org

Cardiology Compass web site, operated
by the Washington University School
of Medicine and Medical Center, provides a list of cardiovascular information
resources.
Web site: http://osler.wustl.edu/~murphy/
cardiology/compass.html
E-mail: murphy@osler.wustl.edu

Children's Heartlink provides treatment
for needy children with heart disease,
support for rheumatic fever prevention
programs, and education and research
information.
Phone: 612-928-4860
Mailing address: 5075 Arcadia Avenue,
Minneapolis, MN 55436-2306

The Heart: An Online Exploration web
site, operated by the Franklin Institute
Science Museum, features a multimedia
tour of the heart.
Web site: http://sln.fi.edu/biosci/heart.html
E-Mail: webteam@sln.fi.edu

The Heart Surgery Forum web site provides information on heart surgery.
Web site: http://www.hsforum.com/
E-mail: moderator@hsforum.com

Mended Hearts provides advice, encouragement, and services to heart disease patients and their families.
Phone: 214-706-1442
Mailing address: 7272 Greenville Avenue, Dallas, TX 75231-4596

HEMOPHILIA

Hemophilia Home Page provides information on hemophilia, a hereditary disease in which blood clotting is abnormally delayed.
Web site: http://www.web-depot.com/hemophilia/autosite/autosite.cgi

National Hemophilia Foundation operates an information center on hemophilia.
Phone: 212-219-8180
Mailing address: 110 Greene Street, Suite 303, New York, NY 10012

World Federation of Hemophilia web site provides information about the disorder.
Web site: http://www.wfh.org/

HEPATITIS

Hepatitis B Foundation web site provides information on the prevention and treatment of hepatitis B.
Web site:
http://www.libertynet.org/~hep-b/

Hepatitis C Information and Support Groups web site provides information on the prevention and treatment of hepatitis C.
Web site: http://planetmaggie.pcchcs.saic.com/hepc.html
E-mail: mccann@fwva.saic.com

Hepatitis/Liver Disease Hotline, operated by the American Liver Foundation, answers questions, provides written information, and makes referrals to physicians and local support groups.
Phone: 800-223-HEPABC
Web site: http://sadieo.ucsf.edu/alf/alffinal/homepagealt.html

HOSPICE CARE

National Hospice Organization provides written information and answers general questions on hospice and makes referrals to local hospices.
Phone: 800-658-8898
Web site: http://www.nho.org
E-mail: drsnho@cais.com

HUNTINGTON'S DISEASE

Huntington's Disease Society of America provides written information to callers who leave their names and addresses on its answering machine 24 hours a day, 7 days a week.
Phone: 800-345-4372
Web site: http://neuro-www2.mgh.harvard.edu/hdsa/hdsamain.nclk

HYPERTENSION

National Heart, Lung, and Blood Institute's Information Line mails written information on high blood pressure and high blood cholesterol to callers who leave their names and addresses on its answering machine.
Phone: 800-575-WELL

National Hypertension Association provides information on hypertension and conducts hypertension and hypercholesterol detection programs.
Phone: 212-889-3557
Mailing address: 324 East 30th Street, New York, NY 10016

HYPOGLYCEMIA

Hypoglycemia Association provides information and support to people with hypoglycemia, a deficiency in the blood sugar that deprives the central nervous system of glucose needed to function normally.
Phone: 202-544-4044
Mailing address: 18008 New Hampshire Avenue, Box 165, Ashton, MD 20861-0165

National Hypoglycemia Association provides informational and support services to individuals with hypoglycemia.
Phone: 201-670-1189
Mailing address: P.O. Box 120, Ridgewood, NJ 07451

IMMUNIZATION

National Immunization Campaign sends information to people who leave a message on their answering machine.
Phone: 800-525-6789

INCONTINENCE

The Simon Foundation for Continence provides free written information and sample products 24 hours a day, 7 days a week.
Phone: 800-237-4666

INJURY CONTROL

Car Accident web site provides information on car accidents and injuries related to car accidents.
Web site: http://www.stresspress.com/car/

Injury Control Resource Information Network web site, operated by the University of Pittsburgh Center for Injury Research and Control, provides a list of resources for treating injuries, and links to data bases and organizations.
Web site:
http://info.pitt.edu/~hweiss/injury
E-mail: hweiss@pitt.edu

KIDNEY DISEASE

American Association of Kidney Patients provides free written information and makes referrals to local support groups.
Phone: 800-749-2257
Mailing address: 100 South Ashley Drive, Suite 280, Tampa, FL 33602-5346
E-mail: AAKPNat@aol.com

American Kidney Fund works to alleviate the financial burdens caused by kidney disease.
Phone: 800-638-8299
Mailing address: 6110 Executive Boulevard, Suite 1010, Rockville, MD 20852

National Kidney Foundation answers questions and provides written information on various types of kidney disease, research, dialysis, transplants, and diet.
Phone: 800-622-9010
Mailing address: 30 East 33rd Street, Suite 100, New York, NY 10016

Renal Net web site provides a clearinghouse of information to patients with renal disorders.
Web site: http://ns.gamewood.net/renalnet/html
E-mail renalnet@ns.gamewood.net

LARYNGECTOMEES

International Association of Laryngectomees offers information and referral for people who have had their larynx removed.
Phone: 404-320-3333
Mailing address: c/o American Cancer Society, 1599 Clifton Road NE, Atlanta, GA 30329

LEAD POISONING

National Lead Information Hotline provides written information on preventing lead poisoning and referrals to agencies that can provide further information to callers who leave their addresses and phone numbers on its answering machine.
Phone: 800-LEAD-FYI; people who are hearing-impaired may call 800-526-5456

LEARNING DISABILITIES

Learning Disabilities Association of America provides information, services, and referrals for parents and children.
Phone: 412-341-1515
Mailing address: 4156 Library Road, Pittsburgh, PA 15234

National Center for Learning Disabilities provides resources and referrals for volunteers, parents, and professionals working with the learning disabled and offers services for children.
Phone: 212-545-7510
Mailing address: 381 Park Avenue South, Suite 1420, New York, NY 10016

National Networker provides peer counseling network and information referrals for learning-disabled adults.
Phone: 602-941-5112
Mailing address: P.O. Box 32611, Phoenix, AZ 85064

LIVER

American Liver Foundation provides information on liver diseases, liver functions, and disease prevention.
Phone: 800-223-0179
Mailing address: 1425 Pompton Avenue, Cedar Grove, NJ 07009

LIVING WILLS

Choice in Dying provides free legal, medical, mental health counseling, and crisis intervention. For a small charge, callers can also obtain state-specific materials for preparing living wills and medical power of attorney documents.
Phone: 800-989-9455
Web site: http://www.choices.org
E-mail: cid@choices.org

LYME DISEASE

Lyme Disease Foundation assists in the formation of support groups, offers referral service, and provides information on Lyme disease, which is spread to humans by ticks. Symptoms include rashes, joint swelling and pain, fever, severe headaches, and heart arrhythmia.
Phone: 800-886-LYME
Mailing address: 1 Financial Plaza, 18th Floor, Hartford, CT 06103

Lyme Disease Information Network web site provides information on the prevention and treatment of the disease.
Web site:
http://www.sky.net/~dporter/lyme1.html

MARFAN SYNDROME

National Marfan Foundation answers questions, sends written information, and makes referrals to local support groups.
Phone: 800-8-MARFAN
Web site: http://www.marfan.org

MENTAL HEALTH

Internet Mental Health web site offers an online encyclopedia of mental health information, such as information on common mood disorders and common psychiatric medications, and it features an online magazine.
Web site: http://www.mentalhealth.com/
E-mail: editor@mentalhealth.com

Mental Health Net web site offers a guide to mental health issues by providing links to more than 3,000 resources.
Web site: http://www.cmhc.com/
E-mail: webmaster@cmhc.com

National Alliance for the Mentally Ill provides written information and makes referrals to support groups to callers who leave their names and addresses on its answering machine. Callers may speak to an information specialist weekdays between 9 a.m. and 5 p.m. Eastern time.
Phone: 800-950-6264
Web site: http://www.cais.com/vikings/nami/index.html
E-mail: namiofc@aol.com

National Foundation for Depressive Illness provides a recorded message describing the symptoms of depression and manic depression.
Phone: 800-248-4344

National Institute of Mental Health sends written information on clinical depression to those who leave their names and addresses on its voice mail.
Phone: 800-421-4211

National Mental Health Association supplies written information on more than 200 mental health topics, makes referrals to local mental health providers, and provides a directory of local mental health associations to callers who leave their names and addresses on its voice mail.
Phone: 800-969-6642

Panic Disorder Information Line, operated by the National Institute of Mental Health, provides written information.
Phone: 800-64-PANIC
Web site: http://www.nimh.nih.gov

MULTIPLE BIRTH

Center for Loss in Multiple Birth provides peer support and information for parents who have experienced the death of one or more multiple-birth children.
Phone: 907-746-6123
Mailing address: P.O. Box 1064, Palmer, AK 99645

Center for Study of Multiple Birth provides information on the medical risks of multiple birth.
Phone: 312-266-9093
Mailing address: 333 East Superior Street, Suite 464, Chicago, IL 60611

National Organization of Mothers of Twins Clubs provides medical research and information on twins.
Phone: 505-275-0955
Mailing address: P.O. Box 23188, Albuquerque, NM 87192-1188

Triplet Connection provides information for parents and expectant parents of triplets or larger multiple births.
Phone: 209-474-0885
Mailing address: P.O. Box 99571, Stockton, CA 95209

Twin Foundation provides information about twins and research on twins and assistance for twins and other multiple births, parents, families; maintains national twin registry.
Phone: 401-729-1000
Mailing address: P.O. Box 6043, Providence, RI 02940-6043

MULTIPLE SCLEROSIS

Multiple Sclerosis Association of America hotline provides an opportunity for people to speak with peer counselors and health-care counselors. Callers also can request written information and referrals to local support groups as well as obtain information on the association's equipment loan program, symptom-management research and therapies, and barrier-free construction assistance.
Phone: 800-833-4672; 800-LEARN MS

Multiple Sclerosis Information Source web site provides information on the disorder.
Web site: http://ils.unc.edu/multiplesclerosis/hopk/mspage.html

National Multiple Sclerosis Society provides educational information about MS, counseling, family and social support, equipment assistance, clinical trials, and employment programs. Callers seeking local services are transferred automatically to their nearest chapters or can speak to trained national staff weekdays from 11 a.m. to 5 p.m. Eastern time.
Phone: 800-FIGHT-MS
Web site: http://www.nmss.org
E-mail: info@nmss.org

MYASTHENIA GRAVIS

Myasthenia Gravis Foundation of America, Inc. answers questions and provides written information.
Phone: 800-541-5454
Web site: http://www.med.unc.edu/mgfa/
E-mail: mgfa@aol.com

NEUROLOGICAL DISORDERS

Cure Paralysis Now web site provides information on research, physical therapy, and technology.
Web site: http://www.cureparalysis.org.

National Institute of Neurological Disorders and Stroke answers questions, provides written information, and makes referrals to local agencies.
Phone: 800-352-9424
Web site: http://www.nih.gov/ninds/

The Neurology, Learning and Behavior Center provides resources on neurological disorders and learning disabilities.
Phone: 801-532-1484
Mailing address: 230 South 500 East, Suite 100, Salt Lake City, UT 84102

Neurosciences on the Internet web site offers a searchable index with resources on neurobiology, neurology, neurosurgery, psychiatry, psychology, and the cognitive sciences.
Web site: http://ivory.lm.com/~nab/
E-mail: nab@telerama.lm.com

NEWS SERVICES ON THE INTERNET

CNN Interactive—Food and Health News web site offers articles related to food and health news items, research developments, tips, guides, and policy decisions.
Web site: http://www.cnn.com/HEALTH/index.html
E-mail: cnn.feedback@cnn.com

Medical Reporter, a monthly healthcare magazine available only on the Internet, provides articles on diseases. treatments, and public policy issues.
Web site: http://www.dash.com/netro/nex/tmr/tmr.html
E-mail: jcooper@medreport.com

NewsFile web site offers medical newsletters that spotlight various healthcare issues.
Web site: http://www.newsfile.com
E-mail:cwhendersonnet.atl.ga.us

New York Times—Your Health Daily web site offers articles on a variety of healthcare topics.
Web site:
http://nytsyn.com/med/index.html
E-mail: nytss@mcimail.com

USA Today Healthline web site provides up-to-date articles on healthcare issues.
Web site: http://www.usatoday.com/life/health/lhd1.htm

ORTHOPEDICS

Ortho Home Page offers an interactive patient's guide on lower back pain, carpal tunnel syndrome, and knee problems, and information on research and advances made in orthopedics.
Web site: http://www.cyberport.net/ortho/ortho.html
E-mail: mmg@cyberport.net

OSTEOPOROSIS

National Osteoporosis Foundation provides written information on the bone disorder.
Phone: 800-223-9994
Web site: http://www.nof.org

PARENTING AND CHILDBIRTH

American Academy of Child and Adolescent Psychiatry offers information related to how the family environment affects children and teen-agers. The web site provides access to more than 45 information sheets published by the AACAP.
Phone: 202-966-7300
Mailing address: AACAP, Public Information, 3615 Wisconsin Avenue, Northwest, Washington, DC 20016
Web site: http://www.psych.med.umich.edu/web/AACAP/factsfam/

Ask NOAH web site, operated by the New York Academy of Medicine and the New York Public Library, provides information on healthcare topics of interest to parents, such as AIDS, sexually transmitted diseases, pregnancy, tuberculosis, and healthy living.
Web site: http://www.noah.cuny.edu
E-mail: noah@noah.cuny.edu

Child Safety Forum web site provides information related to child safety in the home.
Web site: http://www.xmission.com:80/~gastown/safe
E-mail: Pete-NY@ix.netcom.com

Depression After Delivery Information Request Line sends written information to callers who leave their names and addresses on its answering machine.
Phone: 800-944-4773

Families USA offers reports, analyses, and other information related to healthcare legislation that will affect the lives of families.
Phone: 202-628-3030
Mailing address: 1334 G Street, Northwest, Washington, DC 20005
Web site: http://epn.org/families.html
E-mail: info@familiesusa.org

Go Ask Alice web site, operated by Columbia University Health Services, provides explanations and guides to health and nutrition questions.
Web site: http://www.cc.columbia.edu/cu/healthwise/alice/html

La Leche League Helpline answers questions and provides written information on breastfeeding.
Phone: 800-LA LECHE
Mailing address: 1400 Meacham, Schaumburg, IL 60173

Mothers' Network provides information on services for parents with young children.
Phone: 800-779-6667
Mailing address: 70 West 36th Street, Suite 900, New York, NY 10018

National Maternal and Child Health Clearinghouse provides information on maternal and child health, human genetics, nutrition, and pregnancy care, primarily from materials developed by the U.S. Department of Health and Human Services, Health Resources and Services Administration, and Maternal and Child Health Bureau.
Phone: 703-821-8955
Mailing address: 2070 Chain Bridge Road, Suite 450, Vienna, VA 22182-2536

National Parent Information Network provides information on raising and educating children. The web site offers a monthly online newsletter, a parenting discussion group, and resources on child care, health and nutrition, and education.
Phone: 800-583-4135
Mailing address: ERIC/EECE, University of Illinois, 805 West Pennsylvania Avenue, Urbana, IL 61801-4897
Web page: http://ericps.ed.uiuc.edu/npin/npinhome.html
E-mail: rothenbe@uiuc.edu

ParentsPlace web site offers advice, information, and resources in all areas of child rearing.
Web site: http://www.parentsplace.com

Parent Soup web site provides information on child rearing.
Web site: http://www.parentsoup.com/

PARKINSON DISEASE

American Parkinson Disease Association, Inc., sends written information, loans videotapes, and makes referrals to local referral centers. Callers may also leave a message on its answering machine.
Phone: 800-223-2732
Web site: http://neuro-chief-e.mgh.harvard.edu/parkinsonsweb/main/pdmain.html
E-mail: apda@admin.con2.com

National Parkinson Foundation Inc. Hotline answers questions and provides referrals weekdays from 8 a.m. to 5 p.m. Eastern time. An answering machine takes messages outside these hours.
Phone: 800-327-4545; 800-433-7022 within Florida

Parkinson's Disease Information Center web site provides information on the disease and its treatment and news about legislation issues and laws concerning the disease.
Web site:
http://www.efn.org/~jskaye/pd/index.html

PHARMACEUTICALS

Drug Info Net, Inc., provides information related to pharmaceutical issues. The web page offers information on drugs and 15 other major health topics.
Phone: 315-498-5462
Mailing address: 4207 Taylor Road, Jamesville, NY 13078-9618
Web site: http://www.druginfonet.com
E-mail: bhanson@druginfonet.com

Medication Index web site offers information on more than 150 psychiatric medications.
Web site: http://www.fairlite.com/ocd/medications/
E-mail: fairlite@jglou.com

PharmInfoNet web site offers information on thousands of drugs' trade names, generic names, and characteristics.
Web site: http://pharminfo.com

RxList web site offers information on more than 4,000 drug products on the U.S. market.
Web site: http://www.rxlist.com/
E-mail: rx@rxlist.com

PITUITARY DISORDERS

Human Growth Foundation provides information to families of children with physical growth problems.
Phone: 800-451-6434
Mailing address: 777 Leesburg Pike, Falls Church, VA 22043

National Hormone and Pituitary Program provides research information on all pituitary hormones.
Phone: 301-309-3667
Mailing address: 685 Lofstrand Drive, Rockville, MD 20850

PREMENSTRUAL SYNDROME

PMS Access provides recorded information and sends written information to callers who leave their names and addresses on its answering machine.
Phone: 800-222-4767

RARE DISORDERS

National Organization for Rare Disorders collects and provides information on more than 1,000 rare disorders and refers victims of rare disorders to information networks weekdays from 9 a.m. to 5 p.m. Eastern time. NORD also makes referrals to other organizations, support groups, clearing houses, patient services, and registries pertaining to specific rare disorders. An answering machine operates outside regular hours.
Phone: 800-999-6673
Web site:
http://www.nord-rdb.com/~orphan
E-mail: orphan@nord-rdb.com

Office of Orphan Products Development, operated by the United States Food and Drug Administration, sends written information and answers questions on the development of drugs and biological products to treat rare diseases and disorders.
Phone: 800-300-7469

REYE'S SYNDROME

National Reye's Syndrome Foundation answers questions and provides written information.
Phone: 800-233-7393
Mailing address: 426 North Lewis, P.O. Box 829, Bryan, OH 43506

SAFETY

Consumer Product Safety Commission Hot Line provides taped information on product recalls, corrective actions, and other product safety questions 24 hours a day, 7 days a week. Callers also can file complaints about unsafe products.
Phone: 800-638-2772

The National Highway Traffic Safety Administration Auto Safety Hotline provides taped information on recalls, crash-test results, tire quality, and other automotive safety topics 24 hours a day, 7 days a week. Callers can also obtain written information and report auto safety problems.
Phone: 800-424-9393
Mailing address: 400 7th Street Southwest, NTS-13, Washington, DC 20590
Web site: http://www.nhtsa.dot.gov/index.

Occupational Safety and Health Administration (OSHA) web site provides information on OSHA regulations and documents, advisories, legislation, and a list of frequently asked questions about OSHA.
Web site: http://www.osha.gov/
E-mail: webmaster@www.osha.gov

SCLERODERMA

United Scleroderma Foundation answers questions; provides written information; and makes referrals to physicians, local chapters, and support groups.
Phone: 800-722-HOPE
Web site: http://www.scleroderma.com

SCOLIOSIS

International Federation of Scoliosis Associations provides information on scoliosis.
Phone: 919-846-2204
Mailing address: 9908 Cape Scott Court, Raleigh, NC 27614
Web site: http://topbusiness.com/ifosa/index.html

National Scoliosis Foundation provides information on scoliosis.
Phone: 617-926-0397
Mailing address: 72 Mt. Auburn Street, Watertown, MA 02172

Scoliosis Association offers information about scoliosis and a variety of other spinal deviations.
Phone: 800-800-0669
Mailing address: P.O. Box 811705, Boca Raton, FL 33481-1705

SELF-HELP GROUPS

Agoraphobics Anonymous provides support and counseling.
Phone: 201-783-0007
Mailing address: P.O. Box 43982, Upper Montclair, NJ 07043

Agoraphobics in Motion provides support and counseling.
Phone: 810-547-0400
Mailing address: 1729 Crooks, Royal Oak, MI 48067

Anxiety Disorders Association of America provides support and counseling for people experiencing anxiety.
Phone: 301-231-9350
Mailing address: 6000 Executive Boulevard, Rockville, MD 20852

Depressives Anonymous provides help for people who experience anxiety disorders or depression.
Phone: 212-689-2600
Mailing address: 329 East 62nd Street, New York, NY 10021

Emotions Anonymous provides support for people recovering from emotional illness or disorders.
Phone: 612-647-9712
Mailing address: P.O. Box 4245, St. Paul, MN 55104-0245

National Mental Health Consumer Self-Help Clearinghouse offers referrals and consultation.
Phone: 800-553-4539
Mailing address: 311 South Juniper Street, Room 1000, Philadelphia, PA 19107

Neurotics Anonymous offers support for people recovering from an emotional illness or disorder.
Phone: 501-221-2809
Mailing address: 11140 Bainbridge Drive, Little Rock, AR 72212

Obsessive-Compulsive Anonymous offers support and counseling.
Phone: 516-741-4901
Mailing address: P.O. Box 215, New Hyde Park, NY 11040

Schizophrenics Anonymous offers support and counseling.
Phone: 914-337-2252
Mailing address: 1209 California Road, East Chester, NY 10709

Self Abuse Finally Ends offers support and treatment for people with addictive behavior patterns.
Phone: 800-DONTCUT
Mailing address: P.O. Box 267810, Chicago, IL 60626

SEXUALLY TRANSMITTED DISEASES

Centers for Disease Control National STD Hotline answers questions and provides written information and referrals.
Phone: 800-227-8922
Web site: http://sunsite.unc.edu/ASHA/

Sexually Transmitted Disease Gopher web site, operated by the University of Illinois, provides information about prevention and treatment of sexually transmitted diseases.
Web site:
gopher://gopher.uiuc.edu/11/UI/CSF/health/heainfo/sex/std

Sexually Transmitted Disease web site, operated by John Hopkins University School of Medicine, provides information on the prevention, diagnosis, and treatment of sexually transmitted diseases.
Web site:
http://www.jhustd.org/pub/jhustd/

SHINGLES

The VZV Research Foundation provides information on the treatment of shingles.
Phone: 800-472-8478

SICKLE CELL ANEMIA

Sickle Cell Disease Association of America Inc. answers general questions, provides educational materials, and makes referrals to physicians and local chapters.
Phone: 800-421-8453

SLEEP DISORDERS

American Narcolepsy Association offers information to individuals suffering from narcolepsy or sleep apnea.
Mailing address: 1255 Post Street, E.F. Towers, Suite 404, San Francisco, CA 94109

American Sleep Apnea Association offers information on sleep apnea.
Phone: 202-232-1338
Mailing address: P.O. Box 66, Belmont, MA 02178

American Sleep Disorders Association offers information on sleep disorders.
Phone: 507-287-6006
Mailing address: 1610 14th Street Northwest, Suite 300, Rochester, MN 55901

Better Sleep Council provides information about the importance of sleep.
Phone: 703-683-8371
Mailing address: 333 Commerce Street, Alexandria, VA 22314

Narcolepsy Network offers information and a referral service to people suffering from narcolepsy.
Phone: 914-834-2855
Mailing address: P.O. Box 1365, FDR Station, New York, NY 10150

National Sleep Foundation provides information on sleep disorders and on prevention of accidents related to sleep disorders.
Phone: 202-785-2300
Mailing address: 1367 Connecticut Avenue Northwest, Suite 200, Washington, DC 20036

Sleep Medicine Home Page, operated by the National Sleep Foundation, provides information on resources, sleep disorder centers, and educational material.
Web site:
http://www.cloud9.net80/~thropy/

SPINA BIFIDA

Spina Bifida Association of America provides information and a referral service to parents of children suffering from spina bifida.
Phone: 800-621-3141
Mailing address: 4590 MacArthur Boulevard Northwest, Suite 250, Washington, DC 20007-4226

Spina Bifida Information and Referral Hotline sends written information 24 hours a day, 7 days a week to callers who leave their names and addresses on its answering machine.
Phone: 800-621-3141

SPINAL CORD INJURY OR DISORDER

National Spinal Cord Injury Association answers questions, provides written information, makes referrals to facilities, and puts callers in touch with local chapters that know of support groups.
Phone: 800-962-9629
Mailing address: 545 Concord Avenue, No. 29, Cambridge, MA 02138-1122

National Spinal Cord Injury Hotline answers questions weekdays from 9 a.m. to 5 p.m. Eastern time. The hot line also makes referrals to peer support groups, rehabilitation centers, housing advice, and sources of other information to assist people who have suffered paralyzing spinal cord injuries.
Phone: 800-526-3456
Web site: http://users.aol.com/scihotline
E-mail: scihotline@aol.com

Spondylitis Association of America sends written information to callers who leave their names and addresses on its answering machine, and returns the calls of those who leave a phone number.
Phone: 800-777-8189
Web site:
http://www.usa.net/welcome/saapage.html
Online chat room: firenze@aol.com

Think First Foundation: Brain and Spinal Cord Injury Prevention Program provides information to young people about preventing brain and spinal cord injuries.
Phone: 708-692-2740
Mailing address: 22 South Washington Street, Park Ridge, IL 60068

STROKE

American Heart Association Stroke Connection makes referrals to agencies and support groups and provides written information. An answering service operates outside regular hours.
Phone: 800-553-6321
Web site: http://www.amhrt.org/stroke

National Stroke Association answers questions and provides written information about stroke and stroke prevention.
Phone: 800-STROKES
Web site: http://www.stroke.org
E-mail: info@stroke.org

STUTTERING

National Center for Stuttering answers questions, offers suggestions for parents of children who have begun to stutter, makes referrals, and provides written information.
Phone: 800-221-2483
Mailing address: 200 East 33rd Street, New York, NY 10016
Web site: http://www.stuttering.com

Stuttering Foundation of America answers questions, provides written material, and supplies a list of specialists.
Phone: 800-992-9392
Mailing address: P.O. Box 11749, Memphis, TN 38111

SUDDEN INFANT DEATH SYNDROME

American SIDS Institute provides the opportunity to talk with a doctor or social worker. Also sends written information and makes referrals to local support groups. After regular hours, an answering service at the same number will page a doctor or social worker.
Phone: 800-232-7437; 800-847-7437 within Georgia
Web site: http://www.sids.org
E-mail: prevent@sids.org

SIDS Alliance provides written information and referrals to support groups. The alliance also allows SIDS families to speak to a counselor 24 hours a day.
Phone: 800-221-7437

Sudden Infant Death Syndrome Network web site provides articles on SIDS, information on reducing the risk for SIDS, recent research, and legislative updates.
Web site: http://q.continuum.net/~sidsnet/

SUICIDE

American Suicide Foundation provides information on the causes and prevention of suicide.
Phone: 800-AST-4042
Mailing address: 1045 Park Avenue, New York, NY 10028-1030

Suicide Awareness Voices of Education web site provides information about common misconceptions about suicide, what to do if a loved one is suicidal, questions and answers on depression, and a list of books on suicide.
Web site: http://www.save.org/
E-mail: save@winternet.com

Suicide Information and Resources web site provides information on suicide and links to other suicide resources.
Web site:
http://www.paranoia.com/~real/suicide/

Youth Suicide Prevention provides information on the causes and prevention of youth suicide.
Phone: 617-738-0700
Mailing address: 11 Parkman Way, Needham, MA 01292-2863

THYROID DISORDERS

Thyroid Foundation of America Hotline provides written information and referrals to physicians.
Phone: 800-832-8321

TINNITUS

American Tinnitus Association provides information to individuals who suffer from tinnitus.
Phone: 503-248-9985
Mailing address: P.O. Box 5, Portland, OR 97207

TOURETTE SYNDROME

Tourette Syndrome Association sends written information to callers who write to the address given on the answering machine.
Phone: 800-237-0717—answering machine; callers can speak to an information specialist for referrals to physicians and local chapters by calling 718-224-2999

TRANSPLANTATION and ORGAN DONATION

American Association of Tissue Banks provides research and educational information on transplantation.
Phone: 703-827-9582
Mailing address: 1350 Beverly Road, Suite 220-A, McLean, VA 22101

Eye Bank Association of America provides research and educational information.
Phone: 202-775-4999
Mailing address: 1001 Connecticut Avenue Northwest, Suite 601, Washington, DC 20036

Eye Bank for Sight Restoration collects and distributes healthy corneal tissue.
Phone: 212-838-9200
Mailing address: 210 East 64th Street, New York, NY 10021

Lifebanc provides information regarding organ donation.
Phone: 800-558-5433
Mailing address: 20600 Chagrin Boulevard, Suite 350, Cleveland, OH 44122-5343

The Living Bank helps people who, upon their deaths, wish to donate a part or parts of their bodies for the purposes of transplantation, therapy, or medical research.
Phone: 800-528-2971
Mailing address: P.O. Box 6725, Houston, TX 77265

National Bone Marrow Donor Program

provides a registry of bone marrow donors, searches and matches donor recipients, and provides educational and research information.
Phone: 800-627-7692
Mailing address: 3433 Broadway Northeast, Suite 400, Minneapolis, MN 55413-1762

National Temporal Bone Registry serves

as a clearinghouse for information on temporal bone research.
Phone: 800-822-1321
Mailing address: Massachusetts Eye and Ear Infirmary, 243 Charles Street, Boston, MA 02114

Tissue Banks International provides eye

tissue for sight-restoring corneal transplant surgery and distributes bone, skin, and other soft tissues.
Phone: 301-752-3800
Mailing address: 815 Park Avenue, Baltimore, MD 21201

United Network for Organ Sharing sends

organ donor cards and written information to callers who leave their names and addresses on its answering machine.
Phone: 800-243-6667

TRAUMA DISORDERS

Patient's Guide to Cumulative Trauma

Disorders web site provides discussions of trauma disorder, a series of symptoms and syndromes that come about through a repetition of stressful activities, such as overuse of specific muscles, incorrect posture, or excessive muscle tension.
Web site: http://www.cyberport.net/mmg/ctd/stuff.html
E-mail: mmg@cyberport.net

TRAVEL HEALTH

Centers for Disease Control Home Travel

Information Web Page offers a regional breakdown on risks in 16 parts of the world, reference materials for the international traveler, information on countries infected with cholera, yellow fever, and plague and other diseases and epidemics.
Web site: http://www.cdc.gov/travel/travel.html
E-mail: netinfo@cdc1.cdc.gov

Centers for Disease Control

International Travelers' Hotline provides up-to-date information on the prevention and treatment of commonly acquired travel illnesses.
Phone: 404-332-4559

International Association for Medical

Assistance to Travelers offers information and makes physician referrals 24 hours a day to U.S. travelers in foreign countries.
Phone: 716-754-4883
Mailing address: 417 Center Street, Lewiston, NY 14092

International Society of Travel Medicine

provides information on more than 250 travel medicine clinics in the United States.
Phone: 770-736-7060
Web site: http://www.istm.org

Travel Health Information web site,

operated by the Medical College of Wisconsin, provides information on diseases and immunizations, environmental hazards, and other travel-related topics.
Web site:
http://www.intmed.mcw.edu/itc/health.html

Stanford University Hospital's Travel

Medicine Service web site provides basic information for traveling health-care.
Web site: http://www-leland.stanford.edu/~naked/stms.html
E-mail: stms@leland.stanford.edu

ULCER

Cure Foundation provides information on

peptic ulcer disease.
Phone: 213-296-6364
Mailing address: P.O. Box 84513, Los Angeles, CA 90073-0513

National Ulcer Foundation offers infor-

mation on peptic ulcer disease.
Phone: 617-665-6210
Mailing address: 675 Main Street, Melrose, MA 02176

VICTIMS OF VIOLENCE

National Center for Assault Prevention provides information on causes, consequences, and prevention of domestic violence.
Phone: 800-258-3189
Mailing address: 606 Delsea Drive, Sewell, NJ 08080

National Clearinghouse on Marital and Date Rape provides information and educational resources for victims of rape.
Phone: 510-524-1582
Mailing address: 2325 Oak Street, Berkeley, CA 94708

National Coalition Against Sexual Assault provides information and referrals for victims of sexual assault.
Phone: 717-232-6745
Mailing address: 912 North 2nd Street, Harrisburg, PA 17102

National Council on Child Abuse and Family Violence provides assistance for children, women, elderly, and families who are victims of abuse and violence.
Phone: 800-222-2000
Mailing address: 1155 Connecticut Avenue Northwest, Suite 400, Washington, DC 20036

National Victim Center answers questions, sends written materials, and makes referrals to local support groups and organizations for victims of violence.
Phone: 800-FYI CALL
E-mail: nvc@mail.nvc.org
Web site: http://www.nvc.org

WOMEN'S HEALTH

Guide to Women's Health Issues web site, operated by University of Michigan School of Information and Library Studies, serves as a clearinghouse of information related to women's health.
E-mail tsegal@sils.umich.edu
Web site: http://asa.ugl.lib.umich.edu/chdocs/womenhealth/womens_health.html

Institute for Research on Women's Health provides information on women's physical and mental health.
Phone: 202-483-8643
Mailing address: 1616 NW 18th Street, Suite 109B, Washington, DC 20009

National Council on Women's Health provides medical information on women's health.
Phone: 212-535-0031
Mailing address: 1300 York Avenue, Box 52, New York, NY 10021

National Women's Health Resource Center serves as a clearinghouse for women's health information.
Phone: 202-293-6045
Mailing address: 2440 M Street NW, Suite 325, Washington, DC 20037

Women's Health Resources web site, operated by University of Arizona School of Information Resources, provides access to information published by U.S. government agencies.
Web site: http://timon.sir.arizona.edu/govdocs/whealth/agency.htm
E-mail: slollar@ccit.arizona.edu

Women's Medical Health Page web site, operated by the University of California, San Francisco, offers a database of the latest articles on women's health gathered from several professional medical journals.
Web site: http://www.best.com/~sirlou/wmhplist.html
E-mail: coletmc@itsa.ucsf.edu

Directory of
Medical Specialties

PHYSICIANS AND SURGEONS

Allergist-Immunologist—diagnoses and treats patients with allergies or immune system disorders. Prescribes treatment and medication for conditions such as bronchial asthma, connective tissue syndrome, organ transplantation, and autoimmunity.

Anesthesiologist—administers anesthetics so that surgery can be performed without pain to the patient. Examines the patient to determine the degree of surgical risk and the type of anesthetic and sedation to administer. Monitors the progress of the waking patient and watches for developments of complications in the recovery room after surgery.

Cardiologist—diagnoses and treats diseases of the heart. Examines X rays, echocardiograms, and electrocardiograms, and runs stress tests to determine the specific cause of a problem. Refers the patient to a surgeon specializing in cardiac cases when there is a need for corrective surgery.

Dermatologist—diagnoses and treats diseases of the human skin, hair, and nails. Treats abscesses, skin injuries, and other skin infections, and surgically removes malignancies, cysts, birthmarks, and other growths.

Endocrinologist—specializes in diseases and disorders of the endocrine system, which consists of a collection of hormone-producing glands, many regulated by hormones secreted by the pituitary. Patients include people with thyroid disorders or diabetes mellitus.

Family practitioner—provides comprehensive medical services for members of a family. Examines patients, records information about a patient's medical history, performs various tests, administers and prescribes treatments and medications, and promotes health by advising patients on diet, hygiene, and methods of prevention of disease.

Gastroenterologist—specializes in the management of disorders of the digestive system. The major organs involved include the mouth, esophagus, stomach, duodenum, small intestine, colon, and rectum. Also treats diseases of the liver, gallbladder, and pancreas.

Gerontologist—specializes in diseases and disorders that affect the elderly, including the developmental, biological, medical, sociological, and psychological problems associated with aging.

Internist—diagnoses and treats diseases and injuries of the human internal organ systems. Prescribes medication and refers patients to a physician specialist when other medical treatment is necessary.

Neurologist—diagnoses and treats diseases and disorders of the brain and nervous system. Examines a patient's nerves, reflexes, motor and sensory functions, muscles, and blood and spinal fluid to determine the cause and extent of disease or disorder.

Obstetrician/Gynecologist—diagnoses and treats diseases and disorders of female genital, urinary, and rectal organs. Performs surgery to correct problems or to remove a diseased organ. Periodically examines the patient during pregnancy, delivers the infant, and cares for the mother following childbirth.

Oncologist—specializes in the diagnosis and treatment of cancer. Conducts tests to determine the location, type, and extent of the cancer, and administers treatment, which may involve several other specialists. Treatment may take a number of forms, such as radiation therapy, medication, surgery, or a combination of these.

Ophthalmologist—diagnoses and treats diseases and injuries of the eyes. Checks for the presence of disorders such as glaucoma or cataracts. Conducts examinations to determine the quality of vision and the need for corrective glasses or contact lenses. Prescribes glasses and medications and performs surgery when necessary.

 Orthopedist—specializes in problems affecting bones and joints and the muscles, tendons, and ligaments associated with them. Sets broken bones and puts on casts; treats joint conditions such as dislocations, slipped disks, arthritis, and back problems; treats bone tumors and birth defects of the skeleton; and surgically repairs or replaces hip, knee, or finger joints.

 Osteopathic physician—a fully licensed physician with training in the diagnoses and treatment of diseases and injuries of the musculoskeletal system (bones, muscles, tendons, tissues, nerves, and spinal column). Treats disorders through the use of manipulation techniques and medications.

 Otolaryngologist—diagnoses and treats diseases of the ear, nose, and throat. Determines the nature and the extent of the disorder, prescribes and administers medications, and performs surgery when necessary. Treats conditions such as sinus infection, middle-ear infection, tonsillitis, airway problems, and cancer of the larynx and sinuses.

 Pathologist—conducts laboratory studies of the nature, cause, and development of diseases, and structural and functional changes caused by diseases. Performs autopsies to determine the nature and extent of disease, cause of death, and effects of treatment.

 Pediatrician—plans and carries out a medical-care program for children from birth through adolescence to aid in mental and physical growth and development. Determines the nature and extent of disease or injury, prescribes and administers medications and immunizations, and establishes preventive health plans.

 Physiatrist—specializes in the use of exercises to aid in the physical and mental rehabilitation of patients. Prescribes exercises designed to develop functions of specific muscle groups.

 Proctologist—diagnoses and treats diseases and disorders of the anus, rectum, and colon. Treats diseases and disorders by the surgical removal or repair of diseased or malfunctioning parts of the body or by prescription of medication.

 Psychiatrist—diagnoses and treats patients with medical, emotional, and behavioral disorders. Conducts physical examinations, performs laboratory tests, and traces a patient's personal and family history to seek the cause of the problem. Uses physchotherapeutic methods and medications to treat patients.

 Public health physician—plans and participates in medical care or research in a hospital, clinic, or other public medical facility. Institutes programs of preventive health care in a town or city. Gives vaccinations, imposes quarantines, and establishes standards for hospitals, restaurants, and other public places.

 Radiologist—diagnoses and treats diseases of the human body using X-ray and radioactive substances. Examines the internal structure and functions of the organ system and treats growths by exposing them to radiation from X ray, high energy sources, and radioisotopes.

 Rheumatologist—diagnoses and treats arthritis, rheumatism, and other afflictions of the joints, muscles, or connective tissues.

 Surgeon—performs surgery to correct deformities, repair injuries, prevent disease, and improve the body's function. May specialize in a specific type of surgery, such as neurosurgery or plastic surgery.

Urologist—diagnoses and treats diseases and disorders of the urinary organs and tract. Prescribes and administers urinary antiseptics to combat infection and performs surgery when necessary.

DENTAL

 Dental hygienist—during treatment of a patient, passes instruments to the dentist and mixes any materials that are needed such as cement for filings. Cleans teeth, processes X rays, and gives patients instructions on oral hygiene.

 Dentist—diagnoses and treats diseases, injuries, and malformations of teeth and gums. Cleans, fills, extracts, and replaces teeth and provides preventive dental services to patients.

 Endodontist—examines, diagnoses, and treats diseases of the nerve, pulp, and other dental tissues affecting the vitality of the teeth. Treats infected root canal, reinserts teeth that have been knocked out, and bleaches discolored teeth to restore their natural color.

 Oral and maxillofacial surgeon—performs surgery on the mouth and jaws. Treats fracture of the jaws.

 Orthodontist—examines, diagnoses, and treats abnormalities of the jaws, position of the teeth, and other dentalfacial structures. Designs corrective devices, such as retainers, that alter the position and relationship of the teeth and jaws.

 Periodontist—diagnoses and treats inflammatory and destructive diseases of the supporting tissue of the teeth. Performs surgical procedures to remove diseased tissue.

OTHER HEALTH PROFESSIONALS

 Audiologist—determines the type and degree of a hearing impairment.

 Chiropractor—diagnoses and treats disorders of the spinal column through manipulation.

 Dietitian—studies the composition of foods, the effects of cooking and processing, and formulates dietary requirements.

 Optometrist—examines and performs various tests on eyes and prescribes corrective lenses or procedures.

 Psychologist—diagnoses and treats the mental and emotional disorders of individuals. Can not prescribe medication.

 Paramedic—administers life support care to sick and injured individuals at an emergency scene.

 Pharmacist—mixes and dispenses doctor-prescribed medications. Advises patients on medicine and its side effects.

 Physical therapist—administers medically prescribed treatment to restore function and relieve pain from injuries, or from muscle, nerve, joint and bone diseases.

 Podiatrist—diagnoses and treats diseases and deformities of the foot.

 Registered nurse—provides general nursing care to patients in hospitals, nursing homes, infirmaries, or other health-care facilities. Administers prescribed medications and treatments.

 Physician's assistant/Nurse practitioner—provides general medical care and treatment. Performs various duties such as giving physical examinations and ordering and evaluating diagnostic tests.

 Surgical assistant—performs various duties such as helping prepare the patient for surgery, helping position the patient on the surgical table, and holding instruments for the surgeon during the procedure.

Recommended
immunization schedule
for children

	Hepatitis B	DTP (diphtheria, tetanus, pertussis)	Polio	Hib (haemophilis influenza type b)	MMR (measles, mumps, rubella)	Td (tetanus, diphtheria)	Chickenpox
Birth–2 months	X						
1–4 months	X						
2 months		X	X	X			
4 months		X	X	X			
6 months		X		X			
6–18 months	X						
12 months							
12–15 months				X	X		
12–18 months			X				X
15 months							
15–18 months		X					
18 months							
4–6 years		X	X		X		
11–12 years	X					X	
14–16 years							

Source: The Centers for Disease Control and Prevention

336

INDEX

How to use the index
This index covers the contents of the 1996, 1997, and 1998 editions of *The World Book Health & Medical Annual*.

Each entry gives the last two digits of the edition year and the page number or numbers. For example, this entry means that information on skin cancer may be found on page 37 of the 1998 edition.

When there are many references to a topic, some of them are grouped alphabetically by clue words under the main topic. For example, the clue words under Sleep group the major references under several subtopics.

The "see" and "see also" cross-references indicate that references to the topic are listed under another entry in the index.

An entry in all capital letters indicates that there is a Health & Medical Update with that name in at least one of the three volumes covered by this index. Page numbers for these updates appear after these capitalized headings.

An entry that only begins with a capital letter indicates that there are no Health & Medical Update articles with that title but that information on this topic may be found in the edition and on the pages listed.

The indication (il.) after a page number means that the reference is to an illustration only.

ACKNOWLEDGMENTS

The publishers gratefully acknowledge the courtesy of the following artists, photographers, publishers, institutions, agencies, and corporations for the illustrations in this volume. Credits should read from top to bottom, left to right on their respective pages. All entries marked with an asterisk (*) denote illustrations created exclusively for this edition. All maps, charts, and diagrams were prepared by the staff unless otherwise noted.

2 TRW, Vehicle Safety Systems; © Edwin Remsberg, Gamma/Liaison

3 © Will & Deni McIntyre, Tony Stone Images; © Matthew Polak, Sygma

4 © Superstock; Steven Spicer*; CNS, Inc.; © James Schnepf, Gamma/Liaison

5 Cyndy Patrick*; © Dick Luria, FPG; © Oliver Meckes, Photo Researchers; © Merritt Vincent, PhotoEdit

10 © Bruce Ayres, Tony Stone Images; © Arthur Tilley, FPG; © Michael Krasowitz, FPG; © Superstock

11–12 © Ron Routar, FPG

20 © Bruce Ayres, Tony Stone Images

26 © Arthur Tilley, FPG

29 Barbara Cousins*

30 © Michael Krasowitz, FPG

31 Barbara Cousins*

33 © Ron Routar, FPG

36 U.S. Dept. of Agriculture

38 © Superstock

40 Avis Mandel, St. Luke's Medical Center

42 Steven Spicer*; WORLD BOOK photo by David R. Frazier; Steven Spicer*

43 Steven Spicer*

44 Ann Tomasic*

46–54 Steven Spicer*

57 Tom Wrobel

60 WORLD BOOK photo by David R. Frazier

62 Andy Cook

65 WORLD BOOK photo by David R. Frazier

66 Barbara Cousins*; Visual Images West from The Image Works; © James Schnepf, Gamma/Liaison; CNS, Inc.

67 © Billy E. Barnes, PhotoEdit; CNS, Inc.

68 CNS, Inc.

71–74 Barbara Cousins*

76 © Charles Gupton, Tony Stone Images

78 Nellcor Puritan Bennett, Inc.; CNS, Inc.

80 Barbara Cousins*

82 Russell Phillips*

86 © Robert Brenner, PhotoEdit

88 Palmetto SeniorCare

89 © James Schnepf, Gamma/Liaison

90 Visual Images West from The Image Works

94 © L. Mulvehill, The Image Works

96 © Billy E. Barnes, PhotoEdit

98–115 Cyndy Patrick*

130 © Ken Whitmore, Tony Stone Images; © Robert Crandall, Medical Images, Inc.; © Charles Gupton, Tony Stone Images; © Meckes/Ottawa from Photo Researchers

131 © Motta/SPL from Photo Researchers; © Dick Luria, FPG

133 © Robert Crandall, Medical Images, Inc.

136 Shooting Star Graphics

137 © Albert Paglialunga, Phototake

141 © Joseph Lynch, Medichrome

143 © Ken Whitmore, Tony Stone Images

144 © Dick Luria, FPG

146 Donna Kae Nelson*

148 Genentech, Inc.

149 Michael Lilly, M.D., University of Maryland at Baltimore School of Medicine

150 © Paul Conklin, PhotoEdit

151 © Charles Gupton, Tony Stone Images

156 © Meckes/Ottawa from Photo Researchers

157 © Biology Media from Photo Researchers

158 B.B. Finlay et.al. *EMBO Journal*, Vol. 15 No 1. Reprinted with permission of Oxford University Press; © Motta, Andrews, Porter & Vial/SPL from Photo Researchers

159 © CNRI/SPL from Photo Researchers

160 © Motta/SPL from Photo Researchers

161 © Motta & Correr/SPL from Photo Researchers

162 © Motta/SPL from Photo Researchers; © Andrew Syred/SPL from Photo Researchers

164 Steven Spicer*; © Oliver Meckes, Photo Researchers; U.S. Dept. of Agriculture; Century Products Company

165 AP/WideWorld; TRW, Vehicle Safety Systems

166–167 TRW, Vehicle Safety Systems

169–172 Shooting Star Graphics*

174 Jeff Guerrant*; Century Products Company

176 AP/Wide World

180 Archive Photos; U.S. Dept of Agriculture

181 U.S. Dept. of Agriculture

World Book Encyclopedia, Inc., provides high-quality educational and reference products for the family and school. They include THE WORLD BOOK~RUSH-PRESBYTERIAN-ST. LUKE'S MEDICAL CENTER~MEDICAL ENCYCLOPEDIA, a 1,072-page fully illustrated family health reference; THE WORLD BOOK OF MATH POWER, a two-volume set that helps students and adults build math skills; THE WORLD BOOK OF WORD POWER, a two-volume set that is designed to help your entire family write and speak more successfully; and the HOW TO STUDY video, a presentation of key study skills with information students need to succeed in school. For further information, write World Book Encyclopedia, Inc.; Post Office Box 11207; Des Moines, IA 50340-1207.